MW01252909

Chinese Economic Development and the Environment

NEW HORIZONS IN ENVIRONMENTAL ECONOMICS

Series Editors: Wallace E. Oates, *Professor of Economics, University of Maryland, College Park and University Fellow, Resources for the Future, USA* and Henk Folmer, *Professor of Research Methodology, Groningen University and Professor of General Economics, Wageningen University, The Netherlands*

This important series is designed to make a significant contribution to the development of the principles and practices of environmental economics. It includes both theoretical and empirical work. International in scope, it addresses issues of current and future concern in both East and West and in developed and developing countries.

The main purpose of the series is to create a forum for the publication of high quality work and to show how economic analysis can make a contribution to understanding and resolving the environmental problems confronting the world in the twenty-first century.

Recent titles in the series include:

Economic Valuation of River Systems
Edited by Fred J. Hitzhusen

Scarcity, Entitlements and the Economics of Water in Developing Countries
P.B. Anand

Technological Change and Environmental Policy
A Study of Depletion in the Oil and Gas Industry
Shunsuke Managi

Environmental Governance and Decentralisation
Edited by Albert Breton, Giorgio Brosio, Silvana Dalmazzone and Giovanna Garrone

Choice Experiments Informing Environmental Policy
A European Perspective
Edited by Ekin Birol and Phoebe Koundouri

Markets for Carbon and Power Pricing in Europe
Theoretical Issues and Empirical Analyses
Edited by Francesco Gullì

Climate Change and Agriculture
An Economic Analysis of Global Impacts, Adaptation and Distributional Effects
Robert Mendelsohn and Ariel Dinar

Distributional Impacts of Climate Change and Disasters
Concepts and Cases
Edited by Matthias Ruth and María E. Ibarrarán

Governing the Environment
Salient Institutional Issues
Edited by Albert Breton, Giorgio Brosio, Silvana Dalmazzone and Giovanna Garrone

Chinese Economic Development and the Environment
Shunsuke Managi and Shinji Kaneko

Chinese Economic Development and the Environment

Shunsuke Managi

*Associate Professor, Faculty of Business Administration,
Yokohama National University and Institute for Global
Environmental Strategies, Japan*

and

Shinji Kaneko

*Professor, Graduate School for International Development and
Cooperation, Hiroshima University, Japan*

NEW HORIZONS IN ENVIRONMENTAL ECONOMICS

Edward Elgar
Cheltenham, UK • Northampton, MA, USA

Published by
Edward Elgar Publishing Limited
The Lypiatts
15 Lansdown Road
Cheltenham
Glos GL50 2JA
UK

Edward Elgar Publishing, Inc.
William Pratt House
9 Dewey Court
Northampton
Massachusetts 01060
USA

A catalogue record for this book
is available from the British Library

Library of Congress Control Number: 2009936766

Mixed Sources
Product group from well-managed
forests and other controlled sources
www.fsc.org Cert no. SA-COC-1565
© 1996 Forest Stewardship Council

ISBN 978 1 84844 550 5

Printed and bound by MPG Books Group, UK

Physical Processing

Order Type: **NTAS**

Sel ID/Seq No:

231728

/3

Cust/Add: **240950003/02**

Cust PO No.   **new**

BBS Order No: **C1246635**   Ln: **4**   Del: **1**

**1848445504-42351986
(9781848445505)**

TGHR-T   UNIVERSITY OF GUELPH

Cust Ord Date: **19-Mar-2010**

BBS Ord Date: **19-Mar-2010**

Sales Qty: **1**   #Vols: **001**

Chinese economic development and the environment

Subtitle:

Stmt of Resp: **Shunsuke Managi, Shinji Kaneko.**

HARDBACK

Managi, Shunsuke.

Edward Elgar Publishing (US)

Acc Mat:

Pub Year: **2009**   Vol No.: _____   Edition:

Ser. Title:

Profiled	Barcode Label Applicati	Affix Security Device US	Spine Label Protector U!
Tech	Base Charge Processing	Security Device US	
Services:	Circulation (Author/Titl	Affix Spine Label US	TechPro Cataloging US
	Property Stamp US	Spine Label BBS US	

Fund: **BLKW-1604**

Stock Category:

Class #:

Location: **BLKW-1604**

Department: **BLKW-1604**

Cutter:

Collection:

Order Line Notes:

Notes to Vendor:

340306

Blackwell Book Services

To our parents

Contents

Abbreviations

CEBT	China energy balance table
CESY	*China Environmental Statistical Yearbook*
CIESY	*China Industrial Economy Statistical Yearbook*
CO_2	carbon dioxide
COD	chemical oxygen demand
CPI	consumer price index
CRS	constant returns to scale
CSY	*China Statistical Yearbook*
DDF	directional distance function
DEA	data envelopment analysis
EC	efficiency change
EIA	Energy Information Administration
EIA	environmental impact assessment
EKC	environmental Kuznets curve
EMU	European Monetary Union
EPB	environmental protection bureau
EPO	environmental protection office
ERPC	Environment and Resources Protection Committee
FDI	foreign direct investment
GDP	gross domestic product
GMM	generalized method of moments
GRP	gross regional product
GSP	gross state product
IDA	index decomposition analysis
IEA	International Energy Agency
IPCC	Intergovernmental Panel on Climate Change
LMDI	logarithmic mean divisia index
LPI	Luenberger productivity index
MCMC	Markov chain Monte Carlo
MLE	maximum likelihood estimation
NBS	National Bureau of Statistics
NEPA	National Environmental Protection Agency
NIC	newly industrialized country
NO_x	nitrogen oxide
NPC	National People's Congress

OECD	Organization for Economic Cooperation and Development
OLS	ordinary least squares
PACE	pollution abatement cost and expenditure
PEBT	provincial energy balance table
PPP	purchasing power parity
R&D	research and development
SC	scale change
SEPA	State Environmental Protection Administration
SEPC	State Environmental Protection Commission
SETC	State Economic and Trade Commission
SFA	stochastic frontier analysis
SNA	System of National Accounts
SO_2	sulfur dioxide
SOE	state-owned enterprise
SPC	State Planning Commission
TC	technological change
TCE	ton of coal equivalent
TFP	total factor productivity
TOE	ton of oil equivalent
TSP	total suspended particulate matter
VRS	variable returns to scale
WLS	weighted least squares
WUE	water use efficiency

Preface

China's economic growth has been extremely rapid in the past two decades, with an annual growth rate of about 10 percent in the last two decades. Subsequently, environmental problems are threatening China's sustainable future. Pollution damage is estimated to be around $54 billion annually and close to 8 percent of Chinese GDP. Policy makers in China are facing the tradeoffs between economic growth and environmental protection.

The world's most populous country and largest coal producer and consumer, China contributed more than 15 percent of global CO_2 emissions in the year 2007, making it the world's largest emitter of CO_2. Previous studies have suggested that China's energy consumption and CO_2 emissions will continue to rise during the next five decades. This raises a series of questions: what happened during this period? How did underlying forces contribute to the changes in CO_2 emissions? Do the changes represent only a temporary fluctuation or a long-term trend? These can be answered by using energy efficiency or productivity measurement.

Productivity growth plays an important role in GDP growth in China. Technological change is central to maintaining standards of living in modern economies with finite resources and increasingly stringent environmental goals. In addition, the costs (and availability) of alternative production and pollution abatement technologies, which are important determinants of the environmental compliance cost, are also influenced by productivity. Thus, it is important to understand the interaction between productivity change and environmental policies, which influence the compliance costs. In the long run, the most important single criterion on which to judge environmental policies might be the extent to which they spur new technology toward the efficient conservation of environmental quality. There is a burgeoning growth of literature, mainly theoretical, on the effects of environmental policies on technological innovation. In general, the incentive to innovate is stronger under market-based systems (for example, emission fees or permits) than under command and control regulations.

Taking into account the current demand for analysis of a major emerging economy such as China, and also the introduction of more stringent environmental regulations, this is a timely topic to address, particularly with all the media discussion of climate change negotiations, among others. Surprisingly, there is little information on the subject using robust econometric analysis. Incorporating the work of each of the different topics outlined below into one definitive book will result in a reference guide on the subject and on various energy, natural resource and environmental issues.

This study models and measures productivity change, with an application to China using several different measurement techniques. This is an important application because energy resources and environmental attributes are central to sustaining our economy. The traditional issues of measuring productivity change were recast by recognizing that production activity implicitly embodies joint production of market and environmental outputs. Thus, measures of productivity change consider all market, resource and nonmarket outputs.

Our study will analyze how well-designed environmental regulations can be implemented in China. The policies can potentially contribute to productive efficiency in the long run by encouraging innovation. To assess the issue, the productivity of market and environmental outputs is proposed and tested using overall economy- and industry-level data. We suggest that increased stringency of environmental regulation can lead to increased productivity of market outputs and therefore increased industry profits.

Detailed policy scenarios provide quantitative assessments of potential benefits that indicate the significance of the potential benefits of technological change and well-designed environmental policy. We provide a first comprehensive analysis of pollution, resource and efficiency in China using economic methods. Forecasting results are provided and can be used for future policy discussion.

Acknowledgements

In writing this book, we have benefited from the wisdom and generosity of many. But we owe by far the greatest debt to Professor Hidefumi Imura, who has been a constant source of inspiration.

We thank Ryo Fujikura, Libo Wu, Hidemichi Fujii, Katsuya Tanaka, Tomoyo Toyota and Tetsuya Tsurumi, our coauthors, who not only provided insightful comments but made a significant investment in our scholarly development. It has been our pleasure to work with them. Appreciation is also due to participants in various conferences, workshops and seminars for their comments and suggestions. We are also grateful to our parents for their encouragement and support.

We received Grant-in-Aid for Scientific Research from the Japanese Ministry of Education, Culture, Sports, Science and Technology (MEXT), and financial support from the Japan Society for the Promotion of Sciences (JSPS). We express our sincere thanks to both these agencies. The results and conclusions of this research do not necessarily represent the views of the funding agencies.

This monograph contains some revised versions of previously published papers. Permission to reproduce the material published in the following papers was granted by Elsevier, Baltzer Science Publishers B, and Interscience:

Kaneko, S., R. Fujikura and H. Imura (2000), 'A study on experts' judgement on the future perspective of a country: a case study for China', *Environmental Assessment and Modeling*, 1: 87–104.

Kaneko, S., S. Managi, H. Fujii and T. Tsurumi (2009), 'Does an environmental Kuznets curve for waste pollution exist in China?', *International Journal of Global Environmental Issues*, 9 (1/2): 4–19.

Kaneko, S., K. Tanaka, T. Toyoda and S. Managi (2004), 'Water efficiency of agricultural production in China: regional comparison during 1999–2002', *International Journal of Agricultural Resources, Governance and Ecology*, 3 (3/4): 231–51.

Managi, S. and S. Kaneko (2006), 'Economic growth and environment in China: an empirical analysis of productivity', *International Journal of Global Environmental Issues*, 6 (1): 89–133.

Managi, S. and S. Kaneko (2009), 'Environmental performance and returns to pollution abatement in China', *Ecological Economics*, 68 (6): 1643–51.

Wu, L., S. Kaneko and S. Matsuoka (2005), 'Driving forces behind the stagnancy of China's energy-related CO_2 emissions from 1996 to 1999: the relative importance of structural change, intensity change and scale change', *Energy Policy*, **33** (3): 319–35.

Wu, L., S. Kaneko and S. Matsuoka (2006), 'Dynamics of energy-related CO_2 emissions in China during 1980 to 2002: the relative importance of energy supply-side and demand-side effects', *Energy Policy*, **34** (18): 3549–72.

1. Introduction: economic growth and the environment

1 INTRODUCTION

Market transition reforms in China have been shaped by the interaction of a number of factors, including economic conditions, political constraints and official ideology. During this process, transitional institutions took some unconventional forms. However, although these transitions were second-best arrangements, the incentives of economic agents were generally improved. The consequences of this reform process were generally comprehensive, consistent and deep, and this helps to explain why the reform process was more successful in China, as against Eastern Europe, in the period up to 1990.[1] The relation between institutional changes, economic performance and economic conditions are clearly interconnected as the cycle continues and reform moves forward.

China is clearly an economic powerhouse with average economic growth of close to 9 percent per annum over the last 25 years (World Bank, 2001). However, as a result of China's extremely rapid economic growth, the scale and seriousness of its environmental problems are clearly evident. Consequently, a number of environmental problems, including growing energy consumption, heavy reliance on coal and increasing air pollution, are threatening China's sustainable future.[2] For example, the World Bank estimated that economic damage caused by pollution in China cost around $54 billion annually, amounting to close to 8 percent of gross domestic product (GDP) (World Bank, 1997a). Similarly, Economy (2004) reported that in 2000, China had 16 of the 20 most polluted cities in the world, and Bolt et al. (2001) concluded that China's air pollution problem is the world's worst. By the end of the twentieth century, the explosion in economic growth also made China the world's second-largest carbon dioxide (CO_2) emitter and energy consumer after the United States.

In response, from the late 1970s, China began implementing of a number of environmental policies in relation to air and water pollution and solid waste disposal, and the number of these regulations has been steadily increasing (Sinkule and Ortolano, 1995). The State Environmental Protection Administration (SEPA) has also declared control of industrial pollution to be a top priority for Chinese regulators. Responding to this severe environmental pollution, the National Environmental Protection Agency (NEPA) and the State Planning Commission (SPC) jointly proposed China's Environmental Action Plan for 1991–2000. The plan highlights the environmental issues that officials at the national level consider particularly significant. The top three (of seven) problems listed deal with water pollution, air pollution and hazardous waste. The next three involve conservation of natural resources in the form of water, land, and forests and grasslands. The final problem centers on the balance and integrity of China's ecosystems (Ma and Ortolano, 2000). However, weak enforcement of environmental regulations has been recognized as a major problem in China. This chapter reviews the background of economic and environmental policy and conditions.

2   ECONOMIC GROWTH IN CHINA

Reform in the Government System

By 1978, China was one of the most closed economies in the world. The Chinese economy had been closed to Western countries since 1949, and it had been closed to the Eastern bloc since the early 1960s following conflict with the Soviet bloc. The fiscal system as a whole before reform was quite centralized. This is because the SPC had the authority to determine local revenue and expenditure plans on an annual basis, although some fiscal decentralization was implemented. This was known as the principle of 'unified revenue and unified expenditure'. This meant that all government revenue and expenditures had to be directed through the central government.

In December 1978, the Third Plenum of the Eleventh Chinese Communist Party Congress was held. This event is widely regarded as the beginning of the reform era. The main achievement of the meeting was the decision to shift the Communist Party's focus from 'class struggle' to 'economic development'. An intensive ideological debate between Mao Zedong's orthodox version of Marxism–Leninism and pragmatism preceded this meeting in mid-1978.

In 1979, the government decided to welcome foreign investment and expand foreign trade. This allowed a change in ideology from within the Communist Party and paved the way for the initialization of reform. The accepted ideology during the first phase of reform was the idea of 'planning as a principal part and market as a supplementary part'. This was a significant change from Mao's ideology of abolishing markets.

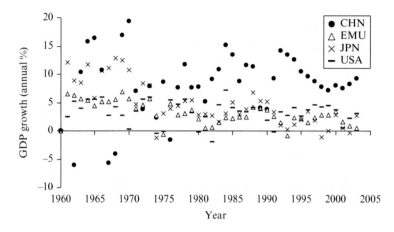

Source: WDI (2005).

*Figure 1.1   Annual GDP growth of China (CHN), the European
Monetary Union (EMU), Japan (JPN) and the United States
(USA)*

As a result of these reforms, there was a significant improvement in
people's standard of living. The state sector was no longer the dominant
part of the economy, and most of the old revolutionaries disappeared from
the political scene. In 1980, a major fiscal reform began, involving central
and provincial relationships. This reform, known as the 'fiscal contracting
system', was colloquially referred to as 'eating from separate kitchens'.
Under this system, budgetary revenue was divided first into 'central fixed
revenue', which was remitted to the center, and then into 'local revenue',
which was shared. The contractual sharing rates varied from province to
province.

Origin of Growth

Before the reform, China was poor, overpopulated, short of human
capital and natural resources, and centrally planned. After more than two
decades of market transition, it progressed into a lower-middle-income,
emerging market economy. During this period, China's per capita GDP
more than quadrupled, and total GDP grew at an average annual rate
of more than 9 percent. In the early 1980s, few economists would have
expected the outcomes seen in China today. This growth is also likely to
continue for the foreseeable future. Figure 1.1 presents the GDP growth
of several major regions, including China, the European Monetary Union

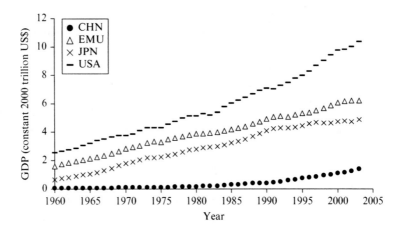

Source: WDI (2005).

Figure 1.2   Gross domestic product

(EMU), Japan and the United States. Clearly, the speed of growth in China is much higher than these other regions. For example, the growth rate in China is around three times higher than that in the USA over the past five years. Even when considered as a developing economy, its more than US$1.3 trillion economy in 2003 is bigger than all other transition economies combined. In 2004, however, GDP in China was still only 13, 22 and 28 percent of GDP in the USA, the EMU and Japan, respectively (see Figure 1.2). However, in GDP dollars expressed in purchasing power parity (PPP) terms (shown in Figure 1.3), putting aside the limitations of GDP conversion at market exchange rates, China surpassed Japan in 1995 and is close to the EMU. China also has a population almost three times the combined size of the eight highest-performing East Asian economies (Japan, South Korea, Taiwan, Hong Kong, Singapore, Malaysia, Thailand and Indonesia).

Conventional economics suggests a basic recipe for transition from a planned to a market economy. This entails stabilization, liberalization and privatization following political democratization. To guarantee sound reforms, this recipe may not be sufficient, but theoretically these essential ingredients are necessary for reform to succeed. Although many of its policies, such as being open to trade and foreign investment, and attention to macroeconomic stability, have been adopted by the government, violations of these standard prescriptions are clear. For the most part, China's reforms in the last two decades succeeded without complete liberalization, privatization and democratization. Therefore, the Chinese path of reform

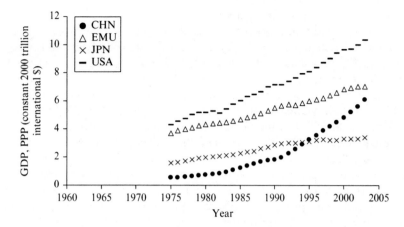

Source: WDI (2005).

Figure 1.3   GDP dollar estimates derived from PPP calculations

and its associated rapid growth is puzzling because it appears to defy conventional wisdom. Blanchard and Fischer (1993), for example, have questioned why China has grown so fast when the conditions thought to be necessary for growth are absent.

Several plausible explanations are provided in the literature. One aspect concerns alternative financing and governance mechanisms. One of the most important of these mechanisms is reputation and relationships (see Allen et al., 2005). This literature indicates that traders' organizations in the eleventh century were able to overcome problems of asymmetric information and the lack of legal and contract enforcement mechanisms (Greif, 1989, 1993). This is because they developed institutions based on reputation, implicit contractual relations and coalitions. China's private sector closely resembles certain aspects of these traders' organizations, especially in terms of how firms raise funds and contract with investors and business partners. Greif (1994) and Stulz and Williamson (2003) have also pointed out the importance of cultural and religious beliefs to the development of institutions, legal origins and investor protections.

The second most important mechanism is competition in product and input markets (see Allen et al., 2005). This mechanism has been shown to work well in both developed and developing countries (for example, McMillan, 1995; Allen and Gale, 2000; Allen et al., 2005).[3] For example, Allen et al. showed how firms in the private sector raise funds, their various growth paths, and the alternative mechanisms employed by owners that can substitute for formal corporate governance mechanisms. Their survey included private sector firms in Wenzhou, a city in Zhejiang province. The survey suggested that it was only those firms that had the strongest comparative advantage in an industry (in the area) that survived and thrived. See also Djankov et al. (2002), which examines entry barriers in 85 countries, including China.

The third mechanism is local government's fiscal incentives (Qian, 2003). China has been viewed as supporting local development and helping local businesses. Specifically, the planning system has been decentralized along regional lines, and local governments have played an important role in economic decision making and resource allocation.[4] Decentralization led to the rise of many small-scale SOEs financed from local government revenues.[5] In addition, they induced collective enterprises, such as commune and brigade enterprises in rural areas, predecessors of township–village enterprises, to emerge outside the state plan before the advent of reform.

Jin et al. (2005) have used panel data on 28 provinces between 1982 and 1992 for local government revenues and expenditures to evaluate the marginal fiscal incentives of provincial governments. They conclude that the new fiscal system did indeed substantially enhance the fiscal incentives for local governments. These results are in contrast to the Russian experience, where increases in a city's own revenue were almost entirely offset by a decrease in shared revenue from the region to the city (Zhuravskaya, 2000).

Incentive theory argues that local government does not have an incentive to support productive local businesses if the central government subtracts all of the locally generated revenue, because it cannot benefit from their support. Conversely, if local government expenditures are closely linked to the revenue they generate, the local governments will more likely support productive local businesses as they benefit directly from their support. The empirical evidence found by Jin et al. (2005) reveals that such incentive effects do exist and are significant. An increase in the marginal fiscal revenue retention rate in a province by 10 percentage points is associated with an increase of one percentage point in the growth rate of employment by nonstate enterprises in that province.

Productivity Growth

The empirical literature on economic growth in China suggests that total factor productivity (TFP) growth has played an import role in increasing GDP during the reform period (for example, World Bank, 1997a; Maddison, 1998). However, there is little consensus on the results in more recent years, that is, economic growth during the 1990s has followed a different pattern from that in the 1980s. For example, Liu (2000) believes that most of the productivity gains in the past two decades stemmed from the rectification of resource misallocations that were the legacy of the central planning era, and from narrowing the technology gap between China and the developed economies. Over time, as China moves closer to a market economy, such gains will inevitably diminish.

In addition, several economists have raised questions regarding the origin of economic growth in China. For instance, Krugman (1994), citing work by Young (1994, 1995), has argued that rapid growth in the East Asian newly industrialized countries (NICs) has been driven mainly by the massive injection of factor inputs, rather than innovation. As China's growth is likened to the East Asian NICs, the same argument is made about the Chinese economy. If this argument is true for China, growth is not sustainable. Sachs and Woo (1997) also pointed out that China's broad growth performance is in line with the performance of other East Asian economies and is attributable mainly to factor accumulation. Characteristics similar to those of other East Asian economies include low initial capital endowment, access to international sea lanes, an export orientation strategy, and a high proportion of the labor force in agriculture. They also find that economic reform has not improved SOE performance, as based on declining profitability, and SOEs have actually become a destabilizer for the economy as a whole (ibid.).[6]

Input-driven growth, such as capital-oriented growth, is also not sustainable in the long term because of diminishing returns to capital. This leaves productivity as the only viable engine of long-term economic growth (Liu, 2000). Young (2000) questions the performance of China's growth by linking his findings on the convergence of the provincial industrial structure to the fragmentation of the domestic market and the distortion of regional production away from patterns of comparative advantage. Young (2003) also shows that one can reduce the growth rate during the reform period to levels previously experienced by other rapidly growing economies, so that TFP growth in the nonagricultural economy is found to be about 1.4 percent per year – a respectable performance, but by no means extraordinary.

In the literature on China's productivity, several studies apply a growth-accounting approach to examine the role of productivity in China's economic growth. For example, by employing Robert Solow's residual growth accounting method, Borensztein and Ostry (1996) and Hu and Khan (1997) found a significant contribution of TFP to growth during the reform period. However, the growth accounting method should be treated with caution since it suffers from some major drawbacks. The method requires the assumption of constant returns to scale, revenue maximization, and the assumption that all decision-making units are efficient, and requires information on cost and/or input and output price data that is often unavailable.

The second assumption especially is questionable when producers' objectives differ, or are unknown or unachieved. The third assumption is crucial if there are situations in which prices are distorted or nonexistent. Finally, and most importantly, the growth-accounting method cannot distinguish between technological progress and changes in technical efficiency.

In this study, we use an alternative technique to overcome these problems. We apply a mathematical programming technique called 'nonparametric frontier analysis' or 'data envelopment analysis' (DEA) (see, for example, Färe et al., 1994) to compute the change in productivity over time. This study decomposes TFP change to provide a better understanding of the relative importance of various components over the study period. The TFP includes all categories of productivity change, which can be decomposed into two components including technological change and efficiency change (ibid.).

Technological change (TC) and efficiency change (EC) have additive or multiple relationships in the composition of TFP. It is then important to analyze these two conceptually different measurements considering the effects of economic reform. TC measures shifts in the production frontier or measures productivity growth by stimulating innovation. EC measures changes in the position of a production unit relative to the frontier – so-called 'catching up'. If existing resources are not fully utilized in production before reform, we can expect a significant increase in EC. Understanding these two components of productivity change is important since it provides valuable insights into understanding the source of a country's spectacular growth. Furthermore, distinction between these two effects provides insights for future growth such that the effect of technological change can be large and sustainable while the effects of efficiency change can be drawn out over time (Lucas, 1988).

The most recent study analyzing productivity in China is provided by Wu (2003), who found that TFP has on average contributed to 13.5 percent of economic growth during the 1981–1997 period using economy-wide province-level data, including the agricultural sector. Wu also found that this contribution is mainly due to technological progress, which tends to accelerate over time. Efficiency change has also been very volatile, reflecting the uncertainties associated with economic reforms and transition (see Figure 1.4). TFP growth was found to be 1.41 percent on average, which has been used to question Chinese growth performance. Significant improvements in productivity are found to appear in the early 1980s; that is, in the years after initiation of the reforms. This is consistent with reforms that began in the agricultural sector in the late 1970s and the success of rural reforms (Lin, 1992).

On the other hand, poor performance is suggested in the second half of

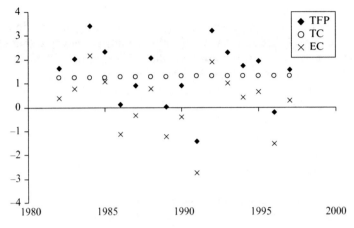

Source: Wu (2003).

Figure 1.4 Total factor productivity, technological change and efficiency change

the 1980s. Efficiency declined every year except 1988 during the 1986–1991 period. The decline in efficiency may well have occurred in many economic sectors during this period. The poorest performances are in the agricultural, industrial and nonstate sectors, including township, village and private enterprises, and these have been well analyzed in the literature (see Kalirajan et al., 1996; Jefferson et al., 1992; Fong and Tong, 1998, respectively). Finally, all three indicators have shown an upward tendency during the early 1990s. This may be the result of reforms initiated in the mid-1980s and more comprehensive reforms implemented in the early 1990s. In particular, price deregulation, which removed price distortions in the early 1990s, created a better business environment for both domestic and foreign investors.

On this basis, Wu (2003) suggests that China's growth will be sustainable in the near future and concludes, unlike Krugman (1994), that productivity increases contributed to economic growth. However, it should be noted that the contribution of productivity increases to economic growth is relatively small compared to that in developed countries or even some developing countries. Economic development in China still clearly depends on the massive injection of factor inputs. For example, Dougherty and Jorgenson (1996) estimate that productivity accounted for 26.2, 49.8 and 57.6 percent of output growth during the 1960–89 period in the United States, Japan and Germany, respectively. These figures are much higher than the Chinese equivalent of 13.5 percent. Chang and Luh (2000) analyze data from 10

Asian economies, including China, Japan, the NICs and the ASEAN-4, using distance-function-based Malmquist productivity indices following Färe et al. (1994). Compared with the other countries, they find that China exhibited productivity regress in both the 1970s and the 1980s. It is thus clear that there is ample scope for improvement in productivity performance in China. Our study evaluates more recent growth, focusing on the industrial sector and using a more sophisticated technique.

3   INSTITUTIONAL DEVELOPMENT OF ENVIRONMENTAL POLICY IN CHINA

Decision-making System of Environmental Policy

As a result of China's rapid economic growth, degradation of the environment has become increasingly severe over the last two decades. For example, the World Bank estimated that economic damage caused by pollution in China cost around $54 billion annually, amounting to close to 8 percent of domestic GDP (World Bank, 1997a). During the 1990s and early 2000s, some mega-cities, including Beijing, Shenyang, Xian, Shanghai and Guangzhou, have always been included among the 10 most polluted cities in the world. Urban pollution in China has also caused significant public health and economic damage. To protect public health and environmental quality, the government has undertaken a series of actions, and various laws, regulations and standards have been promulgated (Sinkule and Ortolano, 1995; Edmonds, 2004).

The decision-making system of environmental policy consists chiefly of three organizations. First, the National People's Congress (NPC) has a committee responsible for environmental policy, called the Environment and Resources Protection Committee (ERPC). The NPC makes policy decisions for environmental protection, passes legislation, and supervises its enforcement. Second, the State Environmental Protection Commission (SEPC) of the State Council drafts policies, regulations and laws for environmental protection. Third, the SEPA administers and supervises the environmental protection laws throughout the country.[7] The local environmental protection bureaus (EPBs) and environmental protection offices (EPOs) at the province, municipality and city levels are directly under the SEPA. EPBs and EPOs are raised to first-tier status under local governments because of the upgrade of the SEPA. The chief responsibility of the EPBs and EPOs is to enforce laws, implement policies and assist in drafting local regulations to supplement central organization. Therefore, EPBs and EPOs work directly with local factories, other polluters and industrial bureaus' local government actors. The industrial bureaus' local government actors include planning commissions, economic commissions, the People's Congress and mayors.

Radical reform of government administration was conducted by the Ninth National People's Congress in 1998 when the environmental protection agency was upgraded to ministerial status and renamed as the SEPA. During this reform period, the number of government ministry-level organizations was reduced from 40 to 29. Around 50 percent of government employees were slated for elimination from the government payroll (Eckholm, 1998). The emergence of the environmental protection administration was an exception during this massive effort to cut central government administration. Whether the administrative reforms of the 1998 Ninth National People's Congress actually changed the performance of environmental management in China is an empirical question.

Before the 1998 administrative reforms, industrial ministries, such as the Ministry of Chemical Industry, were responsible for industry-specific environmental management. They developed their own monitoring stations for specific types of pollution as well as sector-specific environmental regulations to supplement national regulations. After the 1998 reforms, many ministries were abolished, and several were recreated as bureaus under the State Economic and Trade Commission (SETC).

Actual implementation of regulation, at least in part, has depended on the effectiveness of the monitoring system and incentives to use environmental technologies more effectively. Pollution monitoring systems have been established and system management has been improved over time.[8] Furthermore, research and development (R&D) programs for pollution control have been implemented over the past two decades. The government has initiated a series of R&D programs involving studies analyzing atmospheric and water pollutants, solid waste, environmental planning, development of advanced technologies, and demonstration studies of pollution control. Also, many international organizations and foundations, such as the United Nations Development Programme (UNDP), the World Bank, Japan, the United States and others, have provided financial and technological support.[9]

History of Environmental Policy

As the starting point of formal environmental management and administration, the government held the first National Congress of Environmental Protection in 1973. Pollution control during the 1970s, however, concerned only three forms of industrial waste – wastewater, waste gas and solid waste – and no effort was made towards pollution prevention and abatement (Sinkule and Ortolano, 1995). At this stage, the actual authority of the local environmental agency was extremely limited. For example, industry bureaus and local factories resisted efforts by the local environmental agency to implement policy, by delaying or refusing to take action. Local government frequently intervened to help firms. Consequently, environmental protection laws were issued in 1979 and again in 1989.[10]

During 1982 and 1983, the most critical setbacks of these environmental agencies came with the structural reforms of the bureaucracy. As a practical result, the status of the environmental agencies decreased, and this weakened their managerial power. As a response to the damaged environment, changes in policy occurred in 1984, when the State Council established the National Committee for Environmental Protection, responsible for the coordination of environmental activities among the relevant ministries. Several changes in the policy occurred after 1984. For example, on September 15, 1987, the NPC approved the Law on Air Pollution Prevention and Control of the People's Republic of China (LAPPC). According to the law, all plants that discharge pollutants into the air should comply with the rules for pollution control. Consequently, a series of policies and regulations was published by the government and a set of national standards related to air quality was established. In 1988, the status of the environmental agency was raised, and it took a more independent position from the other ministries.

But environmental protection has only really started to exert its full presence on the political agenda in China since the 1990s (Sinkule and Ortolano, 1995). Six environmental laws and regulations were revised and/or issued in the 1990s. One of the most significant changes in policy was the 1997 revision of the Panel Code of the People's Republic of China, which added new articles on a charge of damage to protect natural resources and the environment, and a charge of misconduct in environmental management. In March 1998, the Ninth National People's Congress swept in a radical reform of government administration. By 2001, 430 sets of environmental standards were in place at the central government level and 1,020 sets of laws, regulations, ordinances and rules at the local level.

A formal process for environmental impact assessment (EIA) has been used for more than 20 years. In October 2002, 'The Law of the People's Republic of China on Environmental Impact Assessment', the new EIA law, was approved by the government and came into force on September 1, 2003. This allowed government agencies and other public and private sector bodies affected by the legislation time to prepare for the new requirements. Essentially, the new law superimposed a form of strategic environmental assessment for government plans and programs, but apparently not for policies, on the existing provisions for project-level EIA. In general, the new law does not attempt to modify the existing EIA system in any radical way, suggesting that the government considers that current practices are satisfactory (Wang et al., 2003).

Evaluation of Environmental Management

Although the administrable status of environmental agencies has been enhanced, the actual implementation of environmental regulation has not improved dramatically. Insufficient authority and a lack of coordination between institutional actors appear to be the main reasons. In detail, these are: (i) the low environmental consciousness of managers; (ii) incomplete monitoring and compliance measures; (iii) environmental facilities being easily damaged by lowering maintenance costs; (iv) lack of environmental engineers leading to insufficient management; (v) insurance not supporting maintenance and control expenses; (vi) the low quality of the facilities (sometimes already broken when purchased); and (vii) the fact that it is often cheaper to pay charges than to pay pollution abatement costs (see, for example, Kai, 1996). As a result, environmental facilities often face difficulty in operation. Based on a report to the Fourth National Congress of Environmental Protection in 1996, for example, one-third of environmental facilities in large and medium-sized firms worked properly, another third did not work properly, and the remainder did not work at all. Ma and Ortolano (2000) also find evidence for problems in environmental protection management at the local level, where the administrative rank of the environmental protection bureaus is sometimes lower than that of the enterprises it is intended to oversee (ibid.; Economy, 2004).

Local government, instead of a higher-level environmental protection agency such as SEPA, provides the annual budget, approves institutional advancements in rank, determines changes in personnel, and allocates resources such as office buildings to the local environmental protection administrations such as the EPBs and EPOs. The local environmental protection administrations are then obliged to take local government into account when they regulate industries, since they depend, in part, on the local government.

There are considerable differences in size, funding, staffing and work methods between environmental protection agencies at the province level. Wealthier coastal provinces tend to be better funded, with more staff better technically trained than those in the poorer interior provinces. However, it is not necessarily the case that wealthier regions are more inclined to protect the environment. This is because individual commitment to environmental protection by local officials or leaders plays an important role in policy implementation.

The implementation of environmental policies is also sensitive to differences in economic development and environmental quality (Dasgupta et al., 1997; Wang and Wheeler, 2000). In addition, policy enforcement by local authorities diverges from the legal system established by the central government. In particular, the level of completeness in policy varies across polluting firms: some firms comply perfectly, while others do not (Wang and Wheeler, 1996). Chinese officials are often aware of the problem but have largely responded inadequately, with the demand for continuing economic growth superseding environmental considerations (Economy, 2004).

Wang et al. (2003), for example, concluded that the bargaining power of Chinese factories in enforcing pollutant discharge depended on the type of ownership, profitability and public pressure. Wang and Wheeler (2003) analyzed the determinants of differences in enforcement of the pollution levy system across urban areas. They found that effective levy rates are sensitive to regional ambient quality, local incidence of pollution-related complaints, factory profitability, ownership, production, sales and the sector. Evidence of administrative discretion can also be found in the studies by Wang et al. (2002). They measured townships' environmental performance according to the number of township leaders' visits/inspections, and whether townships provided environmental services. They found that environmental performance is dependent upon upper-level government environmental performance, GDP, the percentage of adult population employed in industries, worker wages, public pressure and environmental quality (Wang and Di, 2002; Wang and Jin, 2002).

For example, firms facing adverse financial conditions have more bargaining power and are more likely to pay lower pollution charges, that is, less enforcement (Wang et al., 2002). However, little is known about how environmental management changes over time.

NOTES

1. See Qian (1999) for an analysis of the institutional foundations of China's market transition. There is a growing literature studying the transition of economies from socialist to market systems. One aspect of this literature examines why the Chinese experience differs from that in other transitional economies, including Russia, Vietnam and those in Eastern Europe. One major difference is that China's economy is much larger and more diversified than most other transitional economies, with the exception of Russia. As a result, countries with a small and homogeneous economy can adjust their legal and financial systems much more easily than large countries (for example, Shleifer and Treisman, 2000). This is probably because it is easier for other countries to adopt drastic reform measures in the short run. China also differs because of the influence of Confucian philosophy. In this regard, people in China believe that fundamental changes in society should be gradual and only fully implemented after they are proved correct (Qian, 2003). This view, however, does not prevent regional experiments being conducted

on a smaller scale. Accordingly, China adopted a gradual, 'dual-track' path in its economic reform, in that the continued enforcement of the existing planning system went alongside the fast-paced development of financial markets, as compared to the 'big bang' approach taken by some other countries (for example, Qian, 1999; Lau et al., 2000).
2. For more information, see World Bank (2001)
3. State-owned enterprise (SOE) reform by the government in this period increased enterprise autonomy and heightened profit incentives. Most economists agree that, despite the great effort in improving SOE performance, the most significant achievement was made by the fast entry and expansion of urban and rural nonstate enterprises. These firms were under tighter budget constraints and had better internal incentive structures. Indirectly, they also benefited from the various reforms aimed at the state sector, including fiscal decentralization, financial reform, the dual-price system and expanding SOE autonomy.
4. Central planning was usually aggregated, crude and not comprehensive, and plan fulfillment often was not a binding constraint. These features represented a significant departure from the textbook model of the Soviet system.
5. We take an example in the banking industry. Before the reform, there was only one bank, the People's Bank of China (PBOC), which served as both the central bank and a commercial bank. In 1983, the State Council granted the PBOC the authority of a central bank and subsequently transferred commercial operations to four specialized banks. After 1984, local governments at provincial, municipal and county levels gained great influence over credit decisions through the regional branches of the central bank and state specialized banks.
6. A number of empirical studies have attempted to measure TFP growth for the Chinese state-owned sector. Although some find that economic reform made little or no contribution to TFP growth in the state sector, most find that such growth has improved since 1978. However, it still lags behind TFP growth in township and village enterprises (Jefferson et al., 1996). We also need to be cautious about the interpretation of SOE TFP because productivity is not necessarily a good indicator of enterprise performance in transition economies, given the nonprofit objectives of SOEs.
7. The National Environmental Protection Bureau, which was established in 1984, was then upgraded to the vice-ministry level as the National Environmental Protection Agency (NEPA). Finally, in 1998, NEPA was further upgraded to ministerial status and renamed SEPA.
8. Urban air pollution monitoring in China started as early as the mid-1970s. For example, more than 350 cities conduct routine urban air quality monitoring of the pollutants SO_2, TSP and NO_x. In addition, Beijing, Shenyang, Shanghai, Guangzhou and Xian joined the Global Environmental Monitoring System.
9. These are provided to help improve the capacity of Chinese experts and researchers to solve pollution challenges for themselves. The investment in environmental infrastructure, including pollution control devices, cleaner production technology and natural gas pipelines, has also increased over time.
10. During this stage, a pollution charge or levy system was set up with Article 18 of the Environmental Protection Law of 1979 specifying that 'in cases where the discharge of pollutants exceeds the limit set by the state, a compensation fee shall be charged according to the quantities and concentration of the pollutants released'. Effective levy rates are the levies actually collected per unit of above-standard wastewater discharge.

REFERENCES

Allen, F. and D. Gale (2000), 'Corporate governance and competition', in X. Vives (ed.), *Corporate Governance: Theoretical and Empirical Perspectives*, Cambridge: Cambridge University Press, pp. 23–94.

Allen, Franklin, Jun Qian and Meijun Qian (2005), 'Law, finance, and economic growth in China', *Journal of Financial Economics*, **77**, 57–116.

Blanchard, Olivier and Stanley Fischer (1993), 'Editorial', in *NBER Macroeconomics Annual 1993*, Cambridge, MA: National Bureau for Economic Research.

Bolt, K., S. Dasgupta, K. Pandey and D. Wheeler (2001), *Cleaning the Air in Developing Countries*, Washington, DC: Forum for Applied Research and Public Policy.

Borensztein, E. and J.D. Ostry (1996), 'Accounting for China's growth performance', *American Economic Review*, **86**, 225–8.

Chang, C.C. and Y.H. Luh (2000), 'Efficiency change and growth in productivity: the Asian growth experience', *Journal of Asian Economics*, **10** (4), 551–70.

Dasgupta, S., M. Huq and D. Wheeler (1997), 'Bending the rules: discretionary pollution control in China', Policy Research Working Paper 1761, Development Research Group, World Bank, Washington, DC.

Djankov, S., R. La Porta, F. Lopez-de-Silanes and A. Shleifer (2002), 'The regulation of entry', *Quarterly Journal of Economics*, **117**, 1–37.

Dougherty, C. and D.W. Jorgenson (1996), 'International comparisons of the sources of economic growth', *American Economic Review*, **86**, 25–9.

Eckholm, Erik (1998), 'New China leader promises reforms for every sector', *New York Times*, 20 March, A1.

Economy, E.C. (2004), *The River Runs Black: The Environmental Challenge to China's Future*, Ithaca, NY: Cornell University Press.

Edmonds, Richard Louis (2004), *Managing the Chinese Environment: Studies on Contemporary China*, Oxford: Oxford University Press.

Färe, R., S. Grosskopf, M. Norris and Z. Zhang (1994), 'Productivity growth, technical progress, and efficiency change in industrialized countries', *American Economic Review*, **84** (1), 66–83.

Fong, R.W.L. and C.S.P. Tong (1998), 'Technological change of China's township and village enterprises (TVPs) and its corresponding spatial disparity: a combined DEA–Poolong approach', Working Paper, Hong Kong Baptist University.

Greif, A. (1989), 'Reputation and coalitions in medieval trade: evidence on the Maghribi traders', *Journal of Economic History*, **49**, 857–82.

Greif, A. (1993), 'Contract enforceability and economic institutions in early trade: the Maghribi traders' coalition', *American Economic Review*, **83**, 525–48.

Greif, A. (1994), 'Cultural beliefs and the organization of society: a historical and theoretical reflection on collectivist and individualist societies', *Journal of Political Economy*, **102**, 912–50.

Hu, Z.F. and M.S. Khan (1997), 'Why is China growing so fast?', *IMF Staff Papers*, **44**, 103–31.

Jefferson, G.H., T.G. Rawski and Y. Zheng (1992), 'Growth, efficiency and convergence in China's state and collective industry', *Economic Development and Cultural Change*, **40**, 239–66.

Jefferson, Gary H., Thomas G. Rawski and Yuxin Zheng (1996), 'Chinese industrial productivity: trends, measurement issues, and recent developments', *Journal of Comparative Economics*, **23** (2), 146–80.

Jin, Hehui, Yingyi Qian and Barry R. Weingast (2005), 'Regional decentralization and fiscal incentives: federalism, Chinese style', mimeo, University of California, Berkeley, CA.

Kai, S. (1996), 'Maintenance and response of wastewater plants', *Environmental Protection*, **222**, 8–9.

Kalirajan, K.P., M.B. Obwona and S. Zhao (1996), 'A decomposition of total factor productivity growth: the case of Chinese agricultural growth before and after reforms', *American Journal of Agricultural Economics*, **78**, 331–8.

Krugman, P. (1994), 'The myth of Asia's miracle', *Foreign Affairs*, **73**, 62–78.

Lau, L., Y. Qian and G. Roland (2000), 'Reform without losers: an interpretation of China's dual-track approach to transition', *Journal of Political Economy*, **108**, 120–43.

Lin, J.Y. (1992), 'Rural reforms and agricultural growth in China', *American Economic Review*, **82**, 34–51.

Liu, M. (2000), 'Dreams as big as the west', *Newsweek*, 2 July.

Lucas, R.E. (1988), 'On the mechanics of economic development', *Journal of Monetary Economics*, **22**, 3–42.

Ma, X. and L. Ortolano (2000), *Environmental Regulation in China*, Lanham, MD: Rowman & Littlefield.

Maddison, A. (1998), *Chinese Economic Performance in the Long Run*, Paris: OECD Development Centre Studies.

McMillan, J. (1995), 'China's nonconformist reform', in P. Edward (ed.), *Economic Transition in Eastern Europe and Russia: Realities of Reform*, Stanford, CA: Hoover Institution Press, pp. 419–33.

Qian, Yingyi (1999), 'The institutional foundations of China's market transition', working paper, Stanford University, Stanford, CA.

Qian, Yingyi (2003), 'How reform worked in China', in Dani Rodrik (ed.), *In Search of Prosperity: Analytic Narratives on Economic Growth*, Princeton, NJ: Princeton University Press, pp. 297–333.

Sachs, J. and W.T. Woo (1997), 'Understanding China's economic performance', NBER Working Paper 5935, Cambridge, MA.

Shleifer, A. and D. Treisman (2000), *Without a Map: Political Tactics and Economic Reform in Russia*, Cambridge, MA: MIT Press.

Sinkule, B.J. and L. Ortolano (1995), *Implementing Environmental Policy in China*, Westport, CT: Praeger.

Stulz, R. and R. Williamson (2003), 'Culture, openness, and finance', *Journal of Financial Economics*, **70**, 261–300.

Wang, H. and W. Di (2002), 'The determinants of government environmental performance: an empirical analysis of Chinese townships', Policy Research Working Paper, World Bank, Washington, DC.

Wang, H. and Y. Jin (2002), 'Industrial ownership and environmental performance: evidence from China', Policy Research Working Paper, World Bank, Washington, DC.

Wang, H. and D. Wheeler (1996), 'Pricing industrial pollution in China: an econometric analysis of the levy system', Policy Research Working Paper 1644, Development Research Group, World Bank, Washington, DC.

Wang, H. and D. Wheeler (2000), 'Endogenous enforcement and effectiveness of China's pollution levy system', Policy Research Working Paper 2336, Development Research Group, World Bank, Washington, DC.

Wang, H. and D. Wheeler (2003), 'Equilibrium pollution and economic development in China', *Environment and Development Economics*, **8**, 451–66.

Wang, H., N. Mamingi, B. Laplante and S. Dasgupta (2002), 'Incomplete enforcement of pollution regulation: bargaining power of Chinese factories', Policy Research Working Paper 2756, Development Research Group, World Bank, Washington, DC.

Wang, Y., R. Morgan and M. Cashmore (2003), 'Environmental impact assessment of projects in the People's Republic of China: new law, old problems', *Environmental Impact Assessment Review*, **23** (5), 543–79.

World Bank (1997a), *China 2020: Development Challenges in the New Century*, Washington, DC: World Bank.

World Bank (1997b), *Clear Water, Blue Skies: China: Environment in the New Century*, Washington, DC: World Bank.

World Bank (2001), *China Air, Land and Water: Environmental Priorities for a New Millennium*, Washington, DC: World Bank.

World Development Indicators (WDI) (2005), *World Development Indicators*, CD-ROM, Washington, DC: World Bank.

Wu, Yanrui (2003), 'Has productivity contributed to China's growth?', *Pacific Economic Review*, **8** (1), 15–30.

Young, A. (1994), 'Lessons from the East Asian NICs: a contrarian view', *European Economic Review*, **110**, 641–80.

Young, A. (1995), 'The tyranny of numbers: confronting the statistical realities of the East Asian growth experience', *Quarterly Journal of Economics*, **110**, 641–80.

Young, A. (2000), 'The razor's edge. Distortions and incremental reform in the People's Republic of China', *Quarterly Journal of Economics*, **115**, 1091–136.

Zhuravskaya, Ekaterina V. (2000), 'Incentives to provide local public goods: fiscal federalism, Russian style', *Journal of Public Economics*, **76** (3), June, 337–68.

2.   Environmental Kuznets curve

1   INTRODUCTION

China is an emerging and leading world economy. The pace of economic change has been tremendously rapid since the beginning of economic reforms. Over the last quarter of a century, China's economy has enjoyed average growth rates close to 9.5 percent (World Bank, 2001). Nationwide income has been doubling every eight years. This boost in output characterizes one of the most sustained and rapid economic transformations in the world economy in the past 50 years.

However, as a result of China's enormously rapid economic expansion, the size and significance of environmental problems is now of concern. As a result, a number of environmental problems such as increasing air pollution are threatening the sustainability of China's growth. For example, the World Bank estimated that economic damage caused by pollution in China costs around $54 billion annually (World Bank, 1997). This is close to 8 percent of domestic GDP. Similarly, Economy (2004) quoted a report by the World Bank that China had 16 of the 20 most polluted cities in the world, and Bolt et al. (2001) concluded that China's air pollution problem is the worst in the world.

In response, China began implementing of a number of environmental policies in relation to air and water pollution and solid waste disposal. The number of these regulations has been steadily increasing since the late 1970s (Sinkule and Ortolano, 1995). The State Environmental Protection Administration (SEPA) has also declared control of industrial pollution to be a top priority for Chinese regulators. Responding to this harsh environmental pollution, the National Environmental Protection Agency and the State Planning Commission jointly proposed China's Environmental Action Plan for 1991–2000. The plan highlighted the environmental issues that officials at the national level consider particularly significant. The top three problems listed dealt with water pollution, air pollution and hazardous waste (Ma and Ortolano, 2000). However, weak enforcement of environmental regulations has been recognized as a major problem in China.

In the last decade, there have been many efforts to assess the impact of economic growth on environmental quality. One important method is testing the existence of an inverted U-shaped relationship between environmental indicators and income. Environmental degradation continues until the middle of the growth stage. However, it eventually reaches a peak and starts declining as income surpasses a certain level. Thus, the income elasticity of environmental degradation turns from positive at lower levels of per capita income to negative at higher levels. This relationship has been called the environmental Kuznets curve (EKC) after Simon Kuznets who first observed a similar relationship between income and inequality.

The principal focus of this chapter is to test the EKC in China using province-level data over the 1992–2003 period. Whether the relationship between income and degradation is monotonic or inverted U-shaped is an empirical question. Despite the importance of the EKC and environmental problems, no previous study has tested China's EKC because of the difficulty in obtaining the data. This study applies nonparametric techniques to estimate the relationship between income and environmental quality. Nonparametric estimation is known to be superior to commonly used parametric functional estimation of quadratic and cubic forms (see Azomahou et al., 2006).

The chapter is structured as follows. Section 2 provides the background to this study. Sections 3 and 4 discuss the data and research methods. Section 5 presents the empirical results, and Section 6 presents a summary and concluding remarks.

2   BACKGROUND

China's extraordinary economic performance has been driven by changes in government economic policies such as the dismantling of price regulations and enforcement of a number of competition laws. This has progressively given greater impetus to market forces.

The government in China has also carried out a series of actions to protect the environment and public health. Several laws, regulations and standards have been promulgated (Sinkule and Ortolano, 1995; Edmonds, 2004; Managi and Kaneko, 2006a,b). Three organizations of the National People's Congress, the State Environmental Protection Commission of the State Council, and the SEPA of the State Council primarily work on the decision-making system of environmental policy.

As the starting point of formal environmental management and administration, the government held the first National Congress of Environmental Protection. However, the actual authority of the local environmental agency was extremely limited at this stage. In 1988, the status of the environmental agency was raised, and it took a more independent position from the other ministries.

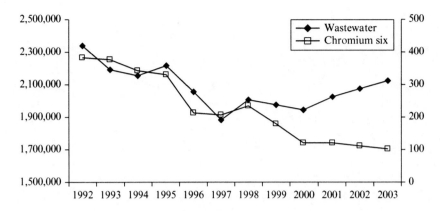

Note: Unit of wastewater discharge is 10,000 ton while unit of chromium six discharge is 1 ton.

Figure 2.1 Annual trend of wastewater and chromium six discharges

The Ninth National People's Congress conducted a radical reform of government administration in 1998 when the environmental protection agency was upgraded to ministerial status and renamed the SEPA. The number of government ministry-level organizations was reduced during this reform period. Therefore, the emergence of the environmental protection administration was an exception during this massive effort to cut central government administration.

Environmental pollutants considered in this study include aggregate measures of wastewater, waste gas and solid waste. Although taking such aggregate measures as pollutants might be questionable, these pollutants are expected to react to improvements in the abatement technologies being applied to corresponding pollutants. This is because environmental policies of the pollution charge system in China directly regulate the volume of wastewater, sulfur dioxide (SO_2) as waste gas, and solid waste. In addition, these three measures are highly correlated with more specific measures of pollutants or costs for damages. Figure 2.1 shows the trend in the national level of wastewater and chromium six discharges over time. These are highly correlated with a correlation coefficient of 0.69. In the same manner, Figures 2.2 and 2.3 show trends in waste gas emissions (with a correlation coefficient of 0.87 to SO_2) and solid waste discharge (with a correlation coefficient of 0.83 to the solid waste levy for the extra discharge of solid waste), respectively. These correlations are not available at the province-level, and therefore our calculations can be considered as a proxy for province level correlations.

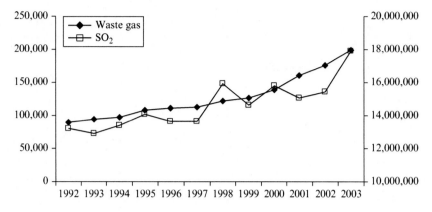

Note: Unit of waste gas emission is 100 million m³ while unit of SO₂ is 1 ton.

Figure 2.2   Annual trend of waste gas emission and SO₂

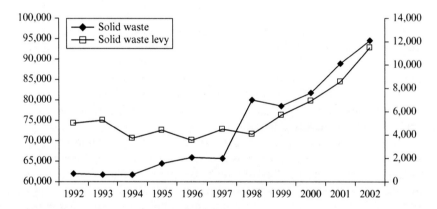

Note: Unit of solid waste generation is 100 million m³ while unit of solid waste levy is 10,000 yuan.

Figure 2.3   Annual trend of solid waste generation and SO₂

These measures are also useful from the viewpoint of saving water and energy. This is because a reduction in wastewater reflects recycling and water saving measures. Reductions in solid waste reflect resource productivity, meaning less use of natural resources. Higher energy use produces higher gas emissions, and therefore a reduction in gas emissions reflects energy saving, at least partially.

Pollution is a byproduct of industrial production. Empirically, environmental degradation has been modeled using the EKC-type specification. Many empirical studies have examined this relationship for various pollutants (for example, Grossman and Krueger, 1995; Dinda, 2004; Azomahou et al., 2006; and Managi, 2007). Researchers have found an inverted U-shaped relationship, monotonically decreasing or increasing, between environmental quality and a rising per capita income level.

Theoretical foundations of the EKC also exist. For example, scale and technique effects are able to explain the pattern of the EKC. In the first stage of development, economic growth demonstrates a scale effect. The effect has a negative impact on the environment. Subsequently, economic growth has encouraging effects on the environment through a technique effect. The shape of the EKC reflects changes in the demand for environmental value. This explanation implies that the link between environmental pollution and income should differ across pollutants according to the difference in their perceived damage.

3   DATA

We use panel data on Chinese manufacturing industrial pollution in this study. This is because manufacturing industries are a primary source of pollution in China. The industries account for about 40 percent of national water pollution and about 80 percent of air pollution from SEPA estimates in 2000. In this study, we use province-by-year panel data covering 29 provinces in the People's Republic of China: Beijing; Tianjin; Hebei; Shanxi; Inner Mongolia; Liaoning; Jilin; Heilongjiang; Shanghai; Jiangsu; Zhejiang; Anhui; Fujian; Jiangxi; Shandong; Henan; Hubei; Hunan; Guangdong; Guangxi; Sichuan and Chongqing; Guizhou; Yunnan; Xizang; Shaanxi; Gansu; Qinghai; Ningxia; Hainan and Xinjiang, including three municipalities. Note that Tibet is excluded because some relevant data are not available. Data for Chongqing, which was separated from Sichuan in 1997, is merged with data for Sichuan. The data cover the 1992–2003 period; data before 1992 are not used because environmental pollution variables are not consistent before and after 1992. Therefore, we are interested in whether these improvements in government policies are reflected in the EKC trend.

Table 2.1 provides definitions and explanations of the variables used in this study. Nominal data are converted into real data using the consumer price index (CPI), and hence the national total is consistent with the sum of regional data in the dataset. Province-level gross state product (GSP) is based on industry and regional government surveys. Note that summation of GSP over the provinces equals GDP, and thus GSP is a province-level

Table 2.1   Data information: 29 provinces for 1993–2003

Variable	Data source
GSP: added value of secondary industry (unit of 10^8 yuan)	1993–1999: *Comprehensive Statistical Data and Materials on 50 Years of New China* 2000–2003: *China Industrial Economy Statistical Yearbook*
Population: year-end population (unit of person)	1993–1999: *Comprehensive Statistical Data and Materials on 50 Years of New China* 2000–2003: *China Industrial Economy Statistical Yearbook*
Wastewater: wastewater quantity measured as the weight of wastewater discharge (unit of 10^4 ton)	1999–2003: *China Environmental Statistical Yearbook*
Waste gas: gas quantity measured as the volume of waste gas emissions, which is not treated (unit of 10^8 m³)	1999–2003: *China Environmental Statistical Yearbook*
Solid waste: waste quantity measured as the discharge amount of solid wastes (unit of 10^4 ton)	1999–2003: *China Environmental Statistical Yearbook*

measure of real GDP in China. Historical GSP data at nominal prices are taken from the *Comprehensive Statistical Data and Materials on 50 Years of New China*. This publication compiles recalculated GSP as far back as 1949 using the System of National Accounts (SNA) method. Population is year-end population obtained from the *Comprehensive Statistical Data and Materials on 50 Years of New China* and the *China Industrial Economy Statistical Yearbook* (CIESY), which is the same source as GSP. Pollution variables of wastewater and solid waste are measured by total weight in each province, while waste gas is measured by total quantity in each province.

Data in the *China Environmental Statistical Yearbook* (CESY) do not cover the entire sample collected in the CIESY or the *China Statistical Yearbook* (CSY). Therefore, direct use of data from the CESY provides biased results. In this study, we adjust the data so as to be able to compare the data to the CSY. Sales data are included in both the CESY and the CIESY. We calculate an adjustment coefficient by taking the ratio of sales data in the CIESY and that in the CESY. The adjustment coefficient varies

Table 2.2   Descriptive statistics

Variable	Unit	Obs	Mean	Std dev.	Min	Max
GSP per capita	yuan	319	6,728.489	3,506.791	1,987.156	19,955.270
Wastewater per capita	ton	319	2.610	1.136	0.969	7.271
Waste gas per capita	m³	319	1,884.638	969.553	475.037	7,536.049
Solid waste per capita	ton	319	0.104	0.058	0.020	0.345

by both year and province and ranges from 1.03 to 7.05, with an average of 1.74. We then multiply the coefficients by the data in the CESY to obtain the adjusted figures. Table 2.2 provides descriptive statistics of the variables used in this study.

The reliability of statistical data in China has been discussed frequently by researchers and policy makers. Economic data are most frequently questioned where the political manipulation of central and local governments are a key issue. The National Bureau of Statistics (NBS) has responsibility for revising the data. The NBS releases the socioeconomic information and makes numerous revisions to the definitions of statistical indicators and the categorization of economic organizations (see Xu, 2004 for details). It revises and adjusts the historical data when: (i) new data sources are found or generated, where such data differ from the original; (ii) changes are made to GDP-related classifications; or (iii) basic concepts, accounting principles, or calculation methods change significantly. Major changes occurred, for instance, in 1995 when the NBS disaggregated the four original secondary industries into five. Documents published by the NBS include *Estimation Methods of China's Annual Gross Domestic Product, Estimation Methods of China's Quarterly Gross Domestic Product* and *Manual of China's Gross Domestic Product Estimation*. Data using the newest methods are from the CSY, while the adjusted data are included in *The Gross Domestic Product of China, 1952–1995*.

Although there may be problems with data reliability, data concerning secondary industries are generally more reliable than those concerning tertiary industries. This is because the value added of many rapidly developing services, such as accounting, legal services, information consultancies and private education, are estimated on the basis of wages and taxes. Province-level GSP is based on industry and regional government surveys. Historical gross regional product (GRP) data for secondary industries at nominal prices are taken from the *Comprehensive Statistical Data and*

Materials on 50 Years of New China. This publication compiles recalculated GRP as far back as 1949 using the SNA method. See Wang and Yao
(2003) for definitions of the other market input variables.

4 MODELS

We employ a nonparametric model to examine the relationship between
environmental degradation data and the economy in order to test the EKC
hypothesis. Computationally intensive nonparametric smoothing methods
have been invented to exploit possible hidden structures and to reduce the
modeling biases of traditional parametric methods demanded by the needs
of nonlinear modeling and fueled by modern computing power.

In parametric regression of the form $y = f(x) + e$, where f is some known,
smooth function, the modeler must determine the appropriate form of f.
In nonparametric regression, f is some unknown, smooth function and is
unspecified by the modeler. A nonparametric smoothing method determines the shape of the curve. Similar to parametric regression, a weighted
sum of the y observations is used to obtain the fitted values. Instead of
using equal weights as in ordinary least squares (OLS), or weights proportional to the inverse of the variance as is often the case in weighted least
squares (WLS), a different rationale determines the choice of weights in
nonparametric regression. Fan (1992) obtained the statistical properties of
the local linear estimator that involves fitting a line locally. This is shown
to be better than the Nadaraya–Watson regression. Fan and Gijbels (1992)
considered the case of local polynomial estimators (also see Hardle and
Linton, 1994). Linton and Gozalo (1996) discussed a related kernel nonparametric regression estimator that can be centered at any parametric
regression model.

Local polynomial regression (see Cleveland, 1979 and Fan and Gijbels,
1992 among others) is the WLS regression that fits to each local data.
An initial kernel regression fitted to the data is used to determine the
weights assigned to the observations. Kernel regression, as described
above, is just a special form of local polynomial regression with polynomials of order (d) equal to zero. Further development of this technique
is provided in Cleveland (1979) and Hastie and Loader (1993), who
generally agreed that for the majority of cases, a first-order fit (local
linear regression) is an adequate choice for d. Local linear regression is
suggested (see Cleveland, 1979) to balance computational ease with the
flexibility to reproduce patterns that exist in the data. Nonetheless, local
linear regression may fail to capture sharp curvature if present in the data
structure (Mays et al., 2001). In such cases, local quadratic regression

($d = 2$) may be needed to provide an adequate fit. Blundell and Duncan (1998) also showed that the fit of a local quadratic regression dominates the local linear and Nadaraya–Watson curves at their respective cross-validated bandwidths. Most modelers now agree that there is usually no need for polynomials of order $d > 2$ (Mays et al., 2001). As a result, only first- and second-order local polynomial regressions are used in the application.

The technique of the local quadratic regression proposed by Cleveland (1979) is usually called locally weighted scatterplot smoother (LOESS) (see also Cleveland and Devlin, 1988). The technique has the advantage of not being sensitive to outliers (therefore, it is robust) and allowing the user to easily adjust the degree of smoothing without the curve having an excessively wiggly shape. It fits a simple straight line or higher-order polynomial function in successive regions of the data, and subsequently iteratively reforms the results to create a smooth, continuous curve. The result of a LOESS regression is a line that best fits the data locally, but is not constrained to be of a particular mathematical form. The resulting curve is not sensitive to missing observations and can be used as a useful tool for finding spurious or outlying observations. The curve is drawn to have the properties the curve needs to be smooth, and that locally, the curve minimizes the variance of the residuals or prediction error. In particular, we apply local polynomial regression (local quadratic fitting) (Cleveland, 1979; Cleveland and Devlin, 1988).

We provide two types of alternative specifications. First, the adjustment coefficients between GSP and environmental variables, which varies over both time and province, directly influence the dependent variables of the regressions. They might be volatile and therefore are affected by the behavior of sales. As alternative specifications, constant values using average adjustment coefficients for all coefficients are used for all three pollutants. Second, we also provide a parametric version of the results from a fixed-effects model for comparison purposes.

5 RESULTS

Three Key Indicators

This study uses a nonparametric model to test the EKC. The three environmental variables are wastewater, waste gas and solid waste. Figures 2.4–2.6 present a summary of the results. Each of the three models includes one of the environmental outputs of waste gas, solid waste and wastewater, respectively.

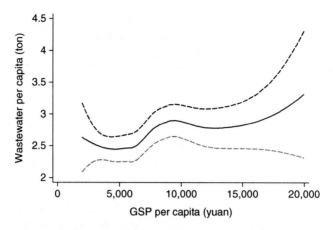

Note: The solid curve represents the estimated line and dashed curves correspond to upper and lower bootstrap 95% pointwise confidence intervals.

Figure 2.4   Nonparametric estimation of the relationship between wastewater and GSP per capita

The results for wastewater are presented in Figure 2.4. This shows an increasing trend on average, or a W-shaped curve, when income levels increase. Thus, we are not able to find an inverted U-shaped curve for wastewater. However, we note that because upper and lower bootstrap 95 percent pointwise confidence intervals show a relatively wide range after 10,000 yuan per capita of GSP, the reliability of its increasing trend is relatively unclear. Waste gas has a more clearly increasing trend, which is presented in Figure 2.5. Its 95 percent pointwise confidence intervals show narrow ranges. Again, we are not able to support the EKC-type curve. Figure 2.6, on the other hand, shows an inverted N-shaped curve, or inverted U-shaped curve, after 5,000 yuan per capita of GSP. We need to be cautious about its statistical reliability because statistical confidence is low for smaller and larger ranges of income per capita. While statistical confidence is high from 5,000 to 12,000 yuan per capita, the trend increases as income levels increase. Therefore, we weakly support the EKC hypothesis for solid waste.

Alternative specifications using constant averaged adjustment co-efficients are employed, and the results are provided in Figures 2.7–9. We obtain very similar trends at the 95 percent confidence level, indicating that our results are robust to changes in the coefficients. Next, the parametric versions of the results using log-cubic regressions are presented in Table 2.3. In the table, the base model uses a time and province varying adjustment

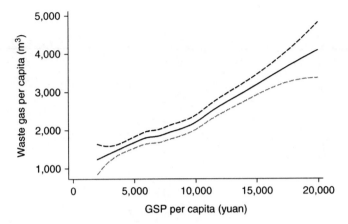

Note: The solid curve represents the estimated line and dashed curves correspond to upper and lower bootstrap 95% pointwise confidence intervals.

Figure 2.5   Nonparametric estimation of the relationship between waste gas and GSP per capita

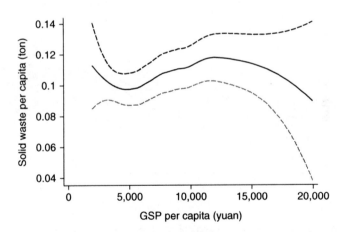

Note: The solid curve represents the estimated line and dashed curves correspond to upper and lower bootstrap 95% pointwise confidence intervals.

Figure 2.6   Nonparametric estimation of the relationship between solid waste and GSP per capita

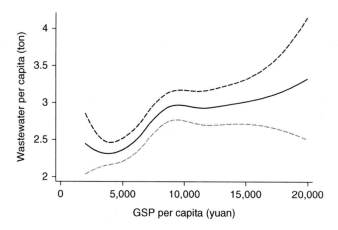

Note: The solid curve represents the estimated line and dashed curves correspond to upper and lower bootstrap 95% pointwise confidence intervals.

Figure 2.7   Alternative specification: nonparametric estimation of the relationship between wastewater and GSP per capita

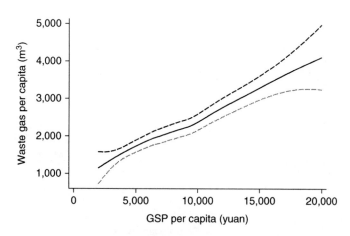

Note: The solid curve represents the estimated line and dashed curves correspond to upper and lower bootstrap 95% pointwise confidence intervals.

Figure 2.8   Alternative specification: nonparametric estimation of the relationship between waste gas and GSP per capita

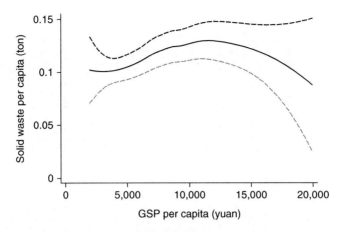

Note: The solid curve represents the estimated line and dashed curves correspond to upper and lower bootstrap 95% pointwise confidence intervals.

Figure 2.9   *Alternative specification: nonparametric estimation of the relationship between solid waste and GSP per capita*

coefficient and the alternative model uses a constant coefficient. Although not all of the linear, square and cubic factors are statistically significant for the three pollutants, generally there are several variables that are significant. The estimated peaks of these pollution estimates show that current income levels for average countries do not reach these points. These are consistent with the results of nonparametric estimations. Summarizing our results, we are not able to support the EKC hypothesis for wastewater and waste gas, and find weak support for solid waste.

The government initiated a series of R&D programs involving studies analyzing atmospheric and water pollutants, solid waste, environmental planning, development of advanced technologies, and demonstration studies of pollution control over decades. Pollution control during the 1970s and 1980s, however, considered only three forms of industrial waste – wastewater, waste gas and solid waste – and no effort was made towards pollution prevention and abatement (Sinkule and Ortolano, 1995). At this stage, the actual authority of the local environmental agency was extremely limited.

Environmental protection has only really started to exert its full presence on the political agenda since the 1990s (ibid.). Six environmental laws and regulations were revised and/or issued in the 1990s. One of the most significant changes in policy was the 1997 revision of the Panel Code of the People's Republic of China, which added a new charge system of

Table 2.3   Parametric estimation of the relationship between pollution and GSP per capita

Variable	Base model			Alternative model		
	Wastewater	Waste gas	Solid waste	Wastewater	Waste gas	Solid waste
GSP per capita	−34.84**	−18.62	−16.78	−55.11***	−38.90**	−37.06*
	(17.64)	(14.56)	(17.13)	(14.59)	(18.01)	(20.42)
(GSP per capita)^2	3.76*	1.85	1.75	6.37***	4.46**	4.35*
	(2.02)	(1.67)	(1.96)	(1.67)	(2.06)	(2.34)
(GSP per capita)^3	−0.14*	−0.06	−0.06	−0.24***	−0.17**	−0.17*
	(0.08)	(0.06)	(0.07)	(0.06)	(0.08)	(0.09)
Constant	108.02**	66.71	49.47	159.14***	117.83***	100.59*
	(51.25)	(42.31)	(49.78)	(42.38)	(52.35)	(59.32)
Observations	319	319	319	319	319	319
Number of states	29	29	29	29	29	29
Turning point1[yuan]	6,504	2,837	2,670	2,613	1,750	1,577
Turning point2[yuan]	17,990	82,1945	218,670	14,875	34,913	24,505

Note: Values in parentheses are standard errors. * Significant at the 10% level. ** Significant at the 5% level. *** Significant at the 1% level. The base model applies a time and province varying adjustment coefficient, while the alternative model applies a constant coefficient.

environmental damage to protect natural resources and the environment, and a charge system of misconduct action in environmental management. In March 1998, the Ninth National People's Congress introduced radical reforms of the government administration.

Therefore, we have reason to expect that environmental qualities will improve when income levels increase (as more environmental policies are implemented). However, we have the following problems. Although the administrative status of environmental agencies has been enhanced, the actual implementation of environmental regulation has not improved dramatically. Insufficient authority and a lack of coordination between institutional actors appear to be the main reasons. Ma and Ortolano (2000) also found evidence for problems in environmental protection management at the local level, where the administrative rank of the environmental protection bureaus is sometimes lower than that of the enterprises it is intended to oversee (ibid.; Economy, 2004). The results of this study confirm the weak status of environmental policies for wastewater, waste gas and solid waste. This evidence might explain why we are not able to find clear signs of an inverted U-shaped relationship between each targeted measure of environmental pollution for wastewater, waste gas, solid waste and per capita income levels.

Detailed Emissions

The nine environmental variables are emissions of SO_2, dust, soot, chemical oxygen demand (COD), lead and chromium six, and domestic demand of coal, oil and fresh water. The first three variables are air pollution indices where SO_2 is the chemical compound and is the main product from the combustion of sulfur compounds, dust is dry particles of matter, and soot is a dark powdery deposit of unburned fuel residues that are hazardous to the lungs and general health. COD is the measure of water quality and the amount of organic pollutants found in surface water (for example, lakes and rivers). Lead and chromium six are metals. Lead is used in building construction among others but also it is a toxic metal. Chromium six is carcinogenic because it is highly reactive, interacting with the body's chemistry and functions. Lastly, coal, oil and fresh water are inputs to production in industry.

Figure 2.10 presents all of the results. The result of SO_2 show a relatively flat trend until about 2,000 yuan per capita, then increase until 7,500 yuan, and finally start declining. This reflects the existence of an EKC relationship. However, we note that, as upper and lower bootstrap 95 percent pointwise confidence intervals show a relatively wide range after 7,500 yuan per capita of income, the reliability of its increasing

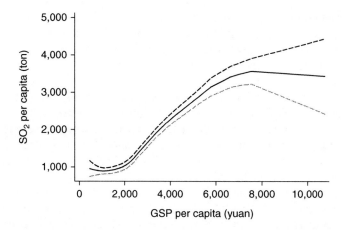

Note: The SO₂ curve represents the estimated line and dashed curves correspond to upper and lower bootstrap 95% pointwise confidence intervals.

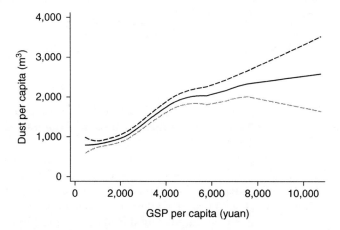

Note: The dust curve represents the estimated line and dashed curves correspond to upper and lower bootstrap 95% pointwise confidence intervals.

Figure 2.10   Relationship between environment and GSP per capita

trend is relatively unclear. This EKC relationship also appears in soot, while the trend of dust is monotonically increasing. In general, relatively hazardous air pollutions of SO₂ and soot show an inverted U-shaped relationship.

Water pollution of COD is known to be difficult to reduce compared to other measures of water quality index such as biochemical oxygen

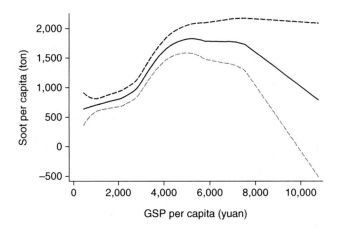

Note: The soot curve represents the estimated line and dashed curves correspond to upper and lower bootstrap 95% pointwise confidence intervals.

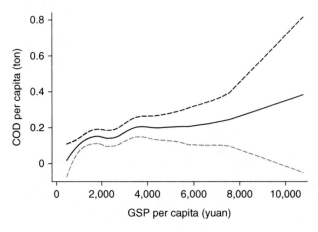

Note: The COD curve represents the estimated line and dashed curves correspond to upper and lower bootstrap 95% pointwise confidence intervals.

Figure 2.10 (continued)

demand. This fact might be a reflection of the monotonically increasing trend of COD. As a toxic metal variable, lead shows a flat trend though higher-income-level reliability is not good. Lead is widely used in industry including building construction, lead-acid batteries, bullets and shot, and is a component of solder, pewter and fusible alloys. Therefore, changes in income level might not matter with regard to its use. However,

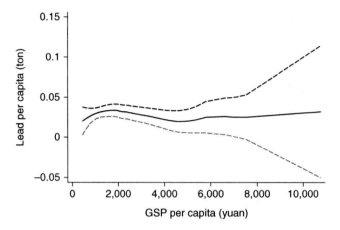

Note: The lead curve represents the estimated line and dashed curves correspond to upper and lower bootstrap 95% pointwise confidence intervals.

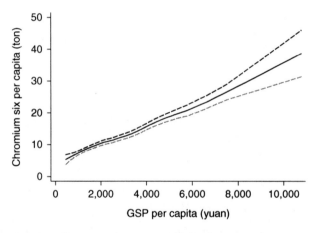

Note: The chromium six curve represents the estimated line and dashed curves correspond to upper and lower bootstrap 95% pointwise confidence intervals.

Figure 2.10 (continued)

we should note that the reliability after 6,000 yuan per capita is rather weak. On the other hand, chromium six has a more clearly increasing trend. Its 95 percent pointwise confidence intervals show narrow ranges. Again, we are not able to support an EKC-type curve. This may be because it is relatively difficult to identify the carcinogenic level in the groundwater.

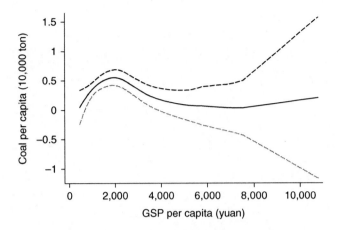

Note: The coal curve represents the estimated line and dashed curves correspond to upper and lower bootstrap 95% pointwise confidence intervals.

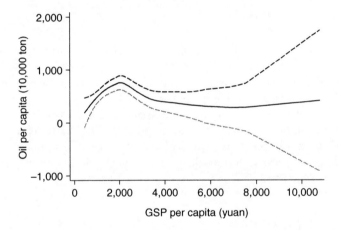

Note: The oil curve represents the estimated line and dashed curves correspond to upper and lower bootstrap 95% pointwise confidence intervals.

Figure 2.10 (continued)

Lastly, all natural resource uses of coal, oil and fresh water are inputs to the industry and therefore less (or efficient) use is preferred. Thus, as in traditional EKC relationships, an inverted U-shape is desirable. All of the results show a similar pattern in that inverted U shapes exist until a middle level of income is reached and then the level of resource uses are flat in higher-income levels. For example, CO_2 emission is directly related to the

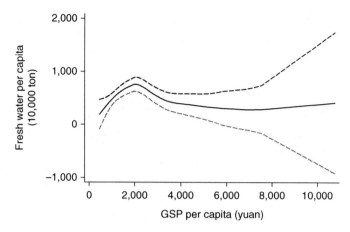

Note: The fresh-water curve represents the estimated line and dashed curves correspond to upper and lower bootstrap 95% pointwise confidence intervals.

Figure 2.10   (continued)

use of energy and, therefore, our results of coal and oil imply that it is difficult to reduce the level of CO_2 by increasing income levels.

We need to be cautious about its statistical reliability at the high-income level since statistical confidence is low at a larger range of income per capita. However, we are able to summarize our results that the SO_2 and soot of air pollution indices seem to support the EKC patterns. The other level of air pollution, water quality measures, toxic metals and natural resource use are either monotonically increasing or show a rather flat trend in high-income levels.

6   CONCLUSION

Because of China's extremely rapid economic growth, the scale and seriousness of environmental problems is no longer in doubt. Considering the importance of the environmental issue, detecting the relationship between economic growth and environmental pollution is important. This study empirically estimates whether there is an EKC, which postulates an inverse U-shaped relationship between a targeted measure of environmental pollution and per capita income levels. None of our results for water pollution, air pollution and solid waste has a significant EKC relationship. We only slightly support the EKC curve for solid waste. Although China has begun to implement a number of environmental policies in relation to air and water pollution and solid waste disposal, our results might imply that enforcement of environmental regulations has been weak, or that the technique effect does not offset the scale effect.

In the future, more stringent comprehensive pollution control needs to be achieved by implementing more effective management. In addition, it will be crucial for China to rely on private initiatives in order to take major steps in addressing the current environmental dilemmas. This is especially so because privately owned firms have less bargaining power in complying with policies than state-owned enterprises (Wang et al., 2002).

However, China faces many challenges in implementing the required strategies. First, China is a developing country, and economic development is a primary consideration. Balancing development with environmental protection to realize sustainable development is difficult. Second, the dominance of 'dirty' industries (for example, coal as an energy source) cannot be changed in the near future. Demand for a better environment is also generally low, so large investment with lengthy delays is required for improvement. Thus, the shift to improved environmental management needs to be cost effective.

REFERENCES

Azomahou, T., F. Laisney and P.N. Van (2006), 'Economic development and CO_2 emissions: a nonparametric panel approach', *Journal of Public Economics*, **90** (6–7), 1347–63.

Blundell, R. and A. Duncan (1998), 'Kernel regression in empirical microeconomics', *Journal of Human Resources*, **33**, 62–87.

Bolt, K., S. Dasgupta, K. Pandey and D. Wheeler (2001), *Cleaning the Air in Developing Countries*, Washington, DC: Forum for Applied Research and Public Policy.

Cleveland, W.S. (1979), 'Robust locally weighted regression and smoothing plots', *Journal of the American Statistical Association*, **74**, 829–36.

Cleveland, W.S. and S.J. Devlin (1988), 'Locally weighted regression: an approach to regression analysis by local fitting', *Journal of the American Statistical Association*, **83**, 596–609.

Dinda, S. (2004), 'Environmental Kuznets curve hypothesis: a survey', *Ecological Economics*, **49** (1), 431–55.

Economy, E.C. (2004), *The River Runs Black: The Environmental Challenge to China's Future*, Ithaca, NY: Cornell University Press.

Edmonds, R.L. (2004), *Managing the Chinese Environment: Studies on Contemporary China*, Oxford: Oxford University Press.

Fan, J. (1992), 'Design-adaptive nonparametric regression', *Journal of the American Statistical Association*, **87**, 998–1004.

Fan, I. and I. Gijbels (1992), 'Variable bandwidths and local linear regression smoothers', *Annals of Statistics*, **20**, 2008–36.

Grossman, G.M. and A.B. Krueger (1995), 'Economic growth and the environment', *Quarterly Journal of Economics*, **110**, 353–77.

Hardle, W. and O. Linton (1994), 'Applied nonparametric methods', in R. Engle and D. McFadden (eds), *Handbook of Econometrics*, Vol. IV, London: Elsevier Science, pp. 2295–339.

Hastie, T. and C. Loader (1993), 'Local regression: automatic kernel carpentry', *Statistical Science*, **8**, 120–43.

Linton, O. and P. Gozalo (1996), 'Using parametric information in non-parametric regression', mimeo, Brown University, Providence, RI.

Ma, X. and L. Ortolano (2000), *Environmental Regulation in China*, Lanham, MD: Rowman & Littlefield.

Managi, S. (2007), *Technological Change and Environmental Policy: A Study of Depletion in the Oil and Gas Industry*, Cheltenham, UK and Northampton, MA, USA: Edward Elgar.

Managi, S. and S. Kaneko (2006a), 'Productivity of market and environmental abatement in China', *Environmental Economics and Policy Studies*, **7** (4), 459–70.

Managi, S. and S. Kaneko (2006b), 'Economic growth and environment in China: an empirical analysis of productivity', *International Journal of Global Environmental Issues*, **6** (1), 89–133.

Mays, J.E., J.B. Birch and B.A. Starnes (2001), 'Model robust regression – combining parametric, nonparametric, and semiparametric methods', *Journal of Nonparametric Statistics*, **13**, 245–77.

Sinkule, B.J. and L. Ortolano (1995), *Implementing Environmental Policy in China*, Westport, CT: Praeger.

Wang, H., N. Mamingi, B. Laplante and S. Dasgupta (2002), 'Incomplete enforcement of pollution regulation: bargaining power of Chinese factories', Policy Research Working Paper 2756, Development Research Group, World Bank, Washington, DC.

Wang, Y. and Y. Yao (2003), 'Sources of China's economic growth 1952–1999: incorporating human capital accumulation', *China Economic Review*, **14**, 32–52.

World Bank (1997), *Clear Water, Blue Skies: China: Environment in the New Century*, Washington, DC: World Bank.

World Bank (2001), *China Air, Land and Water: Environmental Priorities for a New Millennium*, Washington, DC: World Bank.

Xu, X. (2004), 'China's gross domestic product estimation', *China Economic Review*, **15**, 302–22.

3. Efficiency in environment management

1 INTRODUCTION

The principal focus of this chapter is to measure productivity change using a number of approaches, including total factor productivity (TFP), and technological/efficiency change for environmental (that is, nonmarket) outputs in China, using unique province-level secondary industry data over the 1992–2003 period. In addition, the analysis measures market productivity following the traditional productivity literature. It is important to note that the regulations requiring more stringent pollution abatement do not necessarily change environmental productivity. This is because the linear expansion of pollution abatement costs and pollution reduction does not necessarily affect pollution reduction per abatement cost.

Whether pollution abatement technologies are used most efficiently is crucial in the analysis of environmental management because it influences, at least in part, the cost of alternative production and pollution abatement technologies (for example, Jaffe et al., 2003). The role of environmental policy in encouraging or discouraging productivity growth is also well documented in the theoretical literature. As a result of this policy, two possibilities are likely. First, abatement pressures may stimulate technological innovations that reduce the actual cost of compliance below those originally estimated (for example, ibid.). Second, firms may be reluctant to innovate if they believe that regulators will respond by 'ratcheting up' standards (for example, McCain, 1978). In addition to the changes in environmental regulations and technology, management levels also influence environmental productivity. Therefore, whether the productivity and technological frontier expands over time is an empirical question.[1]

2 MODEL

Basic Concept

Productivity is a key concept of production theory. In general, the idea of measuring changes in the productivity of a firm, industry and country is based on comparison of performance in one period relative to another. In other words, a productivity index is defined as the ratio of an index of output growth divided by an index of input growth and inputs over two accounting periods. We focus on the comprehensive productivity measure known as total factor productivity. This measure attempts to include all outputs and all inputs used in the production process. It gives a more accurate picture of performance than partial productivity measures such as labor productivity. Changes in the TFP index tell us how the amount of total output that can be produced from a unit of total input has changed over time. If the firm produces only one output using one input, then a simple measure of productivity change is:

$$TFP = (y_{t+1}/y_t) / (x_{t+1}/x_t), \tag{3.1}$$

where the subscripts t, $t + 1$ indicate the time periods in which x and y are observed. This is also the ratio of the average products of the two periods.

There are two basic approaches to the measurement of productivity change: the econometric estimation of a production, cost or some other function, and the construction of index numbers using nonparametric methods. We adopt the latter because it does not require the imposition of a possibly unwarranted functional form on the structure of production technology as required by the econometric approach.

Nonparametric frontier technologies approaches (for example, Färe et al., 1985, Chambers et al., 1996) can be used to quantify productivity change and can be decomposed into its various components. TFP includes all categories of productivity change, which is decomposed into technological change, or shifts in the production frontier, and efficiency change, or movement of inefficient production units relative to the frontier (for example, Färe et al., 1994).

We measure productivity change in a joint-production model, with a vector of market and nonmarket outputs using production frontier analysis. In the literature of nonparametric frontier technologies approaches, several approaches are proposed, which include the Malmquist productivity index, the Luenberger productivity index, the Hicks–Moorsteen productivity index, and the Luenberger–Hicks–Moorsteen productivity index (see Managi and Aoyagi, 2005). Although each has different characteristics in their assumption and estimation, all of them share the following characteristic: they measure the TFP change between two data points by calculating the ratio (or difference) of two associated distance functions (for example, Caves et al., 1982). A key advantage of the distance function approach is that it provides a convenient way to describe a multi-input, multi-output production technology without the need to specify the functional form. Thus, these approaches allow for a very flexible characterization of productivity change.

Malmquist Productivity Index

Most technology involves more than one output and input. In the presence of multiple outputs, it is not possible to express the production technology in the form of a simple production function since the production function is a 'real-valued function' showing the maximum level of output that can be produced with the given level of inputs. As a result, we need to use sets to represent the technology. The Malmquist productivity index, which is the most frequently used nonparametric frontier technologies approach to measure productivity, requires the choice between an output and an input orientation corresponding to whether one assumes revenue maximization or cost minimization as the appropriate behavioral goal (Färe et al., 1985).

We apply the Malmquist index with an output-based measure of TFP allowing for inefficiency in each decision unit (for example, Färe et al., 1994).[2] Distance functions are a convenient way to describe a multi-input, multi-output production technology without the need to specify a behavioral objective. Using the distance function specification, our problem can be formulated as follows. Let $x = (x^1, \ldots, x^N) \in R_+^N$ and $y = (y^1, \ldots, y^M) \in R_+^M$ be the vectors of inputs and output, respectively, and define the technology set by:

$$P_t \equiv \{(x_t, y_t): x_t \text{ can produce } y_t\}. \tag{3.2}$$

The technology set, P_t, consists of all feasible input, x_t, and output, y_t, vectors, of time period t and satisfies certain axioms sufficient to define meaningful output distance functions (see Shephard, 1970). The estimation of efficiency relative to production frontiers relies on the theory of distance or gauge functions. In economics, distance functions are related to the notion of the coefficient of resource utilization (Debreu, 1951) and to efficiency measures (Farrell, 1957). The distance function at t is defined as:

$$d_0^t(x_t, y_t) = \min \{\phi : (y_t/\phi) \in P_t\}, \text{ on the output set, } P_t, \tag{3.3}$$

where $\tau = 1/\phi$, is the maximal proportional amount that output, y_t, can be expanded while remaining technologically feasible given the technology, P_t, and the input quantities, x_t. The environmental outputs (or pollution) are used as a reciprocal of each value. Therefore, for a given technology and input level, it measures the maximal proportional amount that good outputs and the minimum proportional amount of environmental outputs that can be expanded. Note that $d_0^t(x_t, y_t) \leq 1$ if and only if $(x_t, y_t) \in P_t$, and $d_0^t(x_t, y_t) = 1$ if and only if (x_t, y_t) is on the boundary or production frontier of the technology.

We apply data envelopment analysis (DEA), a nonparametric deterministic technique, to calculate distance functions and construct the productivity measures described below. DEA involves a set of mathematical programming techniques used to estimate the relative efficiency of production units and identify best-practice frontiers.

The DEA formulation calculates the Malmquist productivity index under variable returns to scale by solving the following optimization problem (Färe et al., 1985):

$$[d_0^t(x_t, y_t)]^{-1} = \max_{\tau, \lambda} \tau$$
$$s.t.\ \ Y_t\lambda \geq \tau y_t^i$$
$$X_t\lambda \leq x_t^i \tag{3.4}$$
$$N1'\lambda = 0$$
$$\lambda \geq 0,$$

where $\phi = 1/\tau$ is the efficiency index for province i at year t, $N1$ is an identity matrix, λ is an $N \times 1$ vector of weights, Y_t, X_t are the vectors of output, y_t, and inputs, x_t. The constraints in equation (3.5) construct the reference (or frontier) technology from the information in time t. Every point in this technology set is a linear combination of observed output and input vectors or a point dominated by a linear combination of observed points (see Managi et al., 2004 for an intuitive explanation). To estimate the productivity change over time, several different distance functions, including both the single- and mixed-period distance functions for each province and time period, are necessary. For the mixed-period distance function, we have two years t and $t + 1$. For example, $d_0^t(x_{t+1}, y_{t+1})$ is the value of the distance function for the input–output vector of period $t + 1$ and technology at t.

Caves et al. (1982) introduced two theoretical indices. These indices follow the spirit of Malmquist's quantity index (Malmquist, 1953). Malmquist constructed his quantity index comparing two quantity vectors to an arbitrary indifference curve using radial scaling. Caves et al. offered the multi-output, multi-input productivity measurement (the Malmquist index). They compare two input–output vectors to a reference technology using radial input and output scaling, for the input and output productivity indices, respectively.

The *t*-period output-oriented Malmquist index due to Caves et al. is defined as follows:

$$M_0^t(x_t, y_t, x_{t+1}, y_{t+1}) = \frac{d_0^t(x_{t+1}, y_{t+1})}{d_0^t(x_t, y_t)}. \quad (3.5)$$

This output-oriented Malmquist index treats productivity differences as differences in productivity indices. Two time periods suggested a $t + 1$ productivity index, as follows:

$$M_0^{t+1}(x_t, y_t, x_{t+1}, y_{t+1}) = \frac{d_0^{t+1}(x_{t+1}, y_{t+1})}{d_0^{t+1}(x_t, y_t)}. \quad (3.6)$$

In general, $d_0^t(\cdot)$ and $d_0^{t+1}(\cdot)$ yield different productivity numbers since their reference technologies may differ. The choice between two different productivity indices is arbitrary.

Färe et al. (1994) defined the output-oriented Malmquist productivity index, *TFP(M)*, as the geometric mean of two Malmquist indices. The output-oriented Malmquist index under variable returns to scale is (following Ray and Desli, 1997):

$$
\begin{aligned}
TFP(M) &= [M_0^t(x_t, y_t, x_{t+1}, y_{t+1}) \cdot M_0^{t+1}(x_t, y_t, x_{t+1}, y_{t+1})]^{1/2} \\[2mm]
&= \left[\frac{d_0^t(x_{t+1}, y_{t+1})}{d_0^t(x_t, y_t)} \frac{d_0^{t+1}(x_{t+1}, y_{t+1})}{d_0^{t+1}(x_t, y_t)} \right] \\[2mm]
&= \frac{d_0^{t+1}(x_{t+1}, y_{t+1})}{d_0^t(x_t, y_t)} \left[\frac{d_0^t(x_{t+1}, y_{t+1})}{d_0^{t+1}(x_{t+1}, y_{t+1})} \times \frac{d_0^t(x_t, y_t)}{d_0^{t+1}(x_t, y_t)} \right]^{1/2} \quad (3.7)
\end{aligned}
$$

where the first ratio, which is outside the square brackets, represents efficiency change (EC), and the second geometric product of ratios, which is inside the square brackets, captures technological change (TC).

Luenberger Productivity Index

The Luenberger productivity index is the dual to the profit function and does not require the choice of an input–output orientation (Chambers et al., 1996). Since the Luenberger productivity index can be applied with an output- or input-oriented perspective, it is a generalization of, and superior to, the Malmquist productivity index (Luenberger, 1992a,b, 1995; Chambers et al., 1998; Boussemart et al., 2003). Luenberger

(1992a,b) generalizes the previous notion of distance functions as a shortage function and provides a flexible tool to take account of both input contractions and output improvements when measuring efficiency. This shortage function, also called a 'directional distance function' (DDF), is the dual to the profit function (Luenberger, 1992b, 1995; Chambers et al., 1998).

The DDF involving a simultaneous input and output variation in the direction of a preassigned vector $g_t = (g_t^i, g_t^0) \in R_+^{M+N}$ is defined as follows:

$$D^t(x_t, y_t; g_t) = \max\{\delta:(x_t - \delta g_t^i, y_t + \delta g_t^0) \in P_t\}. \tag{3.8}$$

Considering the special case of a general directional vector $g:g_t^i = x_t$ and $g_t^0 = y_t$, we are able to define the proportional distance function, which is a special case of the shortage function. The proportional distance function is defined at t as:

$$D^t(x_t, y_t) = \max\{\delta:[(1 - \delta)x_t, (1 + \delta)y_t] \in P_t\}, \tag{3.9}$$

where δ is the maximal proportional amount that output, y^t, can be expanded and input, x^t, can be reduced given the technology, P^t. As in the Malmquist index, the DEA formulation calculates the Luenberger productivity index under variable returns to scale by solving the following optimization problem (Chambers et al., 1996):

$$\begin{aligned} D^t(x_t, y_t) &= \max_{\delta,\lambda} \delta \\ \text{s.t. } Y_t\lambda &\geq (1 + \delta)y_t^i \\ X_t\lambda &\leq (1 - \delta)x_t^i \\ N1'\lambda &= 0 \\ \lambda &\geq 0, \end{aligned} \tag{3.10}$$

where $N1$ is an identity matrix, λ is an $N \times 1$ vector of weights, Y^t, and X^t are the vectors of output, y^t, and inputs, x^t.

As in Malmquist indices, several different proportional distance functions are necessary to estimate the change in productivity over time. For the mixed period distance function, we have two years, t and $t + 1$. The t-period and $t + 1$-period Luenberger index due to Caves et al. (1982) are defined as follows:

$$L^t(x_t, y_t, x_{t+1}, y_{t+1}) = D^t(x_t, y_t) - D^t(x_{t+1}, y_{t+1}) \tag{3.11}$$

$$L^{t+1}(x_t, y_t, x_{t+1}, y_{t+1}) = D^{t+1}(x_t, y_t) - D^{t+1}(x_{t+1}, y_{t+1}). \tag{3.12}$$

The Luenberger productivity index, *TFP(L)*, defined by Chambers et al. (1996) is as follows:

$$TFP(L) = \frac{1}{2}\{[D^t(x_t, y_t) - D^t(x_{t+1}, y_{t+1})] + [D^{t+1}(x_t, y_t)$$

$$- D^{t+1}(x_{t+1}, y_{t+1})]\} \tag{3.13}$$

This is an arithmetic mean of period *t* (the first difference) and period *t* + 1 (the second difference) Luenberger indices, as an attempt once again to avoid any arbitrary selection of base years (for example, Balk, 1998). The above index can be decomposed into two components:

$$TFP(L) = [D^t(x_t, y_t) - D^{t+1}(x_{t+1}, y_{t+1})] + \frac{1}{2}\{[D^{t+1}(x_{t+1}, y_{t+1})$$

$$- D^t(x_{t+1}, y_{t+1})] + [D^{t+1}(x_t, y_t) - D^t(x_t, y_t)]\} \tag{3.14}$$

where the first difference represents efficiency changes, and the arithmetic mean of the last two differences represents technological change.

Hicks–Moorsteen Productivity Index

Bjurek (1996) defines an alternative Malmquist TFP (or Hicks–Moorsteen productivity) index, as the ratio of Malmquist output and input indices. The Hicks–Moorsteen productivity index, *TFP(HM)*, with base period *t* is defined as the ratio of a Malmquist output quantity index at base period *t* and a Malmquist input quantity index at base period *t*:

$$TFP(HM)_t = \frac{MO_t(x_t, y_t, y_{t+1})}{MI_t(x_t, x_{t+1}, y_t)}. \tag{3.15}$$

The index is simultaneously oriented, involving both output distance functions and input distance functions. The Malmquist output and input quantity indices are defined as follows, using distance functions, respectively:

$$MO_t(x_t, y_t, y_{t+1}) = \frac{d_0^t(x_t, y_{t+1})}{d_0^t(x_t, y_t)} \tag{3.16}$$

$$MI_t(x_t, x_{t+1}, y_t) = \frac{d_0^t(x_{t+1}, y_t)}{d_0^t(x_t, y_t)}. \tag{3.17}$$

Lovell (2003) decomposes the Hicks–Moorsteen productivity index of the period *t* into efficiency change (EC), technological change (TC), and scale change (SC). Managi and Aoyagi (2005) work further with the geometric mean of period t and period $t + 1$ index and define the Hicks–Moorsteen productivity index with the geometric mean of period t and period $t + 1$ as:

$$TFP(HM) = [TFR(HM)_t \cdot TFP(HM)_{t+1}]^{1/2}$$

$$= \left[\frac{MO_t(x_t, y_t, y_{t+1})\ MO_{t+1}(x_{t+1}, y_{t+1}, y_t)}{MI_t(x_t, x_{t+1}, y_t)\ MI_{t+1}(x_t, x_{t+1}, y_{t+1})} \right]^{1/2}$$

$$= \left[\frac{d_0^t(x_t, y_{t+1})}{d_0^t(x_t, y_t)} \frac{d_0^{t+1}(x_{t+1}, y_{t+1})}{d_0^{t+1}(x_{t+1}, y_t)} \right] \Big/ \left[\frac{d_i^t(x_{t+1}, y_t)}{d_i^t(x_t, y_t)} \frac{d_i^{t+1}(x_{t+1}, y_{t+1})}{d_i^{t+1}(x_t, y_{t+1})} \right], \quad (3.18)$$

where TC, EC and SC of the Hicks–Moorsteen productivity index are defined as follows:

$$TC(HM) = \left[\frac{d_0^t(x_{t+1}, y_{t+1})}{d_0^{t+1}(x_{t+1}, y_{t+1})} \right] \quad (3.19)$$

$$EC(HM) = \left[\frac{d_0^{t+1}(x_{t+1}, y_{t+1})}{d_0^t(x_t, y_t)} \right] \quad (3.20)$$

$$SC(HM) = TFP(HM)/TC(HM) \cdot EC(HM).$$

Lovell (2003) proposes technological change and efficiency change index alternatives to use with an input orientation. In this study, we focus on the output-oriented TC and EC. We should note, however, that SC in *TFP(HM)* is rather difficult to interpret because of its complex formulation. Therefore, the other three indices may be recommended for empirical modeling.

Luenberger–Hicks–Moorsteen Productivity Index

Briec and Kerstens (2004) introduce the difference-based Luenberger–Hicks–Moorsteen productivity index, *TFP(LHM)*. They define *TFP(LHM)* using both input- and output-oriented Luenberger productivity indices. We define input- and output-oriented Luenberger productivity indices with the period t as follows:

$$L_0^t(x_t, y_t, 0, y_{t+1}) = D^t[x_t, y_t; (0, g_0^t)] - D^t[x_t, y_{t+1}; (0, g_0^{t+1})] \quad (3.21)$$

$$L_i^t(x_t, y_t, x_{t+1}, 0) = D^t[x_{t+1}, y_t; (g_i^{t+1}, 0)] - D^t[x_t, y_t; (g_i^t, 0)]. \quad (3.22)$$

The Luenberger–Hicks–Moorsteen productivity index with the period t is defined as follows:

$$TFP(LHM)_t = L_0^t(x_t, y_t, 0, y_{t+1}) - L_i^t(x_t, y_t, x_{t+1}, 0) \qquad (3.23)$$

In the same way, the input and output productivity indices of period $t + 1$ are as follows:

$$L_0^{t+1}(0, y_t, x_{t+1}, y_{t+1}) = D^{t+1}[x_{t+1}, y_t; (0, g_0^t)] - D^{t+1}[x_{t+1}, y_{t+1}; (0, g_0^{t+1})]$$
$$(3.24)$$

$$L_i^t(x_t, 0, x_{t+1}, y_{t+1}) = D^{t+1}[x_{t+1}, y_{t+1}; (g_i^{t+1}, 0)] - D^{t+1}[x_t, y_{t+1}; (g_i^t, 0)].$$
$$(3.25)$$

A base period $t + 1$ Luenberger–Hicks–Moorsteen productivity index can be similarly defined:

$$TFP(LHM)_{t+1} = L_0^{t+1}[0, y_t, x_{t+1}, y_{t+1})] - L_i^{t+1}[x_t, 0, x_{t+1}, y_{t+1})].$$
$$(3.26)$$

The choice between two different Luenberger–Hicks–Moorsteen productivity indices is arbitrary. An arithmetic mean of period t and period $t + 1$ indices is taken as follows:

$$TFP(LHM) = \frac{1}{2}[TFR(LHM)_t + TFP(LHM)_{t+1}]. \qquad (3.27)$$

When $g_i^t = x_t$ and $g_0^t = y_t$, the output- and input-oriented DDFs are as follows:

$$D^t[x_t, y_t; (0, g_0^t)] = \max \{\delta : [x_t, (1 + \delta)y_t] \in P_t\} \qquad (3.28)$$

$$D^t[x_t, y_t; (g_i^t, 0)] = \max \{\delta : [(1 - \delta)x_t, y_t] \in P_t\}. \qquad (3.29)$$

The Luenberger–Hicks–Moorsteen productivity index defined by Briec and Kerstens (2004) is as follows:

$$TFP(LHM) = \frac{1}{2}\{[D_t^0(x_t, y_t) - D_t^0(x_t, y_{t+1})] - [D_t^i(x_{t+1}, y_t) - D_t^i(x_t, y_t)]$$

$$+ [D_{t+1}^0(x_{t+1}, y_t) - D_{t+1}^0(x_{t+1}, y_{t+1})]$$

$$- [D_{t+1}^i(x_{t+1}, y_{t+1}) - D_{t+1}^i(x_t, y_{t+1})]\}. \qquad (3.30)$$

The above index can be decomposed into three components following Managi and Aoyagi (2005):

$$TFP(LHM) = \frac{1}{2}\{[D_t^i(x_t, y_t) - D_{t+1}^i(x_{t+1}, y_{t+1})] - [D_t^0(x_t, y_t)$$

$$- D_{t+1}^0(x_{t+1}, y_{t+1})]\} + \{[D_{t+1}^i(x_{t+1}, y_{t+1})$$

$$- D_t^i(x_{t+1}, y_{t+1})] - [D_{t+1}^0(x_{t+1}, y_{t+1})$$

$$- D_t^0(x_{t+1}, y_{t+1})]\} + \frac{1}{2}\{-D_t^i(x_t, y_t) + 3D_t^0(x_t, y_t)$$

$$- D_{t+1}^0(x_{t+1}, y_{t+1}) - D_{t+1}^i(x_{t+1}, y_{t+1})$$

$$+ 2D_t^i(x_{t+1}, y_{t+1}) - 2D_t^0(x_{t+1}, y_{t+1}) - D_t^0(x_t, y_{t+1})$$

$$- D_t^i(x_{t+1}, y_t) + D_{t+1}^0(x_{t+1}, y_t) - D_{t+1}^i(x_t, y_{t+1})\},$$

$$(3.31)$$

where the first curly brackets measure efficiency changes of the proportional distance function between periods t and $t + 1$, while the second and third curly brackets represent technological change and scale change, respectively.

Environmental Productivity Index

Following Managi et al. (2005), this study uses two datasets, of which one includes only market input/output, TFP_{Market}, and the other includes environmental input/output in addition to the market input/output, TFP_{Joint}, considering the maximum expansion of good outputs and contraction of bad outputs. The TFP associated with environmental outputs, TFP_{Env} or environmental productivity, is then calculated as:

$$TFP_{Env}(M) = TFP_{Joint}(M) / TFP_{Market}(M), \qquad (3.32)$$

$$TFP_{Env}(L) = TFP_{Joint}(L) - TFP_{Market}(L), \qquad (3.33)$$

$$TFP_{Env}(HM) = TFP_{Joint}(HM) / TFP_{Market}(HM), \qquad (3.34)$$

$$TFP_{Env}(LHM) = TFP_{Joint}(LHM) - TFP_{Market}(LHM), \qquad (3.35)$$

where $TFP(M)$ and $TFP(HM)$ are the Malmquist index and the Hicks–Moorsteen productivity index, representing the ratio of the two models. $TFP(L)$ and $TFP(LHM)$ are the Luenberger index and the Luenberger–Hicks–Moorsteen productivity index, respectively, representing the difference between the two models. This is because the Luenberger and Luenberger–Hicks–Moorsteen productivity indices use the difference method while the Malmquist and Hicks–Moorsteen productivity indices use the ratio method (see Färe et al., 1994; Chambers et al., 1998).

In a country-level analysis, TFP includes not only changes in technology but also the effect of management-level changes in institutions, including environmental regulations. Production frontier analysis yields the ratio or difference indices (for example, Malmquist, 1953; Caves et al., 1982; Luenberger, 1995), which can then be used to quantify productivity change. The index-based approach measures the TFP change between two data points by calculating the ratio or difference of two associated distance functions or shortage functions (for example, Caves et al., 1982; Luenberger, 1995). This approach has several advantages. One advantage is the immediate compatibility with multiple inputs and outputs. This is important for environmental applications, since pollutants, as the by-product of market outputs, can be multiple. This technique estimates the weight given to each observation, such as the weight or shadow price for each item of environmental pollution data, and implicitly combines these into a single index. In addition, this approach can incorporate the inefficient behavior of the decision maker and avoid the need for the explicit specification of the production function (see Managi, 2004 and Managi et al., 2004, 2005 for further details).

3 DATA

In this study, we use panel data on Chinese secondary industries, including mining, manufacturing, electricity, gas and water. This study focuses on industrial pollution, since Chinese industry is a primary source of the pollution and industry accounts for about 40 percent of national water pollution and about 80 percent of air pollution according to SEPA estimates in 2000.

The dataset consists of annual data for the 1992–2003 period for 29 of the 31 provinces, including three municipalities, in the People's Republic of China.[3] Definition and explanation of the variables used in this study is provided in Table 3.1. Nominal data are converted into real data using the consumer price index (CPI), hence the national total is consistent with the sum of regional data in the dataset. 'Labor' is quality-adjusted labor in secondary industry. The wages for labor are used to control for quality.[4] Note that, although quality is adjusted in Kaneko and Managi (2005), it is not adjusted in Kaneko and Managi (2004) or Managi and Kaneko (2006). Pollution abatement cost and expenditure (PACE) are funds actually used

Table 3.1   Data information: 29 provinces for 1992–2003

Variable	Data source
GRP: added value of secondary industry (unit: 10^8 yuan)	1992–1999: *Comprehensive Statistical Data and Materials on 50 Years of New China* 2000–2003: *China Industrial Economy Statistical Yearbook*
Number of employees working in secondary industry (unit: 10^4 persons)	1992–1999: *Communication Statistics on 50 Years of China* 2000–2003: *China Industrial Economy Statistical Yearbook*
Wage: Wages paid in industry (unit: 10^4 yuan)	1992–2003: *China Statistical Yearbook*
Capital stock: estimated from annual productive net of depreciation in the secondary industry (unit: 10^8 yuan)	1992–1999: *Communication Statistics on 50 Years of China* 2000–2003: *China Industrial Economy Statistical Yearbook*
Wastewater: wastewater quantity measured as the weight of wastewater discharge (unit: 10^4 ton)	1992–2003: *China Environmental Statistical Yearbook*
Waste gas: gas quantity measured as the volume of waste gas emissions, which is not treated (unit: 10^8 m^3)	1992–2003: *China Environmental Statistical Yearbook*
Solid waste: waste quantity measured as the discharge amount of solid waste (unit: 10^4 ton)	1992–2003: *China Environmental Statistical Yearbook*
PACE: funds actually used for industrial environmental pollution of wastewater, waste gas and solid waste (unit: 10^4 yuan)	1992–2003: *China Environmental Statistical Yearbook*
SO_2: emission refers to volume of SO_2 emission from fuel burning and production process in premises of enterprises (unit: ton)	1992–2003: *China Environmental Statistical Yearbook*
Dust: emission quantity measured as the discharge amount of dust (unit: ton)	1992–2003: *China Environmental Statistical Yearbook*
Soot: soot emission by consumption and others refers to net volume of soot emitted by fuel burning from economic activities and operation of industrial activities.	1992–2003: *China Environmental Statistical Yearbook*

Table 3.1 (continued)

Variable	Data source
It is calculated on the basis of coal consumption (unit: ton)	
COD: Index of water pollution measuring the mass concentration of oxygen consumed by the chemical breakdown of organic and inorganic matter (unit: ton)	1992–2003: *China Environmental Statistical Yearbook*
Lead: discharge of lead emitted by production process of industrial activities (unit: ton)	1992–2003: *China Environmental Statistical Yearbook*
Chromium six: discharge of hexavalent chromium emitted by production process of industrial activities (unit: ton)	1992–2003: *China Environmental Statistical Yearbook*
Oil consumption: total oil consumed as fuel TCE (unit: 10^4 TCE)	1992–2003: *China Environmental Statistical Yearbook*
Coal consumption: total coal consumed as fuel in TCE (unit: 10^4 TCE)	1992–2003: *China Environmental Statistical Yearbook*
Fresh water: use of fresh water in industrial activities (unit: 10^4 ton)	1992–2003: *China Environmental Statistical Yearbook*

to remedy industrial environmental pollution in the form of wastewater, waste gas and solid waste. PACE is considered as an environmental input. Increase in PACE given other input/output will reduce pollution. In addition to PACE and market inputs such as capital and labor, we estimate efficiency with inputs including coal consumption, oil consumption and fresh water use. An increase in coal and oil consumption is associated with an increase in both air pollution and gross regional product (GRP). The explosion in economic growth also made China the world's second largest CO_2 emitter and energy consumer after the United States by the end of the twentieth century (see Figure 3.1).

Crude oil consumption has increased at an average rate of 6 percent per year in the past few decades. China's growing energy consumption, reliance on coal, and air pollution are rapidly emerging as major environmental issues. Coal consumption, the primary energy source accounting for more than 70 percent of total energy consumption, is the main source of anthropogenic air pollution emissions in China. These include TSP pollution, SO_2 pollution and acid rain. Use of fresh water in production process

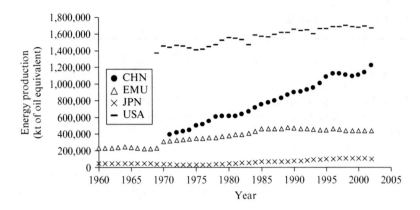

Source: World Development Indicators (WDI, 2005).

Figure 3.1   Energy production

is also necessary to produce goods. The models in this study are able to estimate efficiency improvements in the use of coal and oil consumption to save fuel and fresh water.

Data in the *China Environmental Statistical Yearbooks* (CESY) do not cover the entire sample collected in the other statistical data such as the *China Industrial Economy Statistical Yearbook* (CIESY) and the *China Statistical Yearbook*. Therefore, use of data from the CESY provides biased results. In this study, we adjust the data so as to be able to compare the data to the *China Statistical Yearbook* following Kaneko and Managi (2005). Sales data are included in both the CESY and the CIESY. We calculate an adjustment coefficient by taking the ratio of sales data in the CIESY and that in the CESY. The adjustment coefficient ranges from 1.03 to 7.05, with an average of 1.74. We then multiply the coefficients, which vary by year and province, by the data in the CESY to obtain the adjusted figures.

The reliability of statistical data in China has been discussed frequently by researchers and policy makers. Economic outputs are most frequently questioned where the political manipulation of central and local governments are a key issue. The National Bureau of Statistics (NBS) has responsibility for revising the data. The NBS releases the socioeconomic information and makes numerous revisions to the definitions of statistical indicators and the categorization of economic organizations (see Xu, 2004 for detail). The NBS revises and adjusts the historical data once: (i) new data sources are found or generated, where such data differ from the original; (ii) changes are made to GDP-related classifications; or (iii) basic concepts, accounting principles, or calculation methods change significantly.

Major changes occurred, for instance, in 1995 when the NBS disaggregated the four original secondary industries into five. Documents published by the NBS include *Estimation Methods of China's Annual Gross Domestic Product, Estimation Methods of China's Quarterly Gross Domestic Product,* and the *Manual of China's Gross Domestic Product Estimation.* Data using the newest methods are from the *China Statistical Yearbook,* while the adjusted data are included in *The Gross Domestic Product of China, 1952–1995.*

Although there may be problems with data reliability, data concerning secondary industry in China are generally more reliable than those concerning tertiary industry. This is because the value added of many rapidly developing services, such as accounting, legal services, information consultancies and private education, are estimated on the basis of wages and taxes. Province-level GRP is based on industry and regional government surveys. Historical GRP data for secondary industry at nominal prices are taken from the *Comprehensive Statistical Data and Materials on 50 Years of New China.* This publication compiles recalculated GRP as far back as 1949 using the SNA method. See Wang and Yao (2003) for construction of the other market input variables.

4 EMPIRICAL RESULTS

This study uses different models to measure and decompose productivity change in terms of market outputs, environmental (pollution) outputs, and joint production (so-called 'green' productivity). The vectors of outputs and inputs for each model are listed in Table 3.2. The output variables in our model are GRP, waste gas, solid waste, wastewater, SO_2, dust, soot, COD, lead and chromium six (see Table 3.2). Our input variables include labor, capital, oil consumption, coal consumption, fresh water, PACE, PACE for waste gas, PACE for solid waste, and PACE for wastewater.

Separate frontiers are estimated for each year, and shifts in the frontiers over time are used to measure technological change. We use the geometric mean of the Malmquist indices and the Hicks–Moorsteen productivity indices (both ratio methods), and the arithmetic mean of the Luenberger productivity indices and the Luenberger–Hicks–Moorsteen productivity indices (both difference methods) for each province, to obtain a combined value for each index in each year. See Balk (1998) for theoretical reasoning underlying the use of geometric and arithmetic means to average data. The mean values are presented in each figure. Values larger than one and zero are regarded as increases in productivity using ratio- and difference-based indices, respectively. We estimate the productivity indices in both

Table 3.2   *Model specifications*

Index calculated	Model 1 Base	Model 2 Base (Energy)	Model 3 Base (All)	Model 4 Joint (All1)	Model 5 Joint (All2)	Model 6 Joint (All3)	Model 7 Joint (All4)
Output variables							
GRP	X	X	X	X	X	X	X
Waste gas				X	X	X	X
Solid waste				X	X	X	X
Wastewater				X	X	X	X
SO_2						X	
Dust						X	
Soot						X	
COD						X	
Lead						X	
Chromium six						X	
Input variables							
Labor	X	X	X	X	X	X	X
Capital	X	X	X	X	X	X	X
Oil consumption		X	X		X	X	X
Coal consumption		X	X		X	X	X
Fresh water			X	X	X	X	X
PACE					X	X	X

Index calculated	Model 8 Joint (Gas1)	Model 9 Joint (Gas2)	Model 10 Joint (Gas3)	Model 11 Joint (Gas4)	Model 12 Joint (Gas5)	Model 13 Joint (Solid)	Model 14 Joint (Water1)
Output variables							
GRP	X	X	X	X	X	X	X
Waste gas	X				X		
Solid waste						X	
Wastewater							X
SO_2		X	X	X	X		
Dust			X	X	X		
Soot			X	X	X		
Input variables							
Labor	X	X	X	X	X	X	X
Capital	X	X	X	X	X	X	X
Oil consumption				X	X		
Coal consumption				X	X		
PACE (waste gas)	X	X	X		X		
PACE (solid waste)						X	
PACE (wastewater)							X

Table 3.2 (continued)

Index calculated	Model 15 Joint (Water2)	Model 16 Joint (Water3)	Model 17 Joint (Water4)	Model 18 Joint (Water5)	Model 19 Joint (Water6)	Model 20 Joint (Water7)	Model 21 Joint (Water8)
Output variables							
GRP	X	X	X	X	X	X	X
Wastewater	X	X		X		X	X
COD		X	X	X			
Lead		X	X	X			
Chromium six		X	X	X			
Input variables							
Labor	X	X	X	X	X	X	X
Capital	X	X	X	X	X	X	X
Fresh water	X	X	X	X	X		X
PACE (wastewater)	X	X	X	X			

constant returns to scale (CRS) and variable returns to scale (VRS). Table 3.3 presents the summary of the results, as detailed analyses are provided below. The table shows the results for VRS (Ray and Desli, 1997).

Market Productivity

Centrally planned economies usually commence reform from an extremely inefficient position. Operations would be expected to be far from the Pareto frontier because of the enormous allocative distortions and far below the production possibility set because of the poor incentive mechanisms in the economy. Accordingly, there is great potential for technological and efficiency improvement, which may generate growth opportunities not seen in developed economies. Therefore, once institutions have changed to remove the distortions associated with the centrally planned party system, these economies are able to enjoy great growth potential. The important question for many developing countries is how large the gains are after reform and how to make institutional changes to realize this growth potential when the initial condition has a myriad of distortions. In order to analyze the above questions, this study evaluates the productivity, technological and efficiency change following reform.

Model 1 considers conventional combinations of inputs and output to measure market productivity. The results for annual change of TFP for the several different productivity indices are presented in Figure 3.2.[5] Cumulative values are shown in Figure 3.7 (see below). The TFP of the Malmquist index increases by 22.14 percent between 1992 and 2003. A Malmquist TFP growth of 1.84 percent on average supports the findings of Young (1993), who has questioned Chinese growth performance. The source of the TFP increase appears to come mainly from technological change rather than efficiency change. This reflects the relatively high potential for efficiency improvements. Chen and Feng (2000) estimate a cross-sectional growth equation for 29 Chinese provinces covering the 1978–89 period. They analyze private and semiprivate enterprises, and they find that higher education and international trade all lead to an increase in economic growth. Their evidence indicates that the convergence hypothesis holds. Although their sample period differs, there is the possibility that convergence in growth may have occurred through a lower level of efficiency.

During our study period, several reforms in economic policy occurred. First, reform was introduced in 1993. The Communist Party's Economics and Finance Leading Group, headed by Party Secretary General Jiang Zemin, worked together with economists to prepare a grand strategy for transition to a market system. The Third Plenum of the Fourteenth Party

Table 3.3 Summary of results (VRS): cumulative change in indices

Index	Malmquist			Hicks–Moorsteen			Luenberger			Luenberger–Hicks–Moorsteen		
	TFP	TC	EC	TFP	TC	EC	TFP	TC	EC	TFP	TC	EC
Model 1 (1992–2003)	1.29	1.29	1.00	0.99	1.36	1.00	0.10	0.10	0.05	0.75	0.47	0.30
	(1.02)	(1.02)	(1.00)	(1.00)	(1.03)	(1.00)	(0.01)	(0.01)	(0.00)	(0.07)	(0.04)	(0.03)
Model 2 (1996–2003)	1.21	1.13	1.07	0.88	1.14	1.07	0.15	0.10	0.06	0.44	0.29	0.20
	(1.03)	(1.02)	(1.01)	(0.98)	(1.02)	(1.01)	(0.02)	(0.01)	(0.01)	(0.06)	(0.04)	(0.03)
Model 3 (1996–2003)	1.55	1.47	1.05	0.84	1.88	1.05	0.20	0.16	0.06	0.44	0.14	0.39
	(1.06)	(1.06)	(1.01)	(0.98)	(1.09)	(1.01)	(0.03)	(0.02)	(0.01)	(0.06)	(0.02)	(0.06)
Model 4 (1992–2003)	1.33	1.35	0.98	1.12	1.58	0.98	0.13	0.13	0.04	0.56	0.33	0.37
	(1.03)	(1.03)	(1.00)	(1.01)	(1.04)	(1.00)	(0.01)	(0.01)	(0.00)	(0.05)	(0.03)	(0.03)
Model 5 (1996–2003)	1.48	1.46	1.02	0.85	1.90	1.02	0.20	0.18	0.07	0.38	0.23	0.41
	(1.06)	(1.06)	(1.00)	(0.98)	(1.01)	(1.00)	(0.03)	(0.03)	(0.01)	(0.05)	(0.03)	(0.06)
Model 6 (1996–2003)	1.80	1.71	1.05	1.57	2.31	1.02	0.22	0.23	0.09	0.38	0.07	0.53
	(1.09)	(1.08)	(1.01)	(1.07)	(1.13)	(1.00)	(0.03)	(0.03)	(0.01)	(0.05)	(0.01)	(0.08)
Model 7 (1996–2003)	1.50	1.43	1.05	0.95	1.87	1.05	0.21	0.19	0.06	0.41	0.11	0.39
	(1.06)	(1.05)	(1.01)	(0.99)	(1.09)	(1.01)	(0.03)	(0.03)	(0.01)	(0.06)	(0.02)	(0.06)
Model 8 (1992–2003)	1.21	1.20	1.01	1.15	1.46	1.01	0.12	0.10	0.07	0.47	0.33	0.31
	(1.02)	(1.02)	(1.00)	(1.01)	(1.04)	(1.00)	(0.01)	(0.01)	(0.01)	(0.04)	(0.03)	(0.03)
Model 9 (1992–2003)	1.21	1.21	1.00	0.95	1.46	1.00	0.12	0.10	0.07	0.66	0.38	0.31
	(1.02)	(1.02)	(1.00)	(1.01)	(1.04)	(1.00)	(0.01)	(0.01)	(0.01)	(0.06)	(0.03)	(0.03)
Model 10 (1992–2003)	1.21	1.21	1.00	0.96	1.46	1.00	0.13	0.11	0.07	0.64	0.35	0.30
	(1.02)	(1.02)	(1.00)	(1.00)	(1.04)	(1.00)	(0.01)	(0.01)	(0.01)	(0.06)	(0.03)	(0.03)
Model 11 (1996–2003)	1.24	1.19	1.04	0.81	1.20	1.04	0.12	0.10	0.04	0.32	0.31	0.25
	(1.03)	(1.03)	(1.01)	(0.97)	(1.03)	(1.00)	(0.02)	(0.01)	(0.01)	(0.05)	(0.04)	(0.04)

Model 12 (1992–2003)	1.18	1.14	1.04	0.90	1.20	1.04	0.12	0.10	0.04	0.96	1.03	0.99
	(1.02)	(1.02)	(1.00)	(0.98)	(1.03)	(1.00)	(0.02)	(0.01)	(0.01)	(0.14)	(0.15)	(0.14)
Model 13 (1992–2003)	1.24	1.24	1.01	1.00	1.36	1.01	0.15	0.08	0.03	0.47	0.28	0.27
	(1.02)	(1.02)	(1.00)	(1.00)	(1.03)	(1.00)	(0.01)	(0.01)	(0.00)	(0.05)	(0.03)	(0.03)
Model 14 (1992–2003)	1.53	1.55	0.99	0.93	1.78	0.99	0.14	0.16	0.03	0.63	0.26	0.44
	(1.04)	(1.04)	(1.00)	(0.99)	(1.05)	(1.00)	(0.01)	(0.01)	(0.00)	(0.06)	(0.02)	(0.04)
Model 15 (1996–2003)	1.35	1.40	0.96	0.91	1.56	0.96	0.10	0.10	0.07	0.25	0.16	0.32
	(1.04)	(1.05)	(0.96)	(0.99)	(1.07)	(0.99)	(0.01)	(0.01)	(0.01)	(0.04)	(0.02)	(0.05)
Model 16 (1992–2003)	1.94	1.91	1.02	1.30	3.02	1.02	0.20	0.20	0.03	0.71	0.30	0.82
	(1.06)	(1.06)	(1.00)	(1.02)	(1.11)	(1.00)	(0.02)	(0.02)	(0.00)	(0.06)	(0.03)	(0.07)
Model 17 (1996–2003)	1.05	1.06	0.99	1.47	1.68	0.99	0.13	0.12	0.07	0.26	0.17	1.06
	(1.01)	(1.01)	(1.00)	(1.06)	(1.08)	(1.00)	(0.02)	(0.02)	(0.01)	(0.04)	(0.02)	(0.15)
Model 18 (1996–2003)	1.07	1.09	0.99	1.42	1.76	0.99	0.14	0.13	0.07	0.24	0.14	0.68
	(1.01)	(1.01)	(1.00)	(1.05)	(1.08)	(1.00)	(0.02)	(0.02)	(0.01)	(0.03)	(0.02)	(0.10)
Model 19 (1996–2003)	1.32	1.30	1.01	0.96	1.45	1.01	0.08	0.07	0.05	0.31	0.20	0.27
	(1.04)	(1.04)	(1.00)	(0.99)	(1.05)	(1.00)	(0.01)	(0.01)	(0.01)	(0.04)	(0.03)	(0.04)
Model 20 (1992–2003)	1.30	1.32	0.99	1.02	1.40	0.99	0.10	0.10	0.04	0.68	0.41	0.30
	(1.02)	(1.03)	(1.00)	(1.00)	(1.03)	(1.00)	(0.01)	(0.01)	(0.01)	(0.06)	(0.04)	(0.03)
Model 21 (1996–2003)	1.32	1.31	1.00	0.99	1.49	1.00	0.08	0.07	0.05	0.29	0.15	0.30
	(1.04)	(1.04)	(1.00)	(1.00)	(1.06)	(1.00)	(0.01)	(0.01)	(0.01)	(0.04)	(0.02)	(0.04)

Note: Annual mean values are in parentheses.

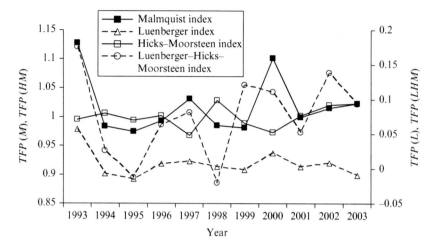

Figure 3.2   Total factor productivity changes (Model 1)

Congress adopted the final output of the 'Decision on Issues Concerning the Establishment of a Socialist Market Economic Structure' in November 1993. This was the turning point on the road to a market system. Several research groups have studied various aspects of the efforts to create a market system. The topics include transition, ranging from taxation, the fiscal system, the financial system and enterprises, to foreign trade. Four major advances in the reform strategy were a rule-based system, building market-supporting institutions, and property rights and ownership, respectively. Our TFP results do not show major change after the initiation of this reform. This may be because the 'Decision' of November 1993 does not consider private ownership as an important player in the economy. State ownership was still regarded as the 'principal component of the economy', while private ownership was a 'supplementary component of the economy'.

A major breakthrough on ownership issues was announced in the Fifteenth Party Congress held in September 1997. Private ownership was elevated to an 'important component of the economy', and state ownership was downgraded to a 'pillar of the economy'. TFP in 1997 increased slightly more than in earlier years, while other Southeast Asian countries faced the Asian financial crisis. In December 1996, current account convertibility of the Chinese currency was announced. It is important to note that the announcement did not move to capital account convertibility but still maintained capital control. This is one reason why the exchange rate remained stable and China weathered the Asian financial crisis relatively well. Even after the Asian financial crisis, China continued to attract foreign direct investment (FDI). A relatively large change in TFP occurred in 2000, which may reflect efforts aimed at enhancing FDI.

We next interpret the remaining TFP indices. The Luenberger TFP growth on average is 0.71 percent, which is much smaller than the 1.84 percent increase in the Malmquist TFP. It is well known that Luenberger indices have smaller magnitudes than comparable Malmquist indices (Boussemart et al., 2003). Luenberger productivity indices can simultaneously contract inputs and expand outputs, and are a dual to profit maximization. The differences of magnitudes between the Malmquist and Luenberger indices are a simple consequence of different behavioral assumptions, where the Luenberger index assumes profit maximization and the Malmquist index assumes revenue maximization. One may be able to assume that provinces, as the decision unit in this study, are able to adjust both inputs and outputs, since their production possibility sets operate in more or less competitive conditions. In this case, the Luenberger productivity index characterizes the true factor productivity growth and the Malmquist productivity indices overestimate true productivity.

Although the values appear to be quite different, both the Malmquist and the Luenberger indices appear to be qualitatively similar (see Figures 3.3 and 3.4). Figure 3.5 plots each province-level change in TFP for Malmquist TFP and Luenberger–Hicks–Moorsteen TFP compared with Luenberger TFP. Although the comparison of Hicks–Moorsteen TFP is not included, all the indices are positively correlated.[6] Figure 3.5 shows the changes in TFP of Model 3. Model 3 includes energy consumption and water use as inputs in addition to the traditional input combination of labor and capital. Although trends are similar to those of Model 1, the values are quantitatively different. Annual change in Malmquist and Luenberger TFP increases are 6.42 and 2.90 percent over 1996 and 2003, respectively. Cumulatively, overall growth is 54.6 and 20.3 percent for these. These results show the possibility of improvements in energy and water use.

Environmental Productivity

Several types of environmental pollution are considered in this section. First, a joint model of all pollutants is provided. Model 5 includes the environmental outputs such as waste gas, solid waste and wastewater. Additionally, Model 6 includes SO_2, dust, soot, COD, lead and chromium six in environmental outputs. Figure 3.6 provides the cumulative Luenberger TFP of both Model 5 and Model 6. Since Luenberger indices are generalizations of Malmquist indices and the other indices, and their

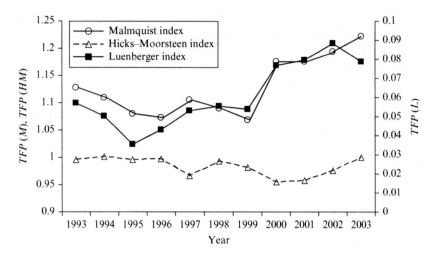

Figure 3.3   Total factor productivity (Model 1)

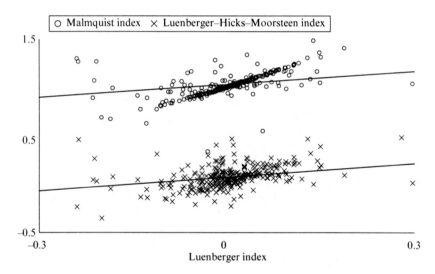

Figure 3.4   Comparison of alternative indices (Model 1)

decomposition is relatively complex, the following analysis focuses on the Luenberger indices. Environmental productivity increases as a cumulative value once the model results of joint output (Model 5 and Model 6) are larger than the base model (Model 3).

Environmental productivity increases by about 1.35 percent, or a mean

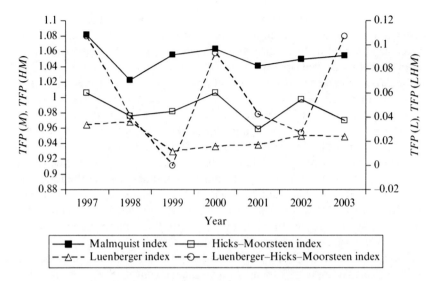

Figure 3.5   Total factor productivity changes (Model 3)

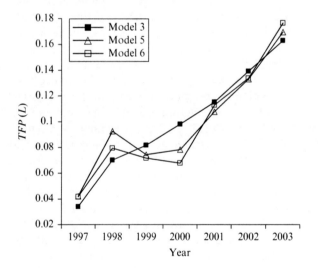

Figure 3.6   Joint model of wastewater, waste gas and solid waste:
Luenberger productivity index

rate of 0.2 percent decrease per year, with the Luenberger indices. In 1998 and 2003, environmental productivity of Model 5 increased, that is, environmental technologies were efficiently utilized and environmental management was well organized. Model 6 has similar results and tends to show larger changes in environmental productivity than Model 5 in many years. Radical reform of government administration was conducted by the Ninth National People's Congress in 1998, and the environmental protection agency was upgraded to ministerial status and renamed as SEPA. However, our study shows that environmental productivity decreased over the 1999–2002 period. This suggests that the reforms were not effective in increasing implementation of environmental management in the long run or, at least, the reforms required several years to increase efficiency. These results, however, do not show which sector (wastewater, waste gas or solid waste) influenced the result. Therefore, we are not able to judge fully the effects of management and policy implementation.

We show the results with more detailed pollutants in the remainder of this section. We especially focus on the management of SO_2 pollution. We are interested in SO_2 since more detailed analysis is available of its policy options than for other pollutants. SO_2 is an important precursor of acid rain and secondary particles, and it severely impairs public health. More than 85 percent of SO_2 comes from coal combustion in China.[7] Since SO_2 emission and coal combustion are closely correlated, the key to reducing the SO_2 emissions is to control the SO_2 emitted from coal combustion (He et al., 2002). A series of laws, regulations and standards to control SO_2 and acid rain were established in the 1990s. In 1995, articles on acid rain control were first listed in the law on air pollution prevention and control. National standards were successively published to limit SO_2 emissions from power plants, coke ovens, cement plants and boilers. In 1999, SEPA distributed the *Control Objectives in Acid Rain Zones and SO_2 Pollution Control Zones in 1999*. This required comprehensive protection plans for the control of SO_2 in every area in the two control zones.[8] All cities within the two control zones are expected to meet the standards by 2010. The following methods are considered: limiting the production and use of high-sulfur coal, promoting coal washing, controlling SO_2 discharge sources, adjusting the spatial layout of SO_2 emission sources, controlling total regional emissions of key pollutants, implementing a discharge license system for regional SO_2 pollution sources, implementing an SO_2 emission trading system, revising SO_2 emission standards, extending the scope of SO_2 emission charges and raising the level of charges, and establishing a national acid rain monitoring network (Tian et al., 2001).

Figure 3.7 shows the results for waste gas. Model 11 includes SO_2, dust and soot in environmental outputs while Model 12 also includes the total quantity of waste gas in the model. TFP for environmental outputs

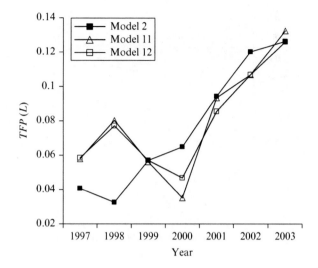

Figure 3.7   Joint model of waste gas: Luenberger productivity index

decreases by 0.02 percent, or a mean rate of 0.003 percent decrease per year, for Luenberger indices. As in Figure 3.6, environmental productivity increased until 1998. The main difference between waste gas and the all-pollutants case is that the increase in environmental productivity before 1998 is larger with waste gas. Again after 1999, environmental productivity decreased until 2002, which also implies ineffectiveness in environmental policy implementation.

We provide a comprehensive review so as to understand fully the relation between air pollution policy focusing on SO_2 and actual outcomes such as environmental productivity. Starting in the 1990s, several policies to control SO_2 were implemented. Experimental imposition of levies on SO_2 started in 1992 and was further expanded in 1995. The SEPA published a notice in April 1998 to Extend Areas for Trial Charges for SO_2 in the Acid Rain Control Zones and SO_2 Pollution Control Zones (SEPA, 1998, No. 6). This notice required the standard charge for SO_2 emissions to be 0.20 RMB/kg. The total revenue from the pollution levies on SO_2 in the power sector increased from 116 million RMB in 1997 to 347 million RMB in 1998. Some power plants installed desulfurization equipment and automatic monitoring systems to control SO_2 emissions as a response to the levy system. The result of Model 11, showing a significant increase in environmental productivity in 1998, may reflect this. In 1999, however, environmental productivity dropped significantly and remained stable until the end of our study period. We suspect that the existing SO_2 emission

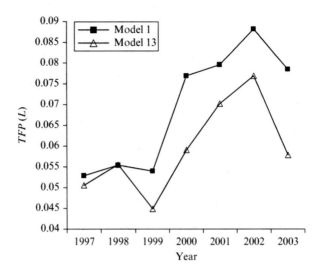

Figure 3.8   Joint model of solid waste: Luenberger productivity index

levy system in China is not an efficient way to control SO_2 pollution, and therefore the environmental productivity does not show continuing growth over the long run.

Several critiques are provided in the literature (for example, Yang et al., 2000). First, the abatement cost of SO_2 is much higher than the amount charged. Thus, it is unreasonable to expect the levy system to motivate compliance and control of SO_2 emissions by power enterprises. For example, the amount charged for SO_2 emissions within the two control zones is only 200 RMB/ton, whereas the average abatement cost is around 1,100 RMB/ton (ibid.). The levy system is different from common taxation in that the plants are able to obtain refunds for 90 percent of the SO_2 levy fees to be used for pollution mitigation. However, the actual amount refunded is much lower than 90 percent. For example, the average refund was only about 12 percent in 1998. In addition, some of the charges not refunded were not actually used for SO_2 pollution control (Wang, 2000).

Solid waste is analyzed in Model 13, and the results are shown in Figure 3.8. Solid waste has not been considered as an important environmental problem in China. In 1996, however, the Law on the Prevention and Control of Pollution of the Environment by Solid Waste was promulgated. With the exception of a slight increase in 1998 and 2001, environmental productivity kept decreasing over our study period. Overall, TFP for environmental outputs decreases by about 2.07 percent, or a mean rate of 0.3 percent decrease per year, for Luenberger indices. The results of wastewater

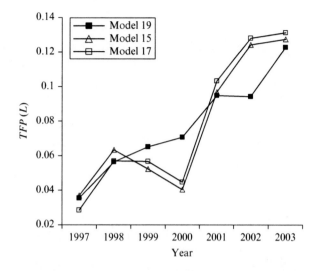

Figure 3.9   Joint model of wastewater: Luenberger productivity index

are analyzed in Model 15 and Model 17. The results are shown in Figure 3.9. Model 15 includes a quantity of total wastewater, while Model 17 includes more specific water pollutants such as COD, lead and chromium six. Both of these show that environmental productivity decreased in 1999 and 2000 but increased significantly in 2001 and 2002. Overall, environmental productivity increased in our study period. Since both Model 15 and Model 17 show similar results, using wastewater quantity may not be a poor approximation for several different wastewater substances. In Model 17, environmental productivity increased by 0.63 percent, or a mean rate of 0.09 percent, over our study period.

With rapid industrialization and a continuous increase in water use, improving the efficiency of water use is an increasingly crucial issue, especially in the northern region. Because of decreased precipitation and increased air temperature over the last 50 years, water resource endowment in the Yellow River has deteriorated: the Yellow River first dried up before reaching the river mouth in 1972. This phenomenon continued chronically until its most serious occurrence in 1997. Water use efficiency has improved over time. As shown in Figure 3.10, the result in 2003 shows the largest increase of TFP in water use. During our study period, environmental productivity increased by about 4.42 percent, or a mean rate of 0.6 percent decrease per year, according to the Luenberger indices. This increase in efficiency may reflect the scarcity of water resources in the past. The problem of scarcity has been dramatically reduced by the enforcement of two new

Chinese economic development and the environment

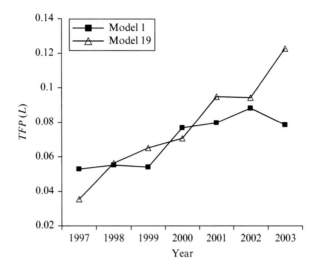

Figure 3.10   Joint model of water use: Luenberger productivity index

water management policies in 1998. One of the new policies is to allocate water drawn from the Yellow River to each province administratively in order to balance water distribution between upper and lower reaches.

Figure 3.11 summarizes the results of environmental productivity as cumulative values. Water use efficiency improved the most. Second, the case of all pollutants and the case of wastewater also showed an increase in environmental productivity. The worst score appears for solid waste treatment management. All of the scores in the figure show an increase in environmental productivity in 1998. The reforms of 1998 appear to affect environmental productivity negatively in the short term. In 2000, none of the values is more than zero. The results show all of the indices in the graph decreasing from 1998 to 2000. With the exception of the results for water use, all of the scores were worse in 2000. All the indices increased from 2000 to 2003, with the exception of the decrease of solid waste TFP in 2003. This study is not able to distinguish whether these increases in environmental productivity are a long-term effect. Further analysis of factors determining changes in environmental productivity is required to evaluate the policies.

5   DISCUSSION AND CONCLUSION

Over the last quarter of a century, China's economy has enjoyed average growth rates close to 9 percent (World Bank, 2001). However, as a result

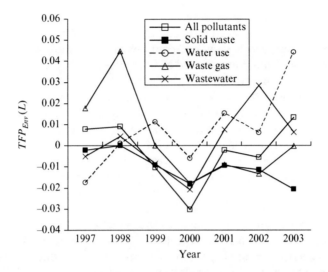

Figure 3.11   Environmental productivity: Luenberger productivity index

of China's extremely rapid economic growth, the scale and seriousness of environmental problems is no longer in doubt. Whether pollution abatement technologies are utilized more efficiently is crucial in the analysis of environmental management because it influences, at least in part, the cost of alternative production and pollution abatement technologies (for example, Jaffe et al., 2003).

Larson et al. (2003) summarize an assessment of future energy-technology strategies in China. One objective of their analysis is to continue social and economic development while ensuring national energy-supply security and promoting environmental sustainability over the next 50 years. Identification of the technological configuration for an energy system is essential, and MARKAL, which is a linear programming model, is used to build a model of China's economic system representing all sectors of the economy and including both energy conversion and end-use technologies.

Their analysis indicates that a business-as-usual strategy that relies on coal combustion technologies would not be able to meet all environmental and energy security goals. However, an advanced technology strategy emphasizing (i) coal gasification technologies coproducing electricity and clean liquid and gaseous energy carriers (polygeneration), with below-ground storage of some captured CO_2; (ii) expanded use of renewable energy sources (especially wind and modern biomass); and (iii) end-use efficiency would enable China to continue its social and economic development through at least the next 50 years while ensuring a steady energy supply and improved local and global environmental quality.

In the future, more stringent comprehensive pollution control and energy strategies could be achieved by implementing new technologies and more effective management. In addition, it will be crucial for China to rely on private initiatives in order to take major steps in turning the current environmental dilemmas around (see Economy, 2004). This is especially so since privately owned firms have less bargaining power in complying with policies than state-owned enterprises (SOEs) (Wang et al., 2002).

However, China faces many challenges in implementing these strategies. First, China is a developing country, and economic development is a primary consideration. Balancing development with environmental protection to realize sustainable development is difficult. Second, the dominance of coal as an energy source cannot be changed in the near future. Production efficiency is also generally very low, so large investment with lengthy delays is required for improvement. Thus, the shift to improved environmental management needs to be cost effective.

It is important to understand the performance of environmental management in order to estimate realistically the future possibility of pollution reduction. This study analyzes how the performance of environmental management has changed over time. Mixed results for environmental productivity are indicated using nonparametric productivity index techniques. Productivity appears to have increased with overall pollution, wastewater and water use. However, it has decreased in the case of solid waste. The case for waste gas remains relatively constant in 2003 compared with 1992, although there was some fluctuation.

Managi and Kaneko (2006) provide three interpretations regarding the changes in environmental productivity. They support the interpretation that if productivity decreases, there is less efficient utilization of pollution abatement technologies and incomplete monitoring and enforcement, although China has implemented many environmental policies in the past, and the stringency of these regulations is increasing. As a short-term outlook prevails, investment in waste treatment or new conservation efforts diminishes (Economy, 2004). The report by Economy suggests that the development of rural areas has contributed to alarming levels of pollution. There is also evidence for problems in environmental protection management at the local level (Ma and Ortolano, 2000). Ma and Ortolano show that the administrative rank of the environmental protection bureaus is sometimes lower than that of the enterprises it is intended to oversee (also see Economy, 2004). For example, several environmental protection offices did not permit officers to monitor wastewater from a paper manufacturing company. This is because the administrative rank of the environmental protection office was lower than that of the company director. Therefore, barriers to effective monitoring and enforcement efforts remain relatively constant, even though the stringency of regulation has increased.

The results of measuring market and environmental productivity and connecting it to policies have several general implications. A number of important factors connecting law, institutions, finance and growth are not well understood. A better understanding of how these nonstandard mechanisms work to promote growth can shed light on optimal development paths for other countries. In the next stage, China would need to achieve at least three objectives: first, to set the goal of transition to a market system; second, to establish market-supporting institutions incorporating international best practices; and third, to privatize and restructure SOEs. For example, the linkages between China and other countries are assessed by Cheung et al. (2003), who recognize that there are non-negligible restrictions on both physical and financial flows between China and other economies. Smooth transitions will encourage the transfer and better use of technology and better management.

NOTES

1. Most empirical research focuses on developed countries. As far as the authors are aware, there are no existing studies that have estimated efficiency changes of environmental technology or management in developing countries with the exception of their own prior work (see Kaneko and Managi, 2004, 2005; Managi and Kaneko, 2006).
2. Although it is usually arbitrary, we employ an output-oriented method since revenue maximization as a behavioral goal for China is more appropriate than cost minimization. This assumption is common in the productivity measurement literature.
3. Beijing, Tianjin, Hebei, Shanxi, Inner Mongolia, Liaoning, Jilin, Heilongjiang, Shanghai, Jiangsu, Zhejiang, Anhui, Fujian, Jiangxi, Shandong, Henan, Hubei, Hunan, Guangdong, Guangxi, Sichuan and Chongqing, Guizhou, Yunnan, Xizang, Shaanxi, Gansu, Qinghai, Ningxia, and Xinjiang. Note that Tibet is excluded because some relevant data are not available. Hainan, a new province from 1988, is also excluded. Data for Chongqing, which was separated from Sichuan in 1997, is merged with data for Sichuan.
4. Note that the labor and capital related to pollution abatement are excluded from these variables. Thus, market inputs and the data on labor, capital and environmental input are independent of one another.
5. The values of geometric and arithmetic mean are presented in Figure 3.3. Choice of geometric and arithmetic mean is based on the theory described in Section 4.
6. $TFP(HM)$ is excluded to simplify the graph. The correlation between each of the two indices appears relatively similar.
7. Industry is a large SO_2 emission source, estimated to account for about one-half of total emissions.
8. The two control zones include 175 cities and districts in 27 provinces, autonomous regions and municipalities accounting for 60 percent of national SO_2 emissions. The zones are characterized by dense populations, developed industries and large flourishing cities important to the national economy.

REFERENCES

Balk, B.M. (1998), *Industrial Price, Quantity, and Productivity Indices: The Micro-Economic Theory and an Application*, Boston, MA: Kluwer.

Bjurek, H. (1996), 'The Malmquist total factor productivity index', *Scandinavian Journal of Economics*, **98** (2), 303–13.

Boussemart, J.P., W. Briec, K. Kerstens and J.C. Poutineau (2003), 'Luenberger and Malmquist productivity indices: theoretical comparisons and empirical illustration', *Bulletin of Economic Research*, **55** (4), 391–405.

Briec, W. and K. Kerstens (2004), 'A Luenberger–Hicks–Moorsteen productivity indicator: its relation to the Hicks–Moorsteen productivity index and the Luenberger productivity indicator', *Economic Theory*, **23**, 925–39.

Caves, D.W., L.R. Christensen and W.E. Diewert (1982), 'The economic theory of index numbers and the measurement of input, output and productivity', *Econometrica*, **50** (6), 1393–414.

Chambers, R.G., Y. Chung and R. Färe (1998), 'Profit, directional distance functions, and Nerlovian efficiency', *Journal of Optimization Theory and Applications*, **98**, 351–64.

Chambers, R.G., R. Färe and S. Grosskopf (1996), 'Productivity growth in APEC countries', *Pacific Economic Review*, **1**, 181–90.

Chen, Baizhu and Yi Feng (2000), 'Determinants of economic growth in China: private enterprise, education, and openness', *China Economic Review*, **11** (1), 1–15.

Cheung, Yin-Wong, Menzie D. Chinn and Eiji Fujii (2003), 'The Chinese economies in global context: the integration process and its determinants', NBER Working Paper 10047, National Bureau of Economic Research, Cambridge, MA.

Debreu, G. (1951), 'The coefficient of resource utilization', *Econometrica*, **19**, 273–92.

Economy, E.C. (2004), *The River Runs Black: The Environmental Challenge to China's Future*, Ithaca, NY: Cornell University Press.

Farrell, M.J. (1957), 'The measurement of productive efficiency', *Journal of the Royal Statistical Society*, **120**, 253–81.

Färe, R., S. Grosskopf and C.A.K. Lovell (1985), *The Measurement of Efficiency of Production*, Boston, MA: Kluwer-Nijhoff.

Färe, R., S. Grosskopf, M. Norris and Z. Zhang (1994), 'Productivity growth, technical progress, and efficiency change in industrialized countries', *American Economic Review*, **84** (1), 66–83.

He, Kebin, Hong Huo and Qiang Zhang (2002), 'Urban air pollution in China: current status, characteristics, and progress', *Annual Review of Energy and Environment*, **27**, 397–431.

Jaffe, A.B., R.G. Newell and R.N. Stavins (2003), 'Technological change and the environment', in Karl-Göran Mäler and Jeffrey Vincent (eds), *Handbook of Environmental Economics*, Amsterdam: North-Holland. Elsevier Science, pp. 462–516.

Kaneko, S. and S. Managi (2004), 'Environmental productivity in China', *Economics Bulletin*, **17** (2), 1–10.

Kaneko, S and S. Managi (2005), 'Environmental productivity modeling in China: stochastic frontier approach', Working Paper, Yokohama National University.

Larson, E.D., Z. Wu, P. DeLaquil, W. Chen and P. Gao (2003), 'Future implications of China's energy-technology choices', *Energy Policy*, **31** (12), 1149–204.

Lovell, C.A.K. (2003), 'The decomposition of Malmquist productivity indexes', *Journal of Productivity Analysis*, **20**, 437–58.

Luenberger, D.G. (1992a), 'Benefit functions and duality, *Journal of Mathematical Economics*, **21**, 461–81.

Luenberger, D.G. (1992b), 'New optimality principles for economic efficiency and equilibrium', *Journal of Optimization Theory and Applications*, **75**, 221–64.

Luenberger, D.G. (1995), *Microeconomic Theory*, New York: McGraw-Hill.

Ma, X. and L. Ortolano (2000), *Environmental Regulation in China*, Lanham, MD: Rowman & Littlefield.

Malmquist, S. (1953), 'Index numbers and indifference curves', *Trabajos de Estatistica*, **4** (1), 209–42.

Managi, S. (2004), 'Competitiveness and environmental policies for agriculture: testing the Porter hypothesis', *International Journal of Agricultural Resources, Governance and Ecology*, **3** (3/4), 310–24.

Managi, S. and S. Aoyagi (2005), 'Forest management and economic policy', Working Paper, Yokohama National University.

Managi, S. and S. Kaneko (2005), 'Productivity of market and environmental abatement in China', *Environmental Economics and Policy Studies*, **7** (4), 459–70.

Managi, S. J.J. Opaluch, D. Jin and T.A. Grigalunas (2004), 'Technological change and depletion in offshore oil and gas', *Journal of Environmental Economics and Management*, **47** (2), 388–409.

Managi, S. J.J. Opaluch, D. Jin and T.A. Grigalunas (2005), 'Environmental regulations and technological change in the offshore oil and gas industry', *Land Economics*, **81** (2), 303–19.

McCain, R.A. (1978), 'Endogenous bias in technical progress and environmental policy', *American Economic Review*, **68**, 538–46.

Ray, Subhash C. and Evangelia Desli (1997), 'Productivity growth, technical progress and efficiency change in industrialized countries: comment', *American Economic Review*, **87** (5), 1033–9.

Shephard, R.W. (1970), *Theory of Cost and Production Functions*, Princeton, NJ: Princeton University Press.

Sinkule, B.J. and L. Ortolano (1995), *Implementing Environmental Policy in China*, Westport, CT: Praeger.

Tian, H.Z., Y.Q. Lu and J.M. Hao (2001), 'The future programming of acid rain and SO_2 control in China', *Electricity*, **12** (2), 35–7.

Wang, H., N. Mamingi, B. Laplante and S. Dasgupta (2002), 'Incomplete enforcement of pollution regulation: bargaining power of Chinese factories', Policy Research Working Paper 2756, Development Research Group, World Bank, Washington, DC.

Wang, Y. and Y. Yao (2003), 'Sources of China's economic growth 1952–1999: incorporating human capital accumulation', *China Economic Review*, **14**, 32–52.

Wang, Z.X. (2000), 'Present situation of charges on pollution discharge of thermal power plants', *Electricity Power*, **33** (1), 77–81.

World Bank (2001), *China Air, Land and Water: Environmental Priorities for a New Millennium*, Washington, DC: World Bank.

World Development Indicators (WDI) (2005), *World Development Indicators*, CD-ROM, Washington, DC: World Bank.

Xu, X. (2004), 'China's gross domestic product estimation', *China Economic Review*, **15**, 302–22.

Yang J.T., D. Cao, J.N. Wang and W.Y. Tian (2000), *SO_2 emission charge in China. SO_2 Emission Trading Program: US Experience and China's Perspective*, Beijing: China Environmental Science.

Young, A. (1993), 'Invention bounded learning by doing', *Journal of Political Economy*, **101**, 443–72.

4. Wastewater, waste gas and solid waste

1 INTRODUCTION

To protect public health and environmental quality, the Chinese government has undertaken a series of actions. Several laws, regulations, and standards have been promulgated (Sinkule and Ortolano, 1995; Edmonds, 2004). Whether pollution abatement technologies are used most efficiently is crucial in the analysis of environmental management because it influences, at least in part, the cost of alternative production and pollution abatement technologies. An extensive theoretical literature examines the role of environmental policy in encouraging productivity growth (see Jaffe et al., 2003). On the one hand, abatement pressures may stimulate innovative responses that reduce the actual compliance cost below the original estimates. On the other, firms might be reluctant to innovate if they believe that regulators will respond by ratcheting up standards even more tightly. In addition to the changes in environmental regulations and technology, management levels also affect environmental productivity. Thus, whether environmental productivity increases over time is an empirical question. The focus of this chapter is to measure technological change both for market and nonmarket (that is, environmental) outputs.

One major problem of measuring the productivity of environmental pollutants is that such pollutants typically are not marketed, and therefore are unpriced. In the market economy, the price mechanism (and property rights) provides incentives that guide the allocation of resources towards their highest-valued uses. However, nonmarket resources frequently have ill-defined property rights, and they lack a price mechanism to guide their allocation. Consequently, we do not have the information to determine whether the environment is being utilized efficiently (that is, less sustainable).

We employ translog multi-input, multi-output specification to estimate the productivity index (and its components of technological change and efficiency change) following Fuentes et al. (2001) and incorporate changes in the state of the environment into a conventional productivity measurement framework to generate an environmentally inclusive measure of productivity change. It is important to note that the regulations requiring more stringent pollution abatement do not necessarily change the efficiency of pollution abatement since the linear expansion of pollution abatement costs and pollution reduction does not necessarily change the pollution reduction per abatement cost. Thus, whether productivity of pollution abatements is increasing over time is an empirical question. This study uses annual data of 29 provinces in China for the 1992–2003 period.

The chapter itself is structured as follows. Section 2 briefly reviews environmental policy in China and provides a literature review of productivity analysis. Section 3 presents the research method. Section 4 discusses the results. The final section presents further discussion and provides some concluding remarks.

2   BACKGROUND

Environmental Policy in China

The implementation of environmental policies is also sensitive to differences in economic development and environmental quality (Dasgupta et al., 1997; Wang and Wheeler, 2003, 2005). In addition, policy enforcement by local authorities diverges from the legal system established by the central government. In particular, the level of completeness in policy varies significantly across polluting firms: some firms comply perfectly, while others do not (Wang and Wheeler, 2003). Chinese officials are often aware of the problem, but have responded inadequately, in large part, to the demand for continuing economic growth superseding environmental considerations (Economy, 2004). For example, firms facing adverse financial conditions have more bargaining power and are more likely to pay lower pollution charges, that is, less enforcement (Wang et al., 2003). However, little is known about how environmental management changes over time. By considering the divergence of policy intention and actual implementation in each province, this study measures the efficiency of environmental management in China using a technique explained in the following subsection.

Productivity Modeling

Total factor productivity (TFP) includes all categories of productivity change and is further decomposed to provide a better understanding of the relative importance of various components, which includes both technological change (TC) and efficiency change (EC) (Färe et al., 1994). TC measures shifts in the production frontier or measures productivity growth

by stimulating innovation. EC measures changes in the position of a production unit relative to the so-called 'catching-up' frontier.

Traditional techniques to measure productivity, including Fisher and
Törnqvist productivity indices value outputs and inputs at their market
prices. Since most environmental impacts are not traded on markets, emission trading prices or shadow prices are required to convert nonmarketed
undesirable byproducts to marketed commodities in the measurements
(Pittman, 1983). Recently developed alternative approaches require only
quantity data for the environmental indicators.

There is a growing literature that develops methodologies for measuring
productive efficiency and productivity in the presence of pollution (Färe
et al., 1989, 1993, 2005; Yaisawarng and Klein, 1994; Chung et al., 1997;
Domazlicky and Weber, 2004). These studies incorporate environmental effects into the output vector, and either adjust conventional indices
of productivity change or adjust conventional measures of technical
efficiency (Hailu and Veeman, 2000; Managi et al., 2005). These studies
approached the problem of environmental output (or undesirable output)
production by using parametric specification of the distance functions (for
example, Färe et al., 1993, 2005; Coggins and Swinton, 1996) and nonparametric specification of the distance functions (for example, Zaim and
Taskin, 2000; Boyd et al., 2002; Färe et al., 2005), respectively. Generally,
pollutants are treated as weakly (costly) disposable outputs while desirable
outputs are strongly (freely) disposable (Färe et al., 1989). Weak disposability involves a constraint on the production possibilities of the producers, that is, producers cannot increase (reduce) undesirable input (output)
levels without costs.

Managi and Kaneko (2006) utilize nonparametric deterministic
approach for province-level data over the 1987–2001 period to measure
various components of productivity within a joint production model that
considers both market and environmental outputs in China. They find that
environmental management is deteriorating, while the productivity level of
joint production is relatively constant. Their study analyzes the quantity
data of wastewater, waste gas and solid wastes together as environmental
(or undesirable) outputs. However, environmental data does not match
with economic data in their sample and, therefore, the measurements are
biased. Furthermore, the labor variable is not quality adjusted. Our study
adjusts these problems and also analyzes more detailed environmental
issues such as use of oil and coal consumption, water use, and pollution
such as SO_2, dust, soot, COD, lead and chromium six, which are not used
in Managi and Kaneko.

This study models the production of market and environmental effects
using parametric specification of the distance functions for three reasons:

(i) parametric specification is preferred to nonparametric specification when either measurement error, management 'luck' or random error needs to be considered, or production is subject to uncontrollable factors including uncertainties in the prices of input and output, and other market situations; (ii) nonparametric measurements of productivity turn out to be infeasibilities under certain weak conditions (Briec and Kerstens, 2006); and (iii) assumption of weak disposability in linear programming of nonparametric specification is shown to have a potential of infeasibility in its solution (Fujii et al., 2006). A recent development in the literature incorporates stochastic characteristics of the production frontier in the distance function estimation and, thus, we utilize this advantage following Fuentes et al. (2001).

3   MODEL

Production frontier analysis provides the Malmquist indices (for example, Caves et al., 1982), which can be used to quantify productivity change and can be decomposed into various constituents, as described below. Malmquist productivity is a specific output-based measure of TFP. It measures the TFP change between two data points by calculating the ratio of two associated distance functions (for example, ibid.). In economics, distance functions are related to the notion of the coefficient of resource utilization and to the efficiency measures (Debreu, 1951). A key advantage of the distance function approach is that it provides a convenient way to describe a multi-input, multi-output production technology without the need to specify functional forms or behavioral objectives, such as cost minimization or profit maximization.

Using the distance function specification, our problem can be formulated as follows. Let $x = (x_1, \ldots, x_N) \in R_+^N$, and $y = (y_1, \ldots, y_M) \in R_+^M$ be the vectors of inputs including capital, labor, oil and coal consumption, water use, and outputs including desirable output of GRP and set of undesirable pollution outputs, respectively, and then define the production possibilities set by:

$$P^t \equiv \{(x^t, y^t): x^t \text{ can produce } y^t\}, \tag{4.1}$$

which is the set of all feasible production vectors. We assume that P^t satisfies standard axioms, which suffice to define meaningful output distance functions. Let ϕ be the reciprocal of scalar valued index that measures efficiency at time $t = 1, \ldots, T$, and the output distance function is defined at t as:

$$d_0^t(x^t, y^t) = \inf \{\phi: (x^t, y^t/\phi) \in P^t\}, \text{ on the output set, } P^t, \quad (4.2)$$

where $1/\phi$ is the maximal proportional amount that the output vector, y^t, can be expanded (that is, expansion of desirable output of GRP and contraction of undesirable pollution outputs) while remaining technologically feasible given the production set, P^t, and the input vector, x^t.[1] Note that $d_0^t(x^t, y^t) \le 1$ if and only if $(x^t, y^t) \in P^t$, and $d_0^t(x^t, y^t) = 1$ if and only if (x^t, y^t) is on the boundary of the production frontier.

We adopt the following translog function to estimate a parametric distance function for the transformation function corresponding to a multi-output, multi-input technology with technological progress defined in the usual form as a trend variable following Grosskopf et al. (1997) and Fuentes et al. (2001):

$$\ln d_0^t(x^{i,t}, y^{i,t}) = \alpha_0 + \sum_k \alpha_k \ln x_k^{i,t} + \frac{1}{2} \sum_k \sum_l \alpha_{kl} \ln x_k^{i,t} \ln x_l^{i,t}$$

$$+ \sum_k \sum_m \delta_{km} \ln x_k^{i,t} \ln y_m^{i,t} + \sum_m \beta_m \ln y_m^{i,t}$$

$$+ \frac{1}{2} \sum_m \sum_n \beta_{mn} \ln y_m^{i,t} \ln y_n^{i,t} + \gamma_1 t + \frac{1}{2} \gamma_2 t^2$$

$$+ \sum_k \eta_k \ln x_k^{i,t} t + \sum_m \mu_m \ln y_m^{i,t} t$$

$$i = 1, \ldots, I; \quad t = 1, \ldots, T; \quad (4.3)$$

where $i \in \{1, \ldots, I\}$ is the index region, $k, l \in \{1, \ldots, K\}$ the index inputs and $m, n \in \{1, \ldots, M\}$ the index outputs.

Symmetry of cross-effects requires:

$$\alpha_{kl} = \alpha_{lk} \text{ and } \beta_{mn} = \beta_{nm} \ \forall k, l, m, n. \quad (4.4)$$

We require the quadratic function to be nondecreasing in pollution output and nonincreasing in market output, and linear homogeneity requires:

$$\sum_n \beta_{mn} = 0, m = 1, \ldots, M; \ \sum_m \delta_{km} = 0, k = 1, \ldots, K; \ \sum_m \mu_m = 0. \quad (4.5)$$

We define the estimated translog distance function (that is, $\ln d_0^t(x^{i,t}, y^{i,t})$) as $\ln TL(x^{i,t}, y^{i,t}, t:\hat{\theta})$ where $\hat{\theta} = [\hat{\alpha}, \hat{\beta}, \hat{\delta}, \hat{\lambda}, \hat{\eta}, \hat{\mu}]$ is a vector of estimated parameters.[2] Following Lovell et al. (1994) and Fuentes et al. (2001), we obtain the following stochastic frontier model by choosing one of the outputs arbitrarily, for example, $y_M^{i,t}$:

$$- \ln y_M^{i,t} = \ln TL(x^{i,t}, y^{i,t}/y_M^{i,t}, t: \theta) + \varepsilon^{i,t}, \varepsilon^{i,t} = v^{i,t} + u^{i,t}, \qquad (4.6)$$

where $\varepsilon^{i,t}$ is the composed error of the following two terms. $v^{i,t}$ is the random noise term, independently and identically distributed as $N(0, \sigma_v^2)$. $u^{i,t}$ accounts for technological inefficiency in production, defined as $u_i \exp[-\eta(t - T)]$ with u_i being a non-negative random variable truncated at 0, and independently and identically distributed as $N(\mu, \sigma_u^2)$. Estimated parameters are used to calculate the following productivity indices.

Following Färe et al. (1994), the Malmquist index defined above can be decomposed into measures associated with TC and EC under constant returns to scale (CRS):

$$TFP(x^{i,t}, y^{i,t}, x^{i,t+1}, y^{i,t+1}) = TC(x^{i,t}, y^{i,t}, x^{i,t+1}, y^{i,t+1}) \, EC(x^{i,t}, y^{i,t}, x^{i,t+1}, y^{i,t+1}).$$
$$(4.7)$$

Traditional measurements of the above indices are nonparametric measurements and therefore measurement error in variables is an important concern for nonparametric DEA. Fuentes et al. (2001) show that the parametric distance functions can be employed for Malmquist productivity measurements and its decomposition as follows:

$$TC(x^{i,t}, y^{i,t}, x^{i,t+1}, y^{i,t+1}) = \exp\left\{ \sum_m \hat{\mu}_m (\ln y_m^{i,t+1} - 2\ln y_m^{i,t}) \right.$$

$$\left. + \sum_k \hat{\eta}_k (\ln x_k^{i,t+1} - 2\ln x_k^{i,t}) - \left[\hat{\gamma}_1 + \hat{\gamma}_2\left(t + \frac{1}{2}\right) \right] \right\},$$

$$EC(x^{i,t}, y^{i,t}, x^{i,t+1}, y^{i,t+1}) = \exp[TL(x^{i,t+1}, y^{i,t+1}/y_M^{i,t+1}, t:\hat{\theta})$$

$$- TL(x^{i,t}, y^{i,t}/y_M^{i,t}, t:\hat{\theta})]. \qquad (4.8)$$

Thus, technological change is evaluated using the estimated parameters in equation (4.6) and efficiency change corresponds to the ratio of two successive distance functions. The value of TFP is calculated as a product of TC and EC.

We estimate productivity improvement associated with the efficient use of environmental abatement efforts or the efficient reduction of pollution. $TFP_{Environment}$ is estimated from two TFP estimates: (i) productivity of market output (that is, GRP), TFP_{Market}; and (ii) productivity of joint outputs of market output and nonmarket output (that is, reduction in environmental pollutants), TFP_{Joint} (so-called 'green' productivity) following Managi et al. (2005).[3] TFP_{Market} includes usual production input and output, and TFP_{Joint} includes environmental degradation and abatement effort in addition to production input/output. Given input level, an increase in market output raises usual productivity, TFP_{Market}. Holding input and environmental output constant, an increase in market output raises TFP_{Joint}. Also, holding input and market output constant, a decrease in environmental output raises TFP_{Joint}. Thus, the residual effects of two factors explain the productivity due to changes in technology for the nonmarket goods (environmental degradation) given by:

$$TFP_{Environment} = TFP_{Joint} / TFP_{Market},$$

where an increase in $TFP_{Environment}$ implies a productivity improvement in abatements or environmental productivity which might be either a reduction of environmental degradation given the same level of abatement effort or the reduction of abatement efforts given the same level of environmental degradation level, or both. Note that both $TFP_{Environment}$ and TFP_{Market} are estimated for each year for each province. Environmental technological change and efficiency change are calculated in the same manner.

4 DATA

In this study, we use panel data on Chinese secondary industries, including mining, manufacturing, electricity, gas and water. This study focuses on industrial pollution, since Chinese industry is a primary source of the pollution and the industry accounting for about 40 percent of national water pollution and about 80 percent of air pollution from SEPA estimates in 2000.

The dataset consists of annual data for the 1992–2003 period for 29 of the 31 provinces, including three municipalities, in the People's Republic of China.[4] Definition and explanation of the variables used in this study is provided in Table 4.1. Nominal data are converted into real data using the CPI, hence the national total is consistent with the sum of regional data in the dataset. 'Labor' is quality-adjusted labor in secondary industry. The wages for labor are used to control for quality where these are not adjusted in Managi and Kaneko (2006).[5] Pollution abatement cost and expenditure (PACE) are funds actually used to remedy industrial environmental pollution in the form of wastewater, waste gas and solid waste. PACE is considered as an environmental input. Increase in PACE given other inputs/outputs will reduce pollution. In addition to PACE and market inputs such as capital and labor, we estimate efficiency with inputs including coal consumption, oil consumption and fresh water use. An increase in coal and oil consumption is associated with an increase in both air pollution and GRP.

Table 4.1   Data information: 29 provinces for 1992–2003

Variable	Data source
GRP: added value of secondary industry (unit: 10^8 yuan)	1992–1999: *Comprehensive Statistical Data and Materials on 50 Years of New China* 2000–2003: *China Industrial Economy Statistical Yearbook*
Number of employees working in secondary industry (unit: 10^4 persons)	1992–1999: *Communication Statistics on 50 Years of China* 2000–2003: *China Industrial Economy Statistical Yearbook*
Wage: wages paid in industry (unit: 10^4 yuan)	*China Statistical Yearbook*
Capital stock: estimated from annual productive net of depreciation in the secondary industry (unit: 10^8 yuan)	1992–1999: *Communication Statistics on 50 Years of China* 2000–2003: *China Industrial Economy Statistical Yearbook*
Wastewater: wastewater quantity measured as the weight of wastewater discharge (unit: 10^4 ton)	1992–2003: *China Environmental Statistical Yearbook*
Waste gas: gas quantity measured as the volume of waste gas emissions, which is not treated (unit: 10^8 m³)	1992–2003: *China Environmental Statistical Yearbook*
Solid waste: wastes quantity measured as the discharge amount of solid wastes (unit: 10^4 ton)	1992–2003: *China Environmental Statistical Yearbook*
PACE: funds actually used for industrial environmental pollution of wastewater, waste gas and solid waste (unit: 10^4 yuan)	1992–2003: *China Environmental Statistical Yearbook*
Soot: soot emission by consumption and others refers to net volume of soot emitted by fuel burning from economic activities and operation of industrial activities. It is calculated on the basis of coal consumption (unit: ton)	1992–2003: *China Environmental Statistical Yearbook*
COD: index of water pollution measuring the mass concentration	1992–2003: *China Environmental Statistical Yearbook*

Table 4.1   (continued)

Variable	Data source
of oxygen consumed by the chemical breakdown of organic and inorganic matter (unit: ton)	
Lead: discharge of lead emitted by production process of industrial activities (unit: ton)	1992–2003: *China Environmental Statistical Yearbook*
Chromium six: discharge of hexavalent chromium emitted by production process of industrial activities (unit: ton)	1992–2003: *China Environmental Statistical Yearbook*
Oil consumption: total oil consumed as fuel in TCE (unit: 10^4 TCE)	1992–2003: *China Environmental Statistical Yearbook*
Coal consumption: total coal consumed as fuel in TCE (unit: 10^4 TCE)	1992–2003: *China Environmental Statistical Yearbook*
Fresh water: use of fresh water in industrial activities (unit: 10^4 ton)	1992–2003: *China Environmental Statistical Yearbook*

China's crude oil consumption has increased at an average rate of 6 percent per year in the past few decades. Growing energy consumption, reliance on coal, and air pollution are rapidly emerging as major environmental issues. Coal consumption, the primary energy source accounting for more than 70 percent of total energy consumption, is the main source of anthropogenic air pollution emissions in China. These include TSP pollution, SO_2 pollution and acid rain. Use of fresh water in production processes is also necessary to produce goods. The models in this study are able to estimate efficiency improvements in the use of oil, coal, and water consumption to save fuel and fresh water.

Data in the *China Environmental Statistical Yearbook* (CESY) do not cover the entire sample collected in the *China Industrial Economy Statistical Yearbook* (CIESY) and the *China Statistical Yearbook*. Therefore, use of data from the CESY provide biased results. In this study, we adjust the data so as to be able to compare the data to the *China Statistical Yearbook*. Sales data are included in both the CESY and the CIESY. We calculate an adjustment coefficient by taking the ratio of sales data in the CIESY and that in the CESY. The adjustment coefficient rages from 1.03 to 7.05, with an average of 1.74. We then multiply the coefficients, which vary by year and province, by the data in the CESY to obtain the adjusted figures.

The reliability of statistical data in China has been discussed frequently by policy makers and researchers. Economic outputs are most frequently questioned where the political manipulation of central and local governments are a key issue. The National Bureau of Statistics (NBS), which has responsibility for revising the data, releases the socioeconomic information and makes numerous revisions to the definitions of statistical indicators and the categorization of economic organizations (see Xu, 2004 for detail). The NBS revises and adjusts the historical data once: (i) new data sources are found or generated, where such data differ from the original; (ii) changes are made to GDP-related classifications; or (iii) basic concepts, accounting principles, or calculation methods change significantly. Major changes occurred, for instance, in 1995 when the NBS disaggregated the four original secondary industries into five. Documents published by NBS include *Estimation Methods of China's Annual Gross Domestic Product*, *Estimation Methods of China's Quarterly Gross Domestic Product*, and the *Manual of China's Gross Domestic Product Estimation*. Data using the newest methods are from the *China Statistical Yearbook*, while the adjusted data are included in *The Gross Domestic Product of China, 1952–1995*.

Although there may be problems with data reliability, data concerning secondary industry in China are generally more reliable than those concerning tertiary industry. This is because the value added of many rapidly developing services, such as accounting, legal services, information consultancies and private education, are estimated on the basis of wages and taxes. Province-level GRP is based on industry and regional government surveys. Historical GRP data for secondary industry at nominal prices are taken from the *Comprehensive Statistical Data and Materials on 50 Years of New China*. This publication compiles recalculated GRP as far back as 1949 using the SNA method. See Wang and Yao (2003) for construction of the other market input variables.

5   APPLICATION

This study uses different models to measure and decompose productivity change in terms of market output, environmental (pollution) outputs and joint production. The vectors of outputs and inputs for each model are listed in Table 4.2. The output variables in our model are GRP, waste gas, solid waste, wastewater, SO_2, dust, soot, COD, lead and chromium six (see Table 4.2). Our input variables include labor, capital, oil consumption, coal consumption, fresh water, PACE, PACE for waste gas, PACE for solid waste, and PACE for wastewater. Most of the estimated parameters of stochastic frontier analysis (SFA) show expected sign with statistical

Table 4.2   Model specifications

Index calculated	Model 1	Model 2	Model 3	Model 4	Model 5	Model 6	Model 7
	Base	Base2 (Energy)	Base3 (Energy & Water)	Joint (All)	Joint (Gas)	Joint (Solid)	Joint (Water)
Output variables							
GRP	X	X	X	X	X	X	X
Waste gas				X	X		
Solid waste				X		X	
Wastewater				X			X
SO$_2$					X		
Dust					X		
Soot					X		
COD							X
Lead							X
Chromium six							X
Input variables							
Labor	X	X	X	X	X	X	X
Capital	X	X	X	X	X	X	X
Oil consumption		X	X	X	X		
Coal consumption		X	X	X	X		
Fresh water			X	X			X
PACE (all)				X			
PACE (gas)					X		
PACE (solid)						X	
PACE (water)							X

significance and tables of estimated parameters are available on request. Annual and cumulative changes in the productivity indices are provided in Table 4.3. The mean values of changes in productivity indices are also presented in each figure of Figure 4.1. Values larger than one are regarded as increases in productivity.

The TFP for the market of Model 1 keeps increasing over the study period and the rate of its change is 35.9 percent with an average of 2.8 percent annual growth. This is relatively higher than previous TFP studies such as Young (2003), who found that average growth is 1.4 percent during the 1978–98 period. We expect this difference to be caused by use of different data and techniques. The source of the TFP increase appears to come mainly from technological change rather than efficiency change. This reflects the relatively high potential for efficiency improvements. With rapid industrialization and a continuous increase in energy and water use, improving the efficiency of energy and water use is an increasingly crucial issue. Previous studies, however, do not take into account energy and water

Table 4.3   *Summary of results: cumulative changes in productivity indices*

Index	Productivity			Environmental productivity		
	TFP	TC	EC	TFP	TC	EC
Model 1	1.3590	1.8693	0.7270	–	–	–
Base	(1.028)	(1.059)	(0.971)			
				Energy (Model 2/Model 1)		
Model 2	1.7735	1.8040	0.9861	1.3050	0.9651	1.3564
Base with energy	(1.056)	(1.060)	(0.997)	(1.027)	(0.998)	(1.028)
				Water (Model 3/Model 2)		
Model 3	2.4338	1.7091	1.4208	1.7908	0.9143	1.9543
Base with energy and water	(1.084)	(1.050)	(1.032)	(1.054)	(0.992)	(1.063)
				All pollutants (Model 4/Model 3)		
Model 4	0.3486	0.3087	1.1214	0.1432	0.1806	0.7892
Base with wastewater, waste gas, solid waste	(0.909)	(0.899)	(1.010)	(0.838)	(0.856)	(0.979)
				Waste gas (Model 5/Model 3)		
Model 5	1.1307	0.9247	1.2163	0.4646	0.5410	0.8561
Base with waste gas	(1.011)	(0.993)	(1.018)	(0.933)	(0.946)	(0.986)
				Solid waste (Model 6/Model 1)		
Model 6	2.6056	2.8275	0.9215	1.9172	1.5126	1.2675
Base with solid waste	(1.091)	(1.099)	(0.993)	(1.061)	(1.038)	(1.022)
				Wastewater (Model 7/Model 3)		
Model 7	5.4461	2.4888	2.1503	2.2377	1.4562	1.5134
Base with wastewater	(1.167)	(1.086)	(1.072)	(1.076)	(1.035)	(1.038)

Note: Annual mean values are in parentheses.

use in China's TFP estimate. Environmental productivity indices as a contribution to joint productivity are provided in Figure 4.2. Contribution of TFP change by efficient use of energy is provided by Model 2/Model 1. The results show that energy is more efficiently used over time with an average of 2.7 percent annual growth in TFP. In contrast to the market case in Model 1, TC decreases while EC increases. Contribution of TFP change by efficient water use is provided by Model 3/Model 2. The results show that energy and water is more efficiently used over time with an average

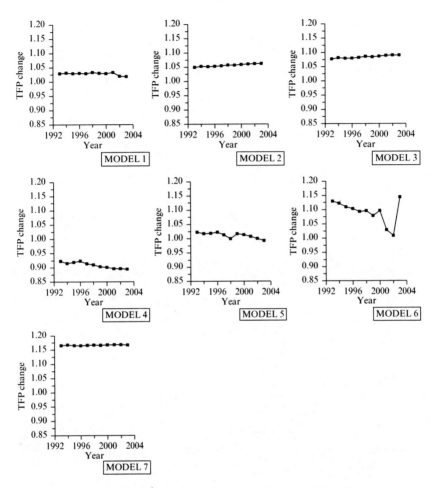

Figure 4.1   Annual change in total factor productivity: Models 1–7

of 5.4 percent annual growth in the TFP. In contrast to the market case in Model 1 again, TC decreases while EC increases. The above two results of energy and water use imply that catch-up of inefficient regions to efficient regions causes a productivity increase, since energy and water have a price and therefore firms in the regions have an incentive to improve efficiency. In particular, the increase in water use efficiency may reflect the scarcity of water resources in the past in China, where its scarcity problem has been dramatically reduced by the enforcement of two new water management policies in 1998.

The results in pollutants provide different stories. Overall results of

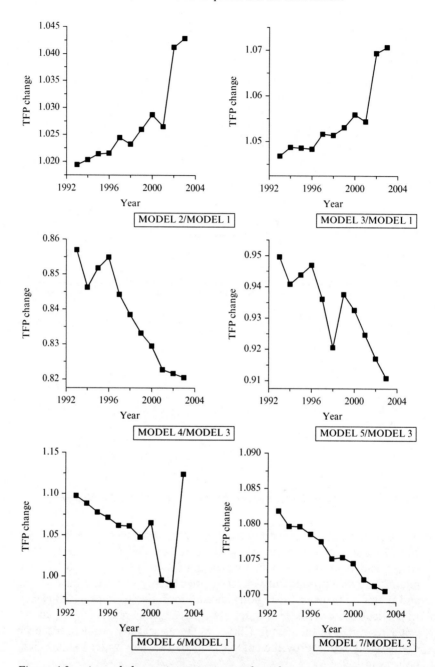

Figure 4.2   Annual change in environmental productivity

wastewater, waste gas and solid waste in Model 4/Model 3 show that overall environmental contribution of TFP, TC and EC decrease. Environmental productivity decreases by about 85.68 percent, or a mean rate of 16.2 percent decrease per year, that is, environmental technologies were less efficiently utilized and environmental management was not well organized. The decrease in environmental TFP over 1992–2003 is consistent with Managi and Kaneko (2006) who study the 1978–2001 period. Although that study uses different period data and their sample is not consistent, it seems that environmental management in China is deteriorating. Radical reform of government administration was conducted by the Ninth National People's Congress in 1998, and the environmental protection agency was upgraded to ministerial status and renamed as SEPA. However, our study shows that environmental productivity decreased over the 1999–2003 period. This suggests that the reforms were not effective in increasing implementation of environmental management in the short run or, at least, the reforms required several more years to increase efficiency. These results, however, do not show which sector of wastewater, waste gas or solid waste is more or less efficient. Therefore, we are not able to judge fully the effects of management and policy implementation. The remaining question is to test comparatively which pollutants are (not) efficiently managed.

The results show that waste gas, which includes SO_2, dust and soot, is less efficiently treated over time with 53.54 percent, or an average of 6.7 percent annual decrease in the TFP. As in Model 4, the all-pollutants case, both TC and EC decrease. The results imply that management of waste gas including SO_2 is deteriorating although a series of laws are being implemented, that is, ineffectiveness in environmental policy implementation.[6] Several critiques are provided in the literature regarding this ineffectiveness (for example, Yang et al., 2000). One of the most important reasons might be that the abatement cost of SO_2 is much higher than the amount charged by the environmental agency. Thus, it is unreasonable to expect the levy system to motivate compliance and control of SO_2 emissions by power enterprises.

Solid waste has not been considered as an important environmental problem in China. In 1996, however, the Law on the Prevention and Control of Pollution of the Environment by Solid Waste was promulgated. Contribution of TFP change by efficient treatment of solid waste is provided by Model 6/Model 1. The results show that environmental productivity of solid waste increases by 91.72 percent, or a mean rate of 6.1 percent annual increase per year in the TFP. Contrary to Model 4, the all-pollutants case, both TC and EC increase. Environmental technologies of solid waste were efficiently utilized and environmental management was improved.

The contribution of TFP change by efficient treatment of wastewater such as COD, lead and chromium six is provided by Model 7/Model 3. The results show that wastewater was more efficiently treated over time with 123.77 percent, or an average of 7.6 percent annual increase in the TFP. In contrast to Model 4, the all-pollutants case, and also for Model 6, the solid waste case, both TC and EC also increase. Overall, environmental management in China has not effectively regulated the all-pollutants case or the waste gas case, but has effectively regulated wastewater and solid waste pollutants over our study periods. We expect that limited enforcement of environmental laws and policies and firms' insufficient environmental management capacity led to this environmental inefficiency where efficiencies decreased.

6   DISCUSSION AND CONCLUSION

Inadequate information inhibits both the ability of private and public managers to make informed decisions having environmental impacts, and the ability of government agencies to enact sound public policy concerning interactions between the economy and the environment. Measurement of environmental productivity provides one important source of information to complement conventional market-based productivity measurements.

Successful economic and environmental policies can contribute to technological or efficiency improvements by encouraging, rather than inhibiting, technological innovation. Although a large number of studies have been made on the measurements of technological change (Griliches, 1994), little is known about the empirical evaluation of environmental management in developing countries. This chapter contributes to the literature on productivity change in several ways. First, we apply a parametric distance function approach to a province-level dataset tracked from 1992 to 2003 to measure various components of TFP within a joint-production model of market and environmental outputs. This contributes to our understanding of the various components of TFP change in China. Our results show that environmental management has not effectively regulated overall pollutants and waste gas, but has effectively regulated wastewater and solid waste pollutant emissions over our study periods.

NOTES

1. Although we do not explicitly impose the translation property with accounting for the polluting outputs as in Färe et al. (2005), our results support the substitutability between the desirable output and the polluting output.

2. The estimated parameters are indicated with hats.
3. The decomposition in productivity is first used in Managi et al. (2004), who analyze the productivity in the oil and gas industry and separate productivity from resource depletion.
4. Beijing, Tianjin, Hebei, Shanxi, Inner Mongolia, Liaoning, Jilin, Heilongjiang, Shanghai, Jiangsu, Zhejiang, Anhui, Fujian, Jiangxi, Shandong, Henan, Hubei, Hunan, Guangdong, Guangxi, Sichuan and Chongqing, Guizhou, Yunnan, Xizang, Shaanxi, Gansu, Qinghai, Ningxia, and Xinjiang. Note; Tibet is excluded because some relevant data are not available. Hainan, a new province from 1988, is also excluded. Data for Chongqing, which was separated from Sichuan in 1997, is merged with data for Sichuan.
5. Note that the labor and capital related to pollution abatement are excluded from these variables. Thus, market inputs and the data on labor, capital and environmental input are independent of one another.
6. We also estimate this model by using SO_2 as the sole environmental output and obtain a similar decreasing trend in the TFP.

REFERENCES

Boyd, G.A. and J.D. McClelland (1999), 'The impact of environmental constraints on productivity improvement in integrated paper plants', *Journal of Environmental Economics and Management*, **38**, 121–42.
Boyd, G.A., G. Tolley and J. Pang (2002), 'Plant level productivity, efficiency, and environmental performance of the container glass industry', *Environmental and Resource Economics*, **23**, 29–43.
Briec, W. and K. Kerstens (2006), 'Well-defined directional distance functions and luenberger productivity indicators: diagnosis of infeasibilities and its remedies', CNRS-LABORES Working Paper, Lille, France.
Caves, D.W, L.R. Christensen and W.E. Diewert (1982), 'The economic theory of index numbers and the measurement of input, output and productivity', *Econometrica*, **50** (6), 1393–414.
Chung, Y.H., R. Färe and S. Grosskopf (1997), 'Productivity and undesirable outputs: a directional distance function approach', *Journal of Environmental Management*, **51**, 229–40.
Coggins, J.S. and J.R. Swinton (1996), 'The price of pollution: a dual approach to valuing SO_2 allowances', *Journal of Environmental Economics and Management*, **30**, 58–72.
Dasgupta, S., M. Huq and D. Wheeler (1997), 'Bending the rules: discretionary pollution control in China', Policy Research Working Paper 1761, Development Research Group, World Bank, Washington, DC.
Debreu, G. (1951), 'The coefficient of resource utilization', *Econometrica*, **19**, 273–92.
Domazlicky, B. and W. Weber (2004), 'Does environmental protection lead to slower productivity growth in the chemical industry?', *Environmental and Resource Economics*, **28** (3), 301–24.
Economy, E.C. (2004), *The River Runs Black: The Environmental Challenge to China's Future*, Ithaca, NY: Cornell University Press.
Edmonds, R.L. (2004), *Managing the Chinese Environment: Studies on Contemporary China*, Oxford: Oxford University Press.
Färe, R., S. Grosskopf, K. Lovell and C. Pasurka (1989), 'Multilateral productivity

comparisons when some outputs are undesirable: a nonparametric approach', *Review of Economics and Statistics*, **71**, 90–98.

Färe, R., S. Grosskopf, C.A.K. Lovell and S. Yaisawarng (1993), 'Derivation of shadow prices for undesirable outputs: a distance function approach', *Review of Economics and Statistics*, **75**, 374–80.

Färe, R., S. Grosskopf, D. Noh and W. Weber (2005), 'Characteristics of a polluting technology: theory and practice', *Journal of Econometrics*, **126**, 469–92.

Färe, R., S. Grosskopf, M. Norris and Z. Zhang (1994), 'Productivity growth, technical progress, and efficiency change in industrialized countries', *American Economic Review*, **84** (1), 66–83.

Fuentes, H.J., E. Grifell-Tatje and S. Parelman (2001), 'A parametric distance function approach for Malmquist productivity index estimation', *Journal of Productivity Analysis*, **15** (2), 79–94.

Fujii, H., S. Kaneko and S. Managi (2006), 'Infeasibility in weak disposality assumption', working paper, Hiroshima University, Hiroshima, Japan.

Griliches, Z. (1994), 'Productivity, R&D and the data constraint', *American Economic Review*, **84** (1), 1–23.

Grosskopf, S., K.J. Hayes, L.L. Taylor and W.L. Weber (1997), 'Budget-constrained frontier measures of fiscal equality and efficiency in schooling', *Review of Economics and Statistics*, **79** (1), 116–24.

Hailu, A. and T.S. Veeman (2000), 'Environmentally sensitive productivity analysis of the Canadian pulp and paper industry, 1959–1994: an input distance function approach', *Journal of Environmental Economics and Management*, **40** (3), 251–74.

Jaffe, A.B., R.G. Newell and R.N. Stavins (2003), 'Technological change and the environment', in Karl-Göran Mäler and Jeffrey Vincent (eds), *Handbook of Environmental Economics*, Amsterdam: North-Holland. Elsevier Science, pp. 462–516.

Kai, S. (1996), 'Maintenance and response of wastewater plants', *Environmental Protection*, **222**, 8–9.

Lovell, C.A.K., S. Richardson, P. Travers and L.L. Wood (1994), 'Resources and functionings: a new view of inequality in Australia', in W. Eichhorn (ed.), *Models and Measurement of Welfare and Inequality*, Berlin: Springer-Verlag, pp. 787–807.

Ma, X. and L. Ortolano (2000), *Environmental Regulation in China*, Lanham, MD: Rowman & Littlefield.

Managi, S. and S. Kaneko (2006), 'Productivity of market and environmental abatement in China', *Environmental Economics and Policy Studies*, **7** (4), 459–70.

Managi, S., J.J. Opaluch, D. Jin and T.A. Grigalunas (2004), 'Technological change and depletion in offshore oil and gas', *Journal of Environmental Economics and Management*, **47** (2), 388–409.

Managi, S., J.J. Opaluch, D. Jin and T.A. Grigalunas (2005), 'Environmental regulations and technological change in the offshore oil and gas industry', *Land Economics*, **81** (2), 303–19.

Pittman, R.W. (1983), 'Multilateral productivity comparisons with undesirable outputs', *Economic Journal*, **93**, 883–91.

Sinkule, B.J. and L. Ortolano (1995), *Implementing Environmental Policy in China*, Westport, CT: Praeger.

Wang, H., N. Mamingi, B. Laplante and S. Dasgupta (2003), 'Incomplete enforcement of pollution regulation: bargaining power of Chinese factories', *Environmental and Resource Economics*, **24**, 245–62.

Wang, H. and D. Wheeler (2003), 'Equilibrium pollution and economic development in China', *Environment and Development Economics*, **8**, 451–66.

Wang, H and D. Wheeler (2005), 'Financial incentives and endogenous enforcement in China's pollution levy system', *Journal of Environmental Economics and Management*, **49** (1), 174–96.

Wang, Y. and Y. Yao (2003), 'Sources of China's economic growth 1952–1999: incorporating human capital accumulation', *China Economic Review*, **14**, 32–52.

Xu, X. (2004), 'China's gross domestic product estimation', *China Economic Review*, **15**, 302–22.

Yaisawarng, S. and J.D. Klein (1994), 'The effects of sulfur dioxide controls on productivity change in the U.S. electric power industry', *Review of Economics and Statistics*, **76**, 447–60.

Yang J.T., D. Cao, J.N. Wang and W.Y. Tian (2000), *SO₂ Emission Charge in China. SO₂ Emission Trading Program: US Experience and China's Perspective*, Beijing: China Environmental Science.

Young, A. (2003), 'Gold into base metals: productivity growth in the People's Republic of China during the reform period', *Journal of Political Economy*, **111** (6), 1220–61.

Zaim, O. and F. Taskin (2000), 'A Kuznets curve in environmental efficiency: an application on OECD countries', *Environmental and Resource Economics*, **17**, 21–36.

5. Foreign direct investment and environmental policies

1 INTRODUCTION

The relationship between environmental policies and technological change is complex, however, and there is no unambiguous case for preferring any of the policy instruments from emissions taxes, auctioned emissions permits and free permits. In practice, there are even more factors that make the evaluation difficult (Fischer et al., 2003). Thus, how actual environmental policies affect technological change positively is an empirical question.

Thorough analyses of technological change are essential for identifying appropriate policy actions to encourage economic growth and mitigate negative effects of environmental problems. The principal focus of this chapter is to measure technological change both for market and non-market (that is, environmental) outputs and to find the determinants of these changes. We employ translog multi-input, multi-output specification to estimate the productivity index (and its components of technological change and efficiency change) following Fuentes et al. (2001).

2 BACKGROUND

Environmental Policies and Technological Change

Numerous works in the literature have examined theoretically the role of environmental policy in encouraging (or discouraging) productivity growth.[1] On the one hand, abatement pressures may stimulate innovative responses that reduce the actual cost of environmental compliance below the original estimates (Downing and White, 1986). Firms might be reluctant to innovate, on the other hand, if they believe that regulators will respond by ratcheting up standards even more tightly (for example, McCain, 1978).

Regarding the environmental technologies, recent empirical studies have found a systematic relationship between environmental regulation and environmental technological progress. Empirical analyses of environmental technologies in the literature focus on the use of patent data, an indirect measurement of innovation. Lanjouw and Mody (1996) found a positive relationship between environmental compliance cost and patenting of new environmental technologies using the data from of the US, Japan and Germany. Jaffe and Palmer (1997) used US data and found no significant relationship between environmental compliance cost and patents.[2] However, they found a significant relationship between compliance costs and R&D expenditure. Brunnermeier and Cohen (2003) analyzed the environmental patent to the US manufacturing industry as a proxy for environmental innovation and found that environmental innovation responded to increases in pollution abatement expenditures. However, problems of using patent data need to be noted. This is because not all inventions that see commercial application are patented, some are subdivided into multiple patents and patent policy changes over time.[3]

Regarding the conventional market technologies, in general, the impact of the regulations on market productivity is expected to be negative since the regulations are likely to induce firms to invest in environmental compliance (or nonproductive inputs) and therefore reduce the investment for market output. Recently, however, researchers have challenged this conventional view with an alternative hypothesis that environmental regulations can encourage productivity growth and ultimately higher profits. This is the well-known Porter hypothesis (Porter, 1991; Porter and van der Linde, 1995). In addition, if the social benefits of regulation were fully taken into account as an additional output, theoretical prediction would be further complicated.

Jaffe et al. (1995) and more recently Gray and Shadbegian (2003) reviewed empirical studies on the subject of environmental regulations on market productivity and showed that the regulations reduced market productivity. For example, Gray and Shadbegian (2002) found that more-regulated firms have significantly lower market productivity growth than less-regulated firms in the US steel, oil and paper industries. In contrast, the recent study of the US oil refiners by Berman and Bui (2001) suggests that environmental regulation is productivity enhancing. These studies, however, did not consider the full range of impacts of environmental regulations, including the possible positive external impact of reducing pollution (for example, Barbera and McConnell, 1990; Repetto, 1996). Thus, the effects of the regulations on productivity need to be tested via both market productivity and pollution control technologies.[4]

Foreign Direct Investment and Productivity

Multinational enterprises possess superior production technology and management techniques, and the entry of an affiliate leads to more severe competition in the host economy (Blomstrom and Kokko, 1998). Thus, foreign direct investment (FDI) might generate productivity spillovers for the host economy. Empirical literature, however, provides little support for this view (Hanson, 2001). For example, Haddad and Harrison (1993) found a weak negative correlation between total FTP and the presence of foreign firms in the Moroccan manufacturing sector. Aitken and Harrison (1999) found mixed results between TFP growth and the presence of foreign firms in the Venezuelan manufacturing sector. These empirical research studies suggest that FDI is sensitive to both host-country tax policies and economic conditions, including the education level of the labor force, overall market size and the size of the local industrial base. Abramovitz (1986) also notes that the adoption of foreign knowledge is a complicated affair since a country must have a factor supplies, production processes and industrial production structure reasonably similar to those of the nation where the technology was created. Thus, whether FDI promotes the productivity growth in a particular region is an empirical question.

China's phenomenal economic growth per capita has been accompanied by a rapid increase in the inflows of FDI (Lin and Song, 2002). The application of FDI is important, since China has become the largest host country for FDI in the developing world (UNCTAD, 2001). To our knowledge, we are not aware of any studies that test the relationship between FDI and productivity 'growth' in China. One recent study shows that FDI is positively related to TFP (Liu and Wang, 2003).

Environmental Policies

China began implementing environmental policies from the late 1970s, such as the Environmental Protection Law in 1979, in response to air pollution, water pollution and solid waste disposal. This development of environmental policies also coincided with and was influenced by the economic reforms of the 1980s and the increased openness to foreign markets (Sinkule and Ortolano, 1995). The pollution levy system is the longest standing component of China's regulatory structure for controlling pollution emissions and discharges (Ellerman, 2002). In the levy system, the government imposes a penalty on emissions and discharges in excess of some standards applying to a particular process or plant. Note, however, that the levy system is legally different from a tax falling within the jurisdiction of the national tax authorities.[5] This is because the levy fee is collected at the local level to fund both the administrative expenses of the local environmental protection bureau and investment in waste control projects. Local governments have the authority to modify the national standards though there is a national fee schedule. In general, the fees levied have not been considered to serve as a strong incentive to clean up waste since they are usually lower than the cost of waste treatment and actual collection is far below the level that emissions data indicate they should be (for example, Sinkule and Ortolano, 1995; Ellerman, 2002). Recent econometric studies, however, show that pollution intensities have been significantly responsive to the levy system (see, for example, Jiang and McKibbin, 2002; Wang and Wheeler, 2003).

3 MODEL

Econometric Model

Our objective is to study the determinants of several productivity indices. In modeling this relationship, we follow the economic growth and industrial organization literature on productivity and add new variables to incorporate the effect of environmental policies on productivity. To analyze the historical development of productivity, we use economy-wide province-level data from 1987 to 2001. We consider changes in productivity (and its components of TC and EC) in both market and nonmarket output. Several variables, such as patent number as a proxy for new invention, in a particular year will affect productivity change several years down the road when the productivity improvement process has been completed. The process of productivity or technological change, however, is quite complex and still poorly understood. Contemporaneous impact analysis of productivity is needed to find the immediate cost of patent, environmental policies and FDI. But time lags are needed to consider the longer-term gains associated with technological change and consequent change in productivity. In particular, we estimate the following equation:

$$\ln A^{i,t} = \sum_z \sum_j \varpi_z^j \ln r_z^{i,t-j}, \tag{5.1}$$

where $A^{i,t}$ is the annual productivity, technological or efficiency change for province i, at time t, A is one of the measurement of joint, market and environmental outputs. $r_z^{i,t-j}$ is the zth independent variable of lag year j, and ϖ_z is the coefficient associated with r_z. In our analysis, we consider a number of independent variables.

In modeling the market and joint-output case, we expect the number of patent applications (*Patent*), as a proxy for invention within a province, to have a positive long-term impact on technological change (Griliches, 1984). Two variables capture environmental abatements and regulations: the ratio of pollution abatement costs and expenditures to GRP (*PACE*), and the actual collected pollution levy rate (*Levy*). *FDI* is included to test the hypothesis that FDI generates productivity growth or 'international spillover' for the host economy. Annual changes in the above invention, environmental and FDI variables are used to capture the effects on productivity measurements. The geometric average of surrounding regions' productivity (*Spillover*) is used to test the 'interregional spillover' effect of accumulated knowledge. Cumulative productivity index (*Productivity*) is included and shows a negative sign if the effect of interregional transfer of technology from rich to poor dominates the effect of larger positive externalities from being a richer province.[6]

Population growth (*Labor*) might capture the tradeoff between family size and the development of human capital of parents and/or children. Therefore, factors that lead to higher population growth such as a decrease in the cost of raising children might reduce productivity (Becker et al., 1990).[7] We include capital intensity (*Capital*) since it might affect the productivity. Given the ambiguity in the literature, however, the sign is difficult to predict (Hughes, 1986; Schmalensee, 1989).[8] The share of secondary industry, which includes such industries as the heavy and chemical industry, to GRP (*Poll-Inten*) is included since the growth of secondary industry becomes the main engine of rapid development for China's economy and the secondary industry tends to be pollution intensive. Note that all the independent variables except *Spillover*, *Productivity* and *Poll-Inten* are expressed in annual change given the nature of our dependent variable. Before proceeding to the model estimation, a discussion of some econometric issues seems in order. If both of the environmental outcome and independent variables are I(1), the static regressions should be interpreted as co-integrating relationships between the environmental outcome and independent variables. Under this interpretation, the residuals should be I(0) if the model is a correct representation of the data-generating process. A test for stationarity of the residuals is thus an important model specification test, and we make use of the panel data unit root test of Im et al. (2003).

4   APPLICATION

This study uses province-level panel data which consists of annual data for 1987–2001, for 28 of the 31 provinces (including three municipalities) (see Appendix 5A1 for the data description). The market output variable is the GRP and the market input variables are labor and capital. The environmental output variables are wastewater, waste gas and solid waste and the environmental input variables are pollution abatement cost and expenditure as a proxy for abatement effort. For the province-level analysis, we estimate our stochastic frontier model (see Chapter 4, equation (4.6)) with two separate specifications, where the first specification excludes environmental input/output and the second includes them. Both of the specifications are estimated using the Frontier Version 4.1 software (Coelli, 1994). The results of the two specifications are summarized in Tables 5A2.1 and 5A2.2. Generally, the estimated coefficients for most variables have the expected sign and reasonable magnitudes. We are able to estimate the changes in productivity indices using equations (4.7) and (4.8) in Chapter 4.

Figure 5.1 presents the results for annual average change in TFP for joint outputs, and changes in the TFP decomposed into the market and environmental outputs. The TFP for the market keeps increasing over the study period and the rate of its change is always larger than 7 percent with an average of 8.6 percent growth. The growth rate of the TFP, however, drops from 9.6 percent in 1988 to 7.6 percent in 2001. A similar trend appeared in TFP change for joint output with an average of 6.8 percent. In contrast, the changes in environmental TFP are always less than one, indicating the inefficiency of environmental management. The magnitude of the change, however, is increasing from −2.2 percent in 1988 to −1.6 percent in 2001.

Figure 5.2 shows the corresponding three indices for TC and has very similar results as shown in Figure 5.1. Their average change in total, market and environmental TC are 8.9, 7.5 and −1.3 percent over the study periods, respectively. The results of EC for joint, market and environmental outputs are presented in Figure 5.3. Although all of the indices are decreasing, indicating that all are becoming less efficient over time, the rates of changes are close to zero. Our result is consistent with the literature that there has been considerable TFP growth (for example, Jefferson et al., 2000). We further find that TC is the main source of TFP growth and there are no catching-up effects (that is, no efficiency improvement) on average.

On the other hand, environmental management has not effectively regulated wastewater, air and solid waste pollutant emissions. It is likely that limited enforcement of environmental laws and policies and firms' insufficient environmental management capacity led to this environmental inefficiency. These seem to dominate the opposing forces that many factories have to shut down facilities since they are not able to satisfy environmental standards, and newly started factories tend to have better environmental technologies[9]. We shall provide some answers as to why there is no progress in environmental productivity in addition to the determinants of market and joint productivity growth.

We estimate the determinants of the productivity measurements over 1987 to 2001. Equation (5.1) is estimated as a two-way fixed-effects model

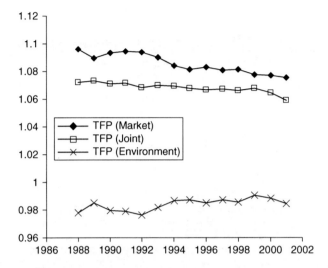

Figure 5.1   Annual total factor productivity change

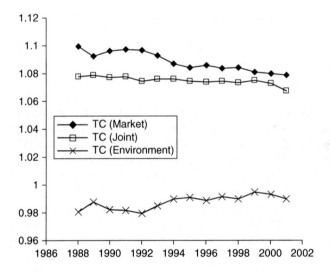

Figure 5.2   Annual technological change

using our cross-section and time-series data. The linear fixed-effects model is given by $y^{i,t} = \alpha^i + \gamma^t + X^{i,t}\beta + \varepsilon^{i,t}$, where $y^{i,t}$ is the log of the dependent variable, $X^{i,t}$ is the vector of the log of explanatory variables, α^i is the province-specific term, γ^t is the time effects, and $\varepsilon^{i,t}$ is a random disturbance

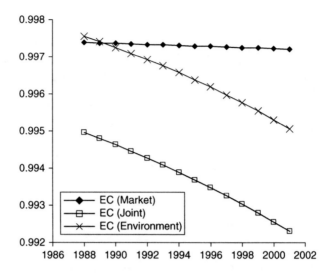

Figure 5.3   Annual efficiency change

term. Since heteroscedasticity is present, the model uses White's hetero-scedasticity adjusted standard errors.

The results of the three model estimates, which are TFP, TC and EC for market output, are presented in Table 5.1. This table provides the determinants of the level of production technology from information on technology-related variables, level of environmental policies, industry characteristic variables and factor endowments.[10] The *Patent*, as a proxy for the invention within the province or 'domestic invention', is not significant for TFP, TC or EC.[11] In contrast, several time lags of FDI, 'international spillover' for the host economy, are significant with a positive sign. Contemporaneous and first lagged terms are significant for TFP and TC while all three lags are significant for EC.[12] The *Spillover* variable, 'interregional spillover' effects of accumulated knowledge, does not have statistical significance. The results indicate that productivity diffusion from adjoining regions does not seem to be easily utilized. Cumulative productivity levels (*Productivity*) are positive with statistical significance for EC showing that the effect of larger positive externalities from being a richer province dominates the effect of interregional transfer of technology from rich to poor province. *Productivity*, however, is not significant for TFP or TC, indicating that either of the effects can dominate the other.

Overall, our result shows that 'international spillover, *FDI*' rather than 'domestic invention, *Patent*' is the major factor for an increase in productivity growth.[13] This result suggests that, although GDP in China is the

Table 5.1   Estimation results of market productivities

Variable	Dependent variable		
	ΔTFP_t (Market)	ΔTC_t (Market)	ΔEC_t (Market)
$\Delta Patent_{t-1}$	−0.0004(−0.87)	0.0003(0.43)	0.000001(1.15)
ΔFDI_t	0.0003(3.03)***	0.00001(2.18)**	0.0000004(2.00)**
ΔFDI_{t-1}	0.0003(2.20)**	0.00001(2.16)**	0.000001(3.29)**
ΔFDI_{t-2}	0.0001(0.87)	0.0001(0.56)	0.0000003(1.88)*
$Spillover_t$	0.0001(0.15)	0.0001(0.10)	−0.0000001(−0.11)
$Productivity_t$	−0.0056(−1.11)	0.0001(0.01)	0.006004(185.69)***
$\Delta PACE_t$	0.0003(0.94)	−0.0032(−5.85)***	−0.0000003(−0.56)
$\Delta PACE_{t-1}$	0.0005(1.57)	−0.0041(−7.82)***	−0.0000001(−0.22)
$\Delta PACE_{t-2}$	0.0002(0.83)	0.0009(1.84)*	0.0000003(0.64)
$\Delta Labor_{t-1}$	−0.0010(−0.14)	−0.0171(−1.43)	−0.000030(−2.18)**
$\Delta Capital_{t-1}$	−0.0001(−0.12)	0.0004(0.52)	−0.000001(−1.67)*
$Poll\text{-}Inten_t$	−0.0028(−1.17)	−0.0004(−0.09)	0.000017(4.41) ***
R-Square	0.9253	0.7559	0.9999
F Test for no fixed effects	76.07***	22.35***	483.36***
Unit root	3.07***	2.65***	2.35***

Note: $\Delta Patent_t$ is equal to $Patent_t / Patent_{t-1}$ in this table. Values in parentheses are *t*-values.
* Significant at the 10% level. ** Significant at the 5% level. *** Significant at the 1% level.

fourth-largest in the world and its growth records are higher than the other developed countries, China is still a developing country and the adoption of new technologies from developed countries, or imitation, is the main source of growth in market productivity. This is consistent with the observations that the number of original innovations is limited, and China lags far behind the world technology frontier (Hu and Jefferson, 2004). Adopting existing technologies from world best practices through FDI might be the best strategy for each province to expand its knowledge stock rather than adopting from neighboring provinces. This might be why the *Spillover* variable does not have statistically significant results.

The first two time lags of PACE are highly significant, with a negative sign for TC, though the third time lag is significant with the opposite sign. A one-year lag of PACE has the largest magnitude to TC, implying the importance of considering time lag as an incentive to technological progress. Summation of the three coefficients is −0.0064, indicating the negative consequence of the increase in PACE to the TC. This might be caused by the inflexibility of financing in that the cost of installing pollution abatement facilities is usually not subject to financial assistance from

Chinese economic development and the environment

Table 5.2   Estimation results of joint output productivities

Variable	Dependent variable		
	ΔTFP_t (Joint output)	ΔTC_t (Joint output)	ΔEC_t (Joint output)
$\Delta Patent_{t-1}$	0.0006(0.81)	−0.0003(−0.80)	0.00001(0.99)
ΔFDI_t	0.0002(2.11)**	0.0003(2.99)***	0.000003(1.00)
ΔFDI_{t-1}	0.0002(2.09)**	0.0003(2.18)**	0.000005(1.90)*
ΔFDI_{t-2}	0.0001(0.38)	0.0001(0.85)	0.000002(0.95)
$Spillover_t$	−0.0006(−0.55)	−0.00003(−0.05)	−0.00002(−1.50)
$Productivity_t$	0.0439(2.06)**	−0.0073(−1.40)	0.03538(248.13)***
$\Delta PACE_t$	0.0034(1.05)	0.0003(0.93)	−0.000003(−0.50)
$\Delta PACE_{t-1}$	0.0039(1.33)	0.0005(1.54)	−0.000004(−0.52)
$\Delta PACE_{t-2}$	0.0009(1.52)	0.0002(0.82)	0.000002(0.32)
$\Delta Labor_{t-1}$	−0.0146(−1.06)	−0.0010(−0.14)	−0.00002(−0.10)
$\Delta Capital_{t-1}$	0.0004(0.43)	−0.0001(−0.28)	−0.000005(−0.43)
$Poll\text{-}Inten_t$	0.0006(0.13)	−0.0028(−1.20)	0.00011(2.07)**
R-Square	0.598	0.9228	0.9999
F Test for no fixed effects	7.85***	66.66***	160.82***
Unit root	2.65***	2.98***	2.76***

Note: Values in parentheses are *t*-values. * Significant at the 10% level. ** Significant at the 5% level. *** Significant at the 1% level.

the commercial banks.[14] In contrast, there are no significant results for TFP and EC, though these have a minus sign.

The *Labor* variable has a negative sign for all cases and is significant for EC. This might imply that higher population growth reduces productivity by decreasing the cost of raising children (Becker et al., 1990). The pollution-intensive variable, *Poll-Inten*, is significant with a positive sign. This is consistent with the idea that higher growth rates of these industries are the main engine of rapid development for China's economy.

Next, we estimate the model separately with three sets of dependent variables, TFP, TC and EC for joint output of market and environmental outputs (see Table 5.2). The results are similar to Table 5.1 in that *Patent* is not significant and FDI is significant for all three cases. This empirical research thus provides support for the idea that promoting FDI is warranted on welfare grounds. In addition to the effects on EC as in Table 5.1, *Productivity* is positive with statistical significance for TFP, showing the effect of larger positive externalities from being a richer province.

Finally, the results of the three models of TFP, TC and EC for

Table 5.3   *Estimation results of environmental productivities*

Variable	Dependent variable		
	ΔTFP_t (Environment)	ΔTC_t (Environment)	ΔEC_t (Environment)
$\Delta PACE_t$	0.003302(5.59)***	0.0033(4.77)***	−0.00003(−1.42)
$\Delta PACE_{t-1}$	0.004172(8.09)***	0.0038(6.36)***	−0.00003(−1.24)
$\Delta PACE_{t-2}$	0.001079(2.13)**	0.0009(1.56)	−0.00002(−0.84)
$\Delta Levy_t$	0.000054(0.52)	0.00003(0.27)	−0.00001(−1.89)*
$\Delta Levy_{t-1}$	0.000027(0.24)	−0.00004(−0.30)	−0.000004(−0.94)
$\Delta Levy_{t-2}$	−0.000120(−1.15)	−0.0002(−1.84)*	−0.000003(−0.69)
ΔFDI_t	−0.000070(−0.36)	−0.0003(−1.34)	−0.00001(−1.08)
ΔFDI_{t-1}	−0.000040(−0.23)	−0.0002(−0.82)	−0.00001(−0.85)
ΔFDI_{t-2}	0.000072(0.41)	0.0001(0.35)	−0.00001(−1.41)
$Spillover_t$	0.000100(0.10)	0.0003(0.42)	0.00002(0.53)
$Productivity_t$	0.010318(1.47)	0.0314(2.70)***	0.04264(78.32)***
$\Delta Labor_{t-1}$	−0.013640(−1.15)	−0.0131(−0.95)	0.00038(0.80)
$\Delta Capital_{t-1}$	0.000122(0.14)	0.0002(0.18)	−0.00011(−3.23)***
$Poll\text{-}Inten_t$	−0.000660(−0.16)	0.0033(0.70)	−0.00040(−2.56)**
R-Square	0.8389	0.69880	0.9984
F Test for no fixed effects	30.63***	12.12***	796.93***
Unit root	2.82***	2.93***	2.70***

Note: Values in parentheses are *t*-values. * Significant at the 10% level. ** Significant at the 5% level. *** Significant at the 1% level.

environmental outputs are presented in Table 5.3. All three time lags of PACE are highly significant with a positive sign for TFP, while the first two time lags are significant for TC and none of the PACE variables is significant for EC. Magnitudes of the coefficients are larger in the second lag than the others for all three models. These results show clearly a strong impact of increase in PACE on environmental productivity and technological progress for consecutive years.[15] None of the Levy variables, however, has a positive sign with statistical significance. These results might be because the levy is set too low to effectively encourage significant pollution abatement.[16]

It is interesting that *Levy* shows a negative effect on TC and EC, where one of the *Levy* variables has significant results for TC and EC, respectively. This observation might be related to the structural set-up of the levy system. The levy is a penalty on emissions or discharges in excess of some standard applying to a particular process or plant. The national government decides the basic guidelines and has legal authority to impose the pollution levy, while the local government is responsible for the assessment, collection and use of funds. Thus, the actual rate of levy imposed may differ between each province and each year. The levy system provides recycling revenues as a subsidy for abatement projects from collected levy payments to local enterprises. Although the targeted rate is 80 percent, the actual percentage is more nearly between 30–50 percent.[17] In addition, this levy system applies only to large and medium-sized sources, and smaller enterprises, particularly town and village enterprises, are not included in their levy system.[18] Since the amount of the penalty is small, even though the rate has increased, it would give no incentive for firms to comply with the regulations. Furthermore, it might actually give a sort of permission for firms to pollute. Thus, the levy system does not function well with regard to encouragement of environmental technological innovation.

In contrast to the market and joint-output cases, FDI, 'international spillover' for the host economy, is not statistically significant for all environmental productivities. Thus, from our empirical research, FDI promotes market and joint-output productivity but not environmental productivity, and provides little support for the idea that promoting FDI is warranted on environmental management grounds. *Spillover*, 'interregional spillover' effects of accumulated knowledge, does not have statistical significance for any of the cases. Thus, technological diffusion from adjacent regions is not utilized for environmental productivity. Cumulative productivity levels (*Productivity*) are positive with statistical significance for TC and EC showing that the effect of larger positive externalities from being a richer province dominates the effect of interregional transfer of technology from rich to poor province. The variable of secondary industry, *Poll-Inten*, is negative and statistically significant for EC. The higher the ratio of pollution-intensive firms in GRP, the lower the efficiency changes. Capital intensity (*Capital*) is negative for EC, meaning less utilization of capital in environmental efficiency improvement.

5   DISCUSSION AND CONCLUSION

Successful economic and environmental policies can contribute to technological or efficiency improvements by encouraging, rather than inhibiting, technological innovation. Although a large number of studies have been made on the constituents of technological change (Griliches, 1994), little is known about the empirical evaluation of policies that encourage (or discourage) productivity progress and/or regress in China. This chapter contributes to the literature on productivity change in several ways. First, we apply a parametric distance function approach to a province-level dataset tracked from 1987 to 2001 to measure various components of TFP within a joint-production model of market and environmental outputs. This contributes to our understanding of the various components of TFP change in China. In addition, this study contributes to better economic and environmental policy design for sustainable development by empirically estimating the role of economic and environmental management on market and nonmarket (that is, environmental) productivity.

Our result for market output is consistent with the literature that there has been considerable TFP growth (for example, Jefferson et al., 2000), while environmental management has not effectively regulated wastewater, air and solid waste pollutants emissions over our study periods. Detecting the determinants of these factors, we found that the 'international spillover, *FDI*' rather than 'domestic invention, *Patent*' is the major factor in an increase in market productivity growth. We also found significant negative impacts of PACE on market technological progress, although elasticity is small. This PACE, in contrast, positively affects environmental productivity and technological progress as expected.

While FDI helps economic development by encouraging market productivity improvements, it does not lead to a positive consequence for environmental technologies where FDI does have negative coefficients, though they are not significant. Thus, we could say that FDI may lead to more environmental damage since firms in advanced countries might avoid stringent environmental regulations.

We find that the levy has a negative consequence with regard to environmental productivity. Therefore, it seems reasonable to conclude that the levy system needs to be re-considered and we highlight several problems with the current system in the following areas: (i) enforcement of environmental laws is limited and policies and firms' environmental management is insufficient. For example, the levy rate is less than the average cost of pollution abatement partially because the levy fees are not indexed for inflation, and, for SOEs, they can be included under costs and later compensated through price increase or tax deductions (Sinkule and Ortolano, 1995); (ii) smaller enterprises tend not to pay a levy though they share a significant rate of total industrial output; and (iii) the cost of installing pollution abatement facilities is usually not subject to financial assistance from the commercial banks.

NOTES

1. Kemp (1997), Jaffe et al. (2003) and Parry (2003) provide thorough surveys of the litera-ture relating policy, technological change and the environment.
2. Note, however, that the patent data include both market and environmental technologies.
3. For example, see Managi et al. (2004) for a review of patent and innovation studies. In addition, even though invention, which is a new idea such as patent, might respond quickly to incentives (Popp, 2002), commercial application of new technologies, which is the actual use of new technologies, might be a more complex issue.
4. Mohr (2002), for example, develops the theoretical model assuming that the new tech-nology enables firms to produce the same amount of output, but with less pollution, and his results support the Porter hypothesis. If market production and pollution control technologies are nonseparable, however, this result may not hold (Nagase, 2004).
5. Note that a new environmental policy was implemented in 2003; its focus is to change the collection mechanism of the levy (see SEPA, 2003 for details).
6. Barro (1991) includes an initial level of per capita GDP to find the relation to the rate of economic growth.
7. Becker et al. (1990) use growth rate of income per capita, instead of productivity, as a dependent variable.
8. Capital intensity is measured as the ratio of capital expenditure to GRP.
9. In particular smaller firms such as township and village enterprises have been forced to shut down their facilities from the mid-1990s. See Arayama and Taketoshi (1998) for further details about the facility shutdown.
10. We examine the stationarity of the residuals using the unit root tests of Im et al. (2003) as discussed in a previous section. In all specifications we are able to reject the null hypothesis of a unit root in the residuals.
11. Choice of time lag does not alter our results, and including several more time lags caused the collinearity problem.
12. Adding more time lags does not show significant results.
13. As described in Section 2, we need to be cautious about the use of patent data.
14. Note that econometric studies generally find significant negative impacts of regulation on productivity, although not always very large ones, while growth-accounting studies use estimates of compliance costs to calculate productivity effects and typically find only a small impact on productivity because compliance costs are a small share of total costs (for example, Denison, 1979; Gray, 1987).
15. The other time lag effects do not show significant results.
16. The levy rate is less than the average cost of pollution abatement (Sinkule and Ortolano, 1995). In addition, the rate of expenditure for actually collected *Levy* to *PACE* decreased from 17.1 percent in 1992 to 8.0 percent in 2000 (*China Environmental Statistical Data and Materials*, 2002).
17. For example, the rate was 44.5 percent in 1992 and decreased to 33.2 percent in 2000 (*China Environmental Statistical Data and Materials*, various years).
18. Although enterprises pay a levy, priority of recycling revenues might be given to larger firms (Arayama and Takeuchi, 1998).

BIBLIOGRAPHY

Abramovitz, M. (1986), 'Catching up, forging ahead, and falling behind', *Journal of Economic History*, **46** (2), 385–406.
Aitken B and A. Harrison (1999), 'Do domestic firms benefit from foreign invest-ment? Evidence from Venezuela', *American Economic Review*, **89**, 605–18.

Arayama, Y. and K. Taketoshi (1998), 'Environmental issues and development of township and village enterprises in China', *Economic Science*, **46**, 15–28.

Barbera, A.J. and V. McConnell (1990), 'The impact of environmental regulations on industrial productivity: direct and indirect effects', *Journal of Environmental Economics and Management*, **18** (1), 50–65.

Barro, R.J. (1991), 'Economic growth in a cross-section of countries', *Quarterly Journal of Economics*, **106**, 407–43.

Becker, G.S., K.M. Murphy and R. Tamura (1990), 'Human capital, fertility, and economic growth', *Journal of Political Economy*, S12–S37.

Berman, E. and Linda T.M. Bui (2001), 'Environmental regulation and productivity: evidence from oil refineries', *Review of Economics and Statistics*, **83** (3), 498–510.

Blomstrom, M. and A. Kokko (1998), 'Multinational corporations and spillovers', *Journal of Economic Surveys*, **12**, 247–77.

Brunnermeier, S. and M. Cohen (2003), 'Determinants of environmental innovation in US manufacturing industries', *Journal of Environmental Economics and Management*, **45**, 278–93.

Caves, D.W., L.R. Christensen and W. Erwin Diewert (1982), 'Multilateral comparisons of output, input and productivity using superlative index numbers', *Economic Journal*, **92** (365), 73–86.

Coelli, T.J. (1994), *A Guide to FRONTIER Version 4.1: A Computer Program for Stochastic Frontier and Cost Function Estimation*, Department of Econometrics, University of New England, Armidale.

Denison, E.P. (1979), *Accounting for Slower Economic Growth: The US in the 1970s*, Washington, DC: Brookings Institution.

Downing, P.G. and L.J. White (1986), 'Innovation in pollution control', *Journal of Environmental Economics and Management*, **13**, 18–29

Ellerman, A.D. (2002), 'Designing a tradable permit system to control SO_2 emissions in China: principles and practice', *Energy Journal*, **23** (2), 1–26

Färe, R., S. Grosskopf, M. Norris and Z. Zhang (1994), 'Productivity growth, technical progress, and efficiency change in industrialized countries', *American Economic Review*, **84** (1), 66–83.

Fischer, I., W.H. Parry and W.A. Pizer (2003), 'Instrument choice for environmental protection when technological innovation is endogenous', *Journal of Environmental Economics and Management*, **45**, 523–45.

Fuentes, H.J., E. Grifell-Tatje and S. Parelman (2001), 'A parametric distance function approach for Malmquist productivity index estimation', *Journal of Productivity Analysis*, **15** (2), 79–94.

Fuss, M. and D. McFadden (1978), *Production Economics: A Dual Approach to Theory and Applications*, Amsterdam: North-Holland.

Gray, W.B. (1987), 'The cost of regulation: OSHA, EPA and the productivity slowdown', *American Economic Review*, **77**, 998–1006.

Gray, W.B. and R.J. Shadbegian (2002), 'Pollution abatement costs, regulation, and plant-level productivity', in W.B. Gray (ed.), *The Economic Costs and Consequences of Environmental Regulation*, Aldershot: Ashgate.

Gray, W.B. and R.J. Shadbegian (2003), 'Plant vintage, technology, and environmental regulation', *Journal of Environmental Economics and Management*, **46** (3), 384–402.

Griliches, Zvi (ed.) (1984), *R&D, Patents, and Productivity*, NBER Conference Report, Chicago and London: University of Chicago Press.

Griliches, Z. (1994), 'Productivity, R&D and the data constraint', *American Economic Review*, **84** (1), 1–23.

Grosskopf, S., K.J. Hayes, L.L. Taylor and W.L. Weber (1997), 'Budget-constrained frontier measures of fiscal equality and efficiency in schooling', *Review of Economics and Statistics*, **79** (1), 116–24.

Haddad, M. and A. Harrison (1993), 'Are there positive spillovers from direct foreign investment?', *Journal of Development Economics*, **42**, 51–74.

Hanson, G. (2001), 'Should countries promote foreign direct investment?', G24 Discussion Paper No. 9, New York and Geneva.

Hu, G.A. and G.H. Jefferson (2004), 'Returns to research and development in Chinese industry: evidence from state-owned enterprises in Beijing', *China Economic Review*, **15** (1), 86–107.

Hughes, K. (1986), *Exports and Technology*, Cambridge and New York: Cambridge University Press.

Im, K., M. Pesaran and Y. Shin (2003), 'Testing for unit roots in heterogeneous panels', *Journal of Econometrics*, **115** (1), 53–74.

Jaffe, A.B., R.G. Newell and R.N. Stavins (2003), 'Technological change and the environment', in Karl-Göran Mäler and Jeffrey Vincent (eds), *Handbook of Environmental Economics*, Amsterdam: North-Holland, pp. 461–5070.

Jaffe, A.B. and K. Palmer (1997), 'Environmental regulation and innovation: a panel data study', *Review of Economics and Statistics*, **79** (4), 610–19.

Jaffe, A.B., S. Peterson, P. Portney and R. Stavins. (1995), 'Environmental regulation and the competitiveness of U.S. manufacturing: what does the evidence tell us?', *Journal of Economic Literature*, **33**, 132–63.

Jefferson, G.H., T.G. Rawski, L. Wang and Y. Zheng (2000), 'Ownership, productivity change, and financial performance in Chinese industry', *Journal of Comparative Economics*, **28** (4), 786–813.

Jiang, T. and W.J. McKibbin (2002), 'Assessment of China's pollution levy system: an equilibrium pollution approach', *Environment and Development Economics*, **7** (1), 75–105.

Kemp, R. (1997), *Environmental Policy and Technical Change: A Comparison of the Technological Impact of Policy Instruments*, Cheltenham, UK and Lyme, USA: Edward Elgar.

Kneese, A.V. and C.L. Schultze (1978), *Pollution, Prices and Public Policy*, Washington, DC: Brookings Institution.

Lanjouw, J.O. and A. Mody (1996), 'Innovation and the international diffusion of environmentally responsive technology', *Research Policy*, **25**, 549–71.

Lin, S. and S. Song (2002), 'Urban economic growth in china: theory and evidence', *Urban Studies*, **39** (12), 2251–67.

Liu, X. and C. Wang (2003), 'Does foreign direct investment facilitate technological progress? Evidence from Chinese industries', *Research Policy*, **32** (6), 945–53.

Lovell, C.A.K., S. Richardson, P. Travers and L.L. Wood (1994), 'Resources and functionings: a new view of inequality in Australia', in W. Eichhorn (ed.), *Models and Measurement of Welfare and Inequality*, Berlin: Springer-Verlag, pp. 787–807.

Malmquist, S. (1953), 'Index numbers and indifference curves', *Trabajos de Estatistica*, **4** (1), 209–42.

Managi, S. J.J. Opaluch, D. Jin and T.A. Grigalunas (2004a), 'Technological change and depletion in offshore oil and gas', *Journal of Environmental Economics and Management*, **47** (2), 388–409.

Managi, S., J.J. Opaluch, D. Jin and T.A. Grigalunas (2005), 'Environmental regulations and technological change in the offshore oil and gas industry', *Land Economics*, **81** (2), 303–19.

McCain, R.A. (1978), 'Endogenous bias in technical progress and environmental policy', *American Economic Review*, **68**, 538–46.

Mohr, R. (2002), 'Technical change, external economies, and the porter hypothesis', *Journal of Environmental Economics and Management*, **43** (1), 158–68.

Nagase, Y. (2004), 'Is a more-output–less-emissions outcome necessarily suboptimal?', Draft, Laurence University, USA.

Parry, I.W.H. (2003), 'On the implications of technological innovation for environmental policy', *Environment and Development Economics*, **8** (1), 57–76.

Popp, D. (2002), 'Induced innovation and energy prices', *American Economic Review*, **92** (1), 160–80.

Porter, M.E. (1991), 'America's green strategy', *Scientific American*, **264**, 168.

Porter, M.E. and C. van der Linde (1995), 'Toward a new conception of the environment–competitiveness relationship', *Journal of Economic Perspectives*, **9** (4), 97–118.

Repetto, R. (1996), *Has Environmental Protection Really Reduced Productivity Growth? We Need Unbiased Measures*, Washington, DC: World Resources Institute.

Robinson, J.C., (1995), 'The impact of environmental and occupational health regulation on productivity growth in U.S. manufacturing', *Yale Journal of Regulations*, **12**, 387–434.

Schmalensee, R. (1989), 'Inter-industry studies of structure and performance', in R. Schmalensee and R. Willig (eds), *Handbook of Industrial Organization*, Vol. II, New York: North-Holland, pp. 951–1010.

Shephard, R.W. (1970), *Theory of Cost and Production Functions*, Princeton, NJ: Princeton University Press.

Sinkule, B.J. and L. Ortolano (1995), *Implementing Environmental Policy in China*, Westport, CT: Praeger.

State Environmental Protection Administration (SEPA) (2003), *The Method to Collect Pollution Levy*, Beijing: SEPA.

United Nations Conference on Trade and Development (UNCTAD) (2001), *World Investment Report*, New York: United Nation.

Wang, H. and D. Wheeler (2003), 'Equilibrium pollution and economic development in China', *Environment and Development Economics*, **8**, 451–66.

Wang, Y. and Y. Yao (2003), 'Sources of China's economic growth 1952–1999: incorporating human capital accumulation', *China Economic Review*, **14** (1), 32–53.

APPENDIX 5A1   DATA INFORMATION

GRP   GRP (or province output) is the dollar of final goods and services produced across the each province economy for each year (unit: 10^8 yuan). Sources: *Comprehensive Statistical Data and Materials on 50 Years of New China* and *China Statistical Yearbook*.

Labor   Number of employees refers to the persons who are engaged in social working and receive remuneration payment or earn business income (unit: 10^4). Source: *Comprehensive Statistical Data and Materials on 50 Years of New China*.

Capital   The capital stock is estimated from annual gross regional investment and depreciation rate (unit: 10^8 yuan). Sources: *China Industrial Economy Statistical Yearbook* and *China Statistical Yearbook*.

FDI   FDI refers to the investments inside China by foreign enterprises and economic organizations or individuals following the relevant Chinese policies and laws (unit: 10^8 yuan). Sources: *China Industrial Economy Yearbook* and *China Statistical Yearbook*.

PACE   PACE is the fund actually used for the environmental wastewater, waste gas and solid waste pollution: (unit: 10^8 yuan). Sources: *Comprehensive Statistical Data and Materials on 50 Years of New China* and *China Statistical Yearbook*.

Water   Wastewater quantity is measured as the weight of wastewater discharge (unit: 10^4 ton). Source: *Comprehensive Statistical Data and Materials on 50 Years of New China* and *China Statistical Yearbook*.

Gas   Waste gas quantity is measured as the volume of waste gas emissions that are not treated (unit: 10^8 m^3). Sources: *China Environmental Statistical Data and Materials*.

Solid   Solid waste quantity is measured as the discharge amount of solid waste (unit: 10^4 ton). Sources: *China Environmental Statistical Data and Materials*.

Patent   Number of patent applications. Source: *China's Statistical Yearbook on Science and Technology*.

Heavy   Ratio of heavy industry in GRP (including mining and quarrying, manufacturing, electricity, water, gas and construction industries). Source: *Comprehensive Statistical Data and Materials on 50 Years of New China.*

Levy   Effective levy rates for excess wastewater, waste gas and solid waste. Sources: *China Environment Yearbook* and *Comprehensive Statistical Data and Materials on 50 Years of New China, and China Statistical Yearbook.*

Provinces in the sample

Beijing, Tianjin, Hebei, Shanxi, Inner Mongolia, Liaoning, Jilin, Heilongjiang, Shanghai, Jiangsu, Zhejiang, Anhui, Fujian, Jiangxi, Shandong, Henan, Hubei, Hunan, Guangdong, Guangxi, Sichuan, Guizhou, Yunnan, Shaanxi, Gansu, Qinghai, Ningxia, Xinjiang. Note: Tibet is excluded because some of the relevant data is not available. Hainan, the new province started in 1988, is also excluded.

APPENDIX 5A2

Table 5A2.1   *Parametric output distance function estimations without environmental variables*

Intercept	−5.253	(−2.74)	Labor*Capital	0.016	(0.39)
Labor	0.518	(0.99)	Time	−0.055	(−2.16)
Capital	−0.246	(−1.45)	Time^2	0.001	(3.57)
Labor^2	−0.061	(−1.56)	Time * Labor	−0.010	(−1.93)
Capital^2	−0.037	(−2.08)	Time * Capital	0.007	(1.63)
$\sigma_s^2 = \sigma_v^2 + \sigma_u^2$	0.079	(3.07)	μ	0.537	(6.25)
$\gamma = \sigma_u^2/\sigma_v^2$	0.912	(36.49)	η	−0.002	(−0.40)
log likelihood	406.80		LR test of the one-sided error		782.93
Time period	1987–2001		No. of observations		420

Note: *t*-tests are in parentheses. GRP is selected as the dependent variable and as the variable of normalization.

Table 5A2.2   *Parametric output distance function estimations with envirnmental variables*

Intercept	5.089	(2.90)	Solid * PACE	−0.001	(−0.04)
Labor	−1.770	(−4.00)	Labor * Water	−0.034	(−0.79)
Capital	−0.109	(−0.36)	Labor * Gas	0.023	(0.35)
Water	−0.792	(−2.17)	Labor * Solid	0.013	(0.30)
Gas	−0.045	(−0.14)	Labor * PACE	0.044	(2.50)
Solid	0.515	(1.84)	Capital * Water	−0.011	(−0.24)
PACE	−0.109	(−0.98)	Capital * Gas	−0.075	(−1.30)
GRP	1.32		Capital * Solid	−0.017	(−0.43)
Labor^2	0.105	(3.05)	Capital * PACE	−0.027	(−1.65)
Capital^2	0.012	(0.49)	GRP * Water	−0.091	
Water^2	0.181	(4.07)	GRP * Gas	0.055	
Gas^2	0.065	(1.24)	GRP * Solid	0.127	
Solid^2	0.071	(2.68)	GRP * PACE	−0.045	
GRP^2	−0.092		Time	−0.069	(−1.92)
PACE^2	−0.003	(−1.13)	Time^2	0.001	(2.10)
Labor * Capital	−0.054	(−1.31)	Time * Labor	−0.008	(−1.51)
GRP * Labor	−0.001		Time * Capital	0.001	(0.25)
GRP * Capital	0.103		Time * PACE	0.003	(1.21)
Water * Gas	−0.007	(−0.09)	Time * Water	0.005	(0.73)

Table 5A2.2 (continued)

Water * Solid	−0.084	(−1.58)	Time * Gas	−0.003	(−0.50)
Water * PACE	−0.014	(−0.52)	Time * Solid	−0.003	(−0.78)
Gas * Solid	−0.114	(−2.06)	Time * GRP	0.002	
Gas * PACE	0.060	(2.26)			
$\sigma_s^2 = \sigma_v^2 + \sigma_u^2$	0.138	(0.88)	μ	−0.242	(−0.34)
$\gamma = \sigma_u^2/\sigma_v^2$	0.965	(23.91)	η	−0.025	(−3.07)
log likelihood	483.42		LR test of the one-sided error		272.50
Time period	1987–2001		No. of observations		420

Note: *t*-tests are in parentheses. GRP is selected as the dependent variable and as the variable of normalization for the other outputs. Note that the estimated results are not affected by this choice.

6. Increasing returns to pollution abatement

1 INTRODUCTION

Because of China's extremely rapid economic growth, the scale and seriousness of environmental problems is no longer in doubt. Whether pollution abatement technologies are utilized more efficiently is crucial in the analysis of environmental management in China. This study analyzes how the performance of environmental management has changed over time using province-level data and particularly estimating the size of increasing returns to pollution abatement.

We first measure the environmental performance index and then measure the effect of returns to pollution abatement efforts. We are not aware of any study that has attempted to test whether efforts to abate environmental pollution involve increasing returns in developing countries. Furthermore, in any such study, it would be important to control the level of abatement technology because, in practice, the technology employed changes over time. Increases in the environmental performance index are expected to be associated with a decrease in pollution. The environmental performance index is used to control this factor.

The chapter is structured as follows. Section 2 provides the background to this study. Section 3 discusses the research methods. Section 4 presents the empirical results, and Section 5 presents a summary and concluding remarks.

2 BACKGROUND

Environment in China

The Chinese government has undertaken a series of actions to protect environmental quality and public health and several laws, regulations and standards have been promulgated (Sinkule and Ortolano, 1995; Edmonds, 2004). The decision-making system of environmental policy consists chiefly of three organizations of the National People's Congress, the State

Environmental Protection Commission of the State Council, and the SEPA of the State Council.

As the starting point of formal environmental management and administration, the government held the first National Congress of Environmental Protection in 1973. At this stage, however, the actual authority of the local environmental agency was extremely limited. In 1988, the status of the environmental agency was raised, and it took a more independent position from the other ministries. But environmental protection has only really started to exert its full presence on the political agenda since the 1990s (Sinkule and Ortolano, 1995). Six environmental laws and regulations were revised and/or issued in the 1990s.

Radical reform of government administration was conducted by the Ninth National People's Congress in 1998 when the environmental protection agency was upgraded to ministerial status and renamed as the SEPA. During this reform period, the number of government ministry-level organizations was reduced (Eckholm, 1998). The emergence of an environmental protection administration was an exception during this massive effort to cut central government administration.

Environmental Quality Model

Pollution is a byproduct of industry production. Environmental quality has been modeled using the environmental Kuznets curve (EKC). The EKC postulates an inverse U-shaped relationship between an environmental quality and per capita income levels. Many empirical studies have examined this relationship for various pollutants (for example, Grossman and Krueger, 1995). Researchers have found an inverted U-shaped relationship, monotonically decreasing or increasing, between environmental quality and a rising per capita income level.

Theoretically, scale and technique effects might explain the pattern of the EKC. In the first phase of development, economic growth exhibits a scale effect that has a negative impact on the environment. This is because the scale effect refers to the fact that higher per capita income creates greater economic activity, thus raising the demand for inputs such as raw materials, transportation services and energy, and consequently creates environmental degradation. Then, economic growth has positive impacts on the environment through a technique effect. The technique effect refers to the changes in production methods that follow higher income. With increased income levels, demand for environmental quality is also likely to increase. Therefore, the pollution level might decrease. The shape of the EKC reflects changes in the demand for environmental quality. This explanation suggests that the relationship between pollution and income should vary across pollutants according to their perceived damage. If we directly estimate the environmental quality without relying on the income-level variable, we might be able to explain the scale and technique effects by using the explanatory variables of industry gross revenue and pollution abatement efforts, respectively.

There are additional theoretical explanations supporting the empirical evidence that an EKC exists. Andreoni and Levinson (2001) provide a simple explanation for the EKC, which is the theory we rely on in this study. Increasing returns to abating pollution implies that the abatement efficiency increases with increases in the scale of abatement. This indicates that doubling the clean-up efforts more than doubles the amount of pollution abated.

There are mechanisms both for not having and for having increasing returns to environmental expenditure. Traditionally in economics, the marginal abatement cost is expected to increase as the level of pollution abatement increases (and consequently with the environmental improvement). For example, moving from 60 percent SO_2 removal to 90 percent removal, cost per unit of emissions reduction typically increases at a much higher rate, for a given technology. On the other hand, there are two mechanisms of increasing returns that are innovations in pollution abatement technologies and learning curve mechanisms. The technologies are unlikely to have remained constant in the time period surveyed and therefore we control this technological change factor by an additional variable. Thus, the remaining possibility is the learning curve mechanism. If the production function follows an initially accelerated S-shaped learning curve in the study periods, we are able to observe increasing returns to abatement. In many of the factories in China, abatements efforts are very small (that is, potential of scale of economy in abatement is large) and therefore we might be able to find increasing returns to abatement.

Andreoni and Levinson demonstrated that EKCs can exist because of increasing returns to scale. They argued that most theoretical explanations of the EKC hypothesis are based on some sort of scale economy and increasing returns to scale in abatement broadly encompass much of the existing EKC theory. An important implication of their research is that explanations of abatement and technologies are central to understanding environmental quality. In the case of pollution from secondary industry production, the inefficiency caused by the lack of cross-regional externalities, such as technology spillovers, might be reduced by scaling up abatement and implementing more effective waste controls.

There are a few empirical studies analyzing increasing returns to abatement. Andreoni and Levinson regressed data on pollution abatement operating costs on a quadratic industry-level gross state product (GSP) in the US. The negative sign of the quadratic term on the GSP indicated that larger industries spend proportionally less on pollution abatement. Managi (2006) tests the hypothesis that there are increasing returns to the abatement of pollution in US agriculture using state-level data by controlling the abatement technology level. He tests this hypothesis by regressing pollution abatement and environmental technology factors using the DEA on pollution. The negative sign of the quadratic term of the abatement variable on pollution supports the increasing returns to abatement.

This study tests the hypothesis that there are increasing returns to the abatement of pollution using the environmental efficiency modeling and econometric approaches, and analyzes the environmental efficiency resulting from China's industry production using data from 1992 to 2003. We are interested in an inter-province comparative analysis because environmental regulations vary between provinces. Our study is different from Managi (ibid.) in estimating environmental efficiency and solving potential serial correlation problems, as described below.

3   DATA

In this study, we use panel data on Chinese secondary industries, including mining, manufacturing, electricity, gas and water.[1] This study focuses on industrial pollution, since these industries are a primary source of pollution and they account for about 40 percent of national water pollution and about 80 percent of air pollution from SEPA estimates in 2000. In this study, we use province-by-year panel data (covering 29 provinces for the 1992–2003 period) on environmental pollutants, real GRP, abatement efforts, capital, labor and the environmental performance index including three municipalities, in the People's Republic of China.[2] The data before 1992 are excluded from our estimation since these are applied as instrumental variables as explained later.

Definition and explanation of the variables used in this study is provided in Table 6.1. Nominal data are converted into real data using the CPI, hence the national total is consistent with the sum of regional data in the dataset. *Labor* is quality-adjusted labor in secondary industries. The wages for labor are used to control for quality where these are not adjusted in Managi and Kaneko (2006). Province-level GRP is based on industry and regional government surveys. Historical GRP data for secondary industries at nominal prices are taken from the *Comprehensive Statistical Data and Materials on 50 Years of New China*. This publication compiles recalculated GRP as far back as 1949 using the SNA method. See Wang and Yao (2003) for construction of the capital and labor variables.

Table 6.1   Data information: 29 provinces for 1992–2003

Variable	Data source
GRP: added value of secondary industry (unit: 10^8 yuan)	1992–1999: *Comprehensive Statistical Data and Materials on 50 Years of New China* 2000–2003: *China Industrial Economy Statistical Yearbook*
Labor: Number of employees working in secondary industry (unit: 10^4 persons)	1992–1999: *Communication Statistics on 50 Years of China* 2000–2003: *China Industrial Economy Statistical Yearbook*
Wage: Wages paid in industry (unit: 10^4 yuan)	*China Statistical Yearbook*
Capital stock: estimated from annual productive net of depreciation in the secondary industry (unit: 10^8 yuan)	1992–1999: *Communication Statistics on 50 Years of China* 2000–2003: *China Industrial Economy Statistical Yearbook*
Wastewater: wastewater quantity measured as the weight of wastewater discharge (unit: 10^4 ton)	1992–2003: *China Environmental Statistical Yearbook*
Waste gas: gas quantity measured as the volume of waste gas emissions that is not treated (unit: 10^8 m^3)	1992–2003: *China Environmental Statistical Yearbook*
Solid waste: waste quantity measured as the discharge amount of solid waste (unit: 10^4 ton)	1992–2003: *China Environmental Statistical Yearbook*
PACE: funds actually used for industrial environmental pollution of wastewater, waste gas and solid waste (unit: 10^4 yuan). Three independent PACE variables of wastewater, waste gas and solid waste are applied for each estimation	1992–2003: *China Environmental Statistical Yearbook*

Pollution indices are each of wastewater and solid waste measured by total weight in each province, while waste gas is measured by total quantity in each province. Pollution abatement cost and expenditure (PACE) are funds actually used to remedy each component of industrial environmental pollution in the form of wastewater, waste gas and solid waste. PACE is considered as an environmental input. Our PACE variables include three independent PACE data for wastewater, waste gas and solid waste, respectively. An increase in PACE given other inputs/outputs will reduce pollution. Our measures of pollution and, therefore, corresponding performance indices in our measures are expected to react on improvements in the abatement technologies being applied to corresponding pollution and the saving of water and energy uses. First, environmental policies of a pollution charge system directly regulate the volume of the wastewater, SO_2 as waste gas, and solid waste.[3] Second, a reduction of the wastewater variable reflects recycling and saving of water use. Reduction of solid waste reflects resource productivity, implying less use of natural resources. Higher energy use leads of higher gas emissions, and therefore, reduction of gas emissions reflects the energy saving at least partially. This contrast of environmental outputs and input uses is consistent with the definition of eco-efficiency defined in the World Business Council for Sustainable Development (2000). Furthermore, we also follow the usual conversion in environmental economics of treating pollution emissions as an input to production (for example, Cropper and Oates, 1992). Thus, a reduction (increase) in the pollution, with all other inputs and outputs held fixed, represents an increase (decrease) in productivity.

Data in the *China Environmental Statistical Yearbook* (CESY) do not cover the entire sample collected in the *China Industrial Economy Statistical Yearbook* (CIESY) and the *China Statistical Yearbook* (CSY). Therefore, direct use of data from the CESY provides biased results. In this study, we adjust the data so as to be able to compare the data to the CSY. Sales data are included in both the CESY and the CIESY. We calculate an adjustment coefficient by taking the ratio of sales data in the CIESY and that in the CESY.[4] We then multiply the coefficients, which vary by year and province, by the data in the CESY to obtain the adjusted figures.

4   MODELS

Technology and its management have been important elements in the theoretical and empirical literature on the determinants of pollution. In the existing literature, time trend variables have been taken into account to test for technology level (for example, Hilton and Levinson, 1998). However, the time trend may capture any effects changing over time, such as changes in relative energy prices (Agras and Chapman, 1999). Explicit consideration of a technology is necessary to capture the technology factors (Stern, 1998). In this study, our specification allows for technological performance differences over provinces and years. This study employed DEA and illustrated the important role played by the environmental performance level in estimating environmental quality. This measurement is especially useful when there are multiple inputs/outputs. This is because DEA estimates the efficiency using environmental pollution with market inputs/outputs.

There is a growing literature that develops methodologies for measuring productive efficiency and productivity in the presence of pollution (Färe et al., 1989, 1993, 2005; Yaisawarng and Klein, 1994; Boyd and McClelland, 1997; Zaim and Taskin, 2000; Domazlicky and Weber, 2004; Kuosmanen, 2005; Kuosmanen and Kortelainen, 2005; Managi et al., 2005). These studies commonly incorporate environmental effects into the output vector, and adjust conventional measures of productivity change or technical efficiency. They approached the problem of environmental (or undesirable) output production and treated pollutants as weakly disposable output while market (or desirable) outputs are strongly disposable.

Researchers commonly assume that a firm is efficient if it can simultaneously produce more market outputs and fewer environmental outputs for the same input vector. However, social and private costs of environmental outputs are usually different since the firm generally has little incentive to reduce pollution more than required by law and has a strong incentive to increase market output. Furthermore, firms have an incentive to reduce market inputs and pollution abatement costs to reduce overall costs. If there is an effective limit on pollution, there is a clear incentive to increase the environmental efficiency of abatement as this efficiency is inversely proportional to abatement cost. The level of abatement is hardly arbitrary as it is determined by environmental policy. Therefore, the firm's decision makers not only have an interest in market technical efficiency but also have an incentive to increase environmental efficiency. Choice of orientation regarding market technical efficiency and environmental efficiency is arbitrary and requires a value judgment. In this study, we simply estimate the environmental efficiency from the social aspect. This is because the objective of this estimation is to control environmental performance, which is expected to reduce the pollution, in the second-step estimation.

Our study is different from Managi (2006), which also tests increasing returns to abatement, in the estimates of an environmental performance index. He includes the pollution abatement efforts of an independent input variable in DEA to estimate the joint productivity of market and environmental output. He calculates the environmental performance index, dividing the joint index by commonly used market productivity. He then uses the pollution abatement efforts in a second-step model to test the increasing returns, by controlling the environmental performance index, which might cause a serial correlation in the second-step estimation. Since we directly estimate the environmental performance index without using pollution abatement efforts, there is no serial correlation problem in the second-step econometric estimation.

Following Tyteca (1997), we define the environmental efficiency measure considering producing minimum environmental outputs given inputs and market outputs. Let $x = (x_1, \ldots, x_M) \in R_+^M$, $b = (b_1, \ldots, b_L) \in R_+^K$, $y = (y_1, \ldots, y_N) \in R_+^N$ be row vectors of inputs, pollution outputs and market outputs, respectively. In this study, inputs correspond to capital and labor, while market output corresponds to GRP in secondary industries. The pollution outputs are wastewater, waste gas and solid waste. Define the technology set (Q) by:

$$Q^t = \{(x^t, b^t, y^t): x^t \text{ can produce } (y^t, b^t)\},$$

where Q^t represents the set of all output vectors, y^t and b^t, that can be produced using the input vector, x^t. The environmental efficiency at time t is defined as:[5]

$$E^t(y^t, x^t, b^t) = \max\{\phi: (y^t, x^t, b^t/\phi) \in Q^t\},$$

A larger value shows that a relatively small amount of pollution is emitted given other input and output levels. We follow productivity literature to measure the environmental performance index over time, which corresponds to the Malmquist index of market productivity indices in variable returns to scale in Ray and Desli (1997). Caves et al. (1982) offered the multi-output, multi-input productivity measurement and compare two input–output vectors to a reference technology using radial input and output scaling, for the input and output productivity indices, respectively. The t-period environmental performance index is defined as follows:

$$EPI^t(y^t, x^t, b^t, y^{t+1}, x^{t+1}, b^{t+1}) = \frac{E^t(y^{t+1}, x^{t+1}, b^{t+1})}{E^t(y^t, x^t, b^t)}. \qquad (6.1)$$

This environmental performance index treats the performance differences as differences in performance indices. Two time periods suggest a $t + 1$ performance index, as follows:

$$EPI^{t+1}(y^t, x^t, b^t, y^{t+1}, x^{t+1}, b^{t+1}) = \frac{E^{t+1}(y^{t+1}, x^{t+1}, b^{t+1})}{E^{t+1}(y^t, x^t, b^t)}. \qquad (6.2)$$

Ray and Desli (1997) defined the output-oriented Malmquist productivity index in variable returns to scale as the geometric mean of two Malmquist indices. The environmental performance under variable returns to scale is:

$$Env.Tech_t^{t+1} = [EPI^t(y^t, x^t, b^t, y^{t+1}, x^{t+1}, b^{t+1})$$

$$\cdot EPI^{t+1}(y^t, x^t, b^t, y^{t+1}, x^{t+1}, b^{t+1})]^{1/2}$$

$$= \left[\frac{E^t(y^{t+1}, x^{t+1}, b^{t+1})}{E^t(y^t, x^t, b^t)} \frac{E^{t+1}(y^{t+1}, x^{t+1}, b^{t+1})}{E^{t+1}(y^t, x^t, b^t)} \right]^{1/2} \quad (6.3)$$

where an increase in *Env. Tech* implies an improvement in abatement performance, which is a greater reduction of environmental pollution given the same level of the other inputs/outputs of labor, capital and market output. Thus, the performance index uses the $E^t(y^t, x^t, b^t)$ directly to evaluate environmental performance. Note that our index is different from traditional eco-efficiency indices. These are simple indices, such as economic output per unit of waste ratios, and provide a very limited perspective. In contrast, our index is able to measure the performance in multi-inputs including the primary production factors labor and capital, and multi-outputs with pollution data. Our index measures the degree to which a firm (or area or industry or plant) has succeeded in a reduction of pollution, given the level of output production from time period t to time period $t + 1$. Furthermore, the use of DEA allows us to distinguish between an inefficient pollution abatement producer and an efficient producer.

Next, we provide the econometric model using environmental performance index and abatement effort to test the returns to abatement hypothesis. This study estimates the following environmental quality model using province-level data. Our level model specification is given by:

$$Y_{ijt} = \alpha_0 + \alpha_1 I_{it} + \alpha_2 I_{it}^2 + \alpha_3 I_{it}^3 + \alpha_4 Abate_{ijt} + \alpha_5 Env.Tech_{ijt} + \varepsilon_{it}, \quad (6.4)$$

where Y is the pollution per capita such as wastewater, waste gas and solid waste for province i and year t, j represents the pollution of wastewater, waste gas and solid waste, I is the real GRP of the province i, *Abate* is the pollution abatement effort represented by the expenditure, and *Env. Tech* is the environmental technological level (environmental performance index) using DEA as described above. Note that the environmental performance index for wastewater, waste gas and solid waste is estimated separately to describe each of the three environmental qualities.

The first three terms of I are variables representing the EKC pattern. We expect a negative sign for the environmental technological level, *Env. Tech*, and the abatement effort variable, *Abate*, because an increase in the pollution abatement technological level and effort reduce the environmental pollution, holding all else constant. The next specification includes the quadratic term of the abatement effort to test the increasing returns, as follows:

$$Y_{ijt} = \beta_0 + \beta_1 I_{it} + \beta_2 I_{it}^2 + \beta_3 I_{it}^3 + \beta_4 Abate_{ijt} + \beta_5 Abate_{ijt}^2$$
$$+ \beta_6 Env.Tech_{ijt} + \eta_{it}. \tag{6.5}$$

A statistically significant negative sign on the quadratic term of abatement implies the existence of increasing returns to pollution abatement. In contrast, a significant positive sign on the quadratic term of abatement implies the existence of decreasing returns to abatement. An insignificant sign implies that we are not able to find any significant evidence of returns to scale.

In the presence of province-specific stochastic trends, neither random effects nor fixed effects estimators will be consistent. In the econometric models, serial correlation must be considered because the dependent variables of environmental pollution have relatively monotonic trends. Although previous studies do not directly control this factor when analyzing the panel data, we correct for the serial correlation. Differencing the data will eliminate potential stochastic trends in the series. Therefore, we take a first differences model as follows:

$$\Delta Y_{ijt} = \alpha_0' + \alpha_1' \Delta I_{it} + \alpha_2' \Delta I_{it}^2 + \alpha_3' \Delta I_{it}^3 + \alpha_4' \Delta Abate_{ijt}$$
$$+ \alpha_5' \Delta Env.Tech_{ijt} + \Delta \varepsilon_{it}, \tag{6.6}$$

$$\Delta Y_{ijt} = \beta_0' + \beta_1' \Delta I_{it} + \beta_2' \Delta I_{it}^2 + \beta_3' \Delta I_{it}^3 + \beta_4' \Delta Abate_{ijt}$$
$$+ \beta_5' \Delta Abate_{ijt}^2 + \beta_6' \Delta Env.Tech_{ijt} + \Delta \eta_{it}. \tag{6.7}$$

which we estimate with a fixed-effects transformation by considering only time effects. The time effects are expected to capture common time-related effects. Province specific effects are eliminated by taking the first difference of the models.

Econometric concerns need to be addressed in order to obtain consistent parameter estimates from the pollution equation. Since GRP data are endogenous, simple OLS can lead to biased estimates. This estimation problem of input endogeneity is addressed by adopting an instrumental variable estimation procedure. Lagged levels, using data before 1992, are also used as instruments in the pollution function in its procedure. If the random factor, ε_{it}, is nonpersistent, a standard generalized method of moments estimator (GMM) is both consistent and efficient (Arellano and Bond, 1991). When the dynamic error processes are highly persistent, however, lagged levels have been shown to be poor instruments for contemporaneous differences and lead to finite sample biases (Blundell and Bond, 1998; Blundell et al., 2000). Both lagged differences and lagged levels are used as instruments in estimating parameters of the pollution function, and the resulting system GMM estimator is both consistent and efficient (Blundell and Bond, 1998). Standard errors are robust and corrected for finite sample biases based on Windmeijer (2005). This estimator, System GMM, also encompasses the standard GMM estimator. Lastly, permanent unobserved heterogeneity is addressed by differencing the data to remove possible correlation between explanatory variables and province-specific effects.

5 RESULTS

This study uses a nonparametric model to measure performance change in terms of joint production of market and environmental outputs (so-called 'green' productivity). The vectors of outputs and inputs are listed in Table 6.1. The output variables in our model are GRP, wastewater, waste gas and solid waste. Our input variables include labor and capital. Separate frontiers are estimated for each year, and shifts in the frontiers over time are used to measure the performance change. The mean values are presented in the following. Values larger than one are regarded as increases in the performance. We use the geometric mean of the indices for each province, to obtain a combined value for each index in each year.

Table 6.2 presents the summary of the results. Each of the three models includes one of the environmental outputs of waste gas, solid waste and wastewater, separately. Table 6.2 provides the cumulative performance of the three results. Environmental performances, on average, increase for the two indices of wastewater and solid waste, but decrease for waste gas. The cumulative changes are 21.2, −42.4 and 8.8 percent changes over wastewater, waste gas and solid waste, respectively. Overall, environmental management in China has not effectively regulated waste gas, but has effectively regulated wastewater and solid waste pollutants over our study periods. One of the reasons why negative results are observed is related to the weak implementation of the policies in waste gas. On September 15, 1987, for example, the NPC approved the Law on Air Pollution Prevention and Control of the People's Republic of China (LAPPC). According to the law, all plants that discharge pollutants into the air should comply with the rules for pollution control. Consequently, a series of policies and regulations was published by the government and a set of national standards related to air quality was established. However, generally the abatement cost is higher than the penalty and the policy does not provide an adequate incentive to the industry. For example, the SEPA published a notice in April 1998 to Extend Areas for Trial Charges for SO_2 in the Acid

Table 6.2   Environmental performance index change

Year	Wastewater	Waste gas	Solid waste
1992–1995	1.123	0.973	0.865
1995–2000	1.078	0.633	1.090
2000–2002	1.001	0.935	1.154
1992–2003	1.212	0.576	1.088

Rain Control Zones and SO_2 Pollution Control Zones. The abatement cost of SO_2 (for example, 1,100 RMB/ton) is much higher than the amount charged (for example, only 200 RMB/ton). Thus, it is unreasonable to expect the levy system to motivate compliance and control of SO_2 emissions by power enterprises (see Yang et al., 2000).

Managi and Kaneko (2006) show an environmental performance index decrease for the joint pollutant case of wastewater, waste gas and solid waste. They conclude that limited enforcement of environmental laws and policies and firms' insufficient environmental management capacity led to this environmental inefficiency where the efficiencies decreased. However, they do not present separate results for the three pollutants. Our results imply that the overall deteriorating trend is caused by waste gas.

We then measure the determinants of each pollutant per capita. All GMM estimates of environmental quality models are based on a two-step System GMM estimator with robust standard errors adjusted for finite sample biases as explained above. Table 6.3 reports the results of estimating equation (6.6). Using *J*-statistics, we are not able to reject the hypothesis that all instruments satisfy orthogonality conditions. The results of the Sargan test of overidentifying restrictions imply that the instruments used in the GMM estimation are valid. We examine the stationarity of the residuals using the unit root tests of Im et al. (2003). In all of the specifications, we are able to reject the null hypothesis of a unit root in the residuals.

We find a statistically significant relationship between province patterns of environmental pollution and the explanatory variables of GRP, environmental performance and abatement efforts. Our studies show that there is no single relationship between environmental quality and per capita GRP that fits all types of pollutants. The environmental performance variable, *Env. Tech.*, shows a negative sign and is statistically significant for all cases. The abatement effort variable, *Abate*, shows a negative sign and is statistically significant. Overall, the results support the argument that performance improvements in environmental technologies and increases in abatement efforts reduce environmental pollution, as expected for all three pollutants. Table 6.3 also presents sensitivity analyses using the same

Table 6.3 GMM parameter estimates (equation (6.6)): base model

Dependent variable	Wastewater	Wastewater	Waste gas	Waste gas	Solid waste	Solid waste
Gross regional product	−53.11***	−55.08***	−0.99	−1.10	0.36**	0.37**
	(−4.76)	(−5.03)	(−1.31)	(−1.49)	(2.36)	(2.45)
(Gross regional product)^2	0.005**	0.005**	0.0003***	0.0003***	−9.61E-6	−2.00E-5
	(2.25)	(2.38)	(2.61)	(2.92)	(−0.16)	(−0.26)
(Gross regional product)^3	−4.28E-8	−5.44E-8	−6.88E-9	−8.11E-9	−5.22E-10	8.34E-10
	(−0.36)	(−0.46)	(−1.20)	(−1.45)	(−0.16)	(0.26)
Abatement effort	−0.80***	−0.76***	−0.01***	−0.02***	−0.03***	−0.03***
	(−2.87)	(−2.66)	(−2.42)	(−2.65)	(−3.65)	(−3.54)
Environmental technology	−15.05**	–	−0.98*	–	−0.91*	–
	(−2.43)		(−1.78)		(−1.76)	
J-statistic (p-value)	0.2204	0.2112	0.2198	0.2043	0.1921	0.1913
Unit root test t-value	−2.401**	−2.398***	−2.265**	−2.112**	−2.361**	−2.207**
Sargan test	0.24	0.23	0.26	0.25	0.24	0.23

Note: Values in parentheses are *t*-values. * Significant at the 10% level. ** Significant at the 5% level. *** Significant at the 1% level.

specification of equation (6.6) without the environmental technology variable and the results are very similar to those with the environmental technology variable.

Next, we add the quadratic term of abatement effort as in equation (6.7). The estimated results are shown in Table 6.4. The *J*-statistics show that we are not able to reject the hypothesis that all instruments satisfy orthogonality conditions. Again we examine the stationarity of the residuals using the unit root tests of Im et al. In all of the specifications, we are able to reject the null hypothesis of a unit root in the residuals. In addition, the results of the Sargan test of overidentifying restrictions imply that the instruments used in this estimation are valid.

The significance level and the magnitude of coefficients for environmental technology in Table 6.4 are similar to those of Table 6.3. Generally, an improvement in environmental technology and management systems, that is, *Env. Tech.*, reduces the environmental pollution. All of the estimates of the quadratic term of the abatement effort show negative signs and all are significant.

Note, however, that the linear abatement terms are positive and statistically significant. In these cases, it is possible that an increased abatement cost is associated with increasing rather than decreasing pollution. The estimated turning points for the abatement and pollution relationships for wastewater, waste gas and solid waste are −0.67, 1.33 and 0.12, respectively. The minimum values for the same three pollutants are 24.25, 11.82 and 0.58, respectively, and their average minimum values are 260.07, 111.32 and 11.1, respectively. As all turning points are much smaller than the average values, the result that increased abatement cost is associated with decreasing pollution remains valid for all of the pollution data. Overall, we support our hypothesis of increasing returns to pollution abatement.

In this study, we show that environmental performance index, abatement effort and increasing returns to pollution abatement play important roles in determining the pollution level over the period of the study. Thus, our important implication of this research is that explanations regarding abatement technology are central to understanding environmental quality in China.

6   CONCLUSION AND DISCUSSION

Because of China's extremely rapid economic growth, the scale and seriousness of environmental problems is no longer in doubt. Whether pollution abatement technologies are utilized more efficiently is crucial in the analysis of environmental management. It is important to understand the performance of environmental management in order to estimate

Table 6.4 GMM parameter estimates (equation (6.7)): test of increasing returns to abating pollution

Dependent variable	Wastewater	Wastewater	Waste gas	Waste gas	Solid waste	Solid waste
Gross regional product	−55.18***	−55.08***	−1.06	−1.10	0.34**	0.38**
	(−5.02)	(−5.03)	(−1.41)	(−1.49)	(2.36)	(2.47)
(Gross regional product)^2	0.004**	0.005**	0.0003***	0.0003***	−9.61E-6	−2.00E-5
	(2.38)	(2.38)	(2.82)	(2.92)	(−0.16)	(−0.26)
(Gross regional product)^3	−5.46E-8	−5.44E-8	−7.83E-9	−8.11E-9	−5.22E-10	8.34E-10
	(−0.47)	(−0.46)	(−1.38)	(−1.45)	(−0.16)	(0.26)
Abatement effort	0.44***	0.43***	0.04***	0.03***	0.03***	0.03***
	(2.69)	(2.73)	(3.25)	(3.22)	(3.65)	(3.66)
(Abatement effort)^2	−2.45 E-3***	−2.49 E-3***	−1.65 E-4***	−1.63 E-4***	−1.42 E-7***	−1.40 E-7***
	(−3.20)	(−3.22)	(−2.35)	(−2.33)	(−3.15)	(−3.13)
Environmental technology	−14.14**	–	−1.03**	–	−0.91*	–
	(−2.19)		(−1.92)		(−1.76)	
J-statistic (p-value)	0.2232	0.2184	0.2234	0.2054	0.1954	0.1929
Unit root test t-value	−2.438**	−2.411**	−2.273**	−2.175**	−2.373**	−2.306**
Sargan test	0.23	0.22	0.24	0.23	0.22	0.21

Note: Values in parentheses are t-values. * Significant at the 10% level. ** Significant at the 5% level. *** Significant at the 1% level.

realistically the future possibility of pollution reduction. This study analyzes how the performance of environmental management has changed over time using province-level data for 1992–2003. Mixed results for environmental performance are indicated using a nonparametric estimation technique. Environmental performance appears to have increased with respect to wastewater and solid waste pollution. However, it has decreased in the case of waste gas.

Considering the importance of the environmental issue, detecting the relationship between abatement and environmental pollution is important. The efficiency increases make abatement less expensive and, thus, environmental quality can increase. We test the hypothesis that pollution abatement efficiency increases as the abatement effort rises. Our estimates for Chinese industries support the hypothesis of increasing returns to abatement.

The numerical results have to be interpreted with care because the evidence of increasing returns to abatement might be short-run results. In the long run, if the environmental technology level remains constant, scale economy effects might be exhausted and change to decreasing returns to abatement. Further evidence of technology is required to answer this question.

NOTES

1. Although the mining industry is not primarily a secondary industry in other countries' definition, it is fully included as a secondary industry in China.
2. Beijing, Tianjin, Hebei, Shanxi, Inner Mongolia, Liaoning, Jilin, Heilongjiang, Shanghai, Jiangsu, Zhejiang, Anhui, Fujian, Jiangxi, Shandong, Henan, Hubei, Hunan, Guangdong, Guangxi, Sichuan and Chongqing, Guizhou, Yunnan, Xizang, Shaanxi, Gansu, Qinghai, Ningxia, and Xinjiang. Note Tibet is excluded because some relevant data are not available. Hainan, a new province from 1988, is also excluded. Data for Chongqing, which was separated from Sichuan in 1997, is merged with data for Sichuan.
3. We note the limitations for the interpretation of our results. That is, definitions of pollution variables might not be ideal measures of pollution in this study though these are the target of the policies in China. This is because there is a different structure in the definitions of the environmental interventions concerning water, air and soil components. Our wastewater variable is water discharge itself and, therefore, the water quality parameter might not react on an avoided pollutant in the wastewater well. Similarly the air pollution variable is measured in volume not treated. Thus, improvements in the abatement technology, such as adding a DeNOx installation to an existing desulfurization installation, might not be adequately measured in our results. The third environmental quality variable of solid waste might not react to improvements of applications shifted from old-style dumping to more controlled landfill. Therefore, these rough definitions chosen in this study might not directly allow for the clear interpretation of wastewater, waste gas and solid waste. Future research needs to disaggregate these variables to a more specific measure of pollutants such as SO_2.
4. The adjustment coefficient rages from 1.03 to 7.05, with an average of 1.74.
5. For example, see Tyteca (1997) for its nonparametric estimation.

REFERENCES

Agras, J.M. and D. Chapman (1999), 'A dynamic approach to the environmental Kuznets curve hypothesis', *Ecological Economics*, **28**, 267–77.

Andreoni, J. and A. Levinson (2001), 'The simple analytics of the environmental Kuznets curve', *Journal of Public Economics*, **80** (2), 269–86.

Arellano, M. and S. Bond (1991), 'Some tests of specification for panel data: Monte Carlo evidence and an application to employment equations', *Review of Economic Studies*, **58**, 277–97.

Blundell, R. and S. Bond (1998), 'Initial conditions and moment restrictions in dynamic panel data models', *Journal of Econometrics*, **87**, 115–43.

Blundell, R., S. Bond and F. Windmeijer (2000), 'Estimation in dynamic panel data models: improving on the performance of the standard GMM estimators', in B. Baltagi (ed.), *Nonstationary Panels, Panel Cointegration, and Dynamic Panels*, Advances in Econometrics, vol. 15, Amsterdam: JAI Press, Elsevier Science, pp. 53–92.

Boyd, G.A. and J.D. McClelland (1999), 'The impact of environmental constraints on productivity improvement in integrated paper plants', *Journal of Environmental Economics and Management*, **38**, 121–42.

Caves, D.W., L.R. Christensen and W.E. Diewert (1982), 'The economic theory of index numbers and the measurement of input, output and productivity', *Econometrica*, **50** (6), 1393–414.

Cropper, M.L. and W.E. Oates (1992), 'Environmental economics: a survey', *Journal of Economic Literature*, **30**, 675–740.

Domazlicky, B. and W. Weber (2004), 'Does environmental protection lead to slower productivity growth in the chemical industry?', *Environmental and Resource Economics*, **28** (3), 301–24.

Eckholm, E. (1998), 'New China leader promises reforms for every sector', *New York Times*, 20 March, A1.

Edmonds, R.L. (2004), *Managing the Chinese Environment: Studies on Contemporary China*, Oxford: Oxford University Press.

Färe, R., S. Grosskopf, K. Lovell and C. Pasurka (1989), 'Multilateral productivity comparisons when some outputs are undesirable: a nonparametric approach', *Review of Economics and Statistics*, **71**, 90–98.

Färe, R., S. Grosskopf, C.A.K. Lovell and S. Yaisawarng (1993), 'Derivation of shadow prices for undesirable outputs: a distance function approach', *Review of Economics and Statistics*, **75**, 374–80.

Färe, R., S. Grosskopf, D. Noh and W. Weber (2005), 'Characteristics of a polluting technology: theory and practice', *Journal of Econometrics*, **126**, 469–92.

Grossman, G.M. and A.B. Krueger (1995), 'Economic growth and the environment', *Quarterly Journal of Economics*, **110**, 353–77.

Hilton, H. and A. Levinson (1998), 'Factoring the environmental Kuznets curve: evidence from automotive lead emissions', *Journal of Environmental Economics and Management*, **35**, 126–41.

Im, K., M. Pesaran and Y. Shin (2003), 'Testing for unit roots in heterogeneous panels', *Journal of Econometrics*, **115** (1), 53–74.

Kuosmanen, T. (2005), 'Weak disposability in nonparametric production analysis with undesirable outputs', *American Journal of Agricultural Economics*, **87** (4), 1077–82.

Kuosmanen, T. and M. Kortelainen (2005), 'Measuring eco-efficiency of production with data envelopment analysis', *Journal of Industrial Ecology*, **9** (4), 59–72.

Managi, S. (2006), 'Are there increasing returns to pollution abatement? Empirical analytics of the environmental Kuznets curve in pesticides', *Ecological Economics*, **58** (3), 617–36.

Managi, S. and S. Kaneko (2006), 'Productivity of market and environmental abatement in China', *Environmental Economics and Policy Studies*, **7** (4), 459–70.

Managi, S., J.J. Opaluch, D. Jin and T.A. Grigalunas (2005), 'Environmental regulations and technological change in the offshore oil and gas industry', *Land Economics*, **81** (2), 303–19.

Ray, S.C. and E. Desli (1997), 'Productivity growth, technical progress, and efficiency change in industrialized countries: comment', *American Economic Review*, **87** (5),1033–9.

Sinkule, B.J. and Ortolano, L. (1995), *Implementing Environmental Policy in China*, Westport, CT: Praeger.

Stern, D.I. (1998), 'Progress on the environmental Kuznets curve?', *Environment and Development Economics*, **3**, 175–98.

Tyteca, D. (1997), 'Linear programming models for the measurement of environmental performance of firms-concepts and empirical results', *Journal of Productivity Analysis*, **8** (2), 182–97.

Wang, Y. and Y. Yao (2003), 'Sources of China's economic growth 1952–1999: incorporating human capital accumulation', *China Economic Review*, **14**, 32–52.

Windmeijer, F. (2005), 'A finite sample correction for the variance of linear efficient two-step GMM estimators', *Journal of Econometrics*, **126** (1), 25–51.

World Business Council for Sustainable Development (2000), *Measuring Eco-efficiency: A Guide to Reporting Company Performance*, Washington DC: World Business Council for Sustainable Development, 1–36.

Xu, X. (2004), 'China's gross domestic product estimation', *China Economic Review*, **15**, 302–22.

Yaisawarng, S. and J.D. Klein (1994), 'The effects of sulfur dioxide controls on productivity change in the U.S. electric power industry', *Review of Economics and Statistics*, **76** (3), 447–60.

Yang J.T., D. Cao, J.N. Wang and W.Y. Tian (2000), SO_2 *Emission Charge in China, SO_2 Emission Trading Program: US Experience and China's Perspective*, Beijing: China Environmental Science.

Zaim, O. and F. Taskin (2000), 'A Kuznets curve in environmental efficiency: an application on OECD countries', *Environmental and Resource Economics*, **17**, 21–36.

7. Causal direction between pollution abatement and environmental efficiency

1 INTRODUCTION

Society faces an important tradeoff between economic output and environmental policy. Both environmental economists and public policy makers in developed and developing countries alike have shown a great deal of interest in the effect of pollution abatement on environmental efficiency. In line with the modern resources available nowadays, there has been a large amount of recent research, but no contribution to the environmental economics field with the Markov chain Monte Carlo (MCMC) application. MCMC techniques enable simulation from a distribution of a Markov chain and simulating from the chain until it approaches equilibrium.

This simulation approach of probability density functions gained prominence through the practice of Bayesian statistics, which has the advantage over classical statistical methods in its simultaneous inference and incorporation of any prior information on all model parameters. The work we carried out concentrated on this point. In this chapter, we apply a Bayesian approach via MCMC simulation to the database of China, the largest developing country. China is the world's third-largest consumer of coal and oil, but much of its energy-producing and -using equipment is both inefficient and highly polluting. As a result, China experiences severe urban air pollution which has a significant impact throughout the region. It is also the world's second-largest source of greenhouse gas emissions. Improving energy efficiency and accelerating the development and application of new and renewable energy and clean coal technologies are therefore very urgent sustainable development and environmental priorities. Public policy makers are facing tradeoffs between economic growth and environmental protection. TFP growth plays an important role in GDP growth.

Whether pollution abatement technologies are utilized more efficiently is crucial for sustainable development. The principal focus of this chapter is to measure the effect of pollution abatement on environmental efficiency using unique province-level secondary industry data over the 1992–2003 period. The pollution variables include wastewater discharge, waste gas emission, solid waste generation, SO_2, dust, soot, COD, lead and chromium six. The capital intensity (*Capital*) is analyzed since it might affect productivity.

In this chapter, we test the causal direction between pollution abatement cost and environmental efficiency with the application of MCMC simulation. In contrast with the models of earlier studies, our model was able to perform a causality test based on a limited dataset. We found that the pollution abatement cost led to an increase in environmental efficiency through the algorithm application, and it is conceivable that environmental policy makers will take more substantial measures to reduce pollution in the near future.

To our knowledge, no previous studies in the environmental economics literature have yet applied the MCMC method. In this study, we apply a Bayesian analysis based on MCMC methods in order to analyze the relationship between environmental efficiency and pollution abatement. The implementation of MCMC techniques is associated with further advantages as discussed below. Statistical inferences on states' variables and parameters are easily performed using Bayesian MCMC methods. The flexibility of MCMC methods allows us to analyze a wide range of models with nonlinear relationships in the dynamic and observation equations, and also in a non-Gaussian error structure. The Bayesian paradigm is efficient for deriving quantitative diagnostics on a probability-based rationale. Outputs of the technique mainly consist of the joint posterior distribution of all the model parameters. Incorporating the likelihood function and the priors, using the Bayesian rule, leads to the conditional posterior distributions for the parameter groupings used in the MCMC sampling scheme.

The use of MCMC is superior to other methods for analysis in a limited dataset. The chapter proceeds as follows. Section 2 discusses China's environmental issues and the theoretical MCMC model. Section 3 describes the empirical model and the data used in the estimation. Section 4 discusses the results, while Section 5 provides conclusions.

2 BACKGROUND

MCMC methods are a class of algorithms for sampling from probability distributions based on constructing a Markov chain that has the desired distribution as its stationary distribution. In very broad terms, Markov chains are processes describing trajectories where successive quantities are described probabilistically according to the value of their immediate predecessors. A good chain will have rapid mixing – the stationary distribution is reached quickly starting from an arbitrary position – described further under Markov chain mixing time. MCMC methods have been applied in economic and social issues because of the simulation of Bayesian posterior density functions. The reason for employing Bayesian inference via MCMC in this chapter is to overcome the drawbacks of maximum likelihood estimation.

In this chapter, the Metropolis–Hastings algorithm is applied to generate a random walk using a proposal density and a method for rejecting proposed moves. The Bayesian approach and its application via MCMC methods have several advantages. First, the subject-specific treatment distributions can be easily computed by simulating the latent variables (see Chib and Hamilton, 2000). Second, we do not have to apply numerical integration methods to evaluate the likelihood function of our model. This is particularly important when more flexible distributions than the normal are assumed for the error terms. Third, it allows us to conduct exact small-sample inference.

3   ESTIMATION

We use economywide province-level data tracked from 1992 to 2003.

The MCMC method is used in the given situation. The main concern is efficient computation. Efficiency can be measured by the ease with which a simulated sample is obtained. We make our inference on the base of a large sample from the posterior distribution, where the sample is generated by designing a Markov chain with a transition kernel. The kernel has an invariant measure equal to the posterior distribution. We refer to this as a 'sequential sampling proposal process'. We now describe a more general Metropolis–Hastings update where the proposal process is a truncated version of the same sequential sampling scheme.

The likelihood function $p(R \perp \Theta)$ is given by:

$$p(R^{2,n} \perp \Theta) = \prod_{t=2}^{n} \left\{ \sum_{j=1}^{2} \frac{\Gamma(v+1)/2}{\Gamma(v/2)\sqrt{(v-2)\pi}} \frac{1}{\sqrt{ht}} \left[1 + \frac{(R_t - \mu_t)^2}{(v-2)h_t} \right]^{-(v+1)/2} I_{jt} \right\},$$

$$(7.1)$$

where p is the posterior distribution, R is the risk of posterior distribution, Θ is the Bayesian estimate, I_{jt} is the indicator variable, $\Gamma(\cdot)$ is the gamma function and v is the degrees of freedom.

We set prior distributions on all model parameters following:

$$p(\Theta) \propto I(\alpha_0^{(1)} > 0, \alpha_1^{(1)} + \beta_1^{(1)} < 1) I(\alpha_0^{(2)} > 0, \alpha_1^{(2)} + \beta_1^{(2)} < 1)$$

$$I(q_1 < rk < q_3), I(d \in 1, 2, 3), I(t \in [0, 0.25]), \qquad (7.2)$$

where $I(\cdot)$ is an indicator function, and q_1 and q_3 are the first and third quantities, respectively, of the required threshold variable. In threshold modeling, we set a minimum number of observations in each regime, so there is sufficient sample size to generate meaningful inference results, driving our prior choice for r_k. We restrict $v > 4$ so that the variance of ε_t is finite, while ensuring that the kurtosis is greater than 3.

Details of the random walk Metropolis–Hastings algorithms are:

Step 1: Generate initial values $p^{[0]}$ from the prior distribution for this parameter vector.

Step 2: At iteration i, generate a point p^* from the kernel density,

$$p^* \sim N(p^{[i-1]}, \alpha\Omega),$$

where $p^{[i-1]}$ is the $(i-1)$th iterate of p.

Step 3: Accept p^* as $p^{[i]}$ with the probability,

$$p = \min\{1, p(p^*|R^{2,n}, \Theta - p)/p(p^{[i-1]}|R^{2,n}, \Theta - p)\}.$$

Otherwise, set $p^{[i]} = p^{[i-1]}$.

To yield good causality properties, the choice of Ω and α for each parameter vector is made to ensure good coverage for each conditional posterior distribution.

4   RESULTS AND DISCUSSION

We investigate the effect of pollution abatement on environmental efficiency in Chinese industry through the estimation of the system equation with the application of Bayesian MCMC methods. The sample ranges from 1992 to 2003. We sample sequentially through the complete set of full conditional distributions of the parameters.

We derive the complete conditional distributions for all parameters in the model to implement the MCMC sampling approach. This procedure produces a set of estimates that converges in the limit to the joint posterior distribution of the parameters (see Gelfand and Smith, 1990). We ran the MCMC algorithm for 5,000 iterations with a burn-in phase of 10,000

Table 7.1   Empirical results for the effect of pollution abatement on environmental efficiency

Year	Posterior mean	Posterior deviation	Standard error
1992	340.32	0.72	0.01
1993	320.34	0.95	0.04
1994	200.21	0.87	0.02
1995	280.98	0.99	0.02
1996	200.72	0.76	0.02
1997	332.01	0.89	0.01
1998	340.25	0.91	0.02
1999	398.32	0.99	0.05
2000	400.62	0.43	0.02
2001	430.02	0.45	0.02
2002	350.23	0.78	0.05
2003	290.98	0.76	0.04

iterations. The posterior standard deviation is used as a measure of our uncertainty about these point estimates. Since we do not have the posterior directly, however, these quantities can be closely approximated by calculating their sample analogues (though they cannot be computed directly).

Table 7.1 shows the results of the hypothesis test of the non-causality on abatements and environmental efficiency regimes. The posterior means were obtained from the marginal posterior densities. The resulting posterior standard deviations are shown in parentheses. For individual periods, however, they express relatively larger posterior standard deviations corresponding to the practical intersection of observations.

The resulting posterior density shown in Figure 7.1 produced numerical quantities indicating that the MCMC methods diverge from corresponding traditional statistics as sample size decreases. In general, the posterior density based directly upon the likelihood function is much more tractable than the sampling distribution of a modal value of that function, which involves the maximization operator. In this study, the limited information analysis can now be carried out under a Bayesian approach, leading to sharper finite sample results.

The costs of alternative production and pollution abatement technologies are important determinants of the environmental compliance cost. In the long run, the most important single criterion on which to judge environmental policies might be the extent to which they spur new technology toward the efficient conservation of environmental quality. We employ economic techniques and find that efficiency in environmental management is improving. Our results show that environmental efficiency (or

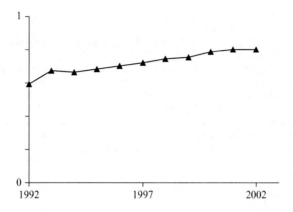

Figure 7.1   Posterior density test results

productivity) is increasing while pollution abatement is improving, though the effect is not always obvious.

5   CONCLUSIONS

Environmental problems have been a top global threat. China is facing daunting challenges in addressing environment pollution and ecosystem degradation with its remarkable economic growth, and its future for sustainable economic development relies on efficiency improvement. Given concerns over the rapid economic growth and severe environmental degradation, our study features various pollutants in 31 provinces from 1992 to 2003. We focus on the estimation of China's dataset using a new method in Bayesian analysis via MCMC simulation.

An advantage of this method is that the normal proposal density for this case becomes adaptive since it depends on the values of the other parameters from the current and previous iterations. This semiautomatic updating feature makes the proposal density closer to the true conditional posterior, which may lead to a more efficient algorithm.

BIBLIOGRAPHY

Afonso, R., M. Tatsutani, T.J. Roskelley and P. Amar (2000), 'The regulation of NOx emissions from coal-fired boilers: a case study', in Amar, P., *Environmental Regulation and Technology Innovation: Controlling Mercury Emissions from*

Coal-Fired Boilers, Northeast States for Coordinated Air Use Management, Boston, MA, pp. III-1-III-17.

Chen, M.H., Q.M. Shao and J.G. Ibrahim (2000), *Monte Carlo Methods in Bayesian Computation*, New York: Springer Verlag.

Chip, S. and B. Hamilton (2000), 'Bayesian analysis of cross-section and clustered data selection models', *Journal of Econometrics*, **97** (1), 25–50.

Chib, S. and I. Jeliazkov (2001), 'Marginal likelihood from the Metropolis–Hastings output', *Journal of the American Statistical Association*, **96**, 270–81.

Chib, S., F. Nardari and N. Shephard (2002), 'Markov chain Monte Carlo methods for stochastic volatility models', *Journal of Econometrics*, **108**, 281–316.

Gelfand, Allan E. and Adrian F.M. Smith (1990), 'Sampling-based approaches to calculating marginal densities', *Journal of the American Statistical Association*, **85**, 398–409.

Geweke, J.F. (1989), 'Bayesian inference in econometric models using Monte Carlo integration', *Econometrica*, **57**, 1317–39.

Geweke, J.F. (1994), 'Bayesian comparison of econometric models', Federal Reserve Bank of Minneapolis Research Department Working Paper 532.

Greene, W.H. (1993), *Econometric Analysis*, New York: Macmillan.

Jaffe, A.B., R.G. Newell, and R. Stavins (2003), 'Technological change and the environment', in Karl-Göran Mäler and Jeffrey Vincent (eds), *Handbook of Environmental Economics*, Amsterdam: North-Holland, Elsevier Science, pp. 462–516.

Jiang, T. and W.J. McKibbin (2002), 'Assessment of China's pollution levy system: an equilibrium pollution approach', *Environment and Development Economics*, **7** (1), 75–105.

Kass, R.E. and A.E. Raftery (1995), 'Bayes factors', *Journal of the American Statistical Association*, **90**, 773–95.

Kim, C.J. and C.R. Nelson (1999), 'Has the US economy become more stable? A Bayesian approach based on a Markov-switching model of the business cycle', *Review of Economics and Statistics*, **80**, 188–201.

Kneese, A.V. and C.L. Schultze (1978), *Pollution, Prices and Public Policy*, Washington, DC: Brookings Institution.

Managi, S., J.J. Opaluch, D. Jin and T.A. Grigalunas (2004), 'Technological change and depletion in offshore oil and gas', *Journal of Environmental Economics and Management*, **47** (2), 388–409.

APPENDIX 7A   DATA SOURCE

Regional Dummy

Provinces: Anhui, Fujian, Gansu, Guangdong, Guizhou, Hainan, Hebei, Heilongjiang, Henan, Hubei, Hunan, Jiangsu, Jiangxi, Jilin, Liaoning, Qinghai, Shaanxi, Shandong, Shanxi, Sichuan, Yunnan and Zhejiang.

Four municipalities: Beijing, Tianjin, Shanghai and Chongqing, administered directly by the central government.

Five autonomous regions: The equivalent of provinces: Guangxi, Inner Mongolia, Ningxia, Tibet and Xinjiang.

Note: Hong Kong and Macao are special administrative regions that are not included in the statistics of the People's Republic of China. The data for Tibet are not fully available, so Tibet is excluded from the computation.

8. Water and agriculture

1 INTRODUCTION

Water efficiency improvement in agricultural production has emerged as a formidable challenge to improve productivity in the water-scarce areas of the world (Qadir et al., 2003). In China, one of the important agricultural bases is located in the Northern semi-arid region from which a large portion of wheat and corn demand is supplied. With rapid industrialization and continuous increase of demand for grain, the role of the Northern region in water efficiency improvement in grain production becomes increasingly significant and crucial.

The deterioration of water resource endowment in the Yellow River due to decreased precipitation and increased air temperature during the last 50 years has been reported (Yang et al., 2004). Since the water in the Yellow River first dried up before reaching the river mouth in 1972, both drying-up period per annum and furthermost distance of dried-up point from the mouth have increased over time. This phenomenon has continued unabated until its most serious position in 1997. However, the situation has dramatically improved since the enforcement of two new water management policies in 1998. One of the new policies administratively allocates water withdrawn from the Yellow River to each province in order to make a balance in water resource distribution between upper and lower reaches (Yellow River Resources Committee, 1998). The agricultural productivity in the region, where supply of agricultural water depends heavily on the river, is expected to be adversely affected by such rapid policy changes.

On the contrary, the Southern part of China is endowed with rich water resources and wet rice agriculture is mainly practiced in this area. There is less pressure on water efficiency improvement in agricultural production compared with the Northern region. Given this background, it is of prime interest for this study to examine the relation between water efficiency and productivity in agricultural production in different regions.

In the field of agricultural science, water use efficiency (WUE) is often employed as a measure of water efficiency in agricultural production (Wang et al., 2000; Kang et al., 2003). The WUE is in principle, a crop-specific physical measurement in relatively small agricultural fields, in which site-specific local parameters including climate, soil conditions and irrigation schemes are assumed to be homogeneous. In Zhang et al. (2003), WUE is generally defined as the ratio of grain yield to actual evapotranspiration, as shown below:

WUE = Grain Yield / Actual Evapotranspiration
   = Grain Yield / (Precipitation + Irrigation − *dSWS*
   − Surface Runoff − Soil Water Drainage),

where *dSWS* denotes the difference in soil water storage between harvest stage and seeding stage and is both supplier and absorber depending on the condition.

The WUE is also regarded as one of the criteria to evaluate various farming technologies in order to maximize grain yield. This is in reference to a unit amount of net water consumption for growing plants regardless of where the water has been sourced originally. Many studies have proposed various methods of farming operation to improve the WUE. For example, the combination of pre-sowing irrigation in semi-arid regions with a plastic mulching technique and phosphorus application (Li et al., 2001a, 2004a), and the ridge and furrow rainfall harvesting system with mulches (Li et al., 2001b; Li and Gong, 2002), are proposed for the crop production in the Loess Plateau. The different long-term crop rotation systems lead to different WUE, and a three-year rotation of corn, wheat and wheat-millet have been found to be most efficient in water use in the Loess Plateau (Huang et al., 2003b). The effects of fertilizer application and the timing of water application to the WUE have also been studied (Huang et al., 2003a; Li et al., 2004b). These experimental findings also show that the role of water in plant growth is highly complex and sensitive to various factors.

Moreover, it is equally important to know the role of irrigation water in the agricultural production function from an economic perspective. With reference to the WUE, irrigation water and natural water supply jointly and alternatively contribute to plant growth. If we specifically focus on irrigation water as a separate component of natural water supply, it is more complex to measure the physical efficiency. Since irrigation water has a certain cost, it can be seen as only one of the input factors of market goods for agricultural production, even though irrigation water price is believed to be very low in China. In this case, natural water supply, as a nonmarket good which is sourced from precipitation and soil moisture, is treated exogenously. Water efficiency refers to the economically efficient use of irrigation water to maximize the output value of production. Therefore,

Table 8.1   Summary of previous studies on productivity

No.	Author(s) and year	Method[1]	Period	Input[2]						Output[3]
				LD	LB	FE	MA	DR	CL	
1	McMillan et al. (1989)	A	1978–1984	X	X	X	X	X		GVAO
2	Lin (1992)	A	1970–1987	X	X	X	X	X		GVAO
3	Wu (1995)	C	1985–1991	X	X	X	X			GVAO
4	Kalirajan et al. (1996)	A	1970–1987	X	X	X	X	X		GVAO
5	Wang et al. (1996)	C	1978–1984	X	X					GVAO
6	Huang and Rozelle (1996)	A	1975–1990	X	X	X				Rice yield
7	Zhang and Carter (1997)	A	1980–1990	X	X	X	X		X	Grain output in tons
8	Mao and Koo (1997)	B	1984–1993	X	X	X	X	X		GVAO and NVAO
9	Bhattacharyya and Parker (1999)	C	1980–1995	X	X	X	X	X		GVAO
10	Zhang and Fan (2001)	D	1979–1996	X	X	X	X	X		GVAO
11	Jin et al. (2002)	A	1979–1995	X	X	X	X	X		GVAO

Notes
1. Method A: decomposition; Method B: DEA; Method C: SFA; Method D: GME (generalized maximum entropy).
2. LD: land area; LB: labor force; FE: fertilizer; MA: machinery; DR: draft animal; CL: climatic condition.
3. GVAO: gross value of agricultural output; NVAO: net value of agricultural output.

the irrigation water use is treated in the same manner as other factor inputs in the production function.

Selected previous studies, which describe the agricultural production function, the measure of productivity and the contributions of various production factors in the agriculture sector, are summarized in Table 8.1. Despite the various different approaches employed in these empirical studies, agricultural land, labor, chemical fertilizer and agricultural machinery are common variables for inputs. This is due to data availability. However, to our best knowledge, there is no previous study that explicitly deals with irrigation water supply in the empirical analyses. Without considering water consumption, the findings from the previous studies are summarized, as follows:

1. The household responsibility system which was introduced in 1978 has contributed to the improvement of productivity until 1984, achieving a 32 percent TFP growth throughout the period. This was also partially

enhanced by good weather conditions in the early 1980s (McMillan et al., 1989; Zhang and Carter, 1997).

2. Slowdown in output growth during the 1984–87 period is mainly due to the decrease in labor and fertilizer inputs (Lin, 1992; Kalirajan et al., 1996).

3. In the late 1980s and early 1990s, technological change largely contributed to productivity improvements, thereby offsetting the reduction in the use of inputs that is due to escalating input prices relative to those of outputs (Wu, 1995; Huang and Rozelle, 1996; Wang et al., 1996; Mao and Koo, 1997; Jin et al., 2002). On the other hand, agricultural labor surplus in most regions was measured to be around 30–40 percent throughout the 1980–95 period (Bhattacharyya and Parker, 1999) period.

4. Land productivity in grain production deteriorated significantly until the mid-1990s (Zhang and Fan, 2001) and the impact of environmental degradation on agricultural productivity emerged in the late 1990s.

Incorporating irrigation water into the sets of production factors in agriculture is needed for better understanding of efficiency in agricultural production. A properly constructed but practical measure of water efficiency is important even under severe data constraints. This measure should provide a useful statistic indicating how each region formulates agricultural water management policy to improve not only water efficiency but also productivity. The objective of the study is to measure the technical and water efficiency in the agricultural sector and to identify the determinants behind these regional differences. We apply stochastic frontier analysis (SFA) techniques to a provincial-level dataset to measure the efficiencies in agricultural production from 1999 to 2002.

2 OUTLINE OF CURRENT REGIONAL AGRICULTURAL PRODUCTION

Because China is a large country, the regional variation of agricultural production practices is considerable, given its diversified climate and geographical conditions, and level and pace of economic development. This study classifies 30 provinces into six economic regions, taking into consideration the homogeneity in economic activities as described in Table 8.2. The regional distribution of major agricultural related statistics is summarized in Figure 8.1.

Two regions, namely the Yellow River and Changjiang, which both

Table 8.2   Regional classification

Region	Provinces
Northeast	Liaoning, Jilin, Heilongjiang
Yellow River	Beijing, Tianjin, Hebei, Shanxi, Shandong, Henan, Shaanxi
Changjiang	Shanghai, Jiangsu, Zhejiang, Anhui, Jiangxi, Hubei, Hunan
South Coast	Fujian, Guangdong, Guangxi, Hainan
Southwest	Sichuan, Guizhou, Yunnan
Northwest	Inner Mongolia, Tibet, Gansu, Qinghai, Ningxia, Xinjiang

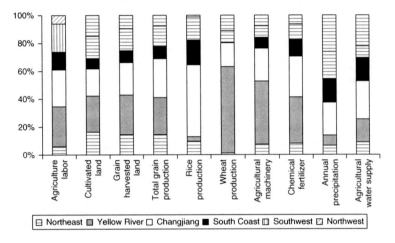

Source: NBS (2003).

Figure 8.1   Regional distribution of major statistics in grain production, 2002

comprise seven provinces, are of particular importance in grain production. In 2002, around 55 percent of the agricultural labor force in these
two regions held 45 percent of the cultivated land area. In these areas more
than half of the harvested land has been utilized, using 44 percent of supplied agricultural water.

The inputs in their production processes also include almost 70 percent
of agricultural machinery power and more than 60 percent of chemical
fertilizer. This results in 55 and 80 percent of rice and wheat productions,
respectively.

Figure 8.2 compares selected productivity indicators of grain production by region with reference to the national average, and shows that the

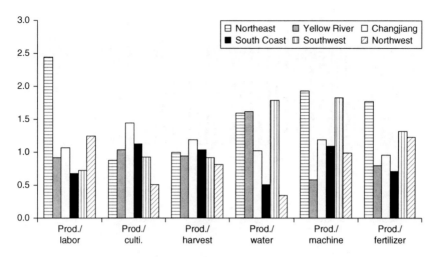

Notes:
Prod./culti. = grain production/cultivated land
Prod./harvest = grain production/harvested land
Harvest/cultivate = harvested land/cultivated land
Prod./labor = grain production/agriculture labor
Water/prod = agricultural water supply/grain production
Machine/harvest = agricultural machine/harvested land
Fertiliz/harvest = chemical fertilizer/harvested land

Source: NBS (2003).

Figure 8.2   Regional variations of selected productivity indicators in agricultural production relative to national average, 2002 (national average = 1)

large gaps among the six regions exist for some indicators. The Northeast demonstrates the highest productivity with regard to the major production inputs such as labor, machinery and fertilizer, whereas land productivity in terms of cultivated land is not especially high. This is partially due to the fact that multi-cropping is not popular in the region. However, considering that productivity in terms of harvested land is the national average, the land is relatively fertile. In contrast, the Yellow River shows the lowest productivity to the machinery input and the second-lowest productivity to fertilizer input. The productivity to the irrigation water input in the Northeast and the Yellow River is higher than the national average by more than 50 percent.

With large-scale agricultural production, Changjiang shapes most of the national averages except productivity with reference to cultivated land.

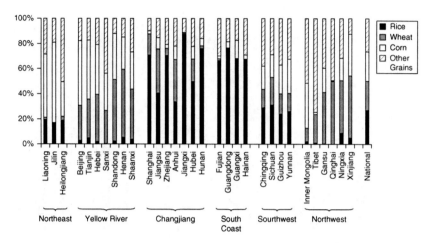

Source: NBS (2003).

Figure 8.3   Provincial share of sown area by major grain crops

This is probably achieved through multiple and diverse cropping sup-
ported by better climatic conditions. The South Coast presents the lowest
productivity in terms of labor and fertilizer inputs despite better land
productivity, following Changjiang. This region also enjoys ample water
resources, as demonstrated in the intensive use of water for grain production. Grain production per water use in the Southwest is quite a contrast
to that in the Northwest. Fifty-four percent of the agricultural water in the
Northwest is used in Xinjian province, where productivity to water input
is the lowest and less than one-sixth of the national average. On the other
hand, the Southwest demonstrates the highest water productivity. The
grain productivity to water input in Sichuan province in this region is 2.4
times higher than the national average.

Rice, wheat and corn are the three major grain crops, accounting for 74
percent of total harvested land area for grain production. Figure 8.3 provides the composition of harvested area for major grain crops by province,
and shows that the classification of six regional economic blocs is applica-
ble and relevant to agricultural analysis. Rice and corn are dominant crops
in the Northeast and wheat and corn are dominant in the Yellow River.
Rice is dominant in Changjiang and in the South Coast, whereas wheat is
also produced to some extent in Changjiang. The Southwest has a well-
balanced combination of crop production where all four of the crops are
grown. The Northwest produces wheat and corn but other grains are also
shared in relatively large proportion.

3   DATA AND METHODOLOGY

Data

The availability of data on cultivated land area and volume of agricultural water use primarily shapes the basic methodological framework of this study. In 1997, the National Bureau of Statistics conducted the first comprehensive land survey which investigated the benchmark data of 1996 (Gale, 2002; Lin and Ho, 2003). The results were finally authorized by the government in the latter part of 1999 (Lomborg, 2001). Results revealed that the total cultivated land area was 130 million hectares, approximately 40 percent less than the figures published in the various issues of the *China Statistical Yearbook* (CSY) before 1998 (NBS, 2000, 2001, 2002, 2003). The CSY in 1999 or later issues provided the cultivated land area statistics based on the 1996 data at the provincial level.

The *China Water Resources Bulletin* (CWRB) is published annually by the Ministry of Water Resources of China and since 1999, the water use in cubic meters by the three major sectors; agriculture, industry and domestic use at the provincial level has been disclosed (Water Resources Committee, 1999, 2000, 2001, 2002).

Based on the above available data, we constructed the panel dataset used in this study for 30 provinces,[1] covering the 1999–2002 period. Much of the information was obtained from the CSY and only two variables, agricultural water use and volume of annual rainfall, were taken from the CWRB. As output variables, total grain production reported in tons, is further subdivided into four major types of crop: rice, wheat, corn and other grain crops. The economic output of agricultural production with constant price is also included. The five variables for input of grain production are as follows: (i) *Land*: cultivated land area in 1996. This is used throughout the study period since the data at the provincial level have not been updated; (ii) *Labor*: the total labor force of primary industry measured in number of persons working in agriculture, forestry, animal husbandry and fishery; (iii) *Machinery*: the total power of agricultural machinery in kilowatts; (iv) *Fertilizer*: the nitrogenous fertilizer and compound chemical fertilizer of nitrogen, phosphate, potash and others, in tons; and (v) *Water*: the total volume of agricultural water use in cubic meters. Complementary data are also added to the dataset for econometric analysis such as capacity and number of reservoirs, irrigation land area, annual rainfall, monthly sunshine hours, mean annual temperature, net income of agricultural employee, and factor price index. Among these, annual rainfall, monthly sunshine hours and mean annual temperature are available only for the capital cities of each province. Therefore, the data for each capital city are representative of the corresponding province.

Methodology

Prior to economic analysis, we first examine the physical determinant structure of the irrigation factor which refers to the unit of water use per irrigation land area. The irrigation factor is reported in the CWRB for major river basins as one of the key parameters for water resource management. The yields of four major grain crops (rice, wheat, corn and others), per cultivated land area are explanatory variables for production capacity. The number of reservoirs per cultivated land area is employed as a variable for irrigation infrastructure, while annual precipitation per hectare, monthly sunshine hours, mean annual temperature and average relative humidity are added to the explanatory variables representing natural conditions. The physical model specification to the provincial-level data from 1999 to 2002 is demonstrated by OLS with time and regional dummy variables.

Following this, we then apply SFA in order to measure the technical and water efficiency in agricultural production from an economic perspective. Specification of the frontier production function is based on the economic production theory employing economic output of agriculture as the independent variable. The input variables are agricultural machinery representing capital, agricultural labor, nitrogen fertilizer and water use, adjusted to the scale of cultivated land area. Finally, the estimated efficiencies by province are further explained by the Tobit model using variables such as farm machinery price index, chemical fertilizer price index, net income of rural households per capita, mean annual temperature, annual precipitation per cultivated land area, monthly sunshine hours and number of reservoirs.

Stochastic Frontier Analysis

Theoretical framework: technical efficiency

The concept of technical efficiency is based on the production frontier. Suppose that a province produces an agricultural output Y using an input X and water W. Assuming that the production possibility set satisfies $T(Y, X, W) \geq 0$, a general representation of the frontier technology is defined as $Y = f(X, W)$. The function $f(\cdot)$ is said to be the production frontier if it gives the upper boundary of T. In other words, given inputs X and W, the frontier output $f(X, W)$ represents the maximum producible output. Then, the production frontier can be expressed in terms of the following maximization problem:

$$f(X, Z) = \text{Max } [Y : T(X, Z, Y) \geq 0]. \qquad (8.1)$$

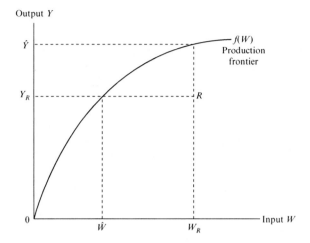

Figure 8.4   Production frontier in output Y and input W space

Given production frontier $f(\cdot)$, Figure 8.4 illustrates the relationship between frontier output $\hat{Y}$ and level of water use W, holding an input X constant. In the figure, the observed output Y_R is inefficient because lies beneath the production frontier. A measure of technical (or output-oriented) inefficiency is defined by the distance between $\hat{Y}$ and Y_R. Thus, the technical efficiency can be expressed as a ratio of the frontier and observed output levels. Therefore, in terms of the maximization problem, the technical efficiency can be defined by:

$$
\begin{aligned}
TE_R &= \{\text{Max}\ [\theta\colon \theta Y_R \le \hat{Y}]\}^{-1} \\
&= \{\text{Max}\ [\theta\colon \theta Y_R \le f(X_R, Z_R)]\}^{-1} \\
&= Y_R/\hat{Y}, \quad\quad\quad\quad\quad\quad\quad\quad\quad (8.2)
\end{aligned}
$$

where θ is a scale parameter representing technical inefficiency. From equation (8.2), Y_R attains its frontier $\hat{Y}$ if and only if $TE_R = 1$. Otherwise $TE_R \in [0, 1]$ provides a measure of the shortfall of observed output from maximum feasible output $\hat{Y}$.

Theoretical framework: environmental efficiency
Following Kopp (1981), we define water efficiency as a ratio of minimum feasible to observed level of water use, at given levels of output and other inputs. Thus, water efficiency is a nonradial input-oriented measure of technical efficiency, allowing a radial reduction of water use.[2] The theoretical

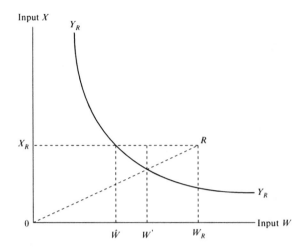

Figure 8.5   Production frontier in input X *and* W *space*

concept of environmental efficiency is illustrated in Figure 8.5. This figure presents the relationship between an input X and water use W, holding an output constant at its observed level Y_R. In Figure 8.4, the observed level of water use W_R is inefficient because (X_R, Y_R) lies above the minimum feasible input requirement set to produce Y_R. Holding an output and input X constant, $\hat{W}$ is the minimum feasible water use. Thus, a measure of water efficiency is given by the non-radial input-oriented measure:

$$WE_R = \text{Min} \ [\mu \colon f(X_R, \mu W_R) \geq Y_R(\hat{W})]$$
$$= \hat{W}/W_R, \tag{8.3}$$

where μ is a scale parameter representing water-use inefficiency. This ratio is presented in both Figures 8.4 and 8.5. Equation (8.3) indicates that W_R attains its minimum feasible value $\hat{W}$ if and only if $WE_R = 1$. Otherwise $WE_R \in [0, 1]$ provides a measure of the surplus of observed water use from the minimum feasible level to produce Y_R.

Empirical framework
There is an extensive literature on empirical techniques of efficiency measurement. Those techniques can be classified broadly into SFA and DEA. In general, because the SFA acknowledges the random error around the estimated production frontier, we can distinguish the effects of uncontrollable exogenous shocks from the effects of inefficiency. In contrast, the DEA method is based on a deterministic production frontier and thus

lumps together random error and inefficiency.[3] Distinction of random error and inefficiency is especially important in this study because agricultural production is highly state contingent due to the stochastic nature of weather as well as other uncontrollable factors (for example, uncertainty in the input and output prices, and market conditions). Thus, this study uses the SFA to estimate technical and water efficiency in the agricultural sector. Once water use is estimated, we then employ the Tobit model to evaluate the determinants of water efficiency.

First-stage stochastic frontier analysis   The SFA treats technical inefficiency as an additional disturbance term with a two-parameter (in our study, half-normal) distribution (Meusen and van den Broeck, 1977; Aigner et al., 1997). Let Y_{it} be the level of observed industrial output in province i at the period t. In the SFA framework, the observed level of industrial output is given by:

$$Y_{it} = f(X_{it}, W_{it}, \beta) \cdot \exp(V_{it} - U_{it}), \qquad (8.4)$$

where X_{it} is a conventional input, W_{it} is the level of water use, and β is a vector of parameters to be estimated. V_{it} is a random error term with $V_{it}^{iid} \sim N(0, \sigma_v^2)$, which absorbs the events beyond the control of agricultural production. U_{it} is a non-negative random error term reflecting technical inefficiency. U_{it} is assumed to be half-normally distributed, $U_{it}^{iid} \sim N^+(0, \sigma_u^2)$. From equation (8.4), the level of technically efficient output can be obtained by setting $U_{it} = 0$. Then, the stochastic version of technical efficiency is defined by:

$$
\begin{aligned}
TE_{it} &= Y_{it} / \hat{Y}_{it} \\
&= Y_{it} / f(X_{it}, Z_{it}, \beta) \cdot \exp(V_{it}) \\
&= \exp(-U_{it}). \qquad (8.5)
\end{aligned}
$$

To derive a stochastic version of the water efficiency defined in equation (8.3), a functional form of the stochastic frontier model needs to be specified. This study uses a standard Cobb–Douglas form to model the production technology in equation (8.1). Under a Cobb–Douglas formulation, equation (8.4) is characterized by:

$$\ln Y_{it} = \beta_0 + \beta_1 \ln K_{it} + \beta_2 \ln L_{it} + \beta_3 \ln N_{it} + \beta_4 \ln W_{it} + V_{it} - U_{it}. (8.6)$$

The logarithm of the technically efficient output $\hat{Y}_{5t}$ is obtained by setting $U_{it} = 0$ in (8.6). The logarithm of the water-efficient output, $\hat{Y}_{it}^W$ is calculated by replacing W_{it} with $\hat{W}_{it}$ and setting $U_{it} = 0$ in (8.6):

$$\ln \hat{Y}_{it}^W = \beta_0 + \beta_k \ln K_{it} + \beta_l \ln L_{it} + \beta_N \ln N_{it} + \beta_W \ln \hat{W}_{it} + V_{it}. \quad (8.7)$$

Setting equations (8.6) and (8.7) equal and solving for $\ln WE_{it} = \ln W_{it} - \ln \hat{W}_{it}$, we have the water efficiency estimator:

$$WE_{it} = \exp(-U_{it}/\beta_w). \quad (8.8)$$

Note that, under a Cobb–Douglas model, a ranking of province by water efficiency is identical to a ranking by technical efficiency. More flexible functional forms, such as a translog model, would be more desirable because those allow rankings by water efficiency and technical efficiency to vary across provinces (Reinhard et al., 1999). However, we detect severe multicollinearity in our data, preventing the specification of any of flexible functional forms.

Second-stage Tobit analysis   Given water efficiency estimated in the first stage, we evaluate the factors affecting water efficiency by regressing the economic and physical variables on water efficiency. Because, by definition, the dependent variable of water efficiency WE_{it} has a discrete jump at zero and one, the OLS produces biased and inconsistent estimates (Greene, 2003). Thus, the censoring of the dependent variables needs to be considered. One of the most commonly used applications to censored data is the Tobit model (also referred to as 'censored regression'). The general formulation of the Tobit model is given by an index function:

$$WE_{it} = \begin{cases} WE_{it}^* & \text{if } 0 < Z_{it}\lambda + \varepsilon_{it} < 1 \\ 0 & \text{if } Z_{it}\lambda + \varepsilon_{it} \leq 0 \\ 1 & \text{if } Z_{it}\lambda + \varepsilon_{it} \geq 1, \end{cases} \quad (8.9)$$

where $WE_{it}^* = Z_{it}\lambda + \varepsilon_{it}$ is an unobserved index variable (also referred to as a latent variable). Z_{it} is a vector of independent variables affecting water efficiency, and ε_{it} is the random disturbance term with the distribution $\varepsilon_{it} \sim N(0, \sigma_\varepsilon^2)$. Let $d_i = 1$ be the noncensored observation and $d_i = 0$ otherwise. Then, the log-likelihood function of equation (8.9) is:

$$\log L = \sum_{d_i=1} -\frac{1}{2}\left[\log(2\pi) + \log\sigma^2 + \frac{(WE_{it} - Z_{it}\lambda)^2}{\sigma^2}\right]$$

$$+ \sum_{d_i=0}\left[1 - \Phi\left(\frac{Z_{it}\lambda}{\sigma}\right)\right], \quad (8.10)$$

where Φ is the cumulative density function. The log-likelihood function in equation (8.10) is computed using the maximum likelihood technique. The resulting parameter estimates are consistent, efficient and asymptotically normally distributed (ibid.). The empirical estimations of both first and second stages are conducted using STATA version 8.

4 RESULTS

Physical Model of the Irrigation Factor

Aside from economic analysis, it is important to study the physical structure of determinants of water use in agriculture production. The result of physical model specification for the irrigation factor is shown in Table 8.3. Due to unavailability of information for some datasets, Tibet is excluded from the sample for this analysis. In addition to time and regional dummy variables, 11 dependent variables are tested using OLS.

The yields of corn and other grain crops are significantly and negatively related to the irrigation factor, while rice and wheat have positive signs but are insignificant. Irrigation infrastructure also plays a more important role in the irrigation factor in terms of capacity rather than in number of reservoirs. The regions with more precipitation use less water per irrigation area, indicating the substitutive relationship between precipitation and irrigation water use. Amount of sunshine and humidity are positively related to water use. Another finding is that even though the analysis period is short, significant change in the irrigation factor over time cannot be observed from the results.

Technical and Water Efficiency in Agriculture

Table 8.4 presents the estimated coefficients for the stochastic frontier production model. Overall, the model fits the data plausibly well. Most coefficients are statistically significant at the 1 percent level. A likelihood-ratio test of the hypothesis that there is no technical inefficiency (that is, $\sigma_u^2 = 0$) is rejected with a test statistic of 10.5. Although labor per hectare is not significant at any level, this may be due to the fact that the values of this variable include a nonagricultural labor force in rural areas. All of the regional dummy variables are significant at the 1 percent level, implying that there are significant geographic variations in agricultural production.

Table 8.5 reports the estimated technical and water efficiency for the six major regions.[4] The highest technical and water efficiency scores are observed in the Southwest region and lowest scores are observed in the South Coast region. Overall, the estimated efficiency rankings are highly

Table 8.3   Estimated coefficients for the physical model (dependent variable: agricultural water use per irrigation area)

	Coefficient	Standard error
Constant	−0.1746**	0.0852
Yield of rice	0.0323	0.0404
Yield of wheat	0.0582	0.0587
Yield of corn	−0.1933**	0.0761
Yield of other grain crops	−0.2559*	0.1319
Capacity of reservoirs	0.1469***	0.0415
Number of reservoirs	0.0100*	0.0054
Annual precipitation per hectare	−0.0340***	0.0088
Monthly sunshine hours	0.0000***	0.0000
Average temperature	0.0019	0.0020
Average relative humidity	0.0031***	0.0009
Dummy for 1999	0.0002	0.0064
Dummy for 2000	−0.0126*	0.0068
Dummy for 2001	−0.0106	0.0065
Dummy for Yellow River	−0.0473**	0.0263
Dummy for Changjiang	−0.0832***	0.0353
Dummy for South Coast	0.0177	0.0215
Dummy for Southwest	−0.0251	0.0185
Dummy for Northwest	0.0636***	0.0852
Number of observations	116	
Adj. *R*-squared	0.793	

Note: One, two and three asterisks indicate statistical significance at the 10%, 5% and 1% levels, respectively.

related to the type of dominant crops in each region. For example, corn is dominant in the Southwest and Yellow River, where the estimated efficiency scores are relatively high. Agronomy information suggests that corn is a less water-intensive and more profitable crop. Such crop characteristics may result in higher technical and water efficiency in those regions. In contrast, rice, a relatively less profitable and more water-intensive crop, is dominant in Changjiang and the South Coast, where efficiency scores are relatively low. The Northwest is reported to be one of the least-productive regions, even though corn is a dominant crop. This can be explained by the climatic conditions in the region: the mean annual temperature is only 8.5°C, although precipitation is abundant. Such climatic conditions may result in less-productive agricultural production.

Finally, Table 8.6 presents the changes in technical and water efficiency scores during the study period. Significant difference in both technical and

Table 8.4   Estimated coefficients for the stochastic frontier production model (dependent variable: agricultural gross output value per hectare)

	Coefficient	Standard error
Constant	−4.04***	0.28
ln Capital per hectare	0.26***	0.07
ln Labor per hectare	0.03	0.06
ln Nitrogen per hectare	0.35***	0.05
ln Water per hectare	0.35***	0.05
Dummy for Northeast	0.50***	0.09
Dummy for Yellow River	0.43***	0.12
Dummy for Changjiang	0.47***	0.11
Dummy for South Coast	0.67***	0.10
Dummy for Southwest	0.52***	0.11
Time trend	0.01	0.02
Number of observations	120	
Log-likelihood ratio	15.08	
σ_u^2/σ_v^2	1.89	

Note: Three asterisks indicates statistical significance at the 1% level.

Table 8.5   Estimated technical and water efficiency by region

Region	Technical efficiency			Water efficiency		
	Mean	Min.	Max.	Mean	Min.	Max.
Northeast	0.80	0.66	0.92	0.55	0.29	0.79
Yellow River	0.81	0.59	0.93	0.57	0.22	0.81
Changjiang	0.80	0.68	0.96	0.54	0.33	0.90
South Coast	0.75	0.52	0.95	0.48	0.15	0.87
Southwest	0.82	0.71	0.91	0.58	0.37	0.75
Northwest	0.77	0.39	0.94	0.53	0.07	0.83
Mean	0.79	0.39	0.96	0.54	0.07	0.90

water efficiency is not observed. This implies that there is little efficiency gain in agricultural output and water use during the period.

The Determinants of Agricultural Water Efficiency

Table 8.7 reports the estimated coefficients for the Tobit model. Most of the estimated coefficients are significant at the 1 percent level and signs of those

Table 8.6   Estimated technical and water efficiency, 1999–2002

Year	Technical efficiency			Water efficiency		
	Mean	Min.	Max.	Mean	Min.	Max.
1999	0.80	0.39	0.95	0.56	0.07	0.87
2000	0.78	0.43	0.93	0.52	0.09	0.82
2001	0.79	0.42	0.95	0.54	0.08	0.86
2002	0.80	0.44	0.96	0.55	0.09	0.90
Mean	0.79	0.39	0.96	0.54	0.07	0.90

Table 8.7   Estimated coefficients and elasticities for the Tobit model (dependent variable: water efficiency)

	Coefficient	Standard error	Elasticity
Constant	-1.18^{***}	0.39	
Farm machinery price index	0.00	0.00	0.93
Chemical fertilizer price index	0.01^{*}	0.00	1.77
Per capita net income of rural households	0.00^{***}	0.00	0.35
Mean annual temperature	0.08^{***}	0.01	2.54
Monthly sunshine hours	0.00^{*}	0.00	-0.45
Annual precipitation per hectare	0.00^{***}	0.00	0.17
Number of reservoirs	0.00^{***}	0.00	-0.16
Dummy for Northeast	0.20^{***}	0.06	
Dummy for Yellow River	-0.41^{***}	0.08	
Dummy for Changjiang	-0.68^{***}	0.11	
Dummy for South Coast	-1.19^{***}	0.16	
Dummy for Southwest	-0.58^{***}	0.11	
Number of observations	110		
Log-likelihood ratio	57.54		
χ^2 (degree of freedom = 97)	60.91		

Note: One and three asterisks indicate statistical significance at the 10% and 1% levels, respectively.

coefficients are consistent with our expectations. In addition, a log-likelihood ratio can reject a null hypothesis that all slope parameters are simultaneously zero with a test statistics of 60.9. The table also shows the estimated elasticity with respect to the major independent variables. The elasticity with respect to the mean annual temperature is 2.54, implying that a 1 percent change in this variable will increase water efficiency by 2.54 percent. This is consistent with agronomy information that the elevated temperature generally facilitates crop growth, which in turn increases the amount of water uptake by the crop. This is particularly true for rice production. The other two climatic variables are estimated to be inelastic. For example, a 1 percent change in monthly sunshine hours will reduce water efficiency by only 0.45 percent. This is reasonable because longer sunshine hours will increase the level of evaporation and decrease the amount of water available for the crops, although the estimated elasticity is relatively small. Finally, the table suggests that the elasticity with respect to the number of reservoir is −0.16. This indicates that a 1 percent increase in the number of reservoirs will reduce water efficiency by 0.16 percent. Although the estimated effect is inelastic, the sign is reasonable because greater water-holding capacity may reduce farmers' incentives to make better use of water for agricultural production. Overall, our results show that water efficiency in the agricultural sector is significantly influenced by the physical variables as well as economic variables such as chemical fertilizers, price index and per capita net income.

5 CONCLUSIONS

This study is a first attempt to measure the water efficiency in agricultural production in China from an economic perspective. The three major findings of the study are summarized below:

1. Dominant crops in the region are significant determinants of the irrigation factor and water efficiency. Corn is found to be one of the most important crops in improving economic and water efficiency.
2. The mean annual temperature is less significant than the water factor, but this is highly elastic to the change in water efficiency. This is consistent with agronomy information which states that an increase in temperature promotes growth of plants while enhancing water intake.
3. Water reservoirs facilitate agricultural water use but may lead to less efficiency in water use. This implies conversely the potential for improvement of water efficiency through the appropriate operation of an agricultural water supply system.

NOTES

1. Due to data unavailability of cultivated land area, all the data for Chongqing is added to Sichuan Province in this study.

2. The standard radial (equiproportionate) measure is not appropriate for identifying the efficiency of individual input use, because it treats the contribution of each input equally to environmental efficiency. See Figure 8.2. See Reinhard et al. (1999) for more detailed discussion.
3. Note that DEA methods have advantages over SFA. In addition, the recent development of DEA incorporates stochastic characteristics of the production frontier.
4. See Appendix 8A for more detailed province-wise efficiency scores.

REFERENCES

Aigner, D.J., C.A.K. Lovell and P. Schmidt (1997), 'Formulation and estimation of stochastic frontier production function models', *Journal of Econometrics*, **6**, July, 21–37.

Bhattacharyya, A. and E. Parker (1999), 'Labor productivity and migration in Chinese agriculture: a stochastic frontier approach', *China Economic Review*, **10**, 59–74.

Gale, F. (2002), 'China's statistics: Are they reliable?', *China's Food and Agriculture: Issues for the 21st Century*, No. 775, pp. 50–53, Market and Trade Economics Division, Economic Research Service, US Department of Agriculture, Agricultural Information Bulletin.

Greene, W.H. (2003), *Econometric Analysis*, 4th edn, Englewood Cliffs, NJ: Prentice-Hall.

Huang, J., and S. Rozelle (1996), 'Technical change: rediscovering the engine of productivity growth in China's rural economy', *Journal of Development Economics*, **49**, 337–69.

Huang, M., T. Dang, J. Gallichand and M. Goulet (2003a), 'Effect of increased fertilizer application to wheat crop on soil-water depletion in the Loess Plateau, China', *Agricultural Water Management*, **58**, 267–78.

Huang, M., M. Shao, L. Zhang and Y. Li (2003b), 'Water use efficiency and sustainability of different long-term crop rotation systems in the Loess Plateau of China', *Soil and Tillage Research*, **72**, 95–104.

Jin, S., J. Huang, R. Hu and S. Rozelle (2002), 'The creation and spread of technology and total factor productivity in China's agriculture', *American Journal of Agricultural Economics*, **84** (4), 916–30.

Kalirajan, K.P., M.B. Obwona and S. Zhao (1996), 'A decomposition of total factor productivity growth: the case of Chinese agricultural growth before and after reforms', *American Journal of Agricultural Economics*, **78**, 331–8.

Kang, S., L. Zhang, Y. Liang and W. Dawes (2003), 'Simulation of winter wheat yield and water use efficiency in the Loess Plateau of China using WAVES', *Agricultural System*, **78**, 355–67.

Kopp, R.J. (1981), 'The measurement of productive efficiency: a reconsideration', *Quarterly Journal of Economics*, **96** (August), 44–60.

Li, F.M., Q.H. Song, H.S. Lie, F.R. Li and X.L. Liu (2001a), 'Effects of Pre-sowing irrigation and phosphorus application on water use and yield of spring wheat under semi-arid conditions', *Agriculture Water Management*, **49**, 173–83.

Li, F.M., P. Wang, J. Wang and J.Z. Xu (2004a), 'Effects of irrigation before sowing and plastic film mulching on yield and water uptake of spring wheat in semiarid Loess Plateau of China', *Agricultural Water Management*, **67**, 77–88.

Li, X.Y. and J.D. Gong (2002), 'Effects of different ridge:furrow ratios and supplemental irrigation on crop production in ridge and furrow harvesting system with mulches', *Agricultural Water Management*, **54**, 243–54.
Li, X.Y., J.D. Gong, Q.Z. Gao and F.R. Li (2001b), 'Incorporation of ridge and furrow method of rainfall harvesting with mulching for crop production under semiarid conditions', *Agricultural Water Management*, **50**, 173–83.
Li, Z.Z., W.D. Li and W.L. Li (2004b), 'Dry-period irrigation and fertilizer application affect water use and yield of spring wheat in semi-arid regions', *Agricultural Water Management*, **65** (2), 133–43.
Lin, G.C.S. and S.P.S. Ho (2003), 'China's land resources and land-use change: insights from the 1996 land survey', *Land Use Policy*, **20**, 87–107.
Lin, J.Y. (1992), 'Rural reforms and agricultural growth in China', *American Economic Review*, **82**, 34–51.
Lomborg, B. (2001), *The Skeptical Environmentalist: Measuring the Real State of the World*, Cambridge: Cambridge University Press.
Mao, W. and W.W. Koo (1997), 'Productivity growth, technological progress, and efficiency change in Chinese agriculture after rural economic reforms: a DEA approach', *China Economic Review*, **8** (2), 157–74.
McMillan, J., J. Whalley and L. Zhu (1989), 'The impact of China's economic reforms on agricultural productivity growth', *Journal of Political Economy*, **97** (4), 781–807.
Meeusen, W. and J. van den Broeck (1977), 'Efficiency estimation from Cobb-Douglas production function with composed error', *International Economic Review*, **18**, June, 435–44.
National Bureau of Statistics (NBS) (2000, 2001, 2002, 2003), *China Statistical Yearbook*, Beijing: China Statistical Publishing House.
Qadir, M., T.M. Boers, S. Schubert, A. Ghafoor and G. Murtaza (2003), 'Agricultural water management in water-starved countries: challenges and opportunities', *Agricultural Water Management*, **62** (3), 165–85.
Reinhard, S., C.A.K. Lovell and G. Thijssen (1999), 'Econometric estimation of technical and environmental efficiency: an application to Dutch dairy farms', *American Journal of Agricultural Economics*, **81**, February, 44–60.
Wang, H., L. Zhang, W.R. Dawes and C. Liu (2000), 'Improving water use efficiency of irrigated corps in the North China Plain – measurements and modeling', *Agricultural Water Management*, **48**, 151–67.
Wang, J., E.J. Wailes and G.L. Cramer (1996), 'A shadow-price frontier measurement of profit efficiency in Chinese agriculture', *American Journal of Agricultural Economics*, **78**, 146–56.
Water Resources Committee, Ministry of Water Resources of China (1999, 2000, 2001, 2002), *China Water Resources Bulletin*, Ministry of Water Resources of China.
Wu, Y. (1995), 'Productivity growth, technological progress, and technical efficiency change in China: a three-sector analysis', *Journal of Comparative Economics*, **21**, 207–29.
Yang, D., C. Li, H. Hu, Z. Lei, S. Yang, T. Kusuda, T. Koike and K. Musiake (2004), 'Analysis of water resources variability in the Yellow River of China during the last half century using historical data', *Water Resources Research*, **40**, 1–12.
Yellow River Water Resources Committee (1998), *Water Resource Bulletin of the Yellow River*.

Zhang, B. and A.C. Carter (1997), 'Reforms, the weather, and productivity growth in China's grain sector', *American Journal of Agricultural Economics*, **79**, 1266–77.

Zhang, X. and S. Fan (2001), 'Estimating crop-specific production technologies in Chinese agriculture: a generalized maximum entropy approach', *American Journal of Agricultural Economics*, **83** (2), 378–88.

Zhang, Y., K. Eloise, Q. Yu, C. Liu, Y. Shen and Z.H. Sun (2003), 'Effect of soil water deficit on evapotranspiration, crop yield, and water use efficiency in the North China Plain', *Agricultural Water Management*, **64** (2), 107–22.

APPENDIX 8A

Table 8A.1   Estimated technical and water efficiency by province

Region	Province	Technical efficiency			Water efficiency		
		Mean	Min.	Max.	Mean	Min.	Max.
Northeast	Heilongjiang	0.69	0.66	0.74	0.35	0.29	0.42
	Jilin	0.82	0.69	0.92	0.58	0.34	0.79
	Liaoning	0.89	0.86	0.92	0.72	0.64	0.78
Yellow River	Beijing	0.88	0.86	0.91	0.69	0.65	0.76
	Hebei	0.70	0.69	0.72	0.36	0.34	0.38
	Henan	0.89	0.88	0.90	0.71	0.70	0.74
	Shaanxi	0.80	0.80	0.81	0.53	0.52	0.54
	Shandong	0.86	0.85	0.86	0.64	0.62	0.65
	Shanxi	0.65	0.59	0.68	0.29	0.22	0.32
	Tianjin	0.90	0.88	0.93	0.74	0.68	0.81
Changjiang	Anhui	0.76	0.73	0.78	0.44	0.40	0.48
	Hubei	0.79	0.76	0.83	0.51	0.45	0.57
	Hunan	0.69	0.68	0.70	0.35	0.33	0.36
	Jiangsu	0.81	0.80	0.83	0.55	0.53	0.59
	Jiangxi	0.79	0.77	0.83	0.51	0.46	0.57
	Shanghai	0.93	0.90	0.96	0.82	0.74	0.90
	Zhejiang	0.84	0.83	0.85	0.60	0.58	0.62
South Coast	Fujian	0.77	0.75	0.78	0.47	0.44	0.49
	Guangdong	0.75	0.73	0.78	0.43	0.40	0.48
	Guangxi	0.55	0.52	0.59	0.18	0.15	0.22
	Hainan	0.94	0.93	0.95	0.83	0.80	0.87
Southwest	Guizhou	0.85	0.82	0.89	0.63	0.56	0.71
	Sichuan	0.89	0.87	0.91	0.71	0.68	0.75
	Yunnan	0.73	0.71	0.74	0.39	0.37	0.42
Northwest	Gansu	0.91	0.88	0.93	0.75	0.69	0.80
	Inner Mongolia	0.87	0.85	0.90	0.67	0.62	0.74
	Ningxia	0.42	0.39	0.44	0.08	0.07	0.09
	Qinghai	0.68	0.63	0.73	0.33	0.26	0.40
	Tibet	0.92	0.91	0.94	0.79	0.75	0.83
	Xinjiang	0.82	0.80	0.85	0.56	0.51	0.63
	Mean	0.79	0.39	0.96	0.54	0.07	0.90

9.   Iron and steel industry

1   INTRODUCTION

The expansion of economic activities in China has led to a rapid increase in consumption of natural resources, resulting in limitations of resources not only domestically but also internationally. In order to alleviate the pressure, especially in energy markets, the government has set a numerical target of 20 percent reduction of energy consumption per GDP during the period of the eleventh five year plan. In the literature, changes in energy efficiencies, which are measured as the input of energy per unit of production output, have been widely analyzed (for example, Feng, 1994; Sinton and Fridley, 2000; Fisher-Vanden et al., 2004; Wu et al., 2005, 2006).

Unlike primary energy resources such as coal, crude oil and natural gas as global commodities, water is a local commodity which is subject to domestic policies. In China, particularly in the northern part, people and industries are suffering from water scarcity due to decreasing precipitation and rapid increase in water consumption (World Bank, 2008). Therefore, efficiency improvement in water usage is another important policy agenda for resource management. In this context, energy and water shortage appears to pose the most urgent environmental risk to China's continued high growth (Woo, 2007). Since government treats energy and water policies differently, the past achievements in efficiency improvements might not be the same when comparing the two.

Energy and water resource efficiency improvement in manufacturing production has emerged as a formidable challenge to improve industry productivity. When compared with other industries, the iron and steel industry requires a relatively large amount of input from both energy and water resources. Therefore the conservation and more efficient usage of these resources are serious issues. The achievements of the iron and steel industry toward increased energy and water efficiency levels during rapid economic development periods may provide important clues to further develop strategic responses to energy and water issues for the entire industrial sector. China became the world's largest crude steel producer in 1996, even though it was only the fifth largest in 1980. The 123 million tons of steel produced in China in 1999, was more than three times the amount produced in 1980, with an average annual growth rate of 6.5

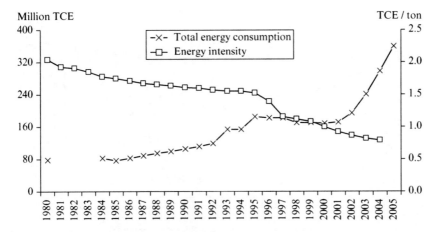

Source: *China Industrial Water Conservation Report* (2004).

Figure 9.1   Energy consumption of the iron and steel sector

percent. Among industrial sectors, the iron and steel industry was the second-largest user of fresh water, accounting for 16 percent of total fresh water consumption of all industrial sectors in 2004 (*China Environmental Yearbook*, 2005). In addition, the water pollution intensity of the iron and steel industry is also higher than others. In this context, it is worth examining the extent to which the modernization of the iron and steel industry has affected the efficiency of resource utilization and pollution management.

The principal focus of this chapter is to measure productivity changes in the Chinese iron and steel industry and analyze how energy and water usage and the associated pollution is hindering productivity during the time when technological modernization occurred. Several studies of energy efficiency exist in the iron and steel sector. However, they exclusively analyze the energy resources (see Kaneko et al., 2006). As previously described, iron and steel processing also requires a large amount of fresh water resources. Therefore, we evaluate the productivity considering the efficient use of not only energy but also water resources.

Here, it is clearly evident that the physical efficiencies of energy and water, which are defined as energy and water inputs per output, had clearly been improved from 1990 to 1999 (see Figures 9.1 and 9.2). However, such physical measurement of efficiency does not fully describe the economic dimensions of productivity such as capital and labor productivities, which are derived from production theories in economics. We apply a nonparametric production frontier approach to firm-level data in order to measure

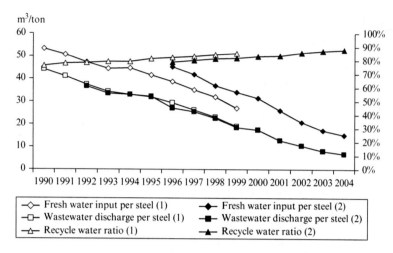

Sources: (1) *China Industrial Water Conservation Report* (2004); (2) *China Environmental Yearbook* (1992–2005).

Figure 9.2   Industrial water use of the iron and steel sector

changes in productivity in the iron and steel industry for the period between 1990 and 1999 and will consider environmental and resource productivity. In order to differentiate the concept of environmental and resource efficiency improvements without hampering economic productivity from the physical environmental and resource efficiency, we hereafter consider the former concept as environmentally sensitive productivity improvement.

The production frontier approach is a set of nonparametric mathematical programming techniques for estimating the relative efficiency of production units, and for identifying best-practice frontiers (see, for example, Färe et al., 1994; Färe and Grosskopf, 2000). As one of those methods, data envelopment analysis (DEA) is a particularly useful tool when assumptions of technological efficiency of every firm in all time periods might be suspect. We also estimate the potential improvements fostered by enhancing energy efficiency, water efficiency and pollution management in the iron and steel sector to better understand the nature of technological advances and their contributions to productivity in our application.

The chapter is structured as follows. Section 2 reviews the iron and steel industry in China and provides a literature review of productivity analysis. Section 3 presents the research method and data description. Section 4 discusses the results. The final section presents further discussion and provides some concluding remarks.

2 BACKGROUND

Iron and Steel Industry

Iron and steel in China had been produced by inefficient facilities and the industry lagged behind developed countries during the 1980s (Wu, 2000). Part of the reason was that there was little technology transfer from developed countries until 1980 due to internal and external political factors. As a result, China was only able to introduce aging technologies and equipment from the former Soviet Union and Eastern European countries. China's iron and steel industry was able to modernize eventually due to economic reforms and liberalization policies.

Around that time, the competitiveness of the country's iron and steel industry was largely influenced by the speed with which they replaced open-hearth furnaces with converter furnaces. Converter furnaces are more energy efficient. By 1980, when Japan ceased production by open-hearth furnaces, 35 percent of production in China was still provided by such furnaces. By the late 1990s, China was in the midst of a major shift from open-hearth to converter furnaces, and production by the former finally ended in 2003 (see Figure 9.3). There were two reasons why China took so long to phase out the open-hearth furnaces. First, significant amounts of monetary investment is required to adopt the technology. Second, the iron and steel industry was running at full capacity in order to meet the rapidly growing demand, making it impossible to quickly phase out production by open-hearth furnaces. At that time, they still accounted for about 30 percent of total iron and steel production.

In addition, casting processes also play an important role in improving energy resource efficiency. The continuous casting ratio increased rapidly during the 1990s, rising from 20 percent in 1990 to almost 90 percent in 1999 (see Figure 9.4). The adaptation of modern production processes led to improvements in productivity as well as energy efficiency. Therefore, energy consumption per unit of crude steel production (that is, energy intensity) improved when open-hearth furnaces were phased out and the continuous casting method came into common use during the 1990s (see Figure 9.4).

Meanwhile, it is important to note that the iron and steel industry also increased its water recycling ratio during the 1990s. The industry utilizes a relatively large amount of industrial water compared to other industries, and therefore, the conservation and efficient use of water resources is a serious issue. It is important to note that China, particularly in the northern areas, is faced with serious constraints on its water resources. Furthermore, increases in water use and wastewater discharge with high

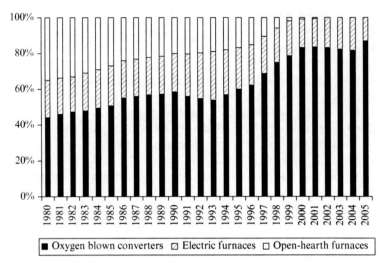

Source: International Iron and Steel Institute (2005a).

Figure 9.3   Share of steel production by operation method

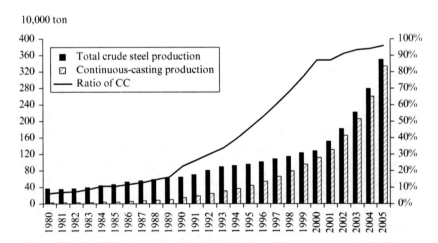

Source: International Iron and Steel Institute (2005b).

Figure 9.4   Crude steel production and continuous casting ratios

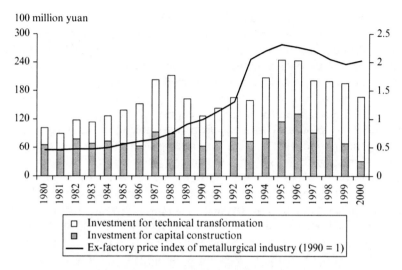

100 million yuan

Figure 9.5 Ex-factory price index and investment

pollutant concentrations threaten to impose further constraints on usable water resources. Thus, water conservation in the industry needs to be treated as an important policy issue.

Three major factors brought improvements in water-utilization efficiency in the iron and steel sector (CIWCR, 2004). First, technological improvements in blast furnaces allowed a reduction in the usage of water resources. Second, the introduction of two new dry methods for removing furnace dust required less water than conventional methods and facilitated water conservation. The third factor was the simplification of production processes by applying electric arc furnaces and using the continuous casting method. These improvements led to a reduction in the amount of water required, and additionally, water recycling rates increased due to further improvements in the quality of wastewater. The water recycling ratio of the iron and steel industry rose from only 57 percent in 1980 to 75 percent in 1990, and later, to 85 percent in 1999 (see Figure 9.2). From 1990 to 1999, the volume of fresh water inputs and industrial wastewater per ton of crude steel dropped by more than half.

The price of steel products was regulated until 1993, when the price was deregulated. This policy change affected the business performance of the iron and steel industry. Figure 9.5 shows that the price of steel increased rapidly after price liberalization. In the case of wire rod, the price was 1,600 yuan per ton in February 1992 before the policy change. Immediately after the change in April 1992, the price was raised to 1,750 yuan per ton. Wire rod reached 3,500 yuan per ton in December 1992, showing that the price more than doubled within a year. Furthermore, although the price of steel continued to increase during 1993, it started declining in late 1993 and the price again returned to 2,000 yuan per ton in December 1993 (Ministry of Metallurgical Industry, *Yearbook of the Iron and Steel Industry of China*, 1994, 1995). Due to this price hike, the firms made large profits, but the change in the sales system of steel products was another reason why firms were able to obtain larger profits during that period. In a conventional sales system called a 'contract management responsibility system', the enterprise was permitted to sell steel products only to customers selected by local governments (Sugimoto, 1993; Ye, 2000), but after price liberalization, many firms began dealing directly in the market. Year by year, this new sales system gained popularity throughout the country. Therefore, the ratio of the steel product sales in direct dealings in the market rose from 27 percent in 1988 to 91.8 percent in 1995 (Ministry of Metallurgical Industry, *Yearbook of the Iron and Steel Industry of China*, 1989, 1996).

The iron and steel firms have increased their profits enormously due to the rise in price and the change in the sales system. As a result, steel firms achieved high returns on sales. This made a significant impact on the technological advancement of iron and steel production. The enlarged profits allowed firms to invest in the introduction of new technologies such as continuous casting equipment, basic oxygen furnaces, and building new manufacturing factories. Furthermore, the demand for high valued-added steel products like seamless pipe and thin steel plate have also increased due to the economic development of the country and export expansion (Figure 9.6), which required advanced technologies (Sugimoto, 1993). This demand further enhanced the acceleration of investments into the advancement of other production technologies. Figure 9.5 shows the coincidence of capital construction and technical advancement after 1993.

Productivity Measurement

Many productivity efficiency evaluation techniques are based on the frontier efficiency originally proposed by Farrell (1957). The idea is to evaluate inefficiency by specifying the production frontier function with the best practical performing samples and measuring the distance of inefficient samples from the frontier. The empirical specification methods of frontier efficiency can be widely divided into two types, namely parametric or nonparametric. The first method is typically represented by stochastic frontier analysis (SFA) developed by Aigner and Chu (1968)

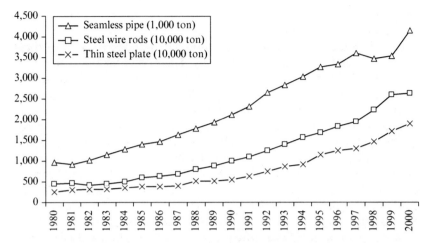

Figure 9.6   Amount of advanced technological steel production

where the production frontier function such as the Cobb–Douglas function and translog function is presumed. The latter method is represented by DEA, developed by Charnes et al. (1978), where nonparametric linear programming techniques are applied. There are already several empirical productivity studies on the Chinese iron and steel industry with either SFA or DEA, or both.

Wu (1995) measured the productivity efficiency of China's 61 iron and steel companies using SFA from 1984 to 1992. Data variables are value added, fixed capital and number of workers. The production function was assumed to fit the Cobb–Douglas function. Wu found that productivity efficiency can be increased by more than 7.0 percent if inefficient performing firms were shut down and their resources transferred to efficient firms. In Wu's study, resources and environmental pollution are not factored into efficiency. Movshuk (2004) measured the productivity of China's state-owned iron and steel firms using SFA applying the firm level data: value added, fixed capital, number of workers and vintage years. They found that productivity increased by 6.4 percent per year on average using the translog function and by 4.4 percent using the Cobb–Douglas function between 1988 and 2000. However, energy consumption for crude steel production is not considered in this model. In contrast, Ma et al. (2002) analyzed the productivity for iron and steel firms applying DEA between 1987 and 1997. They used the variables of total production value, pig iron production, crude steel production, amount of steel products, number of workers, fixed assets, liquid assets, energy consumption and years since establishment. They found that the productivity improved by 3 percent per year. However, no previous studies analyze the effects of water use and pollution in the industry.

Although there are several articles using DEA and SFA, most of them do not consider environmental efficiency. The reason for this is that they encounter difficulties when dealing with undesirable output. To address this issue, Färe et al. (1989) developed the directional distance function (DDF) which can consistently identify undesirable output as an extension of nonparametric approaches. There is a growing literature of methodologies for measuring productivity efficiency including environmental pollution (Färe et al., 1989; Yaisawarng and Klein, 1994; Coggins and Swinton, 1996; Chung et al., 1997; Boyd and McClelland, 1999; Hailu and Veeman, 2000; Zofio and Prieto, 2001; Boyd et al., 2002; Domazlicky and Weber, 2004; Picazo-Tadeo et al., 2005; Managi et al., 2005; Piot-Lepetit and Moing, 2007; Murty et al., 2007). However, few studies employ the DDF to evaluate environmentally sensitive productivity for the iron and steel industry. In the DDF, pollutants are treated as weak disposable outputs where weak disposability involves a constraint on the production possibilities of the producers, that is, producers cannot reduce undesirable output levels without incurring additional costs.

In order to analyze changes in efficiency over time, the aggregated indices such as the Malmquist index and the Luenberger productivity index have been developed (Luenberger, 1992; Chambers et al., 1998). They are derived from the efficiency scores from production frontier models. Those productivity indices can be regarded as a measure of total factor productivity (TFP), when it comes from economic production frontier models. TFP includes all categories of productivity change and can be broken down further in order to provide a better understanding of the relative importance of various components, including 'technical change' and 'efficiency change' (Färe et al., 1994). Technical change measures shifts in the production frontier – so-called 'frontier-shift'; 'efficiency change' measures changes in the position of a production unit relative to the frontier – so-called 'catching up'.

3   METHODS AND DATA

This study measures environmentally sensitive productivity changes in the iron and steel industry. We apply the DDF (Chung et al., 1997) to estimate the Luenberger productivity index (LPI) (Chambers et al., 1998) as a TFP measure. The LPI is considered to be more general than the widely used Malmquist index (Luenberger, 1992; Chambers et al., 1998). The change in the LPI can be further broken down into technical change and efficiency change.

Directional Distance Function (DDF)

Let $x \in \Re_+^L$, $b \in \Re_+^R$, $y \in \Re_+^M$ be vectors of inputs, environmental output (or undesirable output) and market outputs (or desirable output), respectively, and then define the production technology as:

$$P(x) = [(x, y, b): x \text{ can produce } (y, b)] \qquad (9.1)$$

We assume that the good and bad outputs are null-joint; a company cannot produce desirable output without producing undesirable outputs (Shephard and Färe, 1974);

$$(y, b) \in P(x); b = 0 \Rightarrow y = 0. \qquad (9.2)$$

We also assume weak disposability. Weak disposability implies that the pollutant should not be considered to be freely disposable (Färe et al., 1989):

$$(y, b) \in P(x) \text{ and } 0 \le \beta \le 1 \Rightarrow (\beta y, \beta b) \in P(x) \qquad (9.3)$$

Under the null-joint hypothesis and weak disposability, this directional distance function can be computed for firm k solving the following optimization problem:

$$\vec{D}(x, y, b; g_x, g_y, g_b) = \text{Maximize } \beta_k$$

$$\text{s.t.} \sum_{i=1}^{N} \lambda_i x_i \le x_k - \beta_k g_x$$

$$\sum_{i=1}^{N} \lambda_i y_i \ge y_m + \beta_k g_y$$

$$\sum_{i=1}^{N} \lambda_i b_r = b_r - \beta_k g_b$$

$$\lambda_i \ge 0 \ (i = 1, 2, \cdots, N), \qquad (9.4)$$

where x is the input factor in an $L \times N$ input factor matrix, and y is the desirable output in an $M \times N$ desirable output factor matrix, and b is the undesirable output factor in an $R \times N$ undesirable output matrix. In addition, g_x is the directional vector of the input factor, g_y is the directional vector of desirable output factors and g_b is the directional vector of undesirable output factors. β^k is the inefficiency score of the kth firm, and λ_i is the variable weight for the ith firm in estimating β^k. In order to estimate the inefficiency score of all firms, the model must be independently applied N times for each firm.

One objective of this study is to clarify the extent to which the iron and steel industry (a resource-consuming industry) has advanced given the same input levels, as a result of the modernization of facilities. It is therefore desirable to apply a method paying particular attention to the output side of efficiency evaluations. Therefore, we substitute $g_x = 0$ into the directional vector (that is, setting as zero for the total of the inefficiency scores of variables relating to production). In addition, we set: $g_y = y_k$ and $g_b = b_k$. That is, we estimate the following model:

$$\vec{D}(x, y, b: 0, y_k, b_k) = \text{Maximize } \beta_k$$

$$\text{s.t.} \sum_{i=1}^{N} \lambda_i x_i \leq x_k$$

$$\sum_{i=1}^{N} \lambda_i y_i \geq (1 + \beta_k) \times y_k$$

$$\sum_{i=1}^{N} \lambda_i b_i = (1 - \beta_k) \times b_k$$

$$\lambda_i \geq 0 \ (i = 1, 2, \ldots, N), \tag{9.5}$$

where the inefficiency score implies the potential percentage by which each firm can increase desirable output and reduce undesirable output simultaneously without changing input levels, based on the frontier curve. By multiplying these analytical results by the data for each firm, it is possible to calculate the amount of inefficiency production of both desirable and undesirable output. The inefficient production of desirable output based on the frontier line is defined by $\vec{D}(x_i, y_i, b_i; 0, y_i, b_i) \times y_i$ and the inefficient production of undesirable output based on the frontier line is defined by $\vec{D}(x_i, y_i, b_i; 0, y_i, b_i) \times b_i$.

Luenberger Productivity Index

The LPI is computed using the results of the DDF model and derived as follows (Luenberger, 1992; Chambers et al., 1998):

$$LPI_t^{t+1} = TECHCH_t^{t+1} + EFFCH_t^{t+1} \tag{9.6}$$

$$TECHCH_t^{t+1} = [\vec{D}^{t+1}(x_t, y_t, b_t) + \vec{D}^{t+1}(x_{t+1}, y_{t+1}, b_{t+1})$$
$$- \vec{D}^{t}(x_t, y_t, b_t) - \vec{D}^{t}(x_{t+1}, y_{t+1}, b_{t+1})]/2 \tag{9.7}$$

$$EFFCH_t^{t+1} = \vec{D}^{t}(x_t, y_t, b_t) - \vec{D}^{t+1}(x_{t+1}, y_{t+1}, b_{t+1}), \tag{9.8}$$

Table 9.1   Size breakdown of firms in China's iron and steel industry

Total crude steel production (million tons)	Number of iron and steel firms	
	Overall China	Samples in this study
In 1990:		
0.50 to 0.99	12	9
1.00 to 4.99	16	12
5.00 or greater	0	0
Total number of firms	1,589	27
In 2000:		
0.50 to 0.99	13	0
1.00 to 4.99	37	23
5.00 or greater	4	4
Total number of firms	2,997	27

Source: Ministry of Metallurgical Industry, *Yearbook of the Iron and Steel Industry of China* (2003).

where x_t represents input for year t, x_{t+1} is input for year $t + 1$, y_t is desirable output for year t, and y_{t+1} is desirable output for year $t + 1$. b_t is undesirable output for year t, and b_{t+1} is undesirable output for year $t + 1$. $\overrightarrow{D}^t(x_t, y_t, b_t)$ is the inefficiency score of year t based on the frontier curve in year t. Similarly, $\overrightarrow{D}^{t+1}(x_t, y_t, b_t)$ is the inefficiency of year $t + 1$ based on the frontier curve in year $t + 1$.

The LPI score indicates the productivity change comparing benchmark year. The LPI includes all categories of productivity change, which can be broken down into two components including technical change (*TECHCH* indicator) and efficiency change (*EFFCH* indicator). *TECHCH* indicator measures shifts in the production frontier while *EFFCH* indicator measures changes in the position of a production unit relative to the so-called 'catching up' frontier.

Data

Most of our dataset comes from the *China Iron and Steel Industry Fifty-Year Summary* (CISIFS: Ministry of Metallurgical Industry, 2003) and the CIWCR (2004). The 27 firms' data cover the 10 years from 1990 to 1999. The selected firms account for 68 percent of the production of all iron and steel firms in China, based on fiscal year 2000 crude steel production, and most of them are large corporations in the industry (see Table 9.1). The fresh water inputs and industrial wastewater discharge of these 27 firms accounted for about 65 percent of the entire iron and steel

Table 9.2   Selected 27 companies' share of entire steel industry (%)

	1990	1991	1992	1993	1994	1995	1996	1997	1998	1999
Energy	52.1	51.8	54.0	53.8	54.8	55.8	56.6	56.6	58.6	57.0
CO_2	50.9	51.2	52.9	52.6	53.8	54.9	56.3	55.5	57.6	56.5
Fresh water	63.8	66.1	67.0	65.5	66.4	66.7	67.2	68.1	65.9	65.5
Wastewater	56.3	62.7	63.3	62.4	63.4	63.7	63.5	65.7	63.2	63.0
Crude steel	65.7	66.5	63.9	63.6	65.4	66.2	65.7	65.7	67.0	66.1
Value added	56.4	60.3	60.8	57.5	61.0	47.9	64.4	72.3	67.4	65.3
Salary of labor	50.9	51.7	46.1	58.0	61.1	51.3	58.0	50.3	57.5	60.1
Capital stock	63.8	65.9	68.3	68.2	70.1	66.0	64.6	65.5	67.4	69.4

Sources: *China Industrial Water Conservation Report* (2004) and Ministry of Metallurgical Industry (2003), *China Iron and Steel Industry Fifty-Year Summary* (Vols 1 and 2).

industry in 1999, and 48 percent of total energy consumption (see Table 9.2).

Production value (in real value added) and crude steel production are used as the market output data of productivity estimation; fixed capital stock and gross wages are used as input data of productivity estimation; CO_2 emissions and industrial wastewater are used for undesirable output data; and energy consumption and fresh water usage are employed as inputs data of productivity estimation. Energy consumption is calculated from inputs of electricity, coal, coke, oil and natural gas (CISIFS) and net calorific value coefficient (IPCC, 2006). We calculated energy consumption data considering coke making efficiency (CISIFS) and power generation efficiency (China Energy Statistical Yearbook). The CO_2 emission data is calculated from each energy consumption data and the IPCC CO_2 coefficient (IPCC, 2006). Fixed capital stocks, gross wages and value added are deflated to fiscal year 1990 levels using the ex-price indicator for the iron and steel industry (*China Statistical Yearbook*, 2000). We estimate for the four models based on the combinations of input and output data as shown in Table 9.3.

Application of Models

This study conducts an empirical analysis using four DDF models: the *market model* evaluates pure market productivity; the *water model* evaluates water resource sensitive productivity; the *energy model* evaluates energy resource sensitive productivity; and the *joint model* evaluates water and energy sensitive productivity. The market model uses two economic input factors, capital (that is, current value of fixed capital stock) and

Table 9.3   Combinations of data used in each model

		Water model	Energy model	Joint model	Market model
Desirable output	Crude steel	X	X	X	X
	Value added	X	X	X	X
Undesirable output	Wastewater	X	–	X	–
	CO_2	–	X	X	–
Input	Labor	X	X	X	X
	Capital stock	X	X	X	X
	Fresh water	X	–	X	–
	Energy	–	X	X	–

labor (that is, gross wages) and two economic output factors, the economic value of output (value added) and the amount of physical output (crude steel production). The inefficiency scores obtained through this combination of variables are interpreted as corporate economic efficiency. Water and energy resource use efficiency are ignored in the market model. The water model uses fresh-water input and wastewater discharge in addition to the variables used in the market model. The inefficiency scores obtained through this combination of data are interpreted as corporate water resource sensitive productivity. Energy resource use efficiency is ignored in the water model. The energy model uses the amount of energy consumption and CO_2 emissions in addition to the variables used in the market model. The inefficiency scores obtained through this combination of data are interpreted as corporate energy resource sensitive productivity. Water resource use efficiency is ignored in the energy model. The joint model uses the amount of energy consumption, CO_2 emissions, fresh water input, and wastewater discharge as environmental factors in addition to the variables used in the market model. The inefficiency scores obtained through this combination are interpreted as water and energy sensitive productivity. Water and energy resource use efficiency are considered in the joint model.

Many previous studies analyze the simple ratio of energy efficiency of the iron and steel industry as the total energy consumption per crude steel production (for example, Ross and Feng, 1991; Worrel et al., 1997; Kim and Worrell, 2002; Price et al., 2002). However, this approach involves a number of problems including consideration of input factors and additional dimensions of output. During the 1990s, as China's industry strove to improve energy efficiency in crude steel production, it also put much effort into the processing of steel products, and worked to expand the

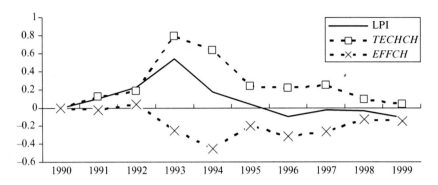

Figure 9.7   Productivity change in the market model

production of high value-added products such as steel plates and steel pipes. The manufacture of such products necessitates the input of additional energy to generate the same output level. Therefore, firms that took the strategy of developing and manufacturing high value-added products during the 1990s may show lower efficiency if efficiency is evaluated as the ratio of total energy consumption to crude steel production. Therefore, the development of new and high value-added products might not reduce energy efficiency, but in fact they may actually increase it. For this reason, we simultaneously used both economic and material outputs as indicators of output for each of the four models.

4   RESULTS

Productivity Analysis

Figures 9.7–9.10 show the productivity of each model. We set the base year as 1990 and the indicator in 1990 equal to zero. The LPI of all models increases rapidly from 1992 to 1993, affected by the price liberalization policy of 1992. Almost all iron and steel firms experienced record profits in 1993 due to the price hikes. However, because the large investments in capital accumulation caused declining capital productivity, the LPI declined after 1993 until 1996.

Because the LPI in the market model is close to zero in 1999, one might say that market productivity changed little compared to 1990. On the other hand, the LPI in the water, energy and joint models had shifted in the same way as the market model from 1990 to 1996. But after 1996, the LPI increased gradually. One could interpret this as advances in water use technologies for

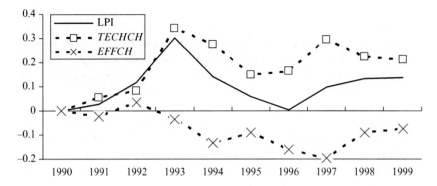

Figure 9.8   Productivity change in the water model

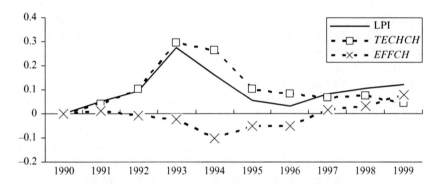

Figure 9.9   Productivity change in the energy model

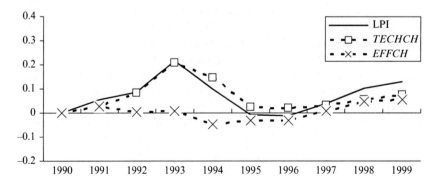

Figure 9.10   Productivity change in the joint model

the entire sample. Furthermore, the average LPI score in the water, energy and joint models was improved to 0.138, 0.121 and 0.129, respectively, from 1990 to 2000. This shows that the productivity considering only water efficiency, only energy efficiency and both of them simultaneously improved in the 1990s. From the joint model result, we can say that water and energy efficiency can be improved similarly in iron and steel firms.

Next, by examining the LPI, and the *TECHCH* and *EFFCH* indicators, we consider how the relationship changed between the efficient firm group performing production frontier analysis and the inefficient firm group among the 27 firms over time. The *TECHCH* indicator was high in 1993 and 1994, while the *EFFCH* indicator was negative in 1993 and 1994. From these results, we can say that there was a significant inefficiency gap between the inefficient group and firms on the frontier line in 1993 and 1994 compared to the year 1990. However, from 1995 to 1999 the efficiency gap was decreasing year by year, in particular, the energy and joint models. The *EFFCH* indicator in the energy and joint models rose significantly after 1994, indicating that during this period inefficient firms reduced the efficiency gap between themselves and the more efficient firms. The most efficient company began continuous casting and discontinued open-hearth furnaces in 1994. But many small and inefficient companies started these equipment improvements after 1994 (CISIFS). For that reason, the energy efficiency gap decreased after 1994.

The *TECHCH* indicator in the market model declined after 1997, because large companies changed their strategy from low value-added products to high which required more technology and larger investments. Therefore, capital productivity was temporarily worse among large companies. This was one reason why the *TECHCH* indicator declined in the market model after 1997. The above examples show the major changes that occurred in China's production facilities during the 1990s. Two factors deserve mention as drivers of modernization: the rising demand for steel products, and the liberalization of steel prices. Rapid economic growth continued through the 1990s, and in addition to the rise in exports of industrial products, China's share of electronic equipment and other high-technology products in global exports also grew. In addition, through cross-industry linkages, industrialization also induced capital investments by the iron and steel industry, an important supplier of the raw materials needed by the economy. Furthermore, the government instituted steel price liberalization in 1992, leading to rapid increases in steel prices between 1992 and 1994. These rapid price increases brought consistently record-setting profits for iron and steel firms, which are believed to have made possible the large-scale investments that resulted in more up-to-date production facilities (see Ye, 2000).

We verify the relationship between the continuous-casting ratio as a modernization indicator and the LPI of each model by using a Spearman correlation analysis. The results show the significantly positive relationship between the continuous-casting ratio and the energy, water and joint models' LPI. Therefore we can conclude that technological modernization brought positive results for improvements in environmentally sensitive productivity including energy and water resource efficiency and environmental efficiency with regard to CO_2 emissions and wastewater.

Evaluation of Water and Energy Resource Efficiency

One objective of this study is to measure the technological progress in water and energy resource utilization by the iron and steel industry. The following analytical results are obtained. The results of inefficiency production and the potential ratio in iron and steel firms each year are shown in Table 9.4. 'Value' indicates value added, 'steel' indicates crude steel production, 'waste' indicates industrial wastewater and 'CO_2' indicates CO_2 emissions.

From Table 9.4, the total inefficient production of 27 firms in the water model in 1999 was 7.6 billion yuan for value added, 21 million tons of crude steel production and 530 million tons of industrial waste water discharge. These account for 24, 26, and 17 percent, respectively of the entire iron and steel industry. Meanwhile, the degree of inefficiency production in the energy model in 1999 was 1.9 billion yuan for value added, 5.8 million tons of crude steel production and 22.7 million tons of CO_2 discharge, which account for 6, 7 and 9 percent, respectively, of the entire iron and steel industry.

To compare the results of the water and the energy models in Table 9.4, there is a greater gap between firms in terms of water resource sensitive technologies than energy resource sensitive technologies in 1999. The following points could be considered as factors to account for the large gap between the analytical results of the two models. Some of the firms in this study introduced technologies from Japan and West Germany, and some were leading-edge firms that began operation after 1985. Therefore these firms' resource-utilization technologies approached the level of developed countries at the time (Ye, 2000). Meanwhile, because water prices in China were low, other firms did not move forward with capital investment and efforts to improve water-use efficiency, so they made little progress with water-use and wastewater treatment technologies. Thus in 1990, there were large disparities between firms, with some possessing leading-edge water resource sensitive technologies, and some that were inefficient in their use of water. On the other hand, when it comes to energy efficiency, corporate management also has an incentive to reduce costs. Therefore, it may have

Table 9.4 *Total inefficiency production of 27 firms*

Year	Water model			Energy model			Joint model			Market model		
	Value	Steel	Waste	Value	Steel	CO_2	Value	Steel	Waste	CO_2	Value	Steel
1990	18.9	462.1	27.0	16.0	376.3	23.9	11.4	264.2	13.9	12.9	37.4	972.0
1991	19.9	498.6	32.4	14.8	354.8	26.0	6.9	157.1	8.6	7.9	45.2	1,159.7
1992	20.9	453.0	25.0	23.4	541.5	30.6	12.6	287.8	14.8	12.5	55.9	1,246.1
1993	53.2	967.1	51.7	35.4	712.2	39.6	14.3	292.8	15.3	13.1	169.4	3,163.3
1994	69.8	1,411.0	69.1	52.0	1,113.6	55.0	27.4	587.5	25.1	27.4	208.6	4,341.3
1995	52.8	1,326.1	62.9	33.0	878.8	42.5	16.6	491.2	25.8	24.8	126.6	3,427.3
1996	70.9	1,881.1	78.5	33.2	931.2	46.2	15.5	489.2	25.6	27.0	162.6	4,455.8
1997	94.7	2,496.4	64.8	29.0	752.8	40.0	18.4	478.1	12.7	21.4	169.3	4,531.6
1998	75.7	2,015.6	56.1	32.2	806.4	34.6	10.4	302.6	8.8	12.9	155.9	4,100.1
1999	75.9	2,100.8	53.3	18.9	577.6	22.7	11.5	365.6	9.1	9.8	170.1	4,574.2

Note: Unit: steel: 10,000 tons; value added: 100 million yuan; CO_2: million tons of CO_2; waste: 10 million tons.

been the case that many firms aggressively pursued energy-related efforts, with the result that the disparities between firms did not increase very much.

The results of the market model in Table 9.4 show that the extent of inefficient production was approximately 46 million tons of crude steel production tons and 17 billion yuan of value added when environment and resource sensitive productivity is not considered. These accounted for 56.0 and 54.2 percent, respectively, of the entire iron and steel industry. The differences between the results of the market model and the other three models show the restriction impacts of environmental and resource efficiencies on business performance.

5   CONCLUSIONS

This study analyzed the impacts on the environmental performance of firms caused by the rapid modernization of production facilities in the 1990s in China's iron and steel industry. The conclusions are summarized below.

First, because of inefficient production, pressures and opportunities for water efficiency improvements are relatively greater than for that of energy. It should be noted that although simultaneous pursuit of energy and water resource sensitive productivity improvements temporarily hamper the economic productivity improvement, water conservation policies should be promoted more through introducing proper pricing systems.

Second, we find that there are significantly positive relationships between the continuous-casting ratio and LPI score of the energy, water and joint models. Therefore we can conclude that technological modernization brought positive results for improvements in environmentally sensitive productivity including energy and water resource efficiency and environmental efficiency with regard to CO_2 emissions and wastewater. The average LPI score in the water, energy and joint models improved to 0.138, 0.121 and 0.129, respectively, from 1990 to 2000. This shows that the productivity considering only water efficiency, only energy efficiency and both of them simultaneously improved in the 1990s. From the joint model result, we can say that water and energy efficiency can be improved similarly in iron and steel firms. Furthermore, we also clarify the differences between the structure productivity change in the three models. LPI in the water model was the catching-up type, while in the energy and joint models it was the frontier-shift type.

Finally, we found that environmentally sensitive productivity had improved even though market productivity had declined in this study

188   *Chinese economic development and the environment*

period. These results indicate that the capital productivity of the iron and steel sector declined temporarily in the 1990s because of the huge investments for modernization of equipment. This modernization enabled steel companies to save resources and reduce environmental damage. Furthermore, modernization helps them to gain competitiveness in the world market when the resource price goes up. Russia still produces 20 percent of its crude steel production from open-hearth furnaces. In addition, Russia and India achieved a continuous-casting ratio of only 54 and 70 percent, respectively, even though they were the fourth- and fifth-largest steel production countries in 2006. They also forecast that steel production would increase rapidly in the future. For that reason, the modernization of equipment in order to achieve sustainable development should be regarded as a top priority.

REFERENCES

Aignar, D.J. and S.F. Chu (1968), 'On estimating the industry production function', *American Economic Review*, **58**, 826–36.
Boyd, G.A. and J.D. McClelland (1999), 'The impact of environmental constraints on productivity improvement in integrated paper plants', *Journal of Environmental Economics and Management*, **38**, 121–42.
Boyd, G.A., G. Tolley and J. Pang (2002), 'Plant level productivity, efficiency, and environmental performance of the container glass industry', *Environmental and Resource Economics*, **23**, 29–43.
Chambers, R.G., Y.H. Chung and R. Färe (1998), 'Profit, directional distance functions, and Nerlovian efficiency', *Journal of Optimization Theory and Applications*, **98** (2), 351–64.
Charnes, A., C.C. Cooper and E. Rhodes (1978), 'Measuring the efficiency of decision making units', *European Journal of Operational Research*, **2** (6), 429–44.
China Energy Statistical Yearbook (1991–1996, 1997–1999, 2005), Beijing: China Statistical Press.
China Environmental Yearbook (1992–2005) (annual), Beijing: China Statistical Press.
China Industrial Water Conservation Report (CIWCR) (2004), Beijing: China Water Power Press.
China Statistical Yearbook (1986–2006) (annual), Beijing: China Statistical Press.
Chung, Y.H., R. Färe and S. Grosskopf (1997), 'Productivity and undesirable output: a directional distance function approach', *Journal of Environmental Management*, **51**, 229–40.
Coggins, J.S. and J.R. Swinton (1996), 'The price of pollution: a dual approach to valuing SO_2 allowances', *Journal of Environmental Economics and Management*, **30**, 58–72.
Domazlicky, B.R. and W.L. Weber (2004), 'Does environmental protection lead to slower productivity growth in the chemical industry?', *Environmental and Resource Economics*, **28**, 301–24.

Färe, R. and S. Grosskopf (2000), 'Theory and application of directional distance functions', *Journal of Productivity Analysis*, **13**, 93–103.
Färe, R., S. Grosskopf, C.A.K. Lovell and C.A. Pasurka Jr. (1989), 'Multilateral productivity comparisons when some outputs are undesirable: a nonparametric approach', *Review of Economics and Statistics*, **71**, 90–98.
Färe, R., S. Grosskopf, M. Norris and Z. Zhang (1994), 'Productivity growth, technical progress and efficiency change in industrialized countries', *American Economic Review*, **84** (1), 66–83.
Farrell, M.J. (1957), 'The measurement of productive efficiency', *Journal of the Royal Statistical Society*, Series A (General), **120** (3), 253–90.
Feng, L. (1994), 'China's steel industry: its rapid expansion and influence on the international steel industry', *Resource Policy*, **20** (4), 219–34.
Fisher-Vanden, K., G. Jefferson, H. Liu and Q. Tao (2004), 'What is driving China's decline in energy intensity?', *Resource and Energy Economics*, **26** (1), 77–97.
Hailu, A. and T.S. Veeman (2000), 'Environmentally sensitive productivity analysis of the Canadian pulp and paper industry, 1959–1994: an input distance function approach', *Journal of Environmental Economics and Management*, **40**, 251–74.
Intergovernmental Panel on Climate Change (IPCC) (2006), *2006 IPCC Guidelines for National Greenhouse Gas Inventories: Volume 1 General Guidance and Reporting*, IPCC.
International Iron and Steel Institute (2005a), *Steel Statistical Yearbook 2005*, Brussels: International Iron and Steel Institute.
International Iron and Steel Institute (2005b), *World Steel in Figures 2005*, Brussels: International Iron and Steel Institute.
Kaneko, S., A. Yonamine and T.Y. Jung (2006), 'Technology choice and CDM projects in China: case study of a small steel company in Shandong Province', *Energy Policy*, **34** (10), 1139–51.
Kim, Y. and E. Worrell (2002), 'International comparison of CO_2 emission trends in the iron and steel industry', *Energy Policy*, **30**, 827–38.
Luenberger, D.G. (1992), 'Benefit function and duality', *Journal of Mathematical Economics*, **21**, 461–81.
Ma, J., D.G. Evans, R.J. Fuller and D.G. Stewart (2002), 'Technical efficiency and productivity change of China's iron and steel industry', *International Journal of Production Economics*, **76**, 293–312.
Managi, S., J.J. Opaluch, D. Jin and T.A. Grigalunas (2005), 'Environmental regulations and technological change in the offshore oil and gas industry', *Land Economics*, **81** (2), 303–19.
Ministry of Metallurgical Industry (2003), *China Iron and Steel Industry Fifty-Year Summary* (Vols 1 and 2), Beijing: Metallurgical Industry Press.
Ministry of Metallurgical Industry *Yearbook of the Iron and Steel Industry of China* (1989–2003) (annual), Beijing: Metallurgical Industry Press.
Movshuk, O. (2004), 'Restructuring, productivity and technical efficiency in China's iron and steel industry, 1988–2000', *Journal of Asian Economics*, **15**, 135–51.
Murty, M.N., S. Kumar and K. Dhavala (2007), 'Measuring environmental efficiency of industry: a case study of thermal power generation in India', *Environmental and Resource Economics*, **38** (1), 31–50.
Picazo-Tadeo, A.J., E. Reig-Martinez and F. Hernandez-Sancho (2005), 'Directional distance functions and environmental regulation', *Resource and Energy Economics*, **27**, 131–42.
Piot-Lepetit, I. and M.L. Moing (2007), 'Productivity and environmental regulation,

the effect of the Nitrate Directive in the French pig sector', *Environmental and Resource Economics*, **38** (4), 433–46.

Price, L., J. Sinton, E. Worrell, D. Phylipsen, H. Xiulian and L. Ji (2002), 'Energy use and carbon dioxide emissions from steel production in China', *Energy*, **27**, 429–49.

Ross, M. and L. Feng (1991), 'The energe efficiency of the steel industry of China', *Energy*, **16**, 833–48.

Shephard, R.W. and R. Färe (1974), 'The law of diminishing returns', *Journal of Economics*, **34** (1), 69–90.

Sinton, J.E. and D.G. Fridley (2000), 'What goes up: recent trends in China's energy consumption', *Energy Policy*, **28**, 671–87.

Sugimoto, T. (1993), 'The Chinese steel industry', *Resource Policy*, **19** (4), 264–86

Woo, W.T. (2007), 'What are the high-probability challenges to continued high growth in China?', Working Paper, Brookings Institution, Washington, DC.

World Bank (2008), *Water Supply Pricing in China: Economic Efficiency, Environment, and Social Affordability*, Washington, DC: World Bank.

Worrell, E., L. Price, N. Martin, J. Farla and R. Schaeffer (1997), 'Energy intensity in the iron and steel industry: a comparison of physical and economic indicators', *Energy Policy*, **25**, 727–44.

Wu, L., S. Kaneko and S. Matsuoka (2005), 'Driving forces behind the stagnancy of China's energy-related CO_2 emissions from 1996 to 1999: the relative importance of structural change, intensity change and scale change', *Energy Policy*, **33** (3), 319–35.

Wu, L., K. Kaneko and S. Matsuoka (2006), 'Dynamics of energy-related CO_2 emissions in China during 1980 to 2002: the relative importance of energy supply-side and demand-side effects', *Energy Policy*, **34** (18), 3549–72.

Wu, Y. (1995), 'The productive efficiency of Chinese iron and steel firms: a stochastic frontier analysis', *Resource Policy*, **21**, 215–22.

Wu, Y. (2000), 'The Chinese steel industry: recent developments and prospects', *Resource Policy*, **26**, 171–8.

Yaisawarng, S. and J.D. Klein (1994), 'The effects of sulfur dioxide controls on productivity change in the U.S. electric power industry', *Review of Economics and Statistics*, **76**, 47–60.

Ye, G. (2000), *The Growth of the Iron and Steel Industry in China*, Tokyo: Yotsuya Round.

Zofio, J.L. and A.M. Prieto (2001), 'Environmental efficiency and regulatory standards: the case of CO_2 emissions from OECD industries', *Resource and Energy Economics*, **23**, 63–83.

10. Stagnancy of energy-related CO_2 emissions

1 INTRODUCTION

The world's most populous country and largest coal producer and consumer, China contributed 12.9 percent of global CO_2 emissions in the year 2000, making it the world's second-largest emitter of CO_2 (IEA, 2002). Previous studies have suggested that China's energy consumption and CO_2 emissions will continue to rise during the next five decades (for example, Ho et al., 1998; Yang et al., 1998; IPCC, 2000; EIA, 2002). CO_2 emissions increased steadily between 1971 and 1996, but contrary to forecasts, they began to decrease thereafter. Figure 10.1 shows recent estimates by the International Energy Agency (IEA, 2002) and the US Energy Information Administration (EIA, 2002). We also estimated CO_2 emissions based on the China energy balance tables from 1980 to 1999 (NBS, 1990a, 1996a, 2000a) following the methodology suggested by the IPCC 1996 Guideline (IPCC/OECD/IEA, 1997). All the above estimates indicate that China's energy-related CO_2 emissions experienced a declining trend from 1996 to 2000. This raises a series of questions: What happened during this period? How did underlying forces contribute to the changes in CO_2 emissions? Do the changes represent only a temporary fluctuation or a long-term trend?

Since fossil fuel combustion is responsible for three-quarters of anthropogenic CO_2 emissions in China (Streets et al., 2001), changes in energy consumption and production are expected to directly influence CO_2 emissions. As shown in Figure 10.2, the decline in CO_2 emissions is a direct result of the decline in energy consumption and production. This decline occurred despite a persistently high growth rate of the GDP. Energy intensity, defined as total final energy consumption per unit of GDP, has continued to decline during the last two decades. Meanwhile, the income elasticity of energy consumption (defined as the change in total final energy consumption divided by the change in economic growth) remained at a comparatively low level (below one) before the mid-1990s and even became negative after 1996. As Zhang (2003) pointed out, such an achievement has rarely been accomplished in any developing or developed

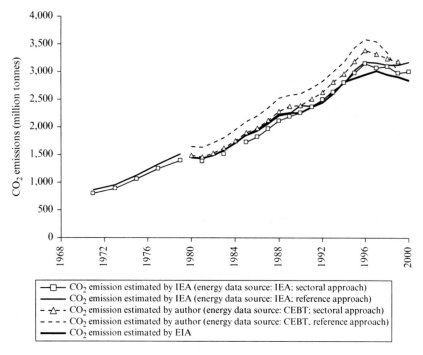

Note: CEBT is the abbreviation for China Energy Balance Table.

Sources: IEA (2002), EIA (2002), Estimation by authors based on the data from NBS (1990a, 1996a, 2000a).

Figure 10.1   *Evolution of energy-related CO_2 emissions in China during
              the last three decades*

country that went through similar growth stages as China. Previous
studies show that the continuous decline in energy intensity from 1980
to the early 1990s can be attributed to the decline in real energy intensity
of industrial sectors (for example, Ang et al., 1998; Sinton et al., 1998;
Fisher-Vanden et al., 2002). Their findings indicate that energy efficiency
improvements in the industrial sector play the most important role in the
evolution of China's energy use; the structural shifts within the manufacturing subsectors or from primary to secondary or tertiary industry play
only a nominal role. Such tendencies do not necessarily support continuity in the long run, however, and they do not definitely result in a sudden
reversal in energy consumption trends (that is, the decline in consumption)
in the late 1990s.

To analyze the paradox of the late 1990s, some research has been

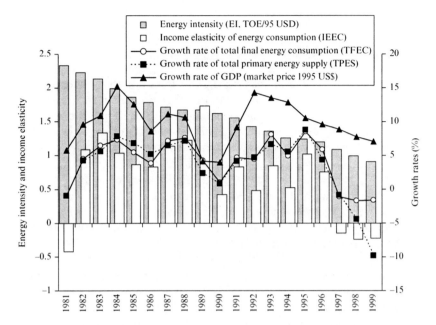

Sources: NBS (1986–1989, 1990a, 1990b, 1991–1994, 1995a, 1996a, 1996b, 1997, 1998a, 1999, 2000a, 2000b).

Figure 10.2   Evolution of energy efficiency in China during the last two decades

carried out either to verify the reliability of the empirical evidence from the estimation side (NRDC, 2001; Sinton, 2001; Streets et al., 2001) or to explore the phenomenon from the policy side (Sinton and Fridley, 2000). The findings from this research show clearly that even though some adjustments have been made to China's energy and economic data, the declining tendency in energy consumption and CO_2 emissions is indisputable. Their conclusions call for further research to explore the underlying driving forces (ibid.). In this chapter, we have explored this phenomenon based on statistics on CO_2 emissions, aggregated from provincial data in China. Attempts have been made to provide a deeper understanding of the driving forces behind the evolution of energy-related CO_2 emissions between 1985 and 1999. A newly proposed three-level factor decomposition method is used to quantify the relative contributions of selected driving forces to the variations in CO_2 emissions.

2   METHODOLOGY AND DATA

Specification on Data Issues

In order to analyze the underlying driving forces of the sudden decline in CO_2 emissions from 1996 to 2000, our first priority in this chapter is to verify the authenticity of this phenomenon by clarifying the accuracy and reliability of the data sources. National-level statistics, such as GDP or coal production in the late 1990s, have been regarded with caution by many scholars and policy analysts in the past. Considering the widespread uncertainty about the quality of China's national energy statistics in the late 1990s (Sinton, 2001), this research sets aside the national-level statistics and traces the national CO_2 emissions back to each province and to each sector and fuel type. At least one study by Fujita and Hu (2002) has used such criteria for collecting data to avoid the bias caused by the data source for their research on China's regional disparity.

To verify the rationale of the above judgment, we compared some indicators generated from national statistics and provincial aggregation. Considering the wide-ranging debate about the coal production and consumption statistics, we decided to track their performance first. Figures 10.3 and 10.4 show the supply, transformation input and final consumption of raw coal based on national statistics and provincial aggregation. National statistics indicate that since the early 1990s, the demand for raw coal from the final consumption and transformation sector exceeded the total supply. This gap became more significant after 1996 and in 1999 the gap was almost half the amount of total final consumption. As for provincial aggregation, in 1985 and 1990, the difference between raw coal supply and demand (final consumption plus transformation) is negligible. For the period from 1995 to 1999, even though some gap appears, it is still comparatively smaller than that in the national statistics. Underestimates of illegal coal production from small-scale mines which were ordered to close after the mid-1990s may account for part of this gap. As a result, the provincial aggregate data are more reliable than the national statistics in capturing this information. In addition to raw coal, we also compared the total energy supply and demand (see Figures 10.5 and 10.6). As stated by Landwehr and Jochem (1997), the ratio of total primary energy supply to final energy consumption depends on the transformation losses, the share of imported secondary energy carriers and the share of primary (unconverted) energy carriers in end use. Figures 10.5 and 10.6 show that the provincial-aggregated transformation losses are comparatively higher than the national estimate. The national estimates indicate that the ratio of total primary energy supply to final energy consumption declined with

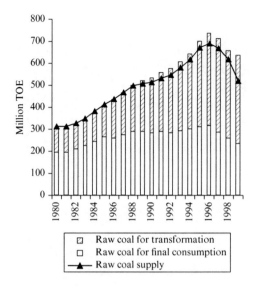

Sources: NBS (1990a, 1996a, 2000a).

Figure 10.3   Raw coal supply and demand based on national statistics

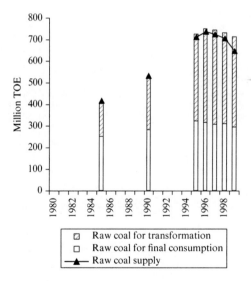

Sources: NBS (1990a, 1996a, 2000a).

Figure 10.4   Raw coal supply and demand based on provincial aggregation

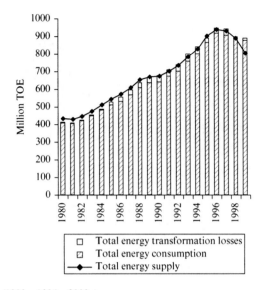

Sources: NBS (1990a, 1996a, 2000a).

Figure 10.5   Total energy supply and demand based on national statistics

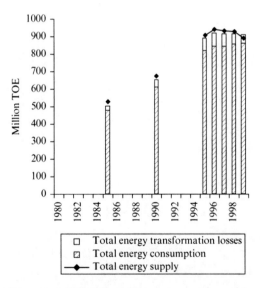

Sources: NBS (1990a, 1996a, 2000a).

Figure 10.6   Total energy supply and demand based on provincial aggregation

time but provincial aggregated estimates show that it remained at the same level. The experiences of developed countries show that such a ratio should increase or at least remain on the same level with the fuel structure transition from primary to secondary energy (ibid.). In China's case, the share of coal production in the total energy supply has continued to decline since the mid-1990s. It is therefore difficult to imagine that this ratio could decline during this period. In this context, the provincial aggregated data also show higher reliability than national statistics.

Of course, the national statistics should be an aggregate of regional data, so our new dataset can only avoid some bias caused by any possible 'adjustment' for the national aggregate data. Problems of data quality arising from regional statistics systems cannot be addressed without intensive empirical surveys, and so far this is beyond our capability. Thus, our analysis based on provincial aggregate data can be taken as a kind of exploration of the same phenomenon, from a different angle. To our knowledge, past studies have not addressed the performance of provincial CO$_2$ emissions. In fact, official estimates of CO$_2$ emissions at the provincial level are still unavailable. Although a study by Auffhammer et al. (2002) estimates CO$_2$ emissions using a simplified function by converting industrial waste gas emissions into CO$_2$ emissions, this methodology is totally different from commonly accepted estimation procedures suggested by the IPCC and is difficult to compare internationally. Furthermore, while Dhakal et al. (2002, 2006) carried out a decomposition analysis for CO$_2$ emissions in China's two mega-cities, Beijing and Shanghai, they did not address the performance of provincial aggregation.

In this study, energy production and consumption data are collected from the *China Energy Statistical Yearbook* (NBS, 1990a, 1996a, 2000a) and the *China Energy Databook* (LBNL/ERI, 2001). The provincial energy balance table is used for our estimate. We followed the *Revised 1996 IPCC Guidelines for National Greenhouse Gas Inventories* (IPCC/OECD/IEA, 1997). Our estimate of CO$_2$ emissions from the supply side follows the *reference* approach, and from the consumption side follows the *sectoral* approach. The reference approach accounts for carbon mainly based on the supply of primary fuels and the net quantities of secondary fuels brought into the economy. The sectoral approach makes a further sectoral breakdown of the aggregate CO$_2$ emissions by using the amount of each fuel consumed in each sector. Given that the more detailed calculating procedures used for these two approaches are essentially similar, the reference approach should be used for the estimate of supply-side energy data and the sectoral approach for the estimate of consumption-side energy data. In this study, sectoral economic outputs and labor force data have been collected from the *China Statistical Yearbook* (NBS, 1986–1989, 1990b,

1991–1994, 1995a, 1996b, 1997, 1998a, 1999, 2000b). Information of the transportation and residential sectors are collected from the *Comprehensive Statistical Data and Materials on 50 Years of New China* (NBS, 2000c). Some other detailed information from the manufacturing sector is collected from the *China Industrial Economy Statistical Yearbook* (NBS, 1995b, 1998b, 2000d).

Methodologies for Three-level Perfect Decomposition

The index decomposition method is a technique for decomposing an aggregate energy or environmental indicator to quantify the relative contributions of pre-defined factors for the change in the aggregate indicator. This technique has been developed since the late 1970s (Ang and Liu, 2001; Ang and Zhang, 2000; Hoekstra and van der Bergh, 2003). A number of studies have appeared since then, enhancing either the methodology or its applications (for example, Ang, 1995, 1999; Schipper et al., 1997, 2001; Ang et al., 1998; Sun, 1998, 2001; Liaskas et al., 2000; Ang and Liu, 2001; Zhang and Ang, 2001; Luukkanen and Kaivo-oja, 2002a, 2002b; Ozawa et al., 2002). Ang and Liu (2001) introduced a new decomposition method, which is accurate in decomposition and consistent in aggregation. The latter attribute makes it feasible to address the issue of two-level decomposition analysis: the pre-defined driving forces can first be quantified on the level of subsectors, which are categorized according to sector, region or fuel type; and then at a more aggregated level, such as a national scale.

The development of our model corresponds well with our own datasets. Thus, in order to fit the three-dimensional data sources, a three-level decomposition model without residual term is proposed in this chapter. This is essentially an extension of the work of Ang and Liu. In contrast to previous studies, which address either a single sector (mainly the industrial sector) or a series of manufacturing subsectors, our research addresses multiple sectors: agriculture, industry, construction, transportation, commercial and residential. Therefore, on the one hand, the definition of the determinants varies by sector due to each sector's intrinsic features. On the other, we categorize all those effects into three broad groups: scale effect, intensity effect and structure effect. Such generalization, based on the essence of each determinant effect, helps us to discuss their performance systematically.

Total CO_2 emissions at the national level can be expressed in the following way:

$$C = \sum_{i=1}^{28} \sum_{j=1}^{6} \sum_{k=1}^{6} C_{ijk}$$

$$
= \sum_{i=1}^{28} \sum_{j=1}^{4} \sum_{k=1}^{6} \frac{C_{ijk}}{E_{ijk}} \times \frac{E_{ijk}}{E_{ij}} \times \frac{E_{ij}}{Y_{ij}} \times \frac{Y_{ij}}{Y_i} \times \frac{Y_i}{L_i} \times L_i
$$

$$
+ \sum_{i=1}^{28} \sum_{j=5}^{} \sum_{k=1}^{6} \frac{C_{ijk}}{E_{ijk}} \times \frac{E_{ijk}}{E_{ij}} \times \frac{E_{ij}}{TD_{ij}} \times VTD_{ij} \times VN_{ij}
$$

$$
+ \sum_{i=1}^{28} \sum_{j=6}^{} \sum_{k=1}^{6} \frac{C_{ijk}}{E_{ijk}} \times \frac{E_{ijk}}{E_{ij}} \times \frac{E_{ij}}{THI_{ij}} \times HI_{ij} \times HN_{ij}, \qquad (10.1)
$$

where i indexes province, $i = 1, 2, \ldots, 28$; j indexes sector, $j = 1, 2, \ldots, 6$, respectively, for the following sectors: agriculture, industry, construction, commercial, transportation and residential; k indexes fuel type, $k = 1, 2, \ldots, 6$, respectively, for coal, coking product, petroleum product, natural gas, heat and electricity. The meaning of each factor in the function is described in Table 10.1.

Table 10.1   Meaning of each factor in function (10.1)

Item	Meaning
C_{ijk}	CO$_2$ emission by fuel k in sector j of province i
E_{ijk}	energy consumption by fuel k in sector j of province i
E_{ij}	energy consumption in sector j of province i
Y_{ij}	economic output of province i
Y_i	total economic output of province i
L_i	total employed labor force of province i
TD_{ij}	traveling distance represented by vehicle-kilometers in transportation sector of province i
VTD_{ij}	vehicle-kilometers per vehicle
VN_{ij}	vehicle numbers of province i
THI_{ij}	total household income in the residential sector of province i
HI_{ij}	average household income in province i
HN_{ij}	total household numbers in province i

Based on this fundamental function, we define the following terms:

$CI_{ijk} = \dfrac{C_{ijk}}{E_{ijk}}$; carbon intensity for fuel k in sector j of province i;

$FS_{ijk} = \dfrac{E_{ijk}}{E_{ij}}$; fuel mix ratio for fuel k in sector j of province i;

$EIP_{ij} = \dfrac{E_{ij}}{Y_{ij}}$; energy intensity in sector j of province i, $j = 1, 2, 3, 4$;

$EIT_{ij} = \dfrac{E_{ij}}{TD_{ij}}$; energy intensity in transportation sector of province i;

$$EIR_{ij} = \frac{E_{ij}}{THI_{ij}}; \text{ energy intensity in residential sector of province } i;$$

$$ES_{ij} = \frac{Y_{ij}}{Y_i}; \text{ share of economic output in sector } j \text{ of province } i,$$
$$j = 1, 2, 3, 4;$$

$$ALPi = \frac{Y_i}{L_i}; \text{ average labor productivity in province } i;$$

$L_i = L_i;$ employed labor force in province i;

$VTD_{ij} = VTD_{ij};$ travelling distance per vehicle

(represented by vehicle–kilometers per vehicle);(

$HI_{ij} = $ per household income;

$VN_{ij} = $ vehicle number;

$HN_{ij} = $ household number.

Function (10.1) can then be transformed as:

$$C = \sum_{i=1}^{28} \sum_{j=1}^{4} \sum_{k=1}^{6} CI_{ijk} \times FS_{ijk} \times EIP_{ij} \times ES_{ij} \times ALP_i \times L_i$$

$$+ \sum_{i=1}^{28} \sum_{j=5}^{6} \sum_{k=1}^{6} CI_{ijk} \times FS_{ijk} \times EIT_{ij} \times VTD_{ij} \times VN_{ij}$$

$$+ \sum_{i=1}^{28} \sum_{j=6}^{6} \sum_{k=1}^{6} CI_{ijk} \times FS_{ijk} \times EIR_{ij} \times HI_{ij} \times HN_{ij}$$

$$\frac{d\ln C}{dt} = \sum_{i=1}^{28} \sum_{j=1}^{4} \sum_{k=1}^{6} \left[\omega_{ijk} \left(\frac{d\ln CI_{ijk}}{dt} + \frac{d\ln FS_{ijk}}{dt} + \frac{d\ln EIP_{ij}}{dt} \right. \right.$$
$$\left. \left. + \frac{d\ln ES_{ij}}{dt} + \frac{d\ln ALP_i}{dt} + \frac{d\ln L_i}{dt} \right) \right]$$

$$+ \sum_{i=1}^{28} \sum_{j=5}^{6} \sum_{k=1}^{6} \left[\omega_{ijk} \left(\frac{d\ln CI_{ijk}}{dt} + \frac{d\ln FS_{ijk}}{dt} + \frac{d\ln EIT_{ij}}{dt} \right. \right.$$
$$\left. \left. + \frac{d\ln VTD_{ij}}{dt} + \frac{d\ln VN_{ij}}{dt} \right) \right]$$

$$+ \sum_{i=1}^{28} \sum_{j=6}^{6} \sum_{k=1}^{6} \left[\omega_{ijk} \left(\frac{d\ln CI_{ijk}}{dt} + \frac{d\ln FS_{ijk}}{dt} + \frac{d\ln EIR_{ij}}{dt} \right. \right.$$
$$\left. \left. + \frac{d\ln HI_{ij}}{dt} + \frac{d\ln HN_{ij}}{dt} \right) \right], \tag{10.3}$$

where $\omega_{ijk} = \dfrac{C_{ijk}}{C}$; and then:

$$\int_0^T \frac{d\ln C}{dt} = \sum_{i=1}^{28}\sum_{j=1}^{4}\sum_{k=1}^{6}\int_0^T \omega_{ijk}\left(\frac{d\ln CI_{ijk}}{dt} + \frac{d\ln FS_{ijk}}{dt} + \frac{d\ln EIP_{ij}}{dt}\right.$$

$$+ \frac{d\ln ES_{ij}^0}{dt} + \frac{d\ln ALP_i}{dt} + \left.\frac{d\ln L_i}{dt}\right)dt$$

$$+ \sum_{i=1}^{28}\sum_{j=5}^{}\sum_{k=1}^{6}\int_0^T \omega_{ijk}\left(\frac{d\ln CI_{ijk}}{dt} + \frac{d\ln FS_{ijk}}{dt} + \frac{d\ln EIT_{ij}}{dt}\right.$$

$$+ \frac{d\ln VTD_{ij}}{dt} + \left.\frac{d\ln VN_{ij}}{dt}\right)dt$$

$$+ \sum_{i=1}^{28}\sum_{j=6}^{}\sum_{k=1}^{6}\int_0^T \omega_{ijk}\left(\frac{d\ln CI_{ijk}}{dt} + \frac{d\ln FS_{ijk}}{dt} + \frac{d\ln EIR_{ij}}{dt}\right.$$

$$+ \frac{d\ln HI_{ij}}{dt} + \left.\frac{d\ln HN_{ij}}{dt}\right)dt \qquad (10.4)$$

$$\frac{C_T}{C_0} \cong \exp\left[\sum_{i=1}^{28}\sum_{j=1}^{6}\sum_{k=1}^{6}\omega_{ijk}(t^*)\ln\frac{CI_{ijk,T}}{CI_{ijk,0}}\right]\exp\left[\sum_{i=1}^{28}\sum_{j=1}^{6}\sum_{k=1}^{6}\omega_{ijk}(t^*)\ln\frac{FS_{ijk,T}}{FS_{ijk,0}}\right]$$

$$\exp\left[\sum_{i=1}^{28}\sum_{j=1}^{4}\sum_{k=1}^{6}\omega_{ijk}(t^*)\ln\frac{EIP_{ij,T}}{EIP_{ij,0}}\right]\exp\left[\sum_{i=1}^{28}\sum_{j=1}^{4}\sum_{k=1}^{6}\omega_{ijk}(t^*)\ln\frac{ES_{ij,T}}{ES_{ij,0}}\right]$$

$$\exp\left[\sum_{i=1}^{28}\sum_{j=1}^{4}\sum_{k=1}^{6}\omega_{ijk}(t^*)\ln\frac{ALP_{i,T}}{ALP_{i,0}}\right]\exp\left[\sum_{i=1}^{28}\sum_{j=1}^{4}\sum_{k=1}^{6}\omega_{ijk}(t^*)\ln\frac{L_{i,T}}{L_{i,0}}\right]$$

$$\exp\left[\sum_{i=1}^{28}\sum_{j=5}^{}\sum_{k=1}^{6}\omega_{ijk}(t^*)\ln\frac{EIT_{ij,T}}{EIT_{ij,0}}\right]\exp\left[\sum_{i=1}^{28}\sum_{j=6}^{}\sum_{k=1}^{6}\omega_{ijk}(t^*)\ln\frac{EIR_{ij,T}}{EIR_{ij,0}}\right]$$

$$\exp\left[\sum_{i=1}^{28}\sum_{j=5}^{}\sum_{k=1}^{6}\omega_{ijk}(t^*)\ln\frac{VTD_{ij,T}}{VTD_{ij,0}}\right]\exp\left[\sum_{i=1}^{28}\sum_{j=5}^{}\sum_{k=1}^{6}\omega_{ijk}(t^*)\ln\frac{VN_{ij,T}}{VN_{ij,0}}\right]$$

$$\exp\left[\sum_{i=1}^{28}\sum_{j=6}^{}\sum_{k=1}^{6}\omega_{ijk}(t^*)\ln\frac{HI_{ij,T}}{HI_{ij,0}}\right]\exp\left[\sum_{i=1}^{28}\sum_{j=6}^{}\sum_{k=1}^{6}\omega_{ijk}(t^*)\ln\frac{HN_{ij,T}}{HN_{ij,0}}\right],$$

$$(10.5)$$

where $\omega_{ijk}(t^*)$ is a weight function given by $\omega_{ijk}(t) = C_{ijk}/C$ at point $t^* \in [0, T]$.

One way to obtain the approximate value of $\omega_{ijk}(t^*)$ is to use the logarithmic mean divisia index method (LMDI), which is able to deal with zero value in the dataset and also leaves no residual term. The logarithmic mean of two positive numbers is defined as:

$$L(x, y) = (y - x)/\ln(y/x) \text{ for } x \neq y$$
$$L(x, x) = x. \tag{10.6}$$

The weight function is then given by

$$\varpi_{ijk}(t^*) = \frac{L(C_{ijk,0}, C_{ijk,T})}{L(C_0, C_T)}. \tag{10.7}$$

Function (10.5) can then be changed to:

$$\frac{C_T}{C_0} \equiv \exp\left[\sum_{i=1}^{28}\sum_{j=1}^{6}\sum_{k=1}^{6}\varpi_{ijk}(t^*)\ln\frac{CI_{ijk,T}}{CI_{ijk,0}}\right]\exp\left[\sum_{i=1}^{28}\sum_{j=1}^{6}\sum_{k=1}^{6}\varpi_{ijk}(t^*)\ln\frac{FS_{ijk,T}}{FS_{ijk,0}}\right]$$

$$\exp\left[\sum_{i=1}^{28}\sum_{j=1}^{4}\sum_{k=1}^{6}\varpi_{ijk}(t^*)\ln\frac{EIP_{ij,T}}{EIP_{ij,0}}\right]\exp\left[\sum_{i=1}^{28}\sum_{j=1}^{4}\sum_{k=1}^{6}\varpi_{ijk}(t^*)\ln\frac{ES_{ij,T}}{ES_{ij,0}}\right]$$

$$\exp\left[\sum_{i=1}^{28}\sum_{j=1}^{4}\sum_{k=1}^{6}\varpi_{ijk}(t^*)\ln\frac{ALP_{i,T}}{ALP_{i,0}}\right]\exp\left[\sum_{i=1}^{28}\sum_{j=1}^{4}\sum_{k=1}^{6}\varpi_{ijk}(t^*)\ln\frac{L_{i,T}}{L_{i,0}}\right]$$

$$\exp\left[\sum_{i=1}^{28}\sum_{j=5}^{6}\sum_{k=1}^{6}\varpi_{ijk}(t^*)\ln\frac{EIT_{ij,T}}{EIT_{ij,0}}\right]\exp\left[\sum_{i=1}^{28}\sum_{j=6}^{6}\sum_{k=1}^{6}\varpi_{ijk}(t^*)\ln\frac{EIR_{ij,T}}{EIR_{ij,0}}\right]$$

$$\exp\left[\sum_{i=1}^{28}\sum_{j=5}^{6}\sum_{k=1}^{6}\varpi_{ijk}(t^*)\ln\frac{VTD_{ij,T}}{VTD_{ij,0}}\right]\exp\left[\sum_{i=1}^{28}\sum_{j=5}^{6}\sum_{k=1}^{6}\varpi_{ijk}(t^*)\ln\frac{VN_{ij,T}}{VN_{ij,0}}\right]$$

$$\exp\left[\sum_{i=1}^{28}\sum_{j=6}^{6}\sum_{k=1}^{6}\varpi_{ijk}(t^*)\ln\frac{HI_{ij,T}}{HI_{ij,0}}\right]\exp\left[\sum_{i=1}^{28}\sum_{j=6}^{6}\sum_{k=1}^{6}\varpi_{ijk}(t^*)\ln\frac{HN_{ij,T}}{HN_{ij,0}}\right] \tag{10.8}$$

Function (10.8) can be written as:

$$D_{tot} = D_{CIN} \cdot D_{FS} \cdot D_{EIP} \cdot D_{EIT} \cdot D_{EIR} \cdot D_{ES} \cdot D_{ALP} \cdot D_L \cdot D_{VTD} \cdot D_{VN} \cdot D_{HI} \cdot D_{HN} \tag{10.9}$$

All the above determinant effects can be further categorized into four groups:

intensity effect: D_{CIN}, D_{EIP}, D_{EIT}, D_{EIR};
structure effect: D_{FS}, D_{ES};
sectoral-specific activity intensity effect: D_{ALP}, D_{VTD}, D_{HI}; and
sectoral-specific activity size effect: D_L, D_{VN}, D_{HN}.

Significance of the Pre-defined Determinant Effects

Figure 10.7 illustrates the framework of our model which clarifies the overall system of this model, the role of each determinant and also the interrelationship among determinants. Several points related to the above determinant effects should be highlighted here.

1. The intensity effect includes the carbon intensity effect (D_{CIN}) and the energy intensity effect (D_{EIP}, D_{EIT}, D_{EIR}). The intensity effect is an indicator of energy efficiency and reflects the role of energy consumption per unit of physical output (energy intensity effect) or carbon emissions per unit of energy consumption (carbon intensity effect). The intensity effect represents the change of carbon or energy intensity in each sector for each fuel type. Therefore, if we further decompose by fuel type (or sector), we can obtain the relative contribution of each fuel's (or sector's) carbon or energy intensity change to the total CO$_2$ emission change. Due to these capabilities, this model can provide a deeper insight into the performance of each determinant.

2. The structural effect consists of the fuel and the economic structural effects. Since these two effects are presented as the change in ratio of each component in the total amount, they actually provide the net effect of changes in fuel or economic structure after the cancellation of positive and negative sectoral impacts. As a result, the net contribution of such structural effects does not follow the degree of structural transition directly.

3. The sector-specific activity intensity effect represents the sector-characterized effect in per unit terms. For industry-related sectors,[1] it represents the changes of average labor productivity in the agriculture, industry, construction and commercial sectors; for the transportation sector, it represents the changes of average traveling distance; for the residential sector, it represents the change in average household income.

4. The sector-specific activity size effect indicates the change of the size of each sector, as measured by the amount of labor for industry-related sectors, the number of vehicles for the transportation sector and the number of households for the residential sector.

It should be pointed out that this model proposes some new definitions: the sector-specific activity intensity effects (see (3) above) and sector-specific activity size effect (see (4) above). The scale effect, commonly discussed in most previous studies, is further decomposed into two parts, namely the sector-specific activity intensity effect and the sector-specific activity size

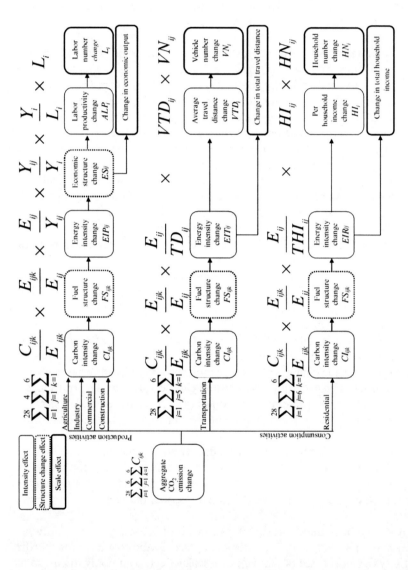

Figure 10.7   Framework of the decomposition model

effect. This clarification will help us to analyze the behavior of each sector in more detail. For example, the traditional model regards the change of economic output only as a proxy indicator for the scale of change in the industry sector. However, commonly accepted production functions reveal that the source of economic growth can be measured as the changes in the amount of capital, changes in the amount of labor and the changes in TFP. Furthermore, the prevalent assumption of constant returns to scale of the production function implies that the size of the economy can be measured by the number of workers and this does not affect the relationship between average labor productivity (economic output per labor) and the physical capital input per labor. So we use the change in average productivity to represent the unitary characteristics of each sector and then the change in the amount of labor to indicate the extension of the scale of each sector. We similarly define such terms for the transportation and residential sectors, to highlight the relative importance of the scale extension and unitary characteristics change. In conclusion, this approach sheds more light on the sector-specific scale effect than earlier approaches.

3   RESULTS AND DISCUSSION

'Stagnancy' versus 'Decline' of CO$_2$ Emissions in China: New Evidence from the Provincial Aggregation

Figure 10.8 shows the estimates of China's energy-related CO$_2$ emissions by different methods and data sources. In this figure, CEBT and PEBT are the corresponding abbreviations for China energy balance table and provincial energy balance table. All of the estimates made by the authors are based on the *China Energy Statistical Yearbook* 1995–1999 (NBS, 1996a, 2000a) and the *China Energy Databook* (LBNL/ERI).The IEA's estimate is based on its own statistics series, *Energy Balances of Non-OECD Countries*. If we trace the data back to their original sources, it appears that some data also came from the China National Bureau of Statistics, although the IEA has made some adjustments to the data source according to its own statistical criteria. Regardless, given the slight difference among the original energy data sources, we can still use the above estimate to shed light on CO$_2$ emission trends. Figure 10.8 compares the provincially aggregated CO$_2$ estimates with other methods for 1985, 1990 and 1995–2000 only, due to data limitations. Estimates for provincially aggregated CO$_2$ emissions in 1985 and 1990 suggest that this approach is consistent with the results of estimates from all other methods, despite some differences in statistical techniques.

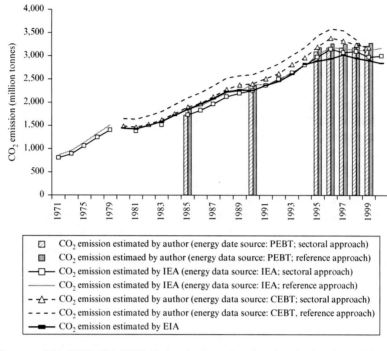

Sources:* IEA (2002), EIA (2002), Estimation by authors based on the data from NBS (1990a, 1996a, 2000a).

Figure 10.8   Comparison of CO_2 emission estimates between the provincial aggregation employed in this study and existing estimates from other sources

For the 1996–2000 period, though, there is some variation due to differences in estimation techniques, but each of them reflects some common behavior (rise and fall). An estimate by the IEA using the sectoral approach reflects an obvious declining trend during that period. As the figure shows, the volume of CO_2 emissions in 2000 is 4.7 percent lower than in 1996. The estimate by the IEA using a reference approach shows a slightly different trend, where the emissions level of 2000 is only a little lower (0.08 percent) than the peak of 1996. Our estimates based on CEBT reveal a more obvious declining tendency for the 1996–99 period. The estimated average annual rate of decline is 1.57 percent when using the sectoral approach (based on consumption-side energy data) and 4.44 percent when using the reference approach (based on supply-side energy data), respectively. In contrast to the above, our new estimates based on the PEBT indicate that there was no obvious declining tendency for China's national CO$_2$ emissions from 1996 to 1999. The results show 'stagnancy' but not a declining trend in CO$_2$ emissions. We could only characterize this period as having some minor fluctuations in CO$_2$ emissions, with no obvious increasing or decreasing trend. Considering the much-discussed doubts regarding China's national energy statistics and the consistency that is evident when comparing all these estimates, we describe China's CO$_2$ emissions as being in transition from a stage of 'stable increase' to a stage of 'stagnancy'. Due to data limitations, we could not validate the 'rebound' in 2000 as estimated by the IEA when using the reference approach.

Contributions of Underlying Driving Forces in CO$_2$ Emissions: 1985–1999

As mentioned in the methodology section, the factor decomposition method is used in this chapter to analyze the relative contribution of driving factors. The essence of a decomposition analysis is to decompose the aggregate change of one variable (such as CO$_2$ emissions) into the relative contributions of a few pre-defined determinants. The positive or negative contribution (higher or lower than 1) is determined by the changing ratio of that determinant factor between the benchmarked years. Figure 10.9 shows the contribution of each pre-defined determinant or driving force on the aggregate CO$_2$ emissions changes over time (the meaning of each determinant effect is described in Section 2). Figure 10.10 highlights the relative importance of each determinant effect within each targeted period. It will help us to identify the leading determinant and disregard some trivial effects in later discussion. Considering that the horizon is the five-year periods from 1985 to 1990 and from 1990 to 1995, we have made an adjustment to reflect the yearly average effect during those periods. To provide a better understanding of the relative importance of each determinant, Table 10.2 ranks the contribution of each determinant by using the yearly average contribution.

The above results lead to a number of findings:

1. Energy-related CO$_2$ emissions during the 1985–99 period were driven by tradeoffs between the positive sector-specific activity size effect and activity intensity effect and the negative energy intensity effects.
2. The dominant positive determinant factors are the sectoral-specific activity intensity effect (change of average labor productivity). The dominant negative factor is the change of energy intensity in each industry-related sector.
3. Sectoral structural change and fuel structural change account for only a small amount in the overall trend of CO$_2$ emissions. These results are consistent with previous studies, in terms of the driving forces of

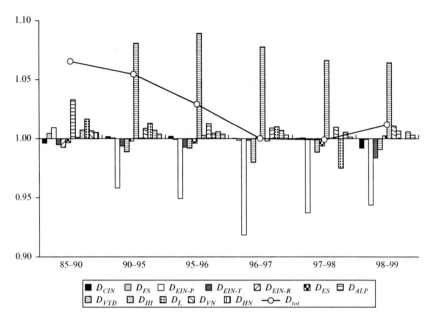

Figure 10.9　Results of factor decomposition analysis for Chinese national CO₂ emission from 1985 to 1999 (provincial aggregation)

China's CO_2 emissions in the 1980s. Furthermore, our analysis reveals that such a trend continued throughout the 1990s.

Contributions of Driving Forces in the 'Stagnancy' Period: 1996–2000

To get a better picture of each determinant's role in the 1996–2009 period, we carried out further decomposition analyses (beyond the description in the previous subsection) at the level of sector or fuel type. Our objective was to clarify the underlying forces that led to the 'sudden stagnancy' that started in 1996.

Carbon intensity effect
Figures 10.9 and 10.10 show that the contribution of the carbon intensity effect fluctuates over time. In Figure 10.11 the D_{CIN} is further decomposed by fuel type. The carbon intensity effects of heating[2] and electricity are major driving forces in the 1996–99 period. The carbon intensity of heating continued to increase prior to 1996, though the growth slowed during 1995–96. After 1996, however, the growth of the carbon intensity of heating became negative. In the case of electricity, its growth rate has slowed since 1996,

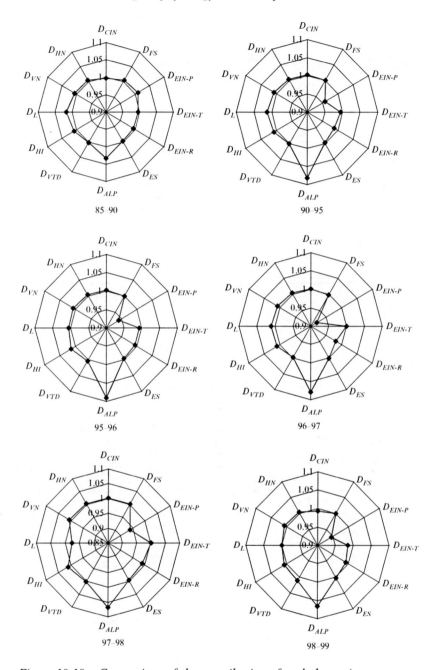

Figure 10.10   Comparison of the contribution of each determinant

Table 10.2   Relative importance of each determinant during 1985–1999

Type of factor	Factor	General quality	YAC (yearly average contribution)	(YAC–1) *100%	Rank
Aggregated	D_{CIN}	Fluctuate	0.9989	(0.110)	*****
intensity effect	D_{EIN-P}	Negative	0.9693	(3.071)	*
	D_{EIN-T}	Negative	0.9941	(0.593)	*
	D_{EIN-R}	Negative	0.9900	(1.003)	**
Aggregated	D_{FS}	Fluctuate	1.0018	0.176	
structural effect	D_{ES}	Fluctuate	0.9976	(0.244)	
Sectoral-specific	D_{ALP}	Positive	1.0616	6.162	*****
activity intensity	D_{VTD}	Positive	1.0013	0.131	*****
effect	D_{HI}	Positive	1.0084	0.837	*
Sectoral-specific	D_L	Fluctuate	1.0098	0.984	*
activity scale	D_{VN}	Positive	1.0068	0.680	*
effect	D_{HN}	Positive	1.0041	0.410	*-

Note: Criteria for ranking: $(YAC-1)*100\%$. 10 stars: 5; 2 stars: 1–1.5; 1 star: 0.5–1; 1 star minus: 0.25–0.5, no star: ≤ 0.25.
Number in (): negative value.

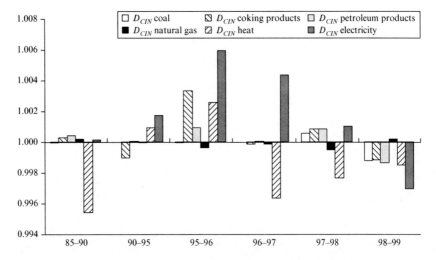

Figure 10.11   Relative contributions of carbon intensity to change in CO_2 emission by energy type

although it played a positive role until 1998. In our estimate, we assumed the same carbon emission factor of primary energy, which means that the above phenomenon must be due to the improvement in energy efficiency from the transformation process, or from fuel structure transition, or from both. Some of the recent policy measures corroborate this trend.

Since 1994, China's electric power industry has undergone considerable transformation. The Electric Power Law was entered into force in April 1996. This was one of the major events in the history of China's electric power industry. The new law aimed at promoting the development of that industry, protecting legal rights of investors, managers and consumers, and regulating generation, distribution and consumption. This law also mandated the prohibition of new small-scale power plants and the closure of existing ones. As a result, 2.84 GW of plants smaller than 100 MW were closed between 1997 and 1998, and an additional 1.8 GW of generation was closed in 1999 (Ling, 1999). Since large power plants are more efficient than small ones, such transformation led to the overall improvement in end-use efficiency. National statistics (SPI, 2003) in China for the 1994–99 period show an increase in the efficiency of coal-generated electricity at the national scale from 414 to 399 grams per kWh; a decrease in the utilization rate of power plants from 6.9 to 6.5 percent; a decrease in losses of power transmission line, from 8.73 to 8.10 percent; and an increase in the aggregate efficiency of thermal power's energy conversion rate, from 38.05 to 38.85 percent. From 1996 to the end of 1999, China invested 539.3 billion yuan in the construction of new power plant projects. Since the late 1990s, China has also unveiled a package of reforms in laws and regulations to ensure better management of the electric power industry, especially in production and operation. These policy measures substantially support improvement in end-use efficiency and, together with fuel structure change, lead to the transition in carbon intensity (reverse from increase to decrease) of the energy transformation sector.

Energy intensity effect
In the case of energy intensity effects, a negative contribution to CO$_2$ emissions is observed in the 1996–2000 period. In terms of contribution to the energy intensity effect, the industry-related sector is ranked first, followed by the residential and the transportation sectors. The industry-related sector provides the strongest negative influence, and this fact is evident in the decline in energy intensity in key sectors, such as agriculture, industry, construction and commerce.

As stated by Sinton et al. (1998) and Zhang (2003), a more detailed sectoral disaggregation could provide a better understanding of the role of underlying driving forces. Figure 10.12 shows the contributions of

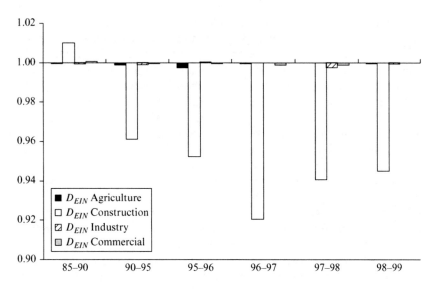

*Figure 10.12   Relative contributions of energy intensity to change in CO_2
emission by production sector*

the carbon intensity effect in each industry-related sector, to CO_2 emissions change. The analyses show that the decline in energy intensity in the industry-related sector is mainly dominated by the changes in the industrial sector. Since the mid-1990s, the rate of decrease in energy intensity in the industrial sector has been more pronounced than that of the early 1990s with an all-time high during the 1996–97 period. This suggests that the industrial structural shift or the energy efficiency improvement in subsectors or both accelerated after the mid-1990s. Due to the lack of provincial-level industrial subsectoral information, we could not identify the relative contributions of sectoral shift and energy efficiency improvements. However, previous studies have shown that the overall energy intensity during the 1980s and early 1990s was mainly driven by end-use efficiency improvement (Huang, 1993; Ang and Pandiyan, 1997; Ang et al., 1998; Sinton et al., 1998; Sun, 1998). For 1990–97, Zhang (2000) indicates the reason for declining energy intensity as energy efficiency improvement in energy-intensive subsectors. Considering these facts, we conclude that the speed of the industrial sector's energy efficiency improvement must have been the dominant contributor to the decrease in CO_2 emissions since 1996.

From a socioeconomic viewpoint, the result could be partly attributed to the change in ownership structure of industrial enterprises. Official statistics (see Figure 10.13) show that the total number of industrial enterprises has been falling since the mid-1990s, notably the number of state- and

Sources: NBS (1986–1989, 1990b, 1991–1994, 1995a, 1996b, 1997, 1998a, 1999, 2000b).

Figure 10.13   Number of industrial enterprises by ownership

collectively owned enterprises, while the number of 'other' enterprises, such as businesses funded by entrepreneurs from Hong Kong, Macao and Taiwan or foreign countries, has increased. Since in general cases the latter categories are more efficient than SOEs (Matsumoto and Imura, 1998), it could have led to the efficiency improvement. Other factors for efficiency improvements could have been the product mix in energy-intensive sectors and the replacement of inefficient equipment.

Fisher-Vanden et al. (2002) employ a unique dataset of approximately 2,500 large and medium-sized industrial enterprises in China for 1997–99 to identify the factors driving the fall in total energy use and energy intensity. Their research shows that changing energy prices and R&D expenditures are significant drivers of declining energy intensity in Chinese industrial enterprises.

Structural effect
The contribution of the structural effect to CO$_2$ emissions was comparatively low during the 1996–2000 period, for both fuel and economic structural changes. For the economic structural changes, our result is consistent with other studies. The contributions of fuel structural changes changed from positive to negative since the mid-1990s (see Figure 10.9 and 10.10)

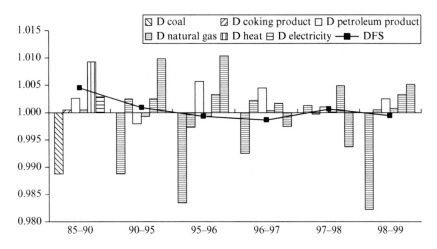

Figure 10.14   Relative contributions of energy structure change to change in CO_2 emission by energy type

but they have comparatively smaller influence on CO_2 emissions. Figure 10.14 shows that, despite its minimal influence on the total CO_2 emissions, fuel structure itself has changed significantly. The increasing share of electricity and decreasing share of coal in total energy consumption suddenly reversed from 1996 to 1998 and again seems to be recovering in 1999. The growth rate of electricity production has slowed down since the 1990s due to the oversupply of electricity in some areas and also due to the shutdown of small-scale power plants (ibid.). In spite of higher end-use efficiency, the transformation losses in the production process of electricity makes the carbon emissions factor per unit of energy supply of electricity higher than that of coal. Such a trend should account for a small, but nonetheless significant portion of the stagnancy in CO_2 emissions.

Scale effect

As mentioned in Section 2, we decomposed the traditionally defined scale effect into the effects of sector specific activity intensity and sectoral-specific activity size. Among the sector-specific activity intensity effects, the change of average labor productivity is found to play a dominant positive role. The technique of growth accounting shows that the growth in average labor productivity depends on the growth in TFP and growth in the capital–labor ratio. The growth in average labor productivity has slowed since the mid-1990s, a fact which indicates a slowdown in either capital accumulation (savings and investment) or factor productivity. A further decomposition in Figure 10.15 shows that such changes in average

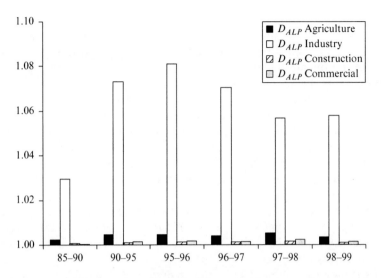

Figure 10.15   *Relative contributions of labor productivity change to change in CO₂ emissions by production sector*

labor productivity are mainly influenced by the industrial sector. Detailed supporting information for the industrial sector (see Figure 10.16) shows that during the 1993–97 period the annual growth rate of the capital–labor ratio in the industrial sector continued to decrease. This growth ratio experienced a sudden rebound in the 1997–98 period and then declined again from 1998 to 1999. Such a trend prevailed in each subsector within the industrial sector. Specifically, the fluctuation of the manufacturing sector is almost the same as the overall industrial sector's performance, since it dominates the industrial sector. The growth rate of the capital–labor ratio in the mining and quarrying sector is a kind of continuous declining trend. The production and supply of gas, electricity and water sectors experienced a jump in 1996–97 and then resumed a general declining trend. Since our discussion is limited to a short period, we may assume that there is no great change with the factor productivity, which is determined by technical and organizational conditions. We can therefore safely say that the slowdown of capital accumulation since the early 1990s has directly led to the slowdown of growth in average labor productivity in industry since the mid-1990s.

In addition to the above analysis by sector, we also measured the performance of enterprises with different registered ownership. Due to data limitations,[3] we can only provide similar support information of the change of the capital–labor ratio by different registered ownership during 1993–97 (see Figure 10.17). We find that the continuous decline of the growth of the capital–labor ratio has prevailed among all types of enterprises. Actually, the total amount of employed labor in SOEs began to decrease in 1995. Thus we may infer that the slowdown of total capital accumulation has accelerated since 1995 in SOEs. McNally (2002) reported that the total losses of those state-owned enterprises exceeded the profits for the first time in early 1996. Despite China's state firms losing their near-monopoly status after 1978, they still form the country's financial and industrial nucleus. So the deterioration of SOEs during the late 1990s unavoidably slowed down the accumulation of capital stock and consequently may have led to the slowdown of average labor productivity and the decrease in the size of the labor force. All these factors affect CO_2 emissions negatively.

The above discussions have illuminated various possibilities for the 'stagnancy' of CO_2 emissions since 1996. In the final part of this section, we shall try to clarify the relative contribution of each possibility mentioned above to the 'stagnancy period'.

As show in function (10.10), the change of D_{tot} should be a product of change of each pre-defined driving force. Since the 'stagnancy period' features a distinct change in the D_{tot}, we can observe such change to the change of each driving force through:

$$\frac{D_{tot}^{96-99}}{D_{tot}^{95-96}} = \frac{D_{CIN}^{96-99}}{D_{CIN}^{95-96}} \cdot \frac{D_{FS}^{96-99}}{D_{FS}^{95-96}} \cdot \frac{D_{EIP}^{96-99}}{D_{EIP}^{95-96}} \cdot \frac{D_{EIT}^{\cdot\ 96-99}}{D_{EIT}^{\cdot\ 95-96}} \cdot \frac{D_{EIR}^{96-99}}{D_{EIR}^{95-96}} \cdot \frac{D_{ES}^{96-99}}{D_{ES}^{95-96}} \cdot$$

$$\frac{D_{ALP}^{96-99}}{D_{ALP}^{95-96}} \cdot \frac{D_{L}^{96-99}}{D_{L}^{95-96}} \cdot \frac{D_{VTD}^{96-99}}{D_{VTD}^{95-96}} \cdot \frac{D_{VN}^{96-99}}{D_{VN}^{95-96}} \cdot \frac{D_{HI}^{96-99}}{D_{HI}^{95-96}} \cdot \frac{D_{HN}^{96-99}}{D_{HN}^{95-96}} \qquad (10.10)$$

following function (10.11):

$$\ln\left(\frac{D_{tot}^{96-99}}{D_{tot}^{95-96}}\right) = \ln\left(\frac{D_{CIN}^{96-99}}{D_{CIN}^{95-96}}\right) + \ln\left(\frac{D_{FS}^{96-99}}{D_{FS}^{95-96}}\right) + \ln\left(\frac{D_{EIP}^{96-99}}{D_{EIP}^{95-96}}\right)$$

$$+ \ln\left(\frac{D_{EIT}^{\cdot\ 96-99}}{D_{EIT}^{\cdot\ 95-96}}\right) + \ln\left(\frac{D_{EIR}^{96-99}}{D_{EIR}^{95-96}}\right) + \ln\left(\frac{D_{ES}^{96-99}}{D_{ES}^{95-96}}\right) + \ln\left(\frac{D_{ALP}^{96-99}}{D_{ALP}^{95-96}}\right)$$

$$+ \ln\left(\frac{D_{L}^{96-99}}{D_{L}^{95-96}}\right) + \ln\left(\frac{D_{VTD}^{96-99}}{D_{VTD}^{95-96}}\right) + \ln\left(\frac{D_{VN}^{96-99}}{D_{VN}^{95-96}}\right) + \ln\left(\frac{D_{HI}^{96-99}}{D_{HI}^{95-96}}\right)$$

$$+ \ln\left(\frac{D_{HN}^{96-99}}{D_{HN}^{95-96}}\right) \qquad (10.11)$$

where the indices for the 1996–99 period are the yearly average in this duration. By using function (10.11) with a logarithmic form, we can get a direct

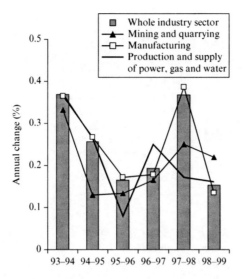

Sources: NBS (1994, 1995a, 1995b, 1996b, 1997, 1998a, 1998b, 1999, 2000b, 2000d).

Figure 10.16 *Annual growth rate of the capital–labor ratio in industrial subsectors*

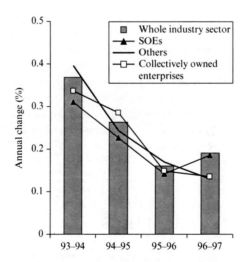

Sources: NBS (1994, 1995a, 1995b, 1996b, 1997, 1998a, 1998b, 1999, 2000b, 2000d).

Figure 10.17 *Annual growth rate of the capital–labor ratio in industrial sector by type of ownership*

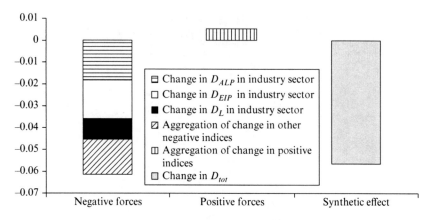

*Figure 10.18   Relative contribution of the possibilities leading to the
stagnancy during 1996–1999*

image of the relative contribution of each index's change to the change of
D_{tot}. According to the quality of each driving force, they are categorized
into positive and negative forces to the change of D_{tot}. Positive forces will
lead to the increase of D_{tot}, and vice versa. The synthetic effect of D_{tot} is
negative since the change of total CO_2 emissions transited from an increasing trend to stagnancy after 1996. Figure 10.18 shows the final result of
the above discussion, where D_{ALP} and D_{EIP} are further decomposed into
two parts: industry sector performance and other industry-related sector
performance.

Figure 10.18 indicates that the change in D_{ALP} in the industry sector and
the change in D_{EIP} in the industry sector play dominant negative roles to
the change of D_{tot}. Combining with the previous discussion, we can draw
a conclusion that the speed of the decrease in energy intensity and the
slowdown of increase in average labor productivity in the industry sector
largely account for the 'stagnancy' of total energy-related CO_2 emissions
since the mid-1990s.

4   CONCLUDING REMARKS

In this chapter, we discussed and estimated trends in China's energy and
CO_2 emissions in the last two decades, paying particular attention to the
much-debated 'decline' in energy consumption and CO_2 emissions since
1996. We also tried to shed light on the role of the driving factors in this
unusual trend.

Our findings, based on the provincially aggregated data, point to a 'sudden stagnancy' of energy consumption and energy-related CO$_2$ emissions, but not an obvious 'decline'. Consistent with previous studies, the decomposition analysis revealed that trends in energy-related CO$_2$ emissions in the 1980s were driven by a tradeoff between the positive sectoral-specific scale effects (including the activity intensity effect and activity size effect) and the negative energy intensity effects. Structural change accounts for only a small portion. This trend continued through the 1990s. The rate of decline in energy intensity and the rate of growth in average labor productivity since the mid-1990s have been the major contributors to this 'stagnancy' of energy-related CO$_2$ emissions. In addition, we note that the share of coal in the energy supply has stopped declining since 1997; the growth of carbon intensity of electricity has slowed since 1996 and reversed in 1998; and that carbon intensity of heating increased steadily until 1996 but declined from then onwards. All of the above characteristics have influenced CO$_2$ emissions negatively (that is, they have played a role in reducing CO$_2$ emissions in absolute terms).

Even though China's state firms lost their near-monopoly status after 1978, they still form the country's financial and industrial nucleus. In early 1996, the total losses of SOEs exceeded their profits for the first time. So it seems that the deterioration of these enterprises in the late 1990s unavoidably slowed the growth of average labor productivity. The changes in the ownership structure of industrial enterprises, and acceleration of energy efficiency improvements stimulated the energy intensity decrease. Furthermore, we have found that the shutdown of small-scale power plants, the oversupply of coal, and some energy and environmental regulations all stimulated end-use efficiency improvements in the energy transformation sector. The stagnancy of fuel structure transition in the 1996–99 period also led to a decline in carbon intensity.

In this chapter, though we tried to provide a detailed insight into the possibilities leading to the 'stagnancy' of China's energy consumption and CO$_2$ emissions since 1996, it is difficult to judge whether these influences are long-term trends or just short-term fluctuations. Zhou (2003) reported that China has plans to construct a number of large thermal power plants. China also plans to rehabilitate old plants with large and relatively efficient units. These initiatives could be expected to play a role in continued reductions in carbon intensity, thus reducing fuel consumption and improving the environment. On the other hand, growth of average labor productivity, which has a dominant positive effect on CO$_2$ emissions, is expected to recover in the near future due to reforms in the industrial sector. In fact, some statistics are already showing that a massive turnaround occurred in 2001 (McNally, 2002). Despite the steady declines in energy intensity during the last two decades, we believe that China's energy consumption and CO_2 emissions have experienced a stagnancy stage in recent years due to special causes, but will resume their increasing trends in the near future, albeit from lower starting points.

NOTES

1.   Industry-related sectors refer to agriculture, industry, construction and commercial sectors.
2.   Heat supply in China is usually distributed through a centralized system and is separated from other energy uses in energy statistics.
3.   We found that since 1998 the statistics criteria for 'Number of staff and workers by status of registration and sector in detail' in China has changed. The shareholding unit and limited liability corporation, which were counted as state-owned units before 1998 have been reclassified as part of other units. Today the numbers of personnel and workers in these two types of enterprises in the industrial sector are no longer available. However, the statistics for total capital assets still treat the contribution from the above two categories as part of SOEs. As a result, we were not able to include the analyses for 1998 and 1999 here.

REFERENCES

Ang, B.W. (1995), 'Decomposition methodology in industrial energy demand analysis', *Energy*, **20**, 1081–95.
Ang, B.W. (1999), 'Is the energy intensity a less useful indicator than the carbon factor in the study of climate change?', *Energy Policy*, **27**, 943–6.
Ang, B.W. and F.L. Liu (2001), 'A new energy decomposition method: perfect in decomposition and consistent in aggregation', *Energy*, **26**, 537–48.
Ang, B.W. and G. Pandiyan (1997), 'Decomposition of energy-induced CO_2 emissions in manufacturing', *Energy Economics*, **19**, 363–74.
Ang, B.W. and F.Q. Zhang (2000), 'A survey of index decomposition analysis in energy and environmental studies', *Energy*, **25**, 1149–76.
Ang, B.W., F.Q. Zhang and K.H. Choi (1998), 'Factorizing changes in energy and environmental indicators through decomposition', *Energy*, **23**, 489–95.
Auffhammer, M., R.T. Carson and T. Garin-Mûnoz (2002), 'Forecasting Chinese carbon dioxide emissions: a provincial approach', working paper presented to the NBER Summer Institute Workshop on Public Policy and the Environment, Cambridge, MA.
Dhakal, S., S. Kaneko and H. Imura (2002), 'An analysis on driving factors for CO_2 emissions from energy use in Tokyo and Seoul by the factor decomposition method', *Environmental Systems Research*, **30**, 295–303, Japan Society of Civil Engineers (JSCE).
Dhakal, S., S. Kaneko and H. Imura (2003), 'CO_2 emissions from energy use in East-Asian mega-cities: driving factors and their contributions', *Environmental Systems Research*, **31**, 209–16, Japan Society of Civil Engineers (JSCE).
Energy Information Administration (EIA) (2002), *International Energy Outlook 2003*, available at: www.eia.doe.gov/oiaf/ieo/index.html, accessed July 2009.
Fisher-Vanden, K., G. Jefferson, H.M. Liu and Q. Tao (2002), 'What is driving

China's decline in energy intensity?', paper presented to the 2002 World Congress of Environmental and Resource Economists, available at: http://weber.ucsd.edu/~carsonvs/papers/787.pdf, accessed July 2009.

Fujita, M. and D.P. Hu (2001), 'Regional disparity in China 1985–1994: the effect of globalization and economic liberalization', *Annals of Regional Science*, **35**, 3–37.

Ho, M.S., D.W. Jorgenson and D.H. Perkins (1998), 'China's economic growth and carbon emissions', in M.B. McElroy, C.P. Nielen and P. Lydon (eds), *Energizing China: Reconciling Environmental Protection and Economic Growth*, Cambridge, MA: Harvard University Press, pp. 301–41.

Hoekstra, R. and J.C.J.M. van der Bergh (2003), 'Comparing structural and index decomposition analysis', *Energy Economics*, **25**, 39–64.

Huang, J.P. (1993), 'Industry energy use and structure change: a case study of the People's Republic of China', *Energy Economics*, **15**, 131–6.

International Energy Agency (IEA) (2002), *CO₂ Emission from Fuel Combustion 1971–2000*, IEA Statistics, Paris.

Intergovernmental Panel on Climate Change (IPCC) (2000), *Special Report on Emission Scenarios: 2000*, Cambridge: Cambridge University Press.

IPCC/OECD/IEA (1997), *Revised 1996 IPCC Guidelines for National Greenhouse Gas Inventories: Reference Manual*, UK Metrological Office.

Lawrence Berkeley National Laboratory (LBNL) and Energy Research Institute (ERI) of the China State Development Planning Commission (2001), *China Energy Databook*, CD-ROM.

Landwehr, M. and E. Jochem (1997), 'From primary energy supply to final energy consumption-analyzing structural and efficiency changes on the energy supply side', *Energy Policy*, **25**, 693–702.

Liaskas, K., G. Mavrotas, M. Mandaraka and D. Diakoulaki (2000), 'Decomposition of industrial CO₂ emissions: the case of the European Union', *Energy Economics*, **22**, 383–94.

Ling, X.G. (1999), 'China's energy reforms', in China Online, July, available at: http://www.chinaonline.com.

Luukkanen, J. and J. Kaivo-oja (2002a), 'A comparison of Nordic energy and CO₂ intensity dynamics in the years 1960–1997', *Energy*, **27**, 135–50.

Luukkanen, J. and J. Kaivo-oja (2002b), 'Asian tigers and sustainability of energy use-decomposition analysis of energy and CO₂ efficiency dynamics', *Energy Policy*, **30**, 281–92.

Matsumoto, T. and H. Imura (1998), 'Foreign-affiliated firms and environmental problems in China: environmental implications of foreign direct investment', *Journal of Global Environmental Engineering*, **4**, 151–67.

McNally, C.A. (2002), 'China's state-owned enterprises: thriving or crumbling?', East–West Center No. 59, Asia Pacific Issues.

National Bureau of Statistics (NBS) (1986–1989, 1990b, 1991–1994, 1995a, 1996b, 1997, 1998a, 1999, 2000b), *China Statistical Yearbook*, Beijing: China Statistical Publishing House.

National Bureau of Statistics (NBS) (1990a, 1996a, 2000a), *China Energy Statistical Yearbook 1989, 1995–1996, 1997–1999*, Beijing: China Statistical Publishing House.

National Bureau of Statistics (NBS) (1995b, 1998b, 2000d), *China Industrial Economy Statistical Yearbook*, Beijing: China Statistical Publishing House.

National Bureau of Statistics (NBS) (2000c), *Comprehensive Statistical Data and Materials on 50 Years of New China*, Beijing: China Statistical Publishing House.

Natural Resources Defense Council (NRDC) (2001), 'China is aggressively reducing its carbon dioxide emissions', available at: http://www.nrdc.org/global Warming/achinagg.asp.

Ozawa, L., C. Sheinbaum, N. Martin, E. Worrell and L. Price (2002), 'Energy use and CO_2 emissions in Mexico's iron and steel industry', *Energy*, **27**, 225–39.

Schipper, L., S. Murtishaw, M. Khrushch, M. Ting, S. Karbuz and F. Unander (2001), 'Carbon emissions from manufacturing energy use in 13 IEA countries: long-term trends through 1995', *Energy Policy*, **29**, 667–88.

Schipper, L., M. Ting, M. Khrushch and W. Golove (1997), 'The evolution of carbon dioxide emission from energy use in industrialized countries: an end-use analysis', *Energy Policy*, **25**, 651–72.

Sinton, J.E. (2001), 'Accuracy and reliability of China's energy statistics', *China Economic Review*, **12**, 373–83.

Sinton, J.E. and D.G. Fridley (2000), 'What goes up: recent trends in China's energy consumption', *Energy Policy*, **28**, 671–87.

Sinton, J.E., M.D. Levine and Q.Y. Wang (1998), 'Energy efficiency in China: accomplishments and challenges', *Energy Policy*, **26**, 813–29.

Solaires Power International (SPI) (2003), 'China power report: 1996 to 2000', available at: http://www.solaires.com/chinapower/reports/1996-2000.htm.

Streets, D.G., K.J. Jiang, X.L. Hu, J.E. Sinton, X.Q. Zhang, D.Y. Xu, M.Z. Jacobson and J.E. Hansen (2001), 'Recent reductions in China's greenhouse gas emissions', *Science*, **294**, 1835–7.

Sun, J.W. (1998), 'Changes in energy consumption and energy intensity: a complete decomposition model', *Energy Economics*, **20**, 85–100.

Sun, J.W. (2001), 'Energy demand in the fifteen European Union countries by 2010 – a forecasting model based on the decomposition approach', *Energy*, **26**, 549–60.

Yang, C., M. May and T. Heller (1998), 'Global carbon dioxide emissions scenarios: sensitivity to social and technological factors in three regions', *Mitigation and Adaptation Strategies for Global Change*, **2**, 373–404.

Zhang, F.Q. and B.W. Ang (2001), 'Methodological issues in cross-country/region decomposition of energy and environment indicators', *Energy Economics*, **23**, 179–90.

Zhang, Z.X. (2000), 'Can China afford to commit itself an emission cap? An economic and political analysis', *Energy Economics*, **22**, 587–614.

Zhang, Z.X. (2003), 'Why did the energy intensity fall in China's industrial sector in the 1990s? The relative importance of structural change and intensity change', East–West Center Working Paper 55, Environmental Change, Vulnerability, and Governance Series.

Zhou, J.P. (2003), 'The current situation of China's electric power industry', available at: http://www.eva.ac.at/(en)/projekte/china_power.htm, accessed July 2009.

11. Energy supply-side and demand-side effects

1 INTRODUCTION

Over the past two decades, the energy intensity of China's economy has fallen rapidly at a rate unparalleled in any other country at a similar stage of industrialization (Fisher-Vanden et al., 2004; Wu et al., 2005). After 1996, the income elasticity of energy consumption even shifted from positive to negative, accompanied by an unprecedented decline in energy-related CO_2 emissions. This shift was contrary to all previous forecasts, which predicted that China's energy consumption and CO_2 emissions would continue to rise during the next five decades (for example, Ho et al., 1998; Yang et al., 1998; IPCC, 2000; EIA, 2004). Our estimates based on newly released energy statistics (NBS, 2004) indicate that energy-related CO_2 emissions kept declining during the years from 1996 to 2000 and rebounded in 2001 and 2002.

What happened to China's energy system over the period from 1980 to 2002, especially from 1996 to 2000? What are the dominant underlying forces driving the unique pattern of change in energy use and CO_2 emissions? In particular, what is the relative importance of those underlying forces? What factors created the ultimate economic and political impetus behind those underlying forces?

A variety of studies have attempted to answer these questions. Index decomposition analysis (IDA), a commonly accepted analytical tool for decomposing the historical evolution of energy or environmental indicators into the contributions of a number of pre-defined factors of interest, has been widely applied for this purpose (see some review papers: Ang, 2004; Ang and Zhang, 2000). In the context of IDA, research done by Huang (1993), Sinton and Levine (1994), Ang et al. (1998), Sinton et al. (1998), Garbaccio et al. (1999) and Zhang (2003) has revealed that from 1980 to the mid-1990s energy efficiency improvement in energy end-use sectors is a dominant contributor to driving trends in CO_2 emissions; the economic and fuel structure changes play only nominal roles. However, such trends do not necessarily support continuity in the long run, and they did not necessarily result in a sudden reversal in energy consumption trends (that is, declines in consumption) in the late 1990s.

To analyze the paradox of the late 1990s, some research has been carried out to either verify the reliability of the empirical evidence from the estimation side (NRDC, 2001; Sinton, 2001; Streets et al., 2001) or explore the phenomenon from the mechanism side (Sinton and Fridley, 2000, 2003; Fisher-Vanden et al., 2004; Wu et al., 2005). Using a newly developed provincially aggregated dataset, Wu et al. point out that the speed of decrease in energy intensity and a slowdown in the growth of average labor productivity in the industrial sectors were the dominant contributors to the atypical change of energy-related CO_2 emissions over the 1996–99 period. Using a unique dataset containing approximately 2,500 of China's most energy-intensive large and medium-sized industrial enterprises, Fisher-Vanden et al. conclude that China's declining energy intensity and use over 1997 to 1999 were principally driven by rising relative energy prices, R&D expenditures and ownership reforms in the enterprise sector, as well as shifts in China's industrial structure.

In general, relying upon descriptive discussion, econometric analysis and IDA, scholars reached a certain degree of consensus about the underlying driving forces as well as the economic and political impetus behind the atypical decline of energy use and CO_2 emissions in China over 1996–99.

It is noteworthy that these previous studies were conducted on the energy demand side, rather than the supply side. In other words, the central target of those studies is the total final energy consumption (TFEC) or the consumption-side derived CO_2 emissions (C-TFEC) but not the total primary energy[1] supply (TPES) or the supply-side derived CO_2 emissions (C-TPES). In fact, the demand and the supply sides are two different angles to look at the energy system. Usually, TPES is not equal to TFEC and the ratio between the two is dependent on several factors: the share of secondary energy carriers[2] in end-use sectors; the input/output ratio in transformation sectors;[3] and the share of international trade of secondary energy in the national energy supply. Figure 11.1 illustrates great differences in the TPES/TFEC ratio in selected countries. In an extreme case, the TFEC may be equal to the TPES and the C-TFEC may be equal to the C-TPES, but further decomposition analysis can provide a totally different image since the components on the demand side are energy end-use sectors, while those on the supply side are the energy supply, transformation and processing sectors.

The structural and efficiency changes on the energy supply side have been scarcely touched upon in studies so far. While the demand-side analyses cover the transformation sectors as well, they simply treat them as end users and thus are only concerned about their own consumption, that is, fuels consumed for heating, pumping, traction and lighting purposes. But they fail to capture the energy utilized as sources for generating

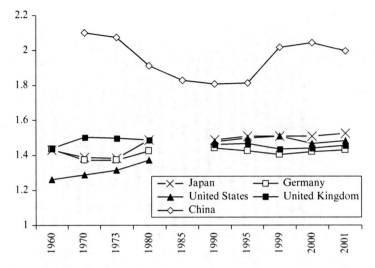

Source: OECD/IEA (2003).

Figure 11.1 Ratio of TPES to TFEC in selected countries

secondary energy carriers. As a result, in the energy demand-side analyses, the secondary energy carriers are usually measured according to the energy service that they can provide (that is, the net calorific value) but not the primary energy equivalent for generating such service.

Theoretically, energy demand-side analyses can certainly touch upon the transformation processes as long as they trace the secondary energy carriers back to their generation base to get the generation-based calorific value. In fact, this is a necessary step to get the carbon emissions factor for electricity and heat. The generation-based calorific value and carbon emissions factor are still limited, however, in terms of reflecting the performance of energy supply processes. For each transformation sector, such single indicators obscure the relative importance of transformation losses, distribution losses, re-use of secondary energy in transformation processes, and the influence of international trade. Therefore, to fully understand changes in scale, structure and efficiency on the energy supply side, we need to develop a new model that decomposes the aggregated TPES and C-TPES into the contributions arising from various energy supply sectors or processes.

Nowadays China's conventional coal-based energy supply system is undergoing great challenges due to the rapidly increasing demand for electricity and petroleum products. Direct consumption of coal is declining (see Figure 11.2); conversely, the prevailing tendency is a dramatic shift

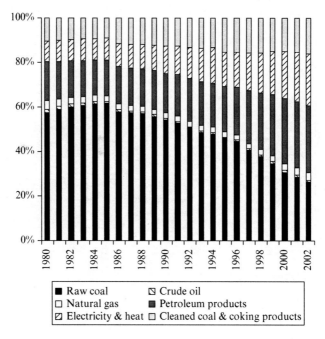

Sources: NBS (1990a, 1996a, 2000a, 2004).

Figure 11.2   Structure of energy consumption by fuel type in China

from direct to indirect use of coal for generating electricity (see Figure 11.3). Hence the transformation sectors, especially the electricity sector, appear to be playing a crucial role in shaping the overall advances in efficiency and changes in CO_2 emissions. Obviously, a new supply-side-based model could help provide a more complete picture of the performance of the transformation sector and thus offer an in-depth understanding about the atypical decline of China's energy supply, demand and CO_2 emissions during the period from 1996 to 2000.

2   MODEL SPECIFICATION

Conceptual Framework of the Overall Energy System

By tracing the energy paths through the economic system, from the desired goods and services to the primary energy required to supply them, we can in principle distinguish energy from other components such as labor

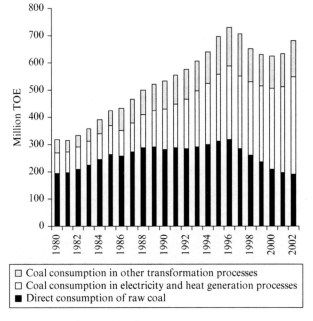

Sources: NBS (1990a, 1996a, 2000a, 2004).

Figure 11.3 Structure of coal consumption by source in China

and capital, and identify a unique 'overall energy system'. The conceptual framework of this system is illustrated in Figure 11.4. Energy supply, transformation and consumption behavior are linked together by energy flows inside the system.

The figure illustrates that when moving from the supply sector across the transformation sector to the final consumption sector, components comprising aggregate TPES are involved in different processes or activities. As with common commercial goods and services, energy is also traded in markets, even though its price may fail to fully reflect its scarcity value under some circumstances. According to Adam Smith's classical statement that 'consumption is the sole end and purpose of all production', changes in energy supply should be driven by changes in transformation and final consumption processes. Thus, by tracing the path of each component in TPES across the overall energy flow, we can clarify the relative contribution of various forces operating in different processes or stages and obtain more detailed insight about change in aggregate TPES and TPES-induced CO_2 emissions.

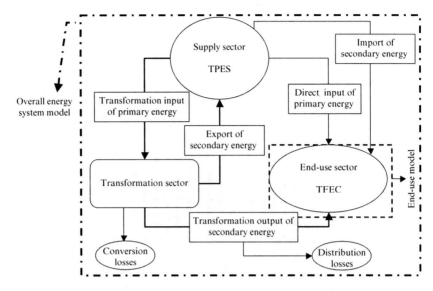

Figure 11.4   Conceptual framework of overall energy system

Comparison between Demand- and Supply-side Analyses

Accounting for national CO_2 emissions can be conducted either from the energy supply side through the 'reference approach' or from the demand side through the 'sectoral approach' (IPCC/OECD/IEA, 1997). Theoretically, these two approaches should result in the same estimates, as long as so-called 'fugitive emissions' can be captured in the sectoral approach. Hence any exploration of the driving forces behind trends in CO_2 emissions can be conducted from either the supply or the demand side. Demand-side analyses specialize in providing a detailed understanding about how changes in economic activity, sectoral and subsectoral shifts, and sectoral energy intensity influence final energy consumption and CO_2 emissions. The supply-side analysis suggested in this chapter can be used as an ancillary tool, capable of elaborating the performance of the overall energy system from a different angle. In demand-side analyses, the behavior of energy supply processes is obscured by each fuel's capability of doing mechanical work, while in supply-side analyses each energy supply, transformation and processing process can be magnified. In demand-side analyses the performance of end users is explored in depth and finer sectoral information is usually preferred, while in supply-side analyses we are just concerned about their cumulative impacts.

National energy or climate change policies can be classified into two major groups: demand- and supply-side policies. Demand-side policies mainly focus on stimulating energy conservation and correspondingly the end-use (demand-side) models specialize in describing some implications about their implementation. Supply-side policies, in reality, can also be adopted in various countries. For example, to meet the increasing demand for electricity in end-use sectors, an energy supply system faces many potential choices, such as re-allocating raw coal by switching from direct combustion to indirect use for generating thermal power; accelerating the development of nuclear and hydro power; or boosting imports of electricity. Tradeoffs must be made among the options, with the goal of achieving a secure energy supply. Obviously, different choices will present different environmental impacts on society. The above-mentioned issues go beyond the scope of end-use models and call for another approach – one that properly covers the energy supply process.

To sum up, while acknowledging that 'end-use models' specialize in interpreting the performance of end-use sectors in terms of energy use and CO_2 emissions, we also realize the necessity to advocate an 'overall energy system model' that integrates the energy supply, transformation and consumption processes, in order to provide an in-depth investigation of the underlying driving forces shaping changes in CO_2 emissions induced from TPES.

Issues to be Explored in this Newly Suggested Model

Based on the conventional Laspeyres index decomposition approach, Landwehr and Jochem (1997) developed a new model dealing with structural and efficiency changes on the energy supply side. While we were illuminated by their way of generating the governing function for decomposition, we also recognize several limitations that need special attention.

Landwehr and Jochem conducted their analysis within the scope of energy supply and could not deal directly with CO_2 emissions. In demand-side analyses, calculating CO_2 emissions from energy end use is straightforward, by multiplying the carbon emissions factor by the amount of each fuel consumed. When we attempt to go from energy supply to CO_2 emissions, however, we must realize that the emissions behavior of each fuel comprising TPES may vary with its original source, and also with the processes that each fuel is involved in across the overall energy system.

The model by Landwehr and Jochem is based on the conventional Laspeyres index decomposition approach, the result of which always leaves a large unexplained residual term and has proven unconvincing to some extent (Ang and Zhang, 2000; Choi and Ang, 2003; Ang, 2004). The appropriate application of a perfect index decomposition approach on the energy supply side is a new challenge confronted by this chapter.

The Landwehr and Jochem model does not distinguish between different fuel mixes for electricity generation; in particular, the role of hydropower is neglected in their analysis. However, the main intension of our analysis is to determine the role of electricity in shaping trends in China's CO_2 emissions; thus some adjustment is undoubtedly needed compared to their approach.

The model suggested in this chapter aims to answer the following questions: (i) How and to what extent do changes in activity scale, energy intensity and fuel structure arising from end-use sectors influence CO_2 emissions? (ii) How and to what extent does hydropower substitution for thermal power influence CO_2 emissions? (iii) How and to what extent do conversion losses, distribution losses, and fuel structure changes arising from transformation processes influence CO_2 emissions? (iv) How and to what extent does the international supply and demand of secondary energy influence domestic CO_2 emissions? And finally, (v) how does a series of 'marginal' factors like 'stock changes', 'non-energy uses' and even 'statistical differences' influence CO_2 emissions?

Model Specification: An Overall Energy System Model

Generation of the governing function
In demand-side models, the left side of the governing function is the aggregate CO_2 emissions derived from TFEC and the right side is the summation of CO_2 emissions arising from various regions, sectors and fuels. Similarly, our overall energy system model uses the aggregate CO_2 emissions derived from TPES as the explained variable (*C-TPES*), which comprises the following items with regard to the energy carriers and sources/sinks of each energy carrier in TPES:

$$C\text{--}TPES = \sum_{n=1}^{4} CP_n + \sum_{n=1}^{4} CS_n, \qquad (11.1)$$

where *CP* and *CS* denote CO_2 emissions corresponding to primary energy carriers and secondary energy carriers respectively; *n* denotes sources or sinks of the primary energy supply; $n = 1$ denotes indigenous production; $n = 2$ denotes imports of energy (including Chinese ships refueling abroad); $n = 3$ denotes exports of energy (including foreign ships refueling in China); and $n = 4$ denotes stock changes. It must be kept in mind that CP_3 and CS_3 have negative value over the targeted period and CP_4 and CS_4 may change over time stochastically. A negative number signifies stock building and a reduced carbon burden on the environment, whereas a positive number means a stock draw and an added carbon burden.

Further decomposition of the above components comprising C-TPES is dependent on what kind of activity each component is involved in. As for CP_n, no matter what kind of origin, there are only two options: direct input into end-use sectors or indirect input into transformation sectors. If we assume that in terms of fuel quality (heat value and carbon content) there is no difference between domestic supply and imports, and also no difference between stock change and current year supply, the components CP_1 to CP_4 can be taken as identical across the overall energy flow, and we do not need to make any distinction among their origins but just use one integrated index CP (net outcome of CP_1 to CP_4) to analyze how CO_2 emissions related to primary energy carriers are influenced by the performance of transformation processes and end-use processes.

In contrast to primary energy carriers, tracing the components of secondary energy carriers in TPES depends on their origins, so these components need to be carefully identified in model development. In reality, imports of secondary energy could be used either in end-use sectors or in transformation sectors. In a theoretical model, however, an allowance for consumption of imported secondary energy in transformation processes requires us to separate this part from the domestic re-use of secondary energy, as the latter has taken part in the transformation process at least once and is then re-used for further conversion. Since such statistics are still unavailable, we need to simplify this issue by assuming that the imported secondary energy is used in the transformation sector only when the domestic supply cannot meet the total demand.

Secondary energy exported is generated domestically but consumed abroad; thus only the transmission and conversion losses related to this part are left in TPES. Since the inputs for generating secondary energy that is later exported have been counted in the net supply of primary energy carriers into transformation and end-use processes, here we should deduct the derived secondary energy in order to avoid overestimating. The route of the stock change of secondary energy is also assumed to be the same as that of the international trade of secondary energy for the same reason.

As mentioned above, there are only two options for primary energy supply in the energy system: direct supply into end-use sectors or indirect supply into transformation sectors. The latter can be further divided into two parts, namely supply for domestic demand, and supply for foreign demand (export). Thus CP can be disaggregated into three parts:[4] $CP1$ (CO_2 emissions related to primary energy supply for end use); $CP2$ (CO_2 emissions related to primary energy supply for transformation of domestic demand of secondary energy); and $CP3$ (CO_2 emissions related to primary energy supply for transformation of exported secondary energy).

$CP1$ will be influenced by the following factors: (a) activity scale, energy intensity and fuel structure with regard to primary energy consumption in end-use sectors; (b) distribution losses during transmission of primary energy; and finally (c) carbon intensity of each fuel. Carbon intensity usually measures the carbon content of each fuel. The direct primary energy input into end-use sectors may be used either for combustion or for non-energy purposes. The latter will lead to a certain amount of carbon storage that will not be released over a certain period. When generating the carbon intensity of each primary energy carrier for direct end use, our model will also take this point into account.

*CP*2 and *CP*3 will be driven by (a) activity scale, energy intensity and fuel structure with regard to secondary energy consumption in end-use sectors; (b) the input/output ratio from primary energy to secondary energy, which is usually decided by conversion losses, distribution losses, and re-use of secondary energy in transformation sectors; (c) competition between imports and domestic supply with regard to secondary energy (given the demand of secondary energy in end-use sectors, increases in imports will lead to declines in domestic primary energy supply and vice versa, and this can be regarded as the indirect impact of imports); (d) the expansion or contraction of exports (the expansion of exports will lead to increases in demand for primary energy input and vice versa, and this can be regarded as the indirect impact of exports); and finally (e) carbon intensity. Since we have to analyze the change in primary energy supply with regard to each transformation process, the carbon intensity corresponding to each process will be decided by each process's carbon content and also the ratio of its products used for only energy purpose. The carbon content of a process is dependent on the fuel mix and the carbon content of each fuel on the input side.

The CO_2 emissions related to imports, exports or stock changes of secondary energy will be influenced by the scale of energy use for each process, the fuel structure and also the carbon content of each fuel. They can be categorized as direct impacts of import, export and stock changes.

Finally, as a statistical artifact, the energy balance table may lose 'balance' in the relationships among TPES, TFEC and the transformation input/output ratio due to statistical errors. The arising differences are usually referred to as 'statistical differences'. A model encompassing the overall energy system must evaluate the contribution of statistical differences. In technical treatment, however, it is difficult to determine the exact stage where statistical differences arise. As stated by OECD/IEA (2004), it is more likely to get a complete and accurate record for energy supply than energy consumption since fuel combustion occurs through a wide range of activities in national economies. A complete and accurate record of the quantities of each fuel type consumed in each 'end-use' activity is often difficult to obtain. Thus, to simplify our discussion, a reasonable approach is to allocate the statistical difference to final consumption data.

The quality of China's energy statistics, especially coal supply data since 1996, has been regarded by scholars as widely suspect (for example, Sinton, 2001). Some argue that a certain amount of supply from prohibited small-scale coal mines may leak into a 'black market', and this market should account for the gap between coal supply and consumption. This argument suggests that the statistical difference for coal should be allocated to the supply side. Furthermore, due to their concentration, transformation sectors usually have more reliable energy input/output data than end-use sectors. In our analysis, we therefore allocate the statistical difference for primary energy carriers to the stage of supply for end-use sectors. For secondary energy carriers, we simply assume that the statistical difference occurs at the final consumption stage.

Decomposition model using LMDI[5] methodology
In the above discussion, we have clarified the potential determinant effects driving changes in C-TPES and established the logical framework of this overall energy system model. The mathematical derivation of this model can be found in Appendix 11A. As emphasized above, in the relevant datasets some variables remain negative or change stochastically over the targeted period, requiring new techniques to deal with such conditions in the field of IDA. The technical appendix offers a detailed discussion of this aspect. Function 11.2 represents the final decomposition function of the overall energy system model:

$$\Delta C\text{-}TPES = D_{E\text{-}SCA} + D_{E\text{-}EI} + D_{E\text{-}FS} + D_{CI} + D_{LO\text{-}P} + D_{STA\text{-}P}$$
$$+ D_{STA\text{-}S} + D_{CYS} + D_{DOS} + D_{FRD} + D_{LO\text{-}S} + D_{RU}$$
$$+ D_{POWST} + D_{GUE} + D_{FST} + D_{TIM} + D_{FS\text{-}IM} + D_{CI\text{-}IM}$$
$$+ D_{TEXP} + D_{FS\text{-}EXPD} + D_{CI\text{-}EXP} + D_{STCH} + D_{CI\text{-}STCH}.$$
$$(11.2)$$

Table 11.1 provides a further interpretation of the significance of each determinant effect in function 11.2. Figure 11.5 clarifies the role of each determinant effect in shaping trends in CO_2 emissions related to the total primary energy supply (TPES).

Data

This model covers the period from 1980 to 2002. All energy data are collected from the *China Energy Statistical Yearbook* (NBS, 1990a, 1996a, 2000a, 2004) and the *China Energy Databook* (LBNL/ERI, 2001). Other economic

Table 11.1   Significance of each determinant effect in function (11.2)

Process	Item	Significance
		Driving forces on energy demand side
End-use processes	$D_{E\text{-}SCA}$	Scale effect — Indicating that sectoral scale changes (measured by economic scale) in end-use processes will entail changes in C-TPES
	$D_{E\text{-}EI}$	Energy intensity effect — Indicating that sectoral energy intensity changes in end-use processes will entail changes in C-TPES
	$D_{E\text{-}FS}$	Fuel structure effect — Indicating that changes in the composition of fuel type in total final energy consumption will entail changes in C-TPES
	D_{CI}	Carbon intensity effect — Measuring the contribution of carbon intensity changes to changes in C-TPES. It is allocated as demand-side effects because it is mainly influenced by non-energy use behavior
		Driving forces on energy supply side
Transformation and distribution processes	D_{CYS}	Current year supply effect — Measuring the indirect impact of stock changes of secondary energy i on changes in C-TPES
	D_{DOS}	Domestic supply effect — Measuring the indirect impact of imports of secondary energy i on changes in C-TPES
	D_{FRD}	Foreign demand effect — Measuring the indirect impact of exports of secondary energy i on changes in C-TPES
	D_{RU}	Re-use effect — Measuring the impact of re-use of secondary energy on changes in C-TPES.
	D_{POWST}	Power substitution effect — Measuring how the substitution of thermal power by hydro power influences changes in C-TPES

	D_{GUE}	Gross unit consumption effect	Measuring the influence of input/output ratio on changes in C-TPES
	D_{FSTR}	Fuel substitution effect	Measuring how the substitute of primary energy by secondary energy on the input side of transformation sector influences the C-TPES
	D_{LO-P}, D_{LO-S}	Distribution losses effect for primary energy	Measuring the contribution of changes in unitary distribution losses (distribution losses per unit of supplied energy) to changes in C-TPES
International trade process	$D_{TIM}, D_{FS-IM}, D_{CI-IM}$	Scale effect, fuel structure effect, carbon intensity effect arising from imports	Indicators measuring the direct impact of imports on the C-TPES: scale changes, fuel structure changes and carbon intensity changes of imported secondary energy carriers. Net impact of imports should be $D_{DOS} + D_{TIM} + D_{FS-IM} + D_{CI-IM}$
	$D_{TEXP}, D_{FS-EXP}, D_{CI-EXP}$	Scale effect, fuel structure effect, carbon intensity effect arising from exports	Indicators measuring the direct impact of exports on the C-TPES: scale changes, fuel structure changes and carbon intensity changes of exported secondary energy carriers. Net impact of exports should be $D_{FRD} + D_{TEXP} + D_{FS-EXP} + D_{CI-EXP}$
Stock change process	$D_{STCH}, D_{CI-STCH}$	Scale effect and carbon intensity effect arising from stock changes	Indicators measuring the direct impact of stock changes on the C-TPES: scale changes and carbon intensity changes of stock changes of secondary energy carriers. Net impact of exports should be $D_{CYS} + D_{STCH} + D_{CI-STCH}$
Others			
Statistical imbalance	D_{STA-S}, D_{STA-P}	Statistical adjustment effect	Measuring the contribution of changes in unitary statistical adjustments to changes in C-TPES. D_{STA-S} corresponds to secondary energy and D_{STA-P} corresponds to primary energy

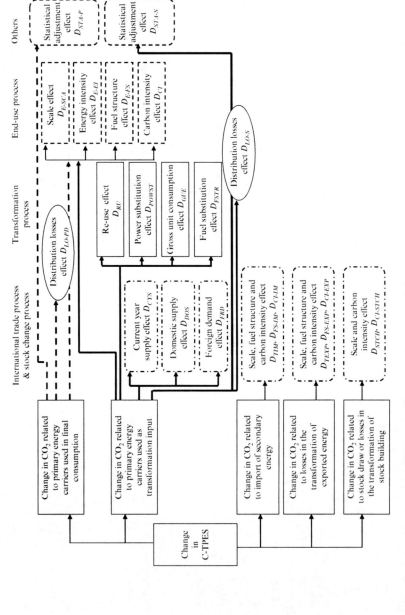

Figure 11.5 Framework of the overall energy system model

236

information is collected from the *China Statistical Yearbook* (NBS, 1986–1989, 1990b, 1991–1994, 1995a, 1996b, 1997, 1998a, 1999, 2000b, 2001, 2002a, 2003), *China Industrial Economy Statistical Yearbook* (NBS, 1995b, 1998b, 2000c), *Comprehensive Statistical Data and Materials on 50 Years of Chinese Industry, Transportation and Energy* (NBS, 2000d) and *The Statistics on Investment in Fixed Assets of China* (1950–2000) (NBS, 2002b).

3   RESULTS AND DISCUSSION

Relative Importance of Each Process to the Real Changes of C-TPES

As shown in Table 11.1, all determinant effects can be classified into two groups: energy demand-side effects and supply-side effects. The demand-side effects are mainly operating in the energy end-use process, while the supply-side effects spread into transformation, distribution, international trade and stock change processes. Figures 11.6–9 show the relative contribution of each process to real changes of C-TPES in different stages.

Figure 11.6 illustrates that for the 1980–90 period, positive economic scale effects and fuel structure effects suppressed the negative energy intensity effects on the demand side, resulting in a net positive influence on C-TPES. On the energy supply side, however, the aggregate effects of

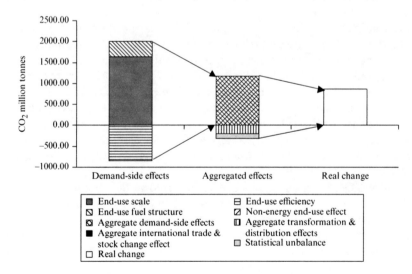

Figure 11.6   Relative contribution of each process to real change of C-TPES (1980–1990)

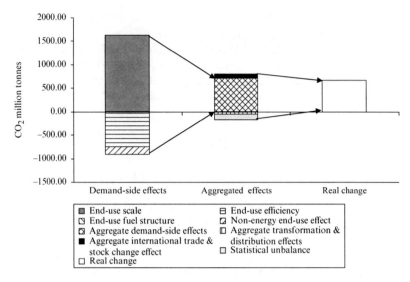

*Figure 11.7   Relative contribution of each process to real change of
C-TPES (1990–1996)*

transformation and distribution processes acted as a negative force, which
to some extent counteracted the demand-side positive effects. Furthermore,
the statistical imbalance between supply and demand, the aggregate effects
of international trade and stock changes played nominal negative roles
over that period. The real change in C-TPES was positive, indicating that
in the 1980s, CO_2 emissions related to the total primary energy supply were
driven primarily by the effects operating in end-use processes.

Figure 11.7 indicates that for the 1990–96 period, the property and scale
of the contribution for each process did not change greatly compared
with that in 1980s. The aggregate influence of demand-side effects played
a persistent positive role, while the aggregate influence of transformation
and distribution processes acted as negative force continuously. The influence of statistical imbalance still remained as negative but the influence of
international trade shifted to positive.

Since 1996, however, great changes occurred in the energy supply and
demand sectors. First, it is noteworthy that CO_2 emissions related to total
primary energy supply kept declining over 1996 to 2000. This was partially
due to the shrinkage of positive aggregate effects on the energy demand
side. As shown in Figure 11.8, economic growth slowed during that period
compared to the early 1990s; simultaneously, declines in energy intensity
accelerated to some extent. These two factors resulted in a great shrinkage
with the net influence of energy demand-side effects. The absolute scale of

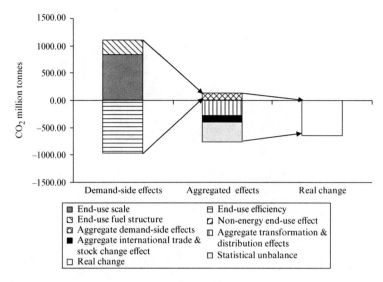

Figure 11.8 Relative contribution of each process to real change in C-TPES (1996–2000)

aggregate energy demand-side effects over the 1996–2000 period was only 20 percent of that over 1990–96. On the other hand, the contribution from transformation and distribution processes expanded dramatically (sixfold) compared with 1990–96. The contributions of statistical imbalance between supply and demand during this period also emerged as significantly negative, which suggests that the apparent decline of CO_2 emissions related to total primary energy supply was partially caused by human error in energy data collection. Finally, the contribution of international trade shifted to negative again, to contribute to a certain extent to the decline of C-TPES.

Since 2001, CO_2 emissions related to total primary energy supply rebounded. As shown in Figure 11.9, the positive force arising from the energy demand side recovered to some extent. Simultaneously, the contributions of international trade and statistical imbalances played important roles in the apparent rebound. All of these effects overwhelmed the persistent negative contribution from energy transformation processes.

To sum up, until 1996 CO_2 emissions related to the total primary energy supply were driven primarily by energy end-use processes. During 1996 to 2000, however, the scale of end-use effects shrank dramatically and simultaneously the negative force arising from transformation processes expanded considerably. The negative force from international trade also reinforced the declining tendency. As shown in Table 11.1, transformation, distribution and international trade are all on the energy supply side.

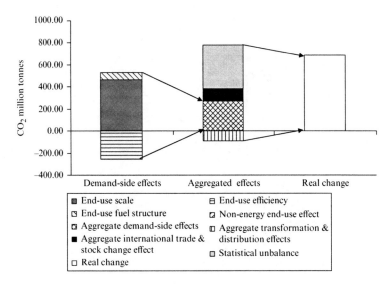

Figure 11.9   Relative contribution of each process to real change of C-TPES (2000–2002)

Therefore, we can safely demonstrate that in spite of the overwhelming role of energy demand-side effects in driving trends in CO_2 emissions, supply-side effects accounted significantly for the special changes in CO_2 emissions over 1996 to 2000.

Performance of Various Effects on the Energy Demand Side

Economic scale, energy intensity and fuel structure as well as carbon intensity are four factors operating on the energy demand side. An in-depth investigation on the performance of the first three factors falls into the scope of an 'end-use model'. Our previous study (Wu et al., 2005) has provided detailed elaboration for the case of China. Thus, our specific goal with this chapter is not to explore detailed sectoral or subsectoral information but to evaluate the relative contribution of the four factors mentioned above, compared with a body of newly defined factors operating on the energy supply side. As for the carbon intensity effect, that is, D_{CI}, it is mainly dependent on the changes in carbon content of the targeted fuel and also on the changes in the non-energy-use ratio of that fuel. Hence, it is necessary to discuss its performance here (see Figure 11.10).

We demonstrated above that our definition of carbon intensity corresponds to a specific process but not to a fuel. When analyzing their performance, we consistently apply our own definition for carbon intensity for

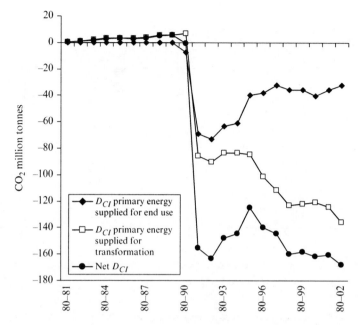

Figure 11.10   Historical change of carbon intensity effect for various processes

different processes. Figure 11.10 indicates that changes in carbon intensity corresponding to primary energy supplied into transformation processes remained slightly above zero during the 1980s and then suddenly shifted from 1990 to 1991. After that it stagnated for some years and then continued declining after 1995. The carbon intensity corresponding to direct end use of primary energy increased over the 1991–95 period but stagnated after that. In our model, the carbon content of each fuel is assumed to be constant over the targeted period, so our analysis reveals that the ratio of secondary energy used for energy purposes continued declining after 1995 and consequently exerted a persistent negative impact on C-TPES. The net outcome of carbon intensity effect was an increase over 1990–95 and a decrease thereafter.

Performance of Various Effects in Transformation and Distribution Processes

Figure 11.11 illustrates the performance of driving forces operating in transformation and distribution processes. This figure indicates that the gross unit consumption effect D_{GUE} played a persistent negative role over

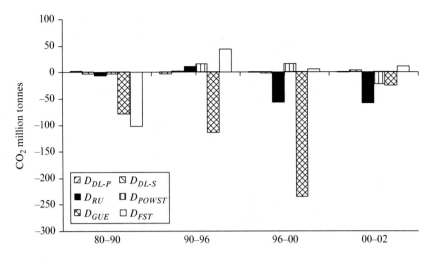

Figure 11.11   Driving forces operating in the transformation and distribution processes

the past two decades and its rate of decrease accelerated during 1996–2000. Gross unit consumption, measuring the input–output ratio of transformation processes, can be taken as a rough indicator of energy efficiency performance. We should not directly link this with the real efficiency performance for a specific production process without clarifying the contribution of fuel structure change. The figure illustrates a positive change in the fuel substitute effect over 1996–2000, which is decided by the ratio of primary energy use on the input side for each transformation process. This means that the fuel structure change positively influenced the CO_2 emissions and therefore the speed of decline of gross unit consumption undoubtedly points to the expansion of energy efficiency improvement in transformation processes.

The transformation processes consist of thermal power generation, heating supply, coal washing, coking processes and petroleum refining. As shown in Figure 11.12, the declining trend of D_{GUE} prevailed in most of the transformation processes for most of the stages. Remarkable efficiency improvement in thermal power generation processes can be observed throughout the 1980s and 1990s; in particular, over the period from 1996 to 2000, such efficiency improvement accelerated to a great extent. A similar acceleration of efficiency improvement in coal washing processes can also be observed since the mid-1990s. Gross efficiency performance in petroleum refinery processes experienced great improvements during 1990–96; but while the pace of such improvements slowed in the late 1990s and early 2000s, it continued to play

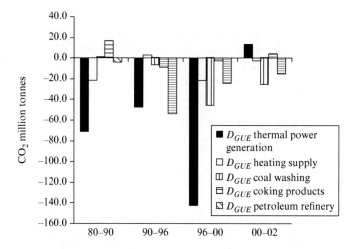

Figure 11.12   Performance of D_{GUE} by transformation processes

Table 11.2   Comparison of performance of power plants of different scales

Capacity(MW)	< 25	25–50	50–100	100–300	300–1000	>1000
Coal consumption (gce/kWh)	705	542	376	366	339	321
SO$_2$ emissions (g/kWh)	15.21	11.7	8.8	7.72	7.78	5.6
CO$_2$ emissions (g-C/kWh)	423	325	226	220	203	193

Source: Adapted from Xue (2002).

a significant role in reducing CO$_2$ emissions. Generally, the speed of decline of gross unit consumption effects in transformation processes as a whole should be mainly attributed to changes in thermal power generation processes and coal washing processes. The efficiency improvements in these two processes are probably two of the most important factors accounting for the decline in CO$_2$ emissions in the late 1990s.

Many economic and political factors provide the impetus behind efficiency improvements in the energy supply sector. First, we can link these efficiency improvements with energy policies calling for the shut down of small-scale power plants in China. Table 11.2 shows that the energy consumption per unit of output of small-scale power plants (with capacity less than 50 MW) is almost double that of large-scale power plants.

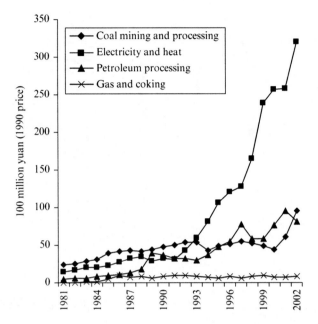

Source: NBS (2002b, 2003).

Figure 11.13   Technical investment in energy sectors over the last two decades

Correspondingly, their CO_2 emissions per kWh of output are also around twice the figure for large ones. After 1986, China began to implement a series of policies to encourage the construction of large-scale power plants, in order to alleviate the problem of power shortages. Negative side-effects appeared quickly, however, due to the inefficiency and high environmental costs of small-scale thermal power plants. From early 1989, therefore, the government began to apply other measures to prohibit the development of small-scale power plants, but the expansion of these plants remained out of control until 1995. After that, stricter policies ensured better control of the development of small-scale plants. The timing of the introduction of such policies is generally consistent with major changes in the 'gross unit consumption' in this sector.

Second, efforts aimed at improving energy efficiency in industrial sectors also played a significant role. Here we use investment in technical upgrades and transformation as a proxy indicator to reflect these efforts. As illustrated in Figure 11.13, investment in technical upgrades and transformation in the electricity sector increased sharply in 1990 and has accelerated further since 1996. This should be one of the most important economic

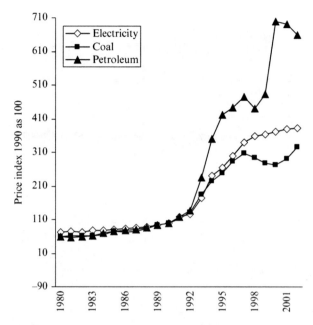

Source: NBS (2002b, 2003).

Figure 11.14 Price index of various fuels over the last two decades

impetuses driving energy efficiency improvements. Government-supported projects and programs accounted for a large source of these investments; furthermore, reforms in energy pricing systems since 1993 led to a dramatic rise in fuel prices (see Figure 11.14) and consequently, better-off economic conditions in the electricity generation, petroleum refinery and coal mining and dressing sectors. These improved conditions reinforced the capability for technical upgrades as well.

Impact of International Trade on C-TPES

Figures 11.15 and 11.16 illustrate the impact of international trade on C-TPES. As clarified above, impacts arising from imports can be classified into two groups: direct impacts (that is, scale changes, fuel structure changes and carbon intensity changes of imported secondary energy products), and indirect impacts (that is, domestic supply effect D_{DOS}). Since we assume that the carbon content of each fuel remained constant over the target period and all imported products were used only for energy purposes, the carbon intensity change can be ignored here. Changes in the

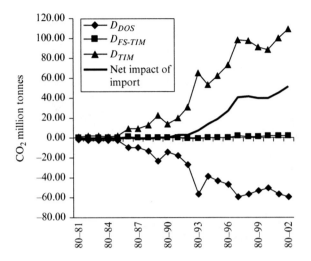

Figure 11.15   Determinants related to import of secondary energy

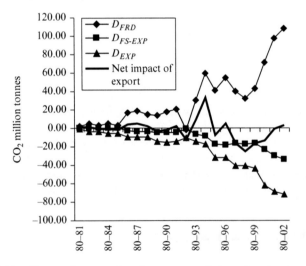

Figure 11.16   Determinants related to export of secondary energy

total amount of imported secondary energy continued playing a positive role in driving national CO_2 emissions during 1980 to 1996; thereafter it became a negative force for four years, and then became positive again in 2001 and 2002. On the other hand, increases in imports compete with the domestic supply and thus reduce the input of primary energy (mainly crude oil) for generating final demand of secondary energy, which is reflected by the trend of D_{DOS}. Figure 11.15 clearly illustrates that trends in domestic supply effect D_{DOS} are symmetrical with D_{TIM}. As for the trend in net impact of imports, we can find that it started to increase gradually from 1990 but has stagnated since 1997. While the absolute level of the contributions arising from imports is comparatively lower than effects operating in end-use or transformation processes, implications drawn from their transition can still provide us with information about how the reliance on foreign supply influences domestic CO_2 emissions.

The fact that changes in exports will entail changes in primary energy input is reflected by the trend of D_{FRD}. Increases in the ratio of exports to domestic demand of secondary energy exert a positive impact on CO_2 emissions related to primary energy input for exports and ultimately on C-TPES. Figure 11.16 shows that D_{FRD} was increasing until 1996, declined during the period from 1996 to 1998 and then increased again. Showing a symmetrical relationship, total exports also stopped increasing during 1996 to 1998 and then resumed again thereafter. Consequently, the 'net impact of exports' became a negative force from 1996 to 1998 but played a positive role for most of the target years. As stated above, the net amount left in the TPES related to exports is the corresponding losses for generating the exported part during transformation processes. Therefore, the decline of 'net impact of exports' was driven not only by the exports themselves, but also by the performance of transformation processes. The accelerated decline of the gross unit consumption effect may be responsible to a certain extent for changes in the net impact of exports.

Relative Contributions of Possible Effects Leading to the Atypical Decline of C-TPES

Based on function (11.3) below, we can evaluate the relative contributions of potential effects leading to the atypical decline of CO_2 emissions related to the total primary energy supply over the period from 1996 to 2000:

$$yearly\ average(\Delta C - TPES)^{90-96} - yearly\ average(\Delta C - TPES)^{96-00}$$

$$= yearly\ average(D_{end-use\ effects})^{90-96}$$

$$- yearly\ average(D_{end-use\ effects})^{96-00}$$

$$+ yearly\ average(D_{transformation\ effects})^{90-96}$$

$$- yearly\ average(D_{transformation\ effects})^{96-00}$$

$$+ yearly\ average(D_{international\ trade\ effects})^{90-96}$$

$$- yearly\ average(D_{international\ trade\ effects})^{96-00}$$

$$+ \text{ } yearly \text{ } average(D_{statistics \text{ } effects})^{90-96}$$

$$- \text{ } yearly \text{ } average(D_{statistics \text{ } effects})^{96-00} \hspace{4cm} (11.3)$$

Figure 11.17 clearly indicates that the speed of energy intensity decline and the slowdown of economic growth in end-use sectors acted as a significant negative force driving the decline of C-TPES on the energy demand side. The fuel structure change contributed positively to the total change of CO_2 emissions. With 1990 as the base year, Figure 11.10 shows a dramatic drop from 1990 to 1996 in carbon intensity. While it kept declining after 1995, the yearly average change over the period from 1996 to 2000 is still much lower than that over 1990 to 1996. Therefore the slowdown of decline of carbon intensity played a positive role here.

It is worth noting that the aggregate effects on the energy demand side are parallel to the aggregate effects on the energy supply side, which includes transformation, distribution and international trade as well as stock changes. Of course, among supply-side effects, the changes in gross unit consumption arising from the transformation sector are overwhelming forces driving the atypical decline of C-TPES. Over the 1996–2000 period, the relative contribution of energy demand processes is around 32.22 percent while that of energy supply processes is around 39.26 percent, among which the transformation processes account for 22.57 percent and international trade processes for 16.68 percent.

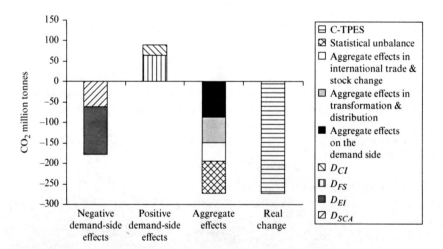

Figure 11.17   Potential factors leading to the atypical decline in C-TPES (1996–2000)

4 CONCLUDING REMARKS

Based on a newly developed model that integrates energy production, transformation and consumption processes, this chapter explores the underlying driving forces behind trends in CO_2 emissions related to the total primary energy supply during the 1980–2002 period in China, paying particular attention to the atypical decline during 1996–2000. A specific intention of this chapter is to compare the relative contribution of some traditionally defined factors operating on the energy demand side with a body of newly defined factors on the energy supply side.

This study reveals that before 1996, changes in C-TPES were mainly driven by changes in economic scale, fuel structure and energy intensity on the energy demand side; the structure and efficiency changes on the energy supply side played only a minor role. During the period from 1996 to 2000, however, the scale of end-use effects shrank dramatically and simultaneously the negative force arising from transformation processes expanded significantly. Such transitions directly resulted in the decline of total CO_2 emissions related to total primary energy supply. The negative force arising from international trade reinforced the declining tendency of C-TPES and the statistical imbalance between supply and demand was also partially responsible for the decline of C-TPES.

The shrinkage of demand-side effects was mainly attributed to the slow-down of economic growth and the speed of energy intensity decrease. On the energy supply side, changes in the gross unit consumption in transformation processes, especially in electricity generation processes, played an overwhelming role. In sum, mainly the speed of efficiency improvement in end-use and transformation processes accounted for the decline of C-TPES.

Many factors provide the impetus behind energy efficiency improvements in either end-use or transformation sectors. To elucidate the economic or political drivers, regression analysis is definitely needed to verify causal linkages between the energy efficiency indicators and some proxy indicators for policy instruments. That analysis would be a massive task, and beyond the main focus of this chapter. By using secondary supporting information, however, we would like to point out some possible factors leading to the speed of efficiency improvements in various sectors. First, investment in technical transformation in industrial sectors has accelerated since the mid-1990s, particularly in the electricity sector. This should contribute to the acceleration of energy efficiency improvements. Meanwhile, the steadily rising prices of electricity, oil and coal since 1993 might have provided strong economic incentives for enterprises to decouple energy use from economic growth, and simultaneously reinforced the potential for technical innovation in the energy sector.

In addition, all of these effects were probably reinforced by policy reforms in the economic system, such as the closing of small-scale energy-intensive enterprises since the mid-1990s, as well as ownership reforms. Finally, some uncontrollable factors, particularly the economic deterioration in heavy industries and slower economic growth, probably led to the slowdown of scale effects. To a certain extent, these factors inevitably contributed negatively to the energy supply, consumption and CO_2 emissions.

NOTES

1. Primary energy refers to fuels which are found in nature, such as raw coal, crude oil, natural gas, hydro power, nuclear power, wind power and so on.
2. Secondary energy carrier refers to fuels that are derived from primary fuels, such as electricity, heat, cleaned and washed coal, coking products, petroleum products and so on.
3. Transformation sectors refer to the sectors where the primary fuels are transformed into secondary fuels by physical or chemical processes (for example, from crude oil to petroleum products, from raw coal to electricity).
4. Note that there are no subscripts with $CP1$, $CP2$ and $CP3$; they are different from CP_n, $n = 1$ to 4.
5. LMDI is the abbreviation for the log-mean divisia index method. For details, see Appendix 11A.

REFERENCES

Ang, B.W. (2004), 'Decomposition analysis for policymaking in energy: which is the preferred method?', *Energy Policy*, **32**, 1131–9.
Ang, B.W. and F.Q. Zhang (2000), 'A survey of index decomposition analysis in energy and environmental studies', *Energy*, **25**, 1149–76.
Ang, B.W., F.Q. Zhang and K.H. Choi (1998), 'Factorizing changes in energy and environmental indicators through decomposition', *Energy*, **23**, 489–95.
Choi, K.H. and B.W. Ang (2003), 'Decomposition of aggregate energy intensity changes in two measures: ratio and difference', *Energy Economics*, **25**, 615–24.
Energy Information Administration (EIA) (2004), *International Energy Outlook 2003*, available at: http://tonto.eia.doe.gov/ftproof/forecasting/0484(2003).pdf, accessed July 2000.
Fisher-Vanden, K., G. Jefferson, H.M. Liu and Q. Tao (2004), 'What is driving China's decline in energy intensity?', *Resource and Energy Economics*, **26**, 77–97.
Garbaccio, R.F., M.S. Ho and D.W. Jorgenson (1999), 'Why has the energy-output ratio fallen in China?', *The Energy Journal*, **20**, 63–91.
Ho, M.S., D.W. Jorgenson and D.H. Perkins (1998), 'China's economic growth and carbon emissions', in M.B. McElroy, C.P. Nielen and P. Lydon (eds), *Energizing China: Reconciling Environmental Protection and Economic Growth*, Cambridge, MA: Harvard University Press, pp. 301–410.
Huang, J.P. (1993), 'Industrial energy use and structural change: a case study of the People's Republic of China', *Energy Economics*, **15**, 131–6.

Intergovernmental Panel on Climate Change (IPCC) (2000), *Special Report on Emission Scenarios: 2000*, Cambridge: Cambridge University Press.

IPCC/OECD/IEA (1997), *Revised 1996 IPCC Guidelines for National Greenhouse Gas Inventories: Reference Manual*, UK Metrological Office.

Landwehr, M. and E. Jochem (1997), 'From primary energy supply to final energy consumption-analyzing structural and efficiency changes on the energy supply side', *Energy Policy*, **25**, 693–702.

Lawrence Berkeley National Laboratory (LBNL) and Energy Research Institute (ERI) of the China State Development Planning Commission (2001), *China Energy Databook*, CD-ROM.

National Bureau of Statistics (NBS) (1986–1989, 1990b, 1991–1994, 1995a, 1996b, 1997, 1998a, 1999, 2000b, 2001, 2002a, 2003), *China Statistical Yearbook*, Beijing: China Statistical Publishing House.

National Bureau of Statistics (NBS) (1990a, 1996a, 2000a, 2004), *China Energy Statistical Yearbook, 1989, 1995–1996, 1997–1999, 2000–2002*, Beijing: China Statistical Publishing House.

National Bureau of Statistics (NBS) (1995b, 1998b, 2000c), *China Industrial Economy Statistical Yearbook*, Beijing: China Statistical Publishing House.

National Bureau of Statistics (NBS) (2000d), *Comprehensive Statistical Data and Materials on 50 Years of Chinese Industry, Transportation and Energy*, Beijing: China Statistical Publishing House.

National Bureau of Statistics (NBS) (2002b),*The Statistics on Investment in Fixed Assets of China (1950–2000)*, Beijing: China Statistical Publishing House.

Natural Resources Defense Council (NRDC) (2001), 'China is aggressively reducing its carbon dioxide emissions, available at http://www.nrdc.org/global Warming/achinagg.asp.

OECD/IEA (2003), *CO_2 emissions from fuel combustion: 1971–2001*, Paris: IEA Statistics.

Sinton, J.E. (2001), 'Accuracy and reliability of China's energy statistics', *China Economic Review*, **12**, 373–83.

Sinton, J.E. and D.G. Fridley (2000), 'What goes up: recent trends in China's energy consumption', *Energy Policy*, **28**, 671–87.

Sinton, J.E. and D.G. Fridley (2003), 'Comments on recent energy statistics from China', *Sinosphere*, **6**, 6–12.

Sinton, J.E. and M. Levine (1994), 'Changing energy intensity in Chinese industry: the relative importance of structural shift and intensity change', *Energy Policy*, **22**, 239–55.

Sinton, J.E., M.D. Levine and Q.Y. Wang (1998), 'Energy efficiency in China: accomplishments and challenges', *Energy Policy*, **26**, 813–29.

Streets, D.G., K.J. Jiang, X.L. Hu, J.E. Sinton, X.Q. Zhang, D.Y. Xu, M.Z. Jacobson and J.E. Hansen (2001), 'Recent reductions in China's greenhouse gas emissions', *Science*, **294**, 1835–7.

Wu, L.B., S. Kaneko and S. Matsuoka (2005), 'Driving forces behind the stagnancy of China's energy-related CO_2 emissions from 1996 to 1999: the relative importance of structural change, intensity change and scale change', *Energy Policy*, **33**, 319–35.

Xue, Z.G. (2002), 'The tendency and strategic options of policies against acid rain and SO_2 emissions in the dual-controlling area in China', *China Energy* (in Chinese), **11**, 4–8.

Yang, C., M. May and T. Heller (1998), 'Global carbon dioxide emissions scenarios:

sensitivity to social and technological factors in three regions', *Mitigation and Adaptation Strategies for Global Change*, **2**, 373–404.

Zhang, Z.X. (2003), 'Why did the energy intensity fall in China's industrial sector in the 1990s? The relative importance of structural change and intensity change', *Energy Economics*, **25**, 625–38.

APPENDIX 11A: MATHEMATICAL DERIVATION OF THE OVERALL ENERGY SYSTEM MODEL

Based on verification, *CP1*, *CP2* and *CP3* can be disaggregated with regard to the energy carriers on the consumption side as follows:

$$CP1 = \sum_{i=1}^{3} Y^t \times \frac{TFC^t}{Y^t} \times \frac{TFC_i^t}{TFC^t} \times \frac{TFC_i^t + DL_i^t}{TFC_i^t}$$
$$\times \frac{TFC_i^t + DL_i^t + STD_i^t}{TFC_i^t + DL_i^t} \times CI_i^t \qquad (11A.1a)$$

$$CP2 = \sum_{i=4}^{8} Y^t \times \frac{TFC^t}{Y^t} \times \frac{TFC_i^t}{TFC^t} \times \frac{TFC_i^t + STD_i^t}{TFC_i^t}$$
$$\times \frac{TFC_i^t + STD_i^t - STCH_i^t}{TFC_i^t + STD_i^t}$$
$$\times \frac{TFC_i^t + STD_i^t - STCH_i^t - IM_i^t}{TFC_i^t + STD_i^t - STCH_i^t}$$
$$\times \frac{Net\text{-}output_i^t + DL_i^t}{Net\text{-}output_i^t} \times \frac{Net\text{-}output_i^t + DL_i^t + RUS_i^t}{Net\text{-}output_i^t + DL_i^t}$$
$$\times \frac{Gross\text{-}output_i^t}{Total\text{-}output^t} \times \frac{Gross\text{-}input_i^t}{Gross\text{-}output_i^t} \times \frac{Net\text{-}input_i^t}{Gross\text{-}input_i^t} \times CI_i^t$$
$$\qquad (11A.1b)$$

$$CP3 = \sum_{i=4}^{8} Y^t \times \frac{TFC^t}{Y^t} \times \frac{TFC_i^t}{TFC^t} \times \frac{TFC_i^t + STD_i^t}{TFC_i^t}$$
$$\times \frac{TFC_i^t + STD_i^t - STCH_i^t}{TFC_i^t + STD_i^t} \times \frac{TFC_i^t + STD_i^t - STCH_i^t - IM_i^t}{TFC_i^t + STD_i^t - STCH_i^t}$$
$$\times \frac{EXP_i^t}{TFC_i^t + STD_i^t - STCH_i^t - IM_i^t} \times \frac{Net\text{-}output_i^t + DL_i^t}{Net\text{-}output_i^t}$$
$$\times \frac{Net\text{-}output_i^t + DL_i^t + RUS_i^t}{Net\text{-}output_i^t + DL_i^t} \times \frac{Gross\text{-}output_i^t}{Total\text{-}output_i^t}$$
$$\times \frac{Gross\text{-}input_i^t}{Gross\text{-}output_i^t} \times \frac{Net\text{-}input_i^t}{Gross\text{-}input_i^t} \times CI_i^t, \qquad (11A.1c)$$

where *i* is the index of energy type differentiated on the consumption side. The meaning of each *i* value is shown in Table 11A.1.

Table 11A.1   Meaning of i *in functions (11A.1a–c)*

Value of i	Meaning	Value of i	Meaning
$i = 1$	Raw coal	$i = 5$	Heat
$i = 2$	Crude oil	$i = 6$	Cleaned and washed coal
$i = 3$	Natural gas	$i = 7$	Coking products
$i = 4$	Electricity (hydro and thermal)	$i = 8$	Petroleum products

Note that changes in *CP* should be partly attributed to the impact of exports themselves, while they are also driven by the performance of the domestic transformation sector.

The statistical meaning of each variable in functions (11A.1a–c) is described in Table 11A.2.

Based on the above three functions, we can further define the following factors:

$EI_i^t = TFC^t/Y^t$ (energy intensity) depicts the energy use per unit of economic output.

$FS_i^t = TFC_i^t/TFC^t$ (fuel structure) depicts the share of fuel i in total final energy consumption.

$LO\text{-}P_i^t = 1 + DL_i^t/TFC_i^t$ (distribution losses factor for primary energy i) depicts the input–output ratio during distribution processes,

$STA\text{-}P_i^t = 1 + STD_i^t/(TFC_i^t + DL_i^t)$ (statistical adjustment factor for primary energy carriers) is decided by the ratio of statistical difference to total supply of primary energy carrier i, which will be referred to as unitary statistical difference in the following discussion.

$STA\text{-}S_i^t = 1 + STD_i^t/TFC_i^t$ (statistical adjustment factor for secondary energy carriers) is decided by the ratio of statistical difference to total final consumption of secondary energy carrier i, which will be referred to as unitary statistical difference in the following discussion.

$CYS_i^t = 1 - STCH_i^t/(TFC_i^t + STD_i^t)$ (current year supply factor) depicts the ratio between current year supply and adjusted total final consumption of fuel i; this factor can measure the impact of stock change of secondary energy i on the supply of primary energy carrier for generating i; given the demand of a specific secondary energy carrier, positive $STCH_i^t$ reduces the supply of primary energy carrier for generating i and vice versa.

$DOS_i^t = 1 - IM_i^t/(TFC_i^t + STD_i^t - STCH_i^t)$ (domestic supply factor) depicts the ratio between domestic supply and total supply (both for

Table 11A.2 Statistical meaning of each variable in functions (11A.1a–c)

Component	Meaning
CI_i^t	Carbon intensity for fuel i at year t
Y^t	Economic output at year t
TFC^t	Total final energy consumption at year t
TFC_i^t	Total final energy consumption of fuel i at year t
STD_i^t	Statistical difference for fuel i at year t; for $i = 1$ to 3, $TFC_i^t + DL_i^t + STD_i^t$ points to the adjusted primary energy supply; for $i = 4$ to 8, $TFC_i^t + STD_i^t$ points to the adjusted final secondary energy consumption
$STCH_i^t$	Stock change for fuel i at year t; $TFC_i^t + STD_i^t - STCH_i^t$ points to the current year supply of fuel i for end use
IM_i^t	Import of fuel i at year t; $TFC_i^t + STD_i^t - STCH_i^t - IM_i^t$ points to the current year supply of fuel i for end use from domestic source
EXP_i^t	Export of fuel i at year t (negative value); $TFC_i^t + STD_i^t - STCH_i^t - IM_i^t + EXP_i^t$ points to the current year domestic net transformation output of fuel i (*Net-output*), which can meet the demand from domestic end-use process and also from the international market
DL_i^t	Distribution losses of fuel i at year t; $TFC_i^t + DL_i^t$ points to the total supply of primary energy carrier i, $TFC_i^t + STD_i^t - STCH_i^t - IM_i^t + EXP_i^t + DL_i^t$ points to transformation output before distribution
RUS_i^t	Re-use of fuel i in transformation process; $TFC_i^t + STD_i^t - STCH_i^t - IM_i^t + EXP_i^t + DL_i^t + RUS_i^t$ points to the 'total output' of secondary energy i; for $i = 4$, it includes both thermal and hydro power
Gross-output$_i^t$	For $i = 4$, it equals total output minus hydro power; for $i = 5$ to 8, it is the same as total output
Gross-input$_i^t$	Gross input includes the primary and secondary energy input for the generation of fuel i
Net-input$_i^t$	Net input refers to the primary energy input for the generation of fuel i
TIM^t	Total amount of import of secondary energy at year t
$TEXP^t$	Total amount of export of secondary energy at year t (negative value)
$TSTCH^t$	Total amount of stock change of secondary energy at year t

current year); this factor can measure the impact of import of secondary energy i on the supply of primary energy carrier for generating i.

$FRD_i^t = EXP_i^t/(TFC_i^t + STD_i^t - STCH_i^t - IM_i^t)$ (foreign demand factor) depicts the ratio of international demand to the domestic demand; this factor can measure the impact of export of secondary energy i on the supply of primary energy carrier for generating i.

$LO\text{-}S_i^t = 1 + DL_i^t/Net\text{-}output_i^t$ (distribution losses factor for secondary energy i) depicts the input–output ratio during the distribution process for secondary energy.

$RU_i^t = 1 + RUS_i^t/(Net\text{-}output_i^t + DL_i^t)$ (unit consumption factor in re-use) depicts the ratio of secondary energy before use and after use.

$POWST_i^t = Gross\text{-}output_i^t/Total\text{-}output_i^t$ (power substitute factor) is only significant for electricity to measure the degree of substitution between thermal power and hydro power; for other secondary energy, it equals 1.

$GUE_i^t = Gross\text{-}input_i^t/Gross\text{-}output_i^t$ (gross unit consumption factor) depicts the ratio between the gross input and gross output for the generation of secondary energy i; this factor can measure the efficiency performance of the transformation sector.

$FST_i^t = Net\text{-}input_i^t/Gross\text{-}input_i^t$ (fuel substitute factor on generation base) depicts the ratio of net input (primary energy) to gross input (all energy types) for generation of fuel i; this factor can measure the impact of fuel substitution of primary energy by secondary energy on the generation base in transformation sector.

Before addressing the contribution of imports and exports to C-TPES, we must make a distinction between their 'direct' and 'indirect' impacts. In the above procedure, the indirect impacts of 'imports' and 'exports' on the supply of primary energy have been taken into consideration. More precisely, given the demand of secondary energy in end-use sectors, production of the domestic transformation sector is limited by imports but simultaneously promoted by exports. Changes occurring in the transformation sector due to the influence of imports and exports will sequentially induce changes in the primary energy input on the generation base. Through this mechanism, international trade exerts a series of 'indirect' impacts on C-TPES. On the other hand, since the imports themselves are a component of TPES, their scale, the composition of fuel types and carbon intensity will also influence the C-TPES directly. As for the CO_2 emissions related to exports, the above-mentioned 'indirect' impacts have been over-estimated and the direct impacts arising from exports themselves should be excluded from TPES. All these direct impacts can be clarified in the following functions (11A.1d) and (11A.1e). The stock change component,

however, is a little bit different from these two items as it may vary from
positive for one fuel to negative for another fuel, or vice versa. Thus composition of the aggregate stock changes as a whole with regard to different
fuel type becomes meaningless and will not be taken into consideration in
our model setting (as shown in function (11A.1f)):

$$CS\text{–}IM = \sum_{i=4}^{8} CS\text{–}IM_i^t = \sum_{i=4}^{8} TIM^t \times \frac{IM_i^t}{TIM^t} \times CI\text{–}IM_i^t \quad (11A.1d)$$

$$CS\text{–}EXP = \sum_{i=4}^{8} CS\text{–}EXP_i^t = \sum_{i=4}^{8} TEXP^t \times \frac{EXP_i^t}{TEXP^t} \times CI\text{–}EXP_i^t \quad (11A.1e)$$

$$CS\text{–}STCH = \sum_{i=4}^{8} CS\text{–}STCH_i^t = \sum_{i=4}^{8} STCH_i^t \times CI\text{–}STCH_i^t. \quad (11A.1f)$$

With reference to functions (11A.1d–f), we define the following terms:

$FS - IM_i^t = IM_i^t/TIM^t$ (fuel structure factor for imports) depicts the
share of fuel i in imported secondary energy.
$FS - EXP_i^t = EXP_i^t/TEXP^t$ (fuel structure factor for exports) depicts
the share of fuel i in exported secondary energy.

By substituting the above indicators for the original components in
functions (11A.1a–f), we can get the following decomposition function
(11A.2).

$$C\text{-}TPES = \sum_{i=1}^{3} Y^t \times EI^t \times FS_i^t \times LO\text{-}P_i^t \times STA\text{-}P_i^t \times CI_i^t$$

$$+ \sum_{i=4}^{8} Y^t \times EI^t \times FS_i^t \times STA\text{-}S_i^t \times CYS_i^t \times DOS_i^t$$

$$\times (1 + FRD_i^t) \times LO\text{-}S_i^t \times RU_i^t \times POWST_i^t$$

$$\times GUE_i^t \times FST_i^t \times CI_i^t + \sum_{i=4}^{8} TIM^t \times FS\text{–}IM_i^t$$

$$\times CI\text{–}IM_i^t + \sum_{i=4}^{8} TEXP^t \times FS\text{–}EXP_i^t$$

$$\times CI\text{–}EXP_i^t + \sum_{i=4}^{8} STCH_i^t \times CI\text{–}STCH_i^t. \quad (11A.2)$$

To disaggregate the changes of C-TPES into the changes of those
pre-defined factors, several perfect decomposition approaches are now
available. As stated by Ang (2004), the multiplicative and additive LMDI

I methods bear several desirable properties due to their theoretical foundations, adaptability, ease of use and results interpretation. The multiplicative LMDI I methods have been applied and extended in a previous study (Wu et al., 2005); in this model, we prefer to choose the additive LMDI I methods based on the following considerations:

1. Ease of interpretation. Note that the governing function of this model contains a number of pre-defined factors, which never appear in previous studies and are not as intuitive. Thus, for ease of interpretation, the additive LMDI I methods are more desirable.
2. Simple and close relationship between the difference approach and ratio approach in the context of LMDI I. As proven by Choi and Ang (2003), through normalization, decomposition in terms of difference can be made consistent with that of the ratio case. Thus we can easily link the present study with previous studies.

According to the LMDI I index decomposition methodology, we must conduct integration over the targeted period. One import precondition for integration is that all of the pre-defined factors should bear positive values over the targeted period. In case a dataset contains a zero value for some variables, Ang et al. (1998) and Ang and Zhang (2000) suggested replacing the zero value by a very small positive number. This way of handling zero value in LMDI I has been widely accepted in the field of IDA. The case of the present analysis, however, is much more complicated: some of the pre-defined factors may bear negative values (exports) or even stochastic changes over time (stock changes). The well-established LMDI I methodology must be further developed to adapt to those specific conditions. Applying differentiation to both sides of function (11A.2), we obtain function (11A.3):

$$
\frac{dC\text{-}TPES^t}{dt} = \sum_{i=1}^{3} \frac{dCP1^t_i}{dt} + \sum_{i=4}^{8} \frac{dCP2^t_i}{dt} + \sum_{i=4}^{8} \frac{dCP3^t_i}{dt} + \sum_{i=4}^{8} \frac{dCS\text{-}IM^t_i}{dt}
$$

$$
+ \sum_{i=4}^{8} \frac{dCS\text{-}EXP^t_i}{dt} + \sum_{i=4}^{8} \frac{dCS\text{-}STCH^t_i}{dt}
$$

$$
= \sum_{i=1}^{3} CP1^t_i \left(\frac{dY^t}{Y^t dt} + \frac{dEI^t}{EI^t dt} + \frac{dFS^t_i}{FS^t_i dt} + \frac{dLO\text{-}P^t_i}{LO\text{-}P^t_i dt} \right.
$$

$$
\left. + \frac{dSTA\text{-}P^t_i}{STA\text{-}P^t_i dt} + \frac{dCI^t_i}{CI^t_i dt} \right) + \sum_{i=4}^{8} CP2^t_i \left(\frac{dY^t}{Y^t dt} + \frac{dEI^t}{EI^t dt} \right.
$$

$$
\left. + \frac{dFS^t_i}{FS^t_i dt} + \frac{dSTA\text{-}S^t_i}{STA\text{-}S^t_i dt} + \frac{dCYS^t_i}{CYS^t_i dt} + \frac{dDOS^t_i}{DOS^t_i dt} \right.
$$

$$+\frac{dLO\text{-}S_i^t}{LO\text{-}S_i^t dt}+\frac{dRU_i^t}{RU_i^t dt}+\frac{dPOWST_i}{POWST_i dt}+\frac{dGUE_i^t}{GUE_i^t dt}$$

$$+\frac{dFST_i}{FST_i dt}+\frac{dCI_i^t}{CI_i^t dt}\Bigg)+\sum_{i=4}^{8}CP3_i^t\Bigg(\frac{dY^t}{Y^t dt}+\frac{dEI^t}{EI^t dt}$$

$$+\frac{dFS_i^t}{FS_i^t dt}+\frac{dSTA\text{-}S_i^t}{STA\text{-}S_i^t dt}+\frac{dCYS_i^t}{CYS_i^t dt}+\frac{dDOS_i^t}{DOS_i^t dt}$$

$$+\frac{dFRD_i^t}{FRD_i^t dt}+\frac{dLO\text{-}S_i^t}{LO\text{-}S_i^t dt}+\frac{dRU_i^t}{RU_i^t dt}+\frac{dPOWST_i}{POWST_i dt}$$

$$+\frac{dGUE_i^t}{GUE_i^t dt}+\frac{dFST_i^t}{FST_i^t dt}+\frac{dCI_i^t}{CI_i^t dt}\Bigg)$$

$$+\sum_{i=4}^{8}CS\text{-}IM_i^t\Bigg(\frac{dTIM^t}{TIM^t dt}+\frac{dFS\text{-}IM_i^t}{FS\text{-}IM_i^t dt}+\frac{dCI\text{-}IM_i^t}{CI\text{-}IM_i^t dt}\Bigg)$$

$$+\sum_{i=4}^{8}CS\text{-}EXP_i^t\Bigg(\frac{dTEXP^t}{TEXP^t dt}+\frac{dFS\text{-}EXP_i^t}{FS\text{-}EXP_i^t dt}$$

$$+\frac{dCI\text{-}EXP_i^t}{CI\text{-}EXP_i^t dt}\Bigg)+\sum_{i=4}^{8}CS\text{-}STCH_i^t\Bigg(\frac{dSTCH_i^t}{STCH_i^t dt}$$

$$+\frac{dCI\text{-}STCH_i^t}{CI\text{-}STCH_i^t dt}\Bigg). \tag{11A.3}$$

In function (11A.3), the components related to *CP*1, *CP*2, *CP*3 and *CS-IM* meet the technical constraint of LMDI I: all of the multipliers comprising them remain positive over the targeted period. Meanwhile, *CS-EXP*$_i^t$ bears negative values due to the negative multipliers of *TEXP*^{t}, which requires special treatment. We can convert the functional form into the following function (11A.3a):

$$\ldots+\sum_{i=4}^{8}CS\text{-}EXP'^t_i\Bigg(\frac{dTEXP^t}{TEXP^t dt}+\frac{dFS\text{-}EXP_i^t}{FS\text{-}EXP_i^t dt}+\frac{dCI\text{-}EXP_i^t}{CI_i^t\text{-}EXP dt}\Bigg)+\ldots$$

$$=\ldots-\sum_{i=4}^{8}-CS3\text{-}EXP_i^t\Bigg[\frac{d(-TEXP^t)}{(-TEXP^t)dt}+\frac{dFS\text{-}EXP_i^t}{FS\text{-}EXP_i^t dt}$$

$$+\frac{dCI\text{-}EXP_i^t}{CI\text{-}EXP_i^t dt}\Bigg]+\ldots \tag{11A.3a}$$

Thus through the above procedure all the factors with a negative sign have been substituted by their opposite numbers and simultaneously the functional form stays exactly the same as before. Integrating functions (11A.3) and (11A.3a) over the time interval [0, *T*] yields function (11A.4):

$$C\text{-}TPES^T - C\text{-}TPES^0 = \sum_{i=1}^{8} \frac{L(CP1_i^T, CP1_{i,}^0)}{L(Y^T, Y^0)}(Y^T - Y^0)$$

$$+ \sum_{i=1}^{8} \frac{L(CP1_i^T, CP1_{i,}^0)}{L(EI^T, EI^0)}(EI^T - EI^0) + \sum_{i=1}^{8} \frac{L(CP1_i^T, CP1_{i,}^0)}{L(FS_i^T, FS_i^0)}(FS_i^T - FS_i^0)$$

$$+ \sum_{i=1}^{8} \frac{L(CP1_i^T, CP1_{i,}^0)}{L(CI_i^T, CI_i^0)}(CI_i^T - CI_i^0)$$

$$+ \sum_{i=1}^{3} \frac{L(CP1_i^T, CP1_{i,}^0)}{L(LO\text{-}P_i^T, LO\text{-}P_i^0)}(LO\text{-}P_i^T - LO\text{-}P_i^0)$$

$$+ \sum_{i=1}^{3} \frac{L(CP1_i^T, CP1_{i,}^0)}{L(STA\text{-}P_i^T, STA\text{-}P_i^0)}(STA\text{-}P_i^T - STA\text{-}P_i^0)$$

$$+ \sum_{i=4}^{8} \frac{L(CP2_i^T, CP2_{i,}^0) + L(CP3_i^T, CP3_{i,}^0)}{L(STA\text{-}S_i^T, STA\text{-}S_i^0)}(STA\text{-}S_i^T - STA\text{-}S_i^0)$$

$$+ \sum_{i=4}^{8} \frac{L(CP2_i^T, CP2_{i,}^0) + L(CP3_i^T, CP3_{i,}^0)}{L(CYS_i^T, CYS_i^0)}(CYS_i^t - CYS_i^0)$$

$$+ \sum_{i=4}^{8} \frac{L(CP2_i^T, CP2_{i,}^0) + L(CP3_i^T, CP3_{i,}^0)}{L(DOS_i^T, DOS_i^0)}(DOS_i^T - DOS_i^0)$$

$$+ \sum_{i=4}^{8} \frac{L(CP3_i^T, CP3_{i,}^0)}{L(FRD_i^T, FRD_i^0)}(FRD_i^T - FRD_i^0)$$

$$+ \sum_{i=4}^{8} \frac{L(CP2_i^T, CP2_{i,}^0) + L(CP3_i^T, CP3_{i,}^0)}{L(LO\text{-}S_i^T, LO\text{-}S_i^0)}(LO\text{-}S_i^T - LO\text{-}S_i^0)$$

$$+ \sum_{i=4}^{8} \frac{L(CP2_i^T, CP2_{i,}^0) + L(CP3_i^T, CP3_{i,}^0)}{L(RU_i^T, RU_i^0)}(RU_i^T - RU_i^0)$$

$$+ \sum_{i=4}^{8} \frac{L(CP2_i^T, CP2_{i,}^0) + L(CP3_i^T, CP3_{i,}^0)}{L(POWST_i^T, POWST_i^0)}(POWST_i^T - POWST_i^0)$$

$$+ \sum_{i=4}^{8} \frac{L(CP2_i^T, CP2_{i,}^0) + L(CP3_i^T, CP3_{i,}^0)}{L(GUE_i^T, GUE_i^0)}(GUE_i^T - GUE_i^0)$$

$$+ \sum_{i=4}^{8} \frac{L(CP2_i^T, CP2_{i,}^0) + L(CP3_i^T, CP3_{i,}^0)}{L(FST_i^T, FST_i^0)}(FST_i^T - FST_i^0)$$

$$- \sum_{i=4}^{8} \frac{L(-CS3_i^T, -CS3_{i,}^0)}{L(-TEXP^t, -TEXP^0)}(-TEXP^T + TEXP^0)$$

$$- \sum_{i=4}^{8} \frac{L(-CS3_i^T, -CS3_{i,}^0)}{L(FS\text{-}EXP_i^t, FS\text{-}EXP_i^0)}(FS\text{-}EXP_i^T - FS\text{-}EXP_i^0)$$

$$- \sum_{i=4}^{8} \frac{L(-CS3_i^T, -CS3_{i,}^0)}{L(CI\text{-}EXP_i^T, CI\text{-}EXP_i^0)}(CI\text{-}EXP_i^T - CI\text{-}EXP_i^0)$$

$$
+ \sum_{i=4}^{8} \frac{L(CS2_i^T, CS2_{i,}^0)}{L(TIM^T, TIM^0)}(TIM^T - TIM^0)
$$

$$
+ \sum_{i=4}^{8} \frac{L(CS2_i^T, CS2_{i,}^0)}{L(FS-IM_i^T, FS-IM_i^0)}(FS-IM_i^T - FS-IM_i^0)
$$

$$
+ \sum_{i=4}^{8} \frac{L(CS2_i^T, CS2_{i,}^0)}{L(CI-IM_i^T, CI-IM_i^0)}(CI-IM_i^T - CI-IM_i^0)
$$

$$
+ ???, \tag{11A.4}
$$

where the logarithmic mean function L is defined as:

$$
L(x, y) = \begin{cases} (x - y)/(\ln x - \ln y), & x \neq y \\ x & x = y \end{cases} \tag{11A.5}
$$

The remaining part in function (11A.4) corresponds to stock changes, which are different from exports, which remain negative continuously over the targeted period. Stock changes, a measurement of the balance of a fuel's stock between the beginning of a year and the end of that year, vary stochastically with time. Hence in some years, they played a positive role in the transition of aggregate CO_2 emissions; in other years, on the other hand, they turn out to be a negative force. There are in total four possible cases with the changes of stock between two successive years (see Table 11A.3).

From function (11A.3) to function (11A.4), integration will be done over a time interval $[0, T]$, which may range from one unitary period (between two successive years) to the overall targeted period. For simplicity, we shall first address the annual change of aggregate CO_2 emissions, which corresponds to a unitary interval and the condition is one of the above four cases. In case 1, stock changes of the previous year and the following year are both positive. This is just a normal situation that can exactly follow the traditional method of LMDI I. Case 2 is a special case that we have discussed above. By substituting the negative value with its opposite number, it can follow the same calculation procedure as case 1. Cases 3 and 4, however, cannot simply follow either of the above two ways without

Table 11A.3 Possible cases for stock changes in the dataset

	Case 1	Case 2	Case 3	Case 4
$STCH_i^{t-1}$	Positive	Negative	Positive	Negative
$STCH_i^t$	Positive	Negative	Negative	Positive

another very important assumption: the function of *STCH* should be either increasing or decreasing between two successive years, without any further fluctuation. In other words, we need to presuppose that the derivative of *STCH* should maintain either not less than zero or not more than zero over each unitary interval.

Why is such an assumption necessary? Since the continuous function of $STCH_i^t$ with respect to time is not available in reality, it is impossible for us to verify any further fluctuation with $STCH_i$ within the temporal unit. The most natural approach therefore is to assume that *SICH* would keep either ascending or descending at least within each unitary interval and any inflexion could only exist at the beginning point of a year (the point that bears an exact value). On the other hand, under such an assumption, a graph of $STCH_i^t(t)$ with respect to t will inevitably intersect with the t axis at some point t^*, so we must make another assumption: that over each unitary interval, $STCH_i^t = 0$ only when $t = t^* = T/2$. Thus, for case 3, over the interval $[0, T/2]$, we should follow the procedure developed for case 1 and over the interval $[T/2, T]$, we should follow the procedure for case 2. The final expression is therefore:

$$
\int_0^T \sum_{i=4}^8 CS\text{-}STCH_i^t \left(\frac{dSTCH_i^t}{STCH_i^t dt} + \frac{dCI\text{-}STCH_i^t}{CI\text{-}STCH_i^t dt} \right)
$$

$$
= \sum_{i=4}^8 \frac{L(CS\text{-}STCH_i^{T/2}, CS\text{-}STCH_i^0)}{L(STCH_i^{T/2}, STCH_i^0)} (STCH_i^{T/2} - STCH_i^0)
$$

$$
+ \sum_{i=4}^8 \frac{L(CS\text{-}STCH_i^{T/2}, CS\text{-}STCH_i^0)}{L(CI\text{-}STCH_i^{T/2}, CI\text{-}STCH_i^0)} (CI\text{-}STCH_i^{T/2} - CI\text{-}STCH_i^0)
$$

$$
- \sum_{i=4}^8 \frac{L(-CS\text{-}STCH_i^T, -CS\text{-}STCH_i^{T/2})}{L(-STCH_i^T, -STCH_i^{T/2})} (-STCH_i^T + STCH_i^{T/2})
$$

$$
- \sum_{i=4}^8 \frac{L(-CS\text{-}STCH_i^T, -CS\text{-}STCH_i^{T/2})}{L(CI\text{-}STCH_i^T, CI\text{-}STCH_i^{T/2})} (CI\text{-}STCH_i^T - CI\text{-}STCH_i^{T/2})
$$

$$
\text{(11A.5a)}
$$

In practical calculation, as we said, this model cannot directly handle zero values. We can therefore replace any zero value of $STCH(T/2)$ with a very small positive number P over the interval $[0, T/2]$ and by a very small negative number $-P$ over the interval $[T/2, T]$ since:

$$
\lim_{t \to T/2} P = \lim_{t \to T/2} (-P) = 0 = STCH(T/2).
$$

This approximation will not violate the basic requirement of functional continuity for an integral but simultaneously meet the requirements of the

LMDI I approach. Adopting the same methodology for case 4, we obtain the following function:

$$\int_0^T \sum_{i=4}^8 CS\text{-}STCH_i^t \left(\frac{dSTCH_i^t}{STCH_i^t dt} + \frac{dCI\text{-}STCH_i^t}{CI\text{-}STCH_i^t dt} \right)$$

$$= -\sum_{i=4}^8 \frac{L(-CS\text{-}STCH_i^{T/2}, -CS\text{-}STCH_i^0)}{L(-STCH_i^{T/2}, -STCH_i^0)} (-STCH_i^{T/2} + STCH_i^0)$$

$$- \sum_{i=4}^8 \frac{L(-CS\text{-}STCH_i^{T/2}, -CS\text{-}STCH_i^0)}{L(CI\text{-}STCH_i^{T/2}, CI\text{-}STCH_i^0)} (CI\text{-}STCH_i^{T/2} - CI\text{-}STCH_i^0)$$

$$+ \sum_{i=4}^8 \frac{L(CS\text{-}STCH_i^T, CS\text{-}STCH_i^{T/2})}{L(STCH_i^T, STCH_i^{T/2})} (STCH_i^T - STCH_i^{T/2})$$

$$+ \sum_{i=4}^8 \frac{L(CS\text{-}STCH_i^T, CS\text{-}STCH_i^{T/2})}{L(CI\text{-}STCH_i^T, CI\text{-}STCH_i^{T/2})} (CI\text{-}STCH_i^T - CI\text{-}STCH_i^{T/2}).$$

$$(11A.5b)$$

As mentioned above, integration over a unitary interval is the way to deal with annual changes of CO_2 emissions. By extending the time interval to a longer period, we can conduct analysis on changes of C-TPES between a base year and any targeted year. In this case, we should check the performance of every unitary interval contained in the interval and adhere to two principles:

1. If over the targeted interval, $STCH_i^t$ only falls into one of the two intervals $[0, +\infty]$ or $[-\infty, 0]$, we can simply follow the procedure for case 1 or case 2.
2. If over the targeted interval, $STCH_i^t$ falls into both of the two intervals $[0,+\infty]$ and $[-\infty,0]$; we should first classify the targeted interval into several subsections, each subsection containing only one case out of the above-mentioned four, and then implement subsectional integration case by case.

12. Experts' judgment on the future perspective

1 INTRODUCTION

The environment is a complex system where social and natural forces are mutually interacting with each other. Without a systematic analysis, forecasting environmental issues is impossible. As human activities become diverse and intensive, the complexity of mutual relations in the system increases, and this makes forecasting more difficult. Since there exists no forecasting model which can perfectly reproduce complicated real-world phenomena, selecting some areas, fields or indices out of a whole system of natural and social systems is a realistic approach.

A number of approaches have been carried out to obtain future perspectives on the condition of the environment and development in a region or the whole world (Morita, 1995; IPCC, 1997). These approaches can be roughly classified into two categories. One of them is a top-down approach where one draws some empirical relationships among indices from a macroscopic viewpoint and forecasts the future based on certain premises or scenarios (for example, Meadows et al., 1972). In order to obtain a reliable result by this approach, it is crucial to determine whether an empirical rule obtained in the past can be applied to the future, and whether scenarios drawn will likely be realized. Another is a bottom-up approach based on the accumulation of very detailed data from finely divided areas and different sectors (for example, Japan Science and Technology Agency, 1992; AIM Project Team, 1995). Models under this approach are becoming larger and more complicated, and intensive effort is needed to establish a complete dataset.

Some factors might cause unexpected changes to some situations that cannot be predicted even by a very sophisticated model. While a rather clear relationship between life expectancy or energy consumption with economic development had been obtained throughout the world, van Asselt et al. (1996) showed a different forecast of populations and life expectancy by integrating people's different preferences into a forecasting model. Policy, culture, people's preferences and other site-specific issues more likely affect motorization, transportation problems, food consumption and supply, and people's lifestyle. Forecasting such situations is difficult using empirical rules obtained from past experience or detailed numerical datasets. However, it is an important task to provide decision makers with information on future situations because government policy and other factors can alter future situations (Dowlatabadi, 1997). In order to forecast them, some studies integrated the opinions of experts into a forecast model (for example, Morgan and Keith, 1995; Anastasi et al., 1997).

Aiming at the incorporation of experts' judgment into integrated assessment models and obtaining future forecasts in a form understandable to non-experts as a final goal, this study collects experts' perspectives of many different indices of a country, and analyzes their characteristics by index and specialty of the experts. It aims at evaluating the difficulty of forecasting each index, and at identifying differences in perspectives among experts. China was selected as a country for this study because its impact on the global environment and resources is of great concern and it is more familiar to Japanese experts than any other developing country.

2 FORECASTING CHINA'S FUTURE

China has accomplished remarkable economic development since the 1980s. The ninth five-year plan and the 2010 long-term objectives have set the economic growth rate at 8 percent by 2000 and 7.2 percent by 2010 and beyond. There is great concern about the impact on both the regional and global environment of the rapid growth of such a large country. The government recognized this serious situation, and adopted its 'Agenda 21' in March 1994. Aimed at attaining sustainable development, it defines numerical targets until 2000 over a broad field, such as population, food, poverty, health, agriculture, industry, energy, the atmosphere and waste.

China has to solve two kinds of environmental problems simultaneously. One is the local environmental issue presented by industrial pollution (Smil, 1993; Imura and Katsuhara, 1995; Geping, 1999). This occurs in a short period of time and in spatially small areas. The other is the long-term, global environmental issue presented by global warming (Watson et al., 1997). Moreover, energy and food consumption in the country is rapidly increasing, and its impact on the whole world is also of great concern.

The answers to the following questions are crucial for not only China's but also global sustainable development: (i) Will the food supply, energy and natural resources be able to support its entire population? (ii) Is the regional imbalance of development solvable? And will the insufficiencies of the traffic network infrastructure between coastal ports and inland be improved? (iii) Will social institutions and laws effectively control the huge country? Macroscopic models by Brown (1995), the East–West Center et al. (1994), and Meadows et al. (1972) forecast mainly to give the answer to the first question. However, few studies have been carried out for the other two questions, although they will also be crucial issues for China's future. Compared with indices regarding resource consumption or population growth, forecasting indices regarding the above issues by numerical models is subject to more uncertain variables. They are likely affected by nonnumerical factors such as policy or changes in the cultural and social structure.

Future forecasts of China's environment have been carried out from various points of view (Meadows et al., 1972; Japan Science and Technology Agency, 1992; East–West Center et al., 1994; AIM Project Team, 1995; Brown, 1995; Matsuoka et al., 1995; Tsuji et al., 1995; Brown and Halweil, 1998; Changming and Xiwu, 1998). These studies can be categorized into two types of approaches: quantitative approaches which develop numerical models such as an economic model (AIM Project Team, 1995; Matsuoka et al., 1995; Tsuji et al., 1995), and heuristic approaches based on interpretation and the intuition of experts (Japan Economic Planning Agency, 1997; Brown and Halweil, 1998; Changming and Xiwu, 1998). The former can quantitatively evaluate the mutual relationship between factors. Among the developing nations, quantitative datasets for China can be obtained rather easily, but their reliability is doubtful. Furthermore, it is difficult for non-experts to understand the model structure and the meaning of the internal variables. The latter approach based on the knowledge and experience of experts is often used to interpret the results obtained by numerical models. Through this approach, interdisciplinary knowledge and various qualitative factors, such as governmental policy or the culture of a region can be taken into account, and a sketch of the future can be drawn (for example, Japan Economic Planning Agency, 1997). The relationships between factors are not necessarily formulated or modeled quantitatively. Therefore, conclusions tend to become ambiguous.

Moreover, in both approaches, future situations are often forecast based on the premise that developing countries will follow similar development patterns as the developed countries, including those Japan has experienced (for example, Kaneko et al., 1996; Kaneko and Imura, 1997). However, China will be able to utilize its latecomer advantages and avoid the pitfalls experienced by developed countries. The fact that factors affecting China could be different from those of former developing countries should also be taken into consideration, but such factors cannot be easily integrated within a numerical model.

3 OBJECTIVES OF THE STUDY

In previous works, the authors obtained some regression curves described in relation to per capita GDP by analysis of various indices of the last 30 years for 24 countries, including several Asian countries and some OECD member states (Kaneko et al., 1996; Kaneko and Imura, 1997). Those indices have changed along a similar trend, despite the different background of the countries, such as climate, geographical conditions, and social systems. Curves on agricultural shares as a percentage of GDP and life expectancy are shown in Figures 12.1 and 12.2. If these curves were applied to the future prediction of a country, the indices could be forecast without large mathematical models as long as the future economic conditions, that is, GDP per capita, were obtained. Based on this assumption, the environmental changes of several Asian countries, including China, have been forecasted (Kaneko et al., 1996). Furthermore, a system dynamics model combining some independent factors was developed, and the framework of future environmental situations in East Asian countries was discussed, considering the result (Kaneko and Imura, 1997).

However, it is hard for this kind of approach to forecast indices that are likely to be influenced by such factors as government policy, culture, or technological innovation. Motorization, transportation problems, food consumption and supply, and people's lifestyle can be regarded as such indices. It is not clear how much the indices are influenced by these factors. Moreover, it is unknown whether and when changes in policies or technological innovation will occur. The judgment and perspectives of experts are

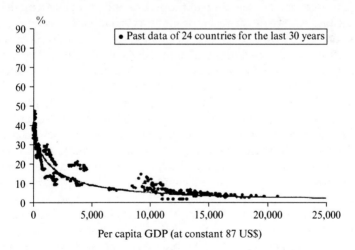

Figure 12.1   Agricultural share of GDP (1)

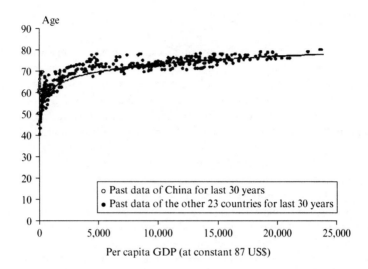

Figure 12.2   Life expectancy

expected to contribute in overcoming this problem. If these experts' views are integrated in the numerical model, forecasting indices will become more meaningful. It could even be utilized to analyze the effectiveness of policies on the indices. The experts' judgment could, therefore, provide useful information urgently needed by decision makers (Morgan and Henrion, 1990).

On the other hand, integration of the experts' judgment into a model may increase uncertainty of the result of model calculation (for example, ibid.; van Asselt et al., 1996). Differences of opinion among experts often significantly affect decision making (Lave and Dowlatabadi, 1993). Therefore, it is important to identify an adequate way to elicit and utilize the judgment and opinions of experts (Anastasi et al., 1997). Morgan and Keith (1995) systematically interviewed leading climate scientists and found great differences between their perspectives on the future of the climate Integration of experts' judgment, however, has been applied mainly to models forecasting global issues such as climate change and world population. Few studies have attempted to apply this approach for forecasting a wide array of factors within a certain region or a country. The present study investigated the judgment and perspectives of experts in terms of various indices on China's resources and environment. It also discussed the divergence of the perspectives in each index and the relationship between each expert's perspectives and his/her specialty. The study was conducted with the use of a questionnaire survey requesting experts to extrapolate the index curves for

China to the year 2050. Each expert drew lines on the graphs based on his/ her own knowledge, experience and judgment.

4   METHOD

One hundred and forty-three China experts were selected in Japan, 69 from universities, 42 from public or private research institutes, and 42 from private companies, and mailed a 58-page questionnaire. The participants were given two weeks to reply. The outline of this survey and the number of collected answers are summarized in Table 12.1. The specialties of the experts encompassed a broad range of fields. Among the 143 experts solicited, 60 experts (42 percent) responded.

Table 12.2 shows the 47 indices which the experts were asked to forecast. They were selected from indices whose past data are relatively complete, and were classified into six fields (economic development, population, food, energy, traffic and environment). Some other indices were calculated from the 47 indices for which replies were obtained. For example, the share for the service industries was obtained from agriculture and manufacturing. As a result, 66 indices as a whole were obtained.

Forty-seven questions were presented in the same format with a diagram. Relevant past data from 1960 to the present (mid-1990s) was shown in each diagram. Some future indices forecast by other groups were shown in a footnote as references. If any reference data existed, such as the numerical targets of China's national policy, the present value of some other countries, or the results of simple scenario prediction, they were also shown in the relevant diagrams. Although giving any of these reference values could cause an anchoring effect leading to a biased result (Morgan and Henrion, 1990), it was believed to be necessary since the fields of the

Table 12.1   Outline of the questionnaire survey

Title	Questionnaire survey for experts about environmental forecast of East Asia–China
Candidates	Experts on the environment and on China in Japan
Persons	Total: 143; universities: 69; research institutes: 32; private companies: 42
Question form	Draw one line (or two if one is not possible) as the most probable path to 2050 in a diagram
Method	Mail survey
Respondents/mailed	60/143 (43%, including preliminary survey)

Table 12.2   Indices to be investigated in this study

No.	Index

Economic Growth and Industrial Structure
Q. 1   GDP growth rate
Q. 2   Per capita GDP
Q. 3   Share of total GDP by industrial sector
Q. 4   Income difference between city and rural
Population and Urbanization
Q. 5   Total fertility rate
Q. 6   Infant mortality
Q. 7   Mortality rate
Q. 8   Life expectancy at birth
Q. 9   Total population
Q. 10   Urban population
Food
Q. 11   Per-day food consumption per capita
Q. 12   Per-day animal foodstuff consumption per capita
Q. 13   Total agricultural land
Q. 14   Total harvested land area for crop production
Q. 15   Total irrigated farmland
Q. 16   Fertilizer input per agricultural land
Q. 17   Number of tractors
Q. 18   Crop yields per harvested land area
Energy
Q. 19   Primary energy consumption per capita
Q. 20   Primary energy consumption per GDP
Q. 21   Income elasticity to primary energy consumption
Q. 22   Crude steel production
Q. 23   Energy demand per steel production
Q. 24   Number of refrigerators per household
Q. 25   Final energy consumption
Q. 26   Share of primary energy supply by energy sources
Q. 27   Share of electricity in final energy consumption
Q. 28   Share of electric power generation by sources
Transportation
Q. 29   Passenger car ownership
Q. 30   Total number of trucks
Q. 31   Total length of road
Q. 32   Total length of railways
Q. 33   Ton-kilometers of freight transportation
Q. 34   Share of freight transportation by mode of transportation
Q. 35   Passenger-kilometers of passenger transport
Q. 36   Share of passenger transport by mode of transportation

Table 12.2   (continued)

No.	Index

Pollution, materials and desertification

Q. 37	Total volume of SO$_2$ emissions
Q. 38	Total volume of dust discharged
Q. 39	Ambient SO$_2$ concentration in Chongqing and Shenyang city
Q. 40	Ambient TSP concentration in Shenyang and Tianjin city
Q. 41	Per-day water consumption for residential use
Q. 42	Per-day industrial wastewater
Q. 43	Access to water supply in urban area
Q. 44	Access to gas in urban area
Q. 45	Industrial solid wastes
Q. 46	Forest area
Q. 47	Desertification speed

indices requested to be forecast were so different and the experts were not all necessarily familiar with all of them.

The following was requested in the questionnaire:

1.   draw a line from the present value to 2050 in each diagram;
2.   evaluate yourself, using five grades of expertise regarding the question and your confidence in your forecast; and
3.   comment on your forecast in the free answer column.

The following were described in notes:

●   draw one line as the 'most probable path' to 2050 in the diagram based on your own knowledge and experiences; and
●   when it is not possible to draw one line, two lines may represent a maximum and a minimum case.

Every line drawn in the diagrams was digitized and synthesized by computer. The accumulation of plotted lines for life expectancy is shown in Figure 12.3 as an example. The distributions of the forecast value by every expert in each year were examined for normality, and the result is shown in Table 12.3. Forecast values of 24 indices (36.4 percent of the whole) present normal distributions for more than 20 different years (75 percent) during 2000–25, while those of 19 (28.8 percent) do for less than six different years (25 percent). In terms of the forecast values for 2026–50, 38 indices (57.6 percent) present normal distributions for more than 20 different years (75 percent), while 16 do at less than six different years. It is not known whether

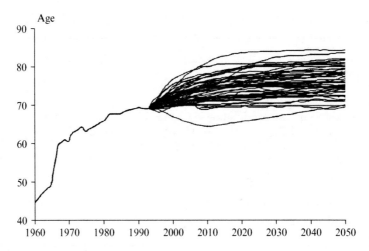

Figure 12.3   Different perspectives of life expectancy

Table 12.3   Normality of forecast values

2000–2025 ratio of number of years when forecast values presenting normal distribution to the forecast periods (25 years)	2026–2050 ratio of number of years when forecast values presenting normal distribution to the forecast periods (25 years)				
	0–25%	25–50%	50–75%	75–100%	Total
0–25%	9	3	2	5	19
	(13.6%)	(4.5%)	(3%)	(7.6%)	(28.8%)
25–50%	3	0	1	7	11
	(4.5%)	(0%)	(1.5%)	(10.6%)	(16.7%)
50–75%	1	1	1	9	12
	(1.5%)	(1.5%)	(1.5%)	(13.6%)	(18.2%)
75–100%	3	1	3	17	24
	(4.5%)	(1.5%)	(4.5%)	(25.8%)	(36.4%)
Total	16	5	7	38	66
	(24.2%)	(7.6%)	(10.6%)	(57.6%)	(100%)

such values should appear in a normal distribution, and some attempts to modify the values taking each expert's specialty into consideration did not succeed in improving the normality. The mean, maximum, minimum and standard deviation had to be adopted as parameters representing the characteristics of forecast values since no other appropriate parameters are available. Those of forecast life expectancy in each year are presented in

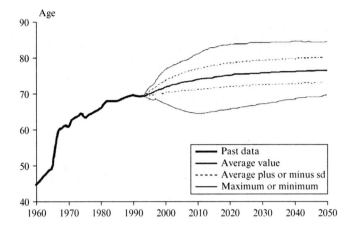

Figure 12.4   Statistical variables of life expectancy

Figure 12.4. The values of the mean and the deviation of forecast indices for 2025 and 2050 are shown in Table 12.4.

5   RESULT OF FORECASTING INDICES

Economic Growth, Industrial Structure and Urbanization

Most of the experts forecast that China's rapid economic growth is expected to continue up to the middle of the twenty-first century. These prospects are based on assumptions that the current trend will continue without any big unexpected change. For example, the following events are considered unlikely to occur: (i) the government will become unstable or will collapse; (ii) progress of democratization and decentralization of authority will be hindered; (iii) investment and financial resources for the establishment of infrastructure from overseas will shrink significantly; and (iv) the prices of natural resources or energy will rise significantly. However, many think that the rate of economic growth will gradually decrease from the present 10 percent to 2 or 3 percent in the future even if China lives up to the experts' assumptions and continues along its current path of development.

The mean value of forecast per capita GDP in 2020 is US$1,571 (at a constant 1987 US$). This represents a similar level to that of Thailand at present. It is expected to reach US$4,000 in 2050, a little less than that of the Republic of Korea at present. The values for 2050 forecast by the experts range from several hundred dollars to US$8,000.

Table 12.4 *Summary of the results (m: mean, sd: standard deviation)*

Parameters	Units	Year					
		2025			2050		
		m + sd	m	m − sd	m + sd	m	m − sd
Economy and industrial structure							
GDP growth rate	%	8~19	5~35	2~52	6~54	2~72	−1~09
Per capita GDP	1987 US$	2,122	1,571	1,020	6,055	4,045	2,036
Agricultural share in total GDP	%	24~7	21~0	17~3	21~3	15~1	8~8
Industrial share in total GDP	%	42~5	38~1	33~6	42~6	36~9	31~3
Service share in total GDP	%	46~7	40~9	35~2	55~3	48~0	40~7
Income difference between urban and rural areas	urban/rural	13~8	3~2	2~6	4~1	2~9	1~7
Population and urbanization							
Total fertility rate	birth/woman	2~1	1~8	1~5	2~3	1~8	1~4
Infant mortality	persons/1,000	23~0	19~5	16~0	19~1	13~5	8~0
Mortality rate	persons/1,000	7~5	6~8	6~2	9~0	7~2	5~4
Life expectancy at birth	age	78~3	75~0	71~8	79~9	76~4	72~9
Total population	millions	1,546	1,471	1,395	1,767	1,552	1,337
Urban population	% of total	51~3	44~9	38~5	73~3	60~9	48.5
Food							
Per-day food consumption per capita	Kcal per capita	3,692	3,371	3,051	4,181	3,601	3,020

		702	610	518	872	718	563
Per-day animal foodstuff consumption per capita	Kcal per capita						
Total agricultural land	million ha	522	483	444	530	460	390
Total harvested land area for crop production	million ha	92~9	88~6	84~2	95~2	88~3	81~5
Total irrigated farmland	million ha	64~1	59~1	54~1	67~4	60~4	53~3
Fertilizer input per agricultural land	kg/ha	237~1	177~5	117~9	330~5	245~2	159~8
Number of tractors cultivated land	no./1,000 ha of	60~4	38~5	16~5	245~7	126~2	6~6
Crop yields per harvested land area	ton/ha	5~8	5~3	4~8	6~4	5~5	4~6
Energy							
Primary energy consumption per capita	TOE per capita	1~81	1~36	0~92	3~47	2~51	1~54
Primary energy consumption per GDP	TOE per 1,000 US$	1~15	0~89	0~62	1~03	0~68	0~33
Income elasticity to primary energy consumption		0~73	0~56	0~39	0~96	0~67	0~37
Crude steel production	tons/year	203	166	128	350	237	124
Energy demand per steel production	TOE/ton	0~91	0~75	0~58	0~70	0~56	0~41
Number of refrigerators per urban household	sets/million houses	106~2	101~7	97~3	111~5	105~3	99~0
Number of refrigerators per rural household	sets/million houses	73~2	55~2	37~2	99~9	78~4	56~8

Table 12.4 (continued)

Parameters	Units	Year					
		2025			2050		
		m + sd	m	m − sd	m + sd	m	m − sd
Final energy consumption for households and commercial sector	million TOE	369	282	196	670	470	271
Final energy consumption for transportation	million TOE	309	229	149	531	364	197
Final energy consumption for industry	million TOE	942	758	573	1,403	1,017	632
Share of primary energy supply (coal)	%	75~7	67~8	59~9	72~7	58~1	43~4
Share of primary energy supply (oil)	%	27~2	20~9	14~7	29~9	20~7	11~6
Share of primary energy supply (gas)	%	7~5	4~8	2~2	15~3	8~7	2~2
Share of primary energy supply (the other)	%	11~7	6~6	1~4	23~1	12~8	2~4
Share of electricity in final energy consumption	%	17~6	15~9	14~3	22~0	18~9	15~9
Share in electric power generation (coal)	%	74~6	65~2	55~9	72~4	57~3	42~2
Share in electric power generation (oil)	%	13~7	8~6	3~6	16~6	9~7	2~7

Share in electric power generation (hydro)	%	22~2	17~9	13~7	24~0	17~3	10~7
Share in electric power generation (nuclear)	%	11~6	6~6	1~6	20~7	11~8	2~9
Share in electric power generation (gas and the others)	%	3~2	1~6	0~0	9~2	3~9	0~0
Transportation							
Passenger car ownership	no./1,000 people	48~6	13~5	0~0	154~0	58~4	0~0
Total number of trucks	no./1,000 people	44~5	24~1	3~6	89~6	55~7	21~9
Total length of road	10,000 km	247~4	201~6	155~8	381~5	282~6	183~7
Total length of railways	10,000 km	8~5	7~2	5~8	12~1	9~0	5~9
Ton-kilometers of freight transportation	ton-km per capita	7,069	5,844	4,619	10,357	7,974	5,591
Share in freight transportation (railways)	%	37~0	31~3	25~6	38~3	28~7	19~1
Share in freight transportation (motor vehicles)	%	24~2	20~0	15~8	39~1	28~3	17~6
Share in freight transportation (shipping)	%	54~3	48~7	43~0	55~3	43~0	30~7
Passenger-kilometers of passenger transport	passenger-km per capita	3,247	2,331	1,414	6,534	4,979	3,424
Share in passenger transport (railways)	%	37~1	31~0	25~0	37~7	26~7	15~7
Share in passenger transport (motor Vehicles)	%	59~6	53~7	47~9	63~2	51~6	40~0

Table 12.4 (continued)

Parameters	Units	Year					
		2025			2050		
		m + sd	m	m – sd	m + sd	m	m – sd
Share in passenger transport (shipping)	%	4~6	2~7	0~9	7~0	3~3	0~5
Share in passenger transport (aircraft)	%	16~2	12~6	9~0	25~7	18~5	11.3
Pollution, materials and desertification							
Total volume of SO_2 emissions	millions of tons per year	44~8	39~2	33~7	98~5	73~2	48~0
Total volume of dust discharged	millions of tons per year	18~7	17~0	15~3	20~1	16~7	13~4
Ambient SO_2 concentration in Chongqing city	mg/m^3	30~35	0~27	0~20	0~30	0~20	0~10
Ambient SO_2 concentration in Shenyang city	mg/m^3	30~16	0~12	0~08	0~13	0~09	0~04
Ambient TSP concentration in Shenyang city	mg/m^3	30~51	0~39	0~26	0~48	0~29	0~10
Ambient TSP concentration in Tianjin city	mg/m^3	30~35	0~26	0~16	0~32	0~18	0~04
Per-day water consumption for daily life	liters per capita	293~8	261~6	229~4	349~2	292~6	236~0
Per-day industrial wastewater	liters per capita	48~7	40~0	31~3	50~0	36~1	22~2

Access to water supply in urban area	% of population	97~4	95~7	94~0	98~5	96~4	94~2
Access to gas in urban area	% of population	90~5	85~0	79~6	93~8	87~4	81~1
Industrial solid waste	100 million tons	10~4	8~9	7~4	13~6	10~2	6~8
Forest area	million ha	132~6	118~0	103~5	134~1	112~8	91~5
Desertification speed	sq. kilometers per year	2,034	1,357	679	1,919	1,168	417

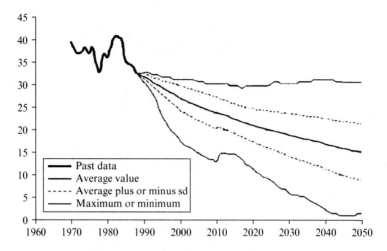

Figure 12.5   Agricultural share of GDP (2)

In this study, experts were requested to forecast GDP growth rate, population and per capita GDP at the same time despite the fact that one of the three indices can be calculated from the other two. Since this study focuses on characteristics of judgment made by various experts, no adjustment was made among the three. Therefore, the values of the three forecast by each expert as well as the mean values are not necessarily consistent. Moreover, the exchange rate was not necessarily taken into account although the income is expressed by a constant US dollar value. Some commented that Chinese economic strength would be underestimated when it is measured in US dollars, and that it should be measured by a comparison of purchasing power.

Figure 12.5 shows the agricultural share of GDP. As most developed countries have experienced, the major industrial sector is expected to shift from agriculture to manufacturing and further to the service industry. However, many consider that an agricultural industry in China will be maintained to some extent, unlike in Japan, because food production will have to be maintained in order to support such a huge population. Some expect certain development of the service industry despite its present underdeveloped state. They think that the government's policy of promoting the service industry and the energy restrictions on heavy manufacturing will accelerate the development of the service industry.

There are different opinions on whether the income gap between city and rural dwellers will increase, while the mean value of the index shows no particular change in the future from the present. The difference of views arises from the following uncertainties: (i) Will agriculture and farm

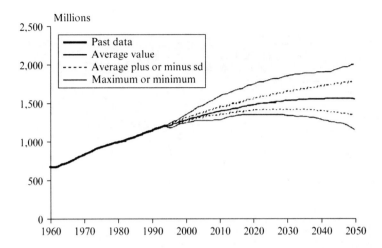

Figure 12.6   Total population

villages be modernized? (ii) How effectively will the inland development policy be enforced? Those who do not forecast a wider gap expect that the government will be concerned about social problems due to such a gap and will enforce effective measures to increase income in rural areas.

The forecast for total population shown in Figure 12.6 shows a trend similar to the one predicted by the middle scenario of the United Nations. Many doubt the effectiveness of the 'One Child Policy' in the future. They think that the government will ease the policy as the economy grows, particularly in urban areas.

It seems that the present trend of urbanization will continue and reach 60 percent by 2050. Some experts suggest that there might be further rapid urbanization as migration to the cities is deregulated. Others hold the view that the regulation restricting immigration to urban areas will be further enforced, and that rapid urbanization will be stemmed, while still others think that rural villages will not entirely collapse because the area of the country is too large for the whole rural population to migrate to urban areas.

Food Production and Consumption

Food consumption on a calorie basis will reach the present level of South Korea by 2020 and then become stable. It will not reach the present US level until 2050. Some have a concern that food consumption will further increase because Chinese people often leave quite a large part of their meal unconsumed. There is another view that their food consumption will

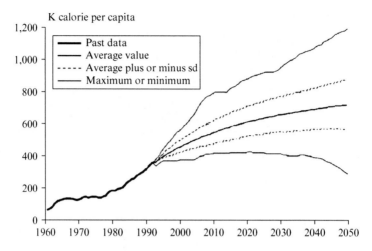

Figure 12.7   Daily consumption of meat

remain at a low level due to worldwide food constraints. Yet others predict
that total food consumption will further increase while 'quality' of diet will
not be improved so much as 'quantity'. They predict that the Chinese will
not consume much more animal foodstuff.

A wider range of views is observed in the forecast of animal foodstuff
consumption than that for total food consumption. Figure 12.7 represents
daily consumption of meat on a calorie basis. By 2030, it will exceed the
present level of Japan, where the consumption is small despite high income.
Some believe that the Chinese people's desire to eat meat, especially pork,
is very strong and think that they will spend a lot of money on meat as
their incomes increase. Others predict slow growth due to insufficient
arable land and limited productivity for meat in the country. There is also
a view that the level of consumption probably will not exceed the Japanese
level as long as the Chinese retain their Asian lifestyle, in which less meat is
consumed than in a Western lifestyle.

It is believed that the land area for crops will probably be maintained
at the current level. Some areas will be transformed to other land use
according to the transition of the economic and social structure. The
government's ability to maintain the cropland areas will depend on the
effectiveness of its food self-sufficiency policy.

Crop yield will reach 5.5 tons per hectare, the present level of Japan,
after 2030 (Figure 12.8). Further yield increases are not expected because
of environmental deterioration such as land degradation and a shortage of
water, as well as because of a shift from crop growing to livestock raising

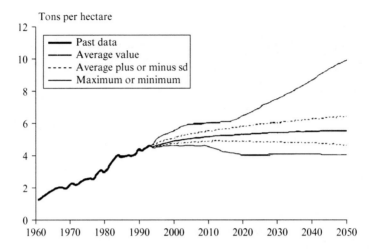

Figure 12.8   Crop yield

and horticulture. Some expect that dramatic improvements in biotechnology will further increase productivity. They think that reforming the grain market is necessary since farmers do not have much incentive for intensive farmland use. There is also an expectation of improvement in productivity with the completion and operation of China's South-to-North Water Transfer project which serves to transfer water from the Yangtze river to northern China.

Energy

Primary energy consumption per capita is shown in Figure 12.9. It will reach the present level of Brazil by 2050. The forecast for this rapid growth is based on the view that energy-intensive industries (steel, cement, chemicals and so on) will have to grow in order to supply basic materials needed for supporting the development. In terms of transportation, some predict a quick motorization up to the level of the United States, whose territory is the same size as China's. Others see a different development because the role of railway transportation is expected to become increasingly important.

Primary energy consumption per capita will be decreased to half of the present level by 2050. Some hold the view that energy efficiency will not be significantly improved because the Chinese economy will further depend on energy-intensive industries. Others expect rapid improvement in energy efficiency because of the development of electronic technology

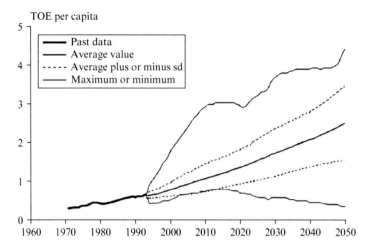

Figure 12.9   Primary energy consumption per capita

and the joint implementation of activities based on the UN Framework Convention on Climate Change. One energy expert suggests that use of non-commercial biomass fuel, which is often excluded from energy statistics, should also be taken into account in the case of developing countries like China. The income elasticity relevant to the amount of primary energy consumption is forecast to gradually rise and converge at around 0.65. Increasing demand, especially in the transportation and residential sectors, will raise the elasticity. However, the insufficient energy supply will hinder its further growth and converge it on a set value.

Industrial Production

Crude steel production will exceed 230 million tons per year by 2050, nearly twice that of the present (Figure 12.10). China is already the largest steel producer in the world, and will probably continue to be so in the future. Some experts think that the production will increase sharply regardless of domestic demand because it is possible for China to become an iron supply center for other Asian countries. There are other views, especially concerning the long term, which predict that production will not increase because labor costs will rise and China will lose its international competitiveness. Passenger car ownership will reach 60 cars per 1,000 persons (similar to the present level in South Korea) by 2050 from 0.24 cars per 1,000 persons in 1995 (equivalent to 1 = 2 of South Korean level in 1965). However, some doubt such a rapid increase because the development of a road network

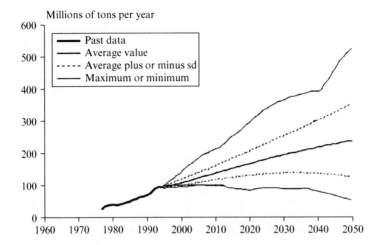

Figure 12.10   Crude steel production

is not expected to meet the increasing demand for car ownership. Others forecast slower motorization because China has already developed a better railway network than those in other developing countries like Thailand.

Pollution and Others

Air pollution, specifically ambient SO_2 concentration in Chongqing city, where it is currently the highest in China, will decrease by 23 percent to 0.27 mg/m^3 in 2030 (Figure 12.11). Yet many hold the view that rapid improvement cannot be expected due to its dependence on high-sulfur coal and geographical location. Chongqing is surrounded by mountains. Energy conservation, the development of a simplified desulfurizer, and the introduction of cleaner production methods are required for further improvement. Some consider that effective measures will not be taken before 2020.

Water use will amount to 260 liters per person per day in 2020. This increasing trend will continue, but it will not reach the present level of Japan (350 liters per person a day) before 2050. Many forecasters believe that the government has to take substantial water conservation measures because the actual water supply will not meet the increasing demand. One expert thinks that the wider use of flush toilets will increase demand significantly. Continuous shortages of water will likely occur in some areas.

Industrial solid waste will reach 890 million tons in 2020. While most of the experts predict an increase, some forecast that it will remain at the present level.

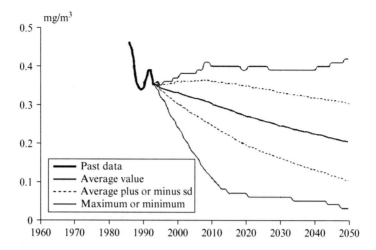

Figure 12.11   Ambient SO₂ concentration in Chongqing city

Some 1,200 square kilometers of land per year will turn to desert by 2020. The government is trying to slow down the process of desertifica- tion to 1,000 square kilometers per year. However, some experts think that desertification is a phenomenon caused by complex combinations of natural, social and economic factors, and that stopping desertification is technically and economically very difficult. They think that the achieve- ment of this target by the beginning of the twenty-first century is difficult even though desertification prevention programs have been successful in some areas such as in the Changchiang basin.

6   INVESTIGATION OF THE CHARACTERISTICS OF THE INDICES

Purpose

The difficulty of forecasting future values of indices varies depending on their characteristics. Forecasting indices whose future value will not likely change much is easy. Life expectancy or per-day food consumption per capita are such indices. On the other hand, it is difficult to forecast indices that will likely change to a great extent or are likely to be affected by other factors. Passenger car ownership in China is one of them. Many people think that it will increase rapidly, but their estimation of how much of an increase varies. Government traffic policy, development of a road network, and market price of fuel are key factors likely to affect passenger car ownership. This section attempts to categorize indices into several groups depending on the uncertainty of future values and magnitude of the change of each index.

Forecast values of all 66 indices for the short-term future (2010) and for the long-term (2050) future were analyzed. Their average paths were regarded as the probable paths represented by experts. The deviation of each path of indices, that is the width of the cluster of paths drawn, represents the difference in the opinion of the experts. Indices showing greater deviation seem to be more difficult to forecast than those with a smaller deviation (that is, narrow width). If a future forecasting model includes such indices, the results of the model simulation will be less certain than that without them.

Method

Changes in the indices from 2010 to 2050 and their deviation at these years were analyzed. The nondimensional variables were defined. $T_{i,2010}$ represents the magnitude of change of the mean value of index from 1995 to 2010. Hereafter $T_{i,2010}$ is referred to as 'transition'. A large transition means that the magnitude of the index would change to a great extent in the next 15 years. They might increase to several times larger than today. Per-day industrial wastewater and total volume of SO_2 emissions are such indices. On the other hand, indices such as life expectancy at birth and total population show a small transition, indicating that such a big change would unlikely occur for them. Transition could be, therefore, regarded as an indicator representing difficulty of forecasting the index.

However, transition is a difference of mean values during a certain period and does not represent disagreement of experts regarding future value. For example, significant disagreement is not found on life expectancy, and most experts think that it will gradually increase (see Figure 12.4). On the other hand, there are different opinions regarding desertification speed, whose transition is even smaller than life expectancy. Some experts forecast that desertification will be accelerated, but others show opposite views. As a consequence, its transition becomes small. In order to represent a different aspect of difficulty of forecast from transition, $U_{i,2010}$, the deviation of the experts' forecasts for index at 2010, is introduced. Hereafter, $U_{i,2010}$ is referred to as 'uncertainty'. Uncertainty in this chapter simply represents the degree of difference among future perspectives of an index. Who is likely to be correct or not among the experts has not been investigated. Uncertainty of desertification speed is larger than that of life expectancy. Therefore, forecasting the former is regarded as being more difficult than the latter.

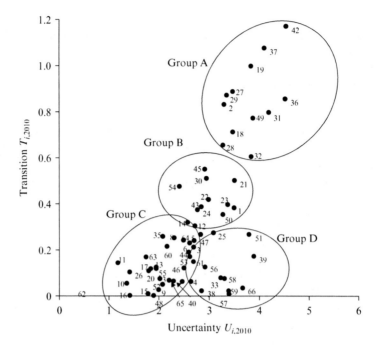

Figure 12.12   Transition and uncertainty

It should be noted that both transition and uncertainty represent qualitative characteristics of the indices and that their absolute value does not
have any substantial bearing. Transition and uncertainty are shown in
Figure 12.12. The indices are categorized into four groups: A, B, C and D.
The indices of each group are shown in Table 12.5. One parameter, No. 41,
passenger car ownership, which is assigned to group A is not shown on the
graph, because both its transition and uncertainty are too large.

Results

Indices showing large transition and uncertainty are categorized in group
A. In other words, forecasting these indices is difficult at best. This group
includes indices related to motorization, such as ownership of passenger
cars, trucks and passenger traffic per capita. Indices related to energy
consumption such as new energy sources (gas or biomass), and primary
energy consumption for the transportation section also belong to group
A. They will likely change to a great extent in the short term as China's
economy develops. This makes a quantitative estimate of the change difficult to forecast. It should be noted that per capita GDP also belongs to

Table 12.5   Classification of indices

No.	Group A	No.	Group B
2	Per capita GDP	1	GDP growth rate
18	Fertilizer input per agricultural land	3	Agricultural share in total GDP
19	Number of tractors	5	Service share in total GDP
27	Number of refrigerators per rural household	6	Income difference between urban and rural areas
28	Final energy consumption for households and commercial	8	Infant mortality
29	Final energy consumption for transportation	12	Urban population
31	Share of primary energy supply (the other)	14	Per-day animal foodstuff consumption per capita
32	Share of primary energy supply (gas)	21	Primary energy consumption per capita
36	Share in electric power generator (gas and others)	22	Primary energy consumption per GDP
37	Share in electric power generation (nuclear)	23	Income elasticity to primary energy consumption
41	Passenger car ownership	24	Crude steel production
42	Total number of trucks	25	Energy demand per steel production
49	Passenger-kilometers of passenger transport	30	Final energy consumption for industry
		43	Total length of road
		45	Ton-kilometers of freight transportation
		47	Share in freight transportation (motor vehicles)
		50	Share in passenger transport (aircraft)
		54	Total value of SO_2 emissions
		64	Industrial solid wastes

No.	Group C	No.	Group D
7	Total fertility rate	4	Industrial share in total GDP
9	Mortality rate	33	Share of primary energy supply (oil)
10	Life expectancy at birth	38	Share in electric power generation (hydro)
11	Total population	39	Share in electric power generation (oil)

Table 12.5   (continued)

No.	Group C	No.	Group D
13	Per-day food consumption per capita	51	Share in passenger transport (shipping)
15	Total agricultural land	56	Ambient SO_2 concentration in Chongqing city
16	Total harvested land area for crop production	57	Ambient SO_2 concentration in Shenyang city
17	Total irrigated farmland	58	Ambient TSP concentration in Shenyang city
20	Crop yields per harvested land area	59	Ambient TSP concentration in Tianjin city
26	Number of refrigerators per urban household	66	Desertification speed
34	Share of primary energy supply (coal)		
35	Share of electricity in final energy consumption		
40	Share in electric power generation (coal)		
44	Total length of railways		
46	Share in freight transportation (railways)		
48	Share in freight transportation (shipping)		
52	Share in passenger transport (motor vehicles)		
53	Share in passenger transport (railways)		
55	Total volume of dust discharged		
60	Per-day water consumption for daily life		
61	Per-day industrial wastewater		
62	Access to water supply in urban area		
63	Access to gas in urban area		
65	Forest area		

this group. Since many forecasts are based on the prospect of a growing per capita GDP, this presents a fundamental difficulty for forecasting the future.

Group B contains indices whose magnitude of transition and uncertainty are medium. They are important factors for viewing the transition of social structures, such as the GDP share of agriculture and the service industry, the income gap between urban and rural areas, and the rate of urbanization. Some of the indices are related to energy efficiency, such as primary energy consumption, both per capita and per GDP, elasticity of primary energy consumption to GDP, and energy efficiency in steel production. Indices indicating social infrastructures such as the volume of steel production and the total extended distance of a road also belong to group B. The policy of the government and the change of the social structure could alter them. Like those in group A, many of them are influenced by the progress of technology.

The indices in group C show relatively moderate changes both in transition and uncertainty over the short term. Some of them have already reached their limits: total fertility rate, mortality rate, life expectancy, total population, total food consumption, grain yield, and availability of waterworks and city gas. Some other parameters will not change very much unless effective policy is enforced, for example, land use for farmland and forests. The transition of parameters in group D is relatively small, but the uncertainty is large. There are many different views regarding the future of these indices. While some experts think there will be upward change, others downward. The indices in group D are air pollution in some cities, the share of petroleum as a source of energy, the GDP share of industry and desertification. They would be greatly affected by policy.

Figure 12.13 shows how the center of gravity of each group classified at 2010 will change by 2050. The center of group A moves upward showing a small horizontal shift. The centers of groups B and D move up and to the right. Group C moves to the right, suggesting no major change in the magnitude, but rather in uncertainty.

7   PERSPECTIVES

Experts' Bias

It was reported that the environmental consciousness of Japanese experts varied according to their particular field of study (Naito et al., 1991). This section analyzes how the experts' fields affect their judgment. Experts were classified into four groups according to their specialties: (i) economists, (ii) sociologists, (iii) engineers and (iv) other scientists. Sociologists, political scientists, jurists and journalists were included in the sociologist group. Physicists, chemists, biologists and agriculturists were included in the 'other scientists' group. The forecast tendency of each group was analyzed,

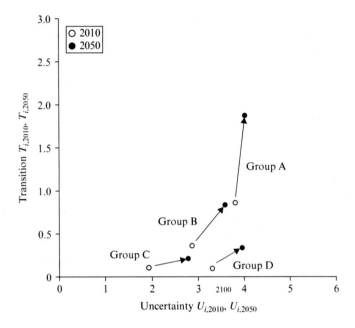

Figure 12.13   Changes in transition and uncertainty toward 2050

using the values of indices belonging to groups A and B at 2030 and 2050 as the medium- and long-term perspectives. The number of experts who forecast larger values than the mean and those forecasting smaller values within each group of experts was examined.

These results indicate that economists forecast further rapid development of the economy such as the GDP growth rate and GDP per capita. They also tend to forecast larger increases in indices such as the number of tractors, crude steel production, final energy consumption by the residential sector and the industrial sector, freight traffic per capita, and total SO_2 emissions. The view of the economists seems to be similar to the 'business-as usual' (BaU) scenario used in ordinary models.

Engineers forecast that the present rapid economic growth will not continue. They forecast smaller increases in production of raw materials and manufacturing (chemical fertilizer, tractors and crude steel), and they think that a shortage in these materials will hinder further economic growth. Regarding energy consumption, they also anticipate relatively conservative prospects for the development of new energy sources and nuclear power generation as compared with other groups of experts. However, they hope that SO_2 emissions will be reduced by certain technology innovations.

The sociologist and other scientists groups drew a slower development

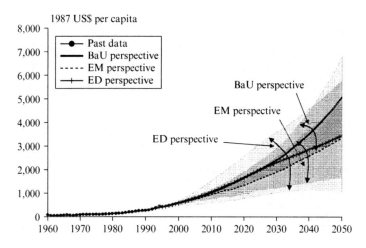

Figure 12.14   Perspectives of per capita GDP

path for the indices of the number of tractors in use, freight traffic per capita, and final energy consumption of the residential and industrial sectors. They forecast increasing environmental loads, such as total SO_2 emissions, and industrial solid wastes. They express grave concern about environmental deterioration. The variation of perspectives of the other scientists group is large probably because this group consists of scientists with different backgrounds, while the sociologist group presents a small deviation.

Perspectives of Three of the Groups

The perspectives of the experts' groups are as follows, and their characteristics are illustrated using some typical indices:

1.   BaU perspective by economists;
2.   environmental management (EM) perspective by engineers; and
3.   environmental deterioration (ED) perspective by other scientists.

The mean value and standard deviation of GDP per capita, crude steel production and total SO_2 emissions were calculated for each group. They represent living standards, industrialization, and effectiveness of environmental measures and technologies, respectively.

GDP per capita will further increase until 2050 in both the BaU and the EM perspectives (Figure 12.14). The EM perspective shows slower growth than the BaU perspective does. The ED perspective predicts similar growth

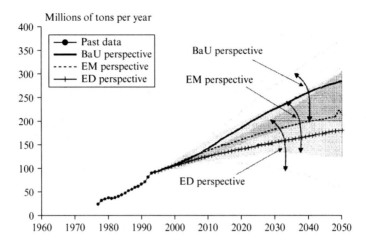

Figure 12.15   Perspectives of crude steel production

to that in the BaU perspective up to 2030, but a slower increase after that. Previous research by the authors showed that significant improvement in the living environment, particularly indices on sanitation, can be expected when GDP per capita exceeds US$5,000 (Kaneko et al., 1996). The BaU perspective alone expects this achievement by 2050.

In terms of crude steel production (Figure 12.15), the BaU perspective expects 280 million tons per year by 2050. The EM and the ED perspectives forecast a growth limit around twice the present level (about 200 million tons).

The ED perspective predicts the smallest increase in GDP per capita, and forecasts the largest amount of SO_2 emissions (Figure 12.16). The EM perspective forecasts the smallest amount of emissions reaching 60 million tons per year.

This result may suggest that economists are unlikely to expect any substantial changes that affect the indices. Engineers are more or less likely to expect such changes. Other experts think that environmental conditions will worsen and that the pace of economic development will become slower. Morgan and Henrion (1990) suggest that the use of a heuristic model is likely to lead to overestimates if solely recall or imagination is relied upon. Economists study, analyze, interpret past and current issues, and then extrapolate past trends to forecast the future. Engineers work toward improvement of current situations under given conditions considering capacity and limit. They are likely to recall technological innovations for environmental management and expect future improvement. Other scientists are more likely to recall the current worsening environmental

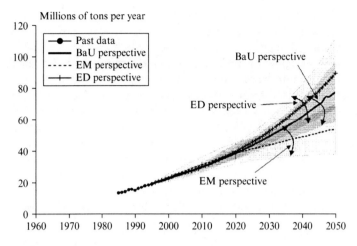

Figure 12.16   Perspectives of total SO₂ emissions

situation in China and have a 'pessimistic' outlook. These might explain the differences in judgment among experts.

8   CONCLUDING REMARKS

The results of this study are as follows:

1. Sixty Japanese specialists drew the future paths of 66 economic and environmental indices for China according to their own judgment based on their expertise.
2. The indices obtained are classified according to future change and uncertainty. The uncertainty of indices referencing GDP, transportation, and new energy development, which are greatly dependent on policy and selection of technology, is large.
3. Forecasts are influenced by the respective specialties of the experts. Economists are likely to forecast a BaU perspective. Engineers predict some kind of limitation to economic growth but expect technological innovation.

As shown above, the forecast of per capita GDP itself is difficult and many different views exist among experts. Since many models use future values of per capita GDP as a premise, this uncertainty indicates the fundamental difficulty of the forecast. Perspectives of many other indices are not as different as per capita GDP. Although much further study is needed

to investigate the characteristics of the indices, it might be possible to forecast 'difficult' indices such as per capita GDP by using forecast values for
'easily' predicted ones.

If experts' judgment is integrated into a quantitative model calculation,
some issues need to be resolved. First, development of a selection method
of experts is needed. Because their specialties are found to affect the results,
the selection of experts itself would determine the result of the forecast.
The necessity of an interface to feed back the result to the experts and for
further amendment of their previous forecast, like the Delphi method,
should be considered. This process, however, requires a great deal of work.
For example, the process of digitizing every line drawn on the graph was
extremely labor intensive. A simple system of data processing or an on-line
questionnaire system should be developed for any further detailed study.

REFERENCES

AIM Project Team (1995), AIM Interim paper.
Anastasi, C. et al. (1997), Integrated assessment – visions for sustainable develop-
ment' (Background paper), paper presented at the 2nd Open Meeting of IHDP.
Brown, L.R. (1995), *Who Will Feed China? Wake Up Call for a Small Planet*, New
York: Norton.
Brown, L.R. and B. Halweil (1998), 'China's water shortage could shake world food
security', *Worldwatch*, **11**.
Changming, L. and H. Xiwu (1998), *Water Problem Strategy for China's 21st
Century*, Beijing: China Science Press (in Chinese).
Dowlatabadi, H. (1997), 'Cultural content of integrated assessment and models',
in IPCC, pp. 509–15.
East–West Center, Argonne National Laboratory and Tsingha University (1994),
*National Response Strategy for Global Climate Change: People's Republic
of China*, Final report of the Technical Assistance Project funded by the
Office of Environment, Asian Development Bank and implemented by the
Department of Science and Technology for Social Development, State Science
and Technology Commission of China.
Geping, Q. (ed.) (1999), *The Knowledge for Environmental Protection*, Beijing:
Hong Qi Press (in Chinese).
Imura, H. and T. Katsuhara (eds) (1995), *Environmental Issues in China*, Tokyo:
Toyokeizai Shinpo-sha (in Japanese).
Intergovernmental Panel on Climate Change (IPCC) (1997), *Climate Change and
Integrated Assessment Models (IAMs) – Bridging the Gaps*, Proceedings of the
IPCC Asia-Pacific Workshop on Integrated Assessment Models, Tokyo.
Japan Economic Planning Agency (1997), *Some Scenarios on China's 21st Century*,
Tokyo (in Japanese).
Japan Science and Technology Agency (1992), *Energy Usage and Environmental
Forecasting in the Asia-Pacific Region*, Tokyo (in Japanese).
Kaneko, S. and H. Imura (1997), 'Long-term perspective on population and food

supply and demand in Asia based on empirical equations and BaU scenarios', *Journal of Global Environmental Engineering*, **3**, 99–119.

Kaneko, S.,T. Matsumoto, R. Fujikura and H. Imura (1996), 'Development and the environment: forecasting the future of Asia – an empirical analysis using learning curves', *Journal of International Development Studies*, **5**, 17–29 (in Japanese).

Lave, L.B. and H. Dowlatabadi (1993), 'Climate change: the effects of personal beliefs and scientific uncertainty', *Environmental Science and Technology*, **27**, 1962–72.

Matsuoka, Y., T. Kainuma and T. Morita (1995), 'Scenario analysis of global warming using the Asia-Pacific integrated model (AIM)', *Energy Policy*, **23**, 257–371.

Meadows, D.H., D.L.R. Meadows and W.W. Behrens III (1972), *The Limits to Growth*, New York: Universe Book.

Morgan, M.G. and M. Henrion (1990), *Uncertainty – A Guide to Dealing with Uncertainty in Quantitative Risk and Policy Analysis*, Cambridge and New York: Cambridge University Press.

Morgan, M.G. and D.W. Keith (1995), 'Subjective judgments by climate experts', *Environmental Science and Technology*, **29**, 468–76.

Morita, T. (1995), 'New trends in policy science', *Environmental Research Quarterly*, **100**, 34–9.

Naito, M., T. Morita, H. Ono and N. Sasahara (1991), 'A questionnaire study of experts on the environmental consciousness of Japanese experts', *Environmental Science*, **4**, 289–94 (in Japanese).

Smil, V. (1993), *China's Environmental Crisis: An Inquiry into the Limits of National Development*, An East Gate Book, New York: Sharpe.

Tsuji, K., Y. Sekiguchi and R. Makita (1995), 'Food demand prospects in China and proposals for agricultural development policy', Kaihatsu Enjo Kenkyu, Research Institute of Development Assistance, The Overseas Economic Cooperation Fund 2, 38–75.

van Asselt, M.B.A., H.H.W. Beusen and H.B.M. Hilderink (1996), 'Uncertainty in integrated assessment: a social scientific perspective', *Environmental Modeling and Assessment*, **1**, 71–90.

Watson, R.T., M.C. Zinyowera and R.H. Moss (eds) (1997), *The Regional Impacts of Climate Change: An Assessment of Vulnerability*, Special Report of the IPCC Working Group II, Cambridge: Cambridge University Press.

13. Conclusion

1 FORECASTING

Applying an EKC framework, we aimed to show basic forecasting results of Chinese pollution. It is not surprising that resource uses and pollution emissions are growing much faster than anticipated. Considering China's recent economic growth, it is important to apply the most recent economic data to forecast future scenarios. In this concluding chapter, we show the forecasting results using detailed province-level information from within China. Following an EKC framework, results up to 2025 are provided. The emission data is produced by the following equation:

$$\ln E_{it}^k = C_1 + \alpha_1 \ln E_{it-1} + \alpha_2 (\ln GSP_{it})^2 + \alpha_3 (\ln GSP_{it})^3$$
$$+ \alpha_4 \ln GSP_{it} + \gamma_i + \varepsilon_{it},$$

where i is the province, t is the time and GSP indicates per capita real GSP. The E is each of per capita SO_2, dust, soot, COD, coal, and fresh water. As discussed in previous chapters, these are important indicators for environmental management. For example, SO_2 gas is produced not only from anthropogenic sources such as the burning of fossil fuels but also from natural sources such as transboundary movement.

Key factors that affect emissions are size of economic growth and population in each province. Table 13.1 lists the 12 scenarios of economic environment and population change.

In scenarios 1–3, changes in population are not considered. Average economic growth rate over the past five years (that is, 1999–2003) is 9.43 percent per year. In scenario 1, the growth rate is assumed to continue until 2025. In scenario 2, the rate is assumed to decrease at a constant rate and end up with a 1 percent increase in 2025. In scenario 3, it is assumed to end in a 5 percent increase in 2025.

In scenarios 4–12, changes in population are taken into account. As in economic growth, the average change is taken, that is, about 0.42 percent increase per year for population change. One scenario considers this rate to be the same until 2025. The other two scenarios assume constant change over the forecasting periods and reach +/− 1 percent change in 2025.

Table 13.1   Forecasting scenarios

Scenario	Economic growth	Population change
1	Current growth rate until 2025	Constant to current population
2	Reach annual 1% increase in 2025	Constant to current population
3	Reach annual 5% increase in 2025	Constant to current population
4	Current growth rate until 2025	Current growth rate until 2025
5	Current growth rate until 2025	Reach annual 1% increase in 2025
6	Current growth rate until 2025	Reach annual −1% increase in 2025
7	Reach annual 1% increase in 2025	Current growth rate until 2025
8	Reach annual 1% increase in 2025	Reach annual 1% increase in 2025
9	Reach annual 1% increase in 2025	Reach annual −1% increase in 2025
10	Reach annual 5% increase in 2025	Current growth rate until 2025
11	Reach annual 5% increase in 2025	Reach annual 1% increase in 2025
12	Reach annual 5% increase in 2025	Reach annual −1% increase in 2025

Data over 1993 and 2003 are used to estimate the parameters. Then, the estimated parameters with predicted values with scenarios are used to calculate the forecasting results. Table 13.2 shows the estimated results of the parameters. To obtain statistically significant results, we include only the single GSP variable in soot and COD, while the others include all factors in the estimations.

The forecasting results based on the 12 scenarios are provided in Figures 13.1–13.5. Figures 13.1a–d show the SO_2 results. In most of the cases, as China's economy is growing rapidly, the byproduct of SO_2 is expected to increase. Especially, here, we examine the three cases of scenarios 5, 12 and 3. In scenario 5, the aggregated emissions increase most, while the other two show decreasing trends. In all of the cases, Guangdong shows the highest emissions, which peak at 2023 (in scenario 12) and at 2017 (in scenario 3). In scenario 5, 2025 emissions in Guangdong are around 7.5 times larger than the second-largest province of Gansu. It is clear from our results that reducing the pollution from Guangdong is key to solving the overall pollutions. Guangdong is a province on the southern coast; its

Table 13.2   Estimated results

	SO$_2$	Dust	Soot	COD	Water	Coal
ln E_{it-1}	0.44***	0.15***	0.42***	0.47***	00.30***	0.59***
	(7.14)	(2.52)	(7.56)	(9.06)	(4.26)	(10.38)
ln GSP_{it}	−50.55**	−53.72**	0.087***	−0.91***	−78.57*	−49.27***
	(−2.93)	(−2.27)	(0.06)	(−6.11)	(−1.90)	(−2.64)
(ln GSP_{it})^2	5.87***	6.43***			9.26*	5.59**
	(2.88)	(2.30)			(1.94)	(2.54)
(ln GSP_{it})^3	−0.23***	−0.26**			−0.36*	−0.21**
	(−2.83)	(−2.36)			(−1.96)	(−2.43)
Constant	151.96***	161.55	7.21***	14.08	228.25*	146.95
	(3.12)	(2.42)	(5.34)	(8.98)	(1.93)	(2.80)
Observations	290	290	290	290	290	290
No. of groups	29	29	29	29	29	29
R^2	0.22	0.19	0.18	0.27	0.16	0.37

Note: Values in parentheses are t values. *, ** and *** indicate 'significant' at the 10%, 5% and 1% levels, respectively.

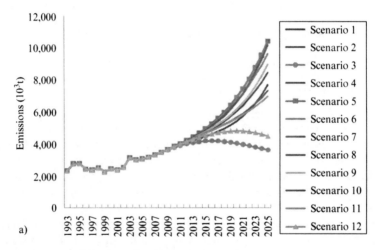

Figure 13.1a   Sulfur dioxide: forecasting results

provincial capital Guangzhou and economic hub Shenzhen are among the most populous and important cities in China.

Although Shanghai is often cited as evidence of China's success, Guangdong's economic boom exemplifies the reality of the vast labor-intensive manufacturing powerhouse of industries such as car manufacturing and chemicals that China has become. Guangdong is the country's richest province with the highest total GDP among all the provinces. Its

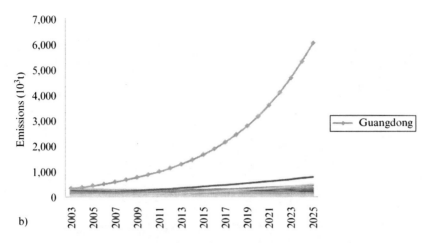

Figure 13.1b   Sulfur dioxide: forecasting results (Scenario 5)

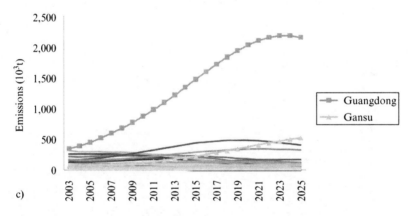

Figure 13.1c   Sulfur dioxide: forecasting results (scenario 12)

nominal GDP for 2003 was US$165 billion, increasing to US$265 billion in 2005, which is about the same size as Denmark. Its nominal GDP for 2007 was 3.07 trillion yuan (US$422 billion), a rise of 14.5 percent on a year-on-year basis. Guangdong contributes approximately 12.5 percent of national economic output.

Guangdong has three of the six special economic zones of Shenzhen, Shantou and Zhuhai. However, the affluence of Guangdong remains very much concentrated near the Pearl River Delta. In 2007 its foreign trade also grew 20 percent compared to the previous year and is also by far the largest: its foreign trade accounts for 29 percent of China's US$2.17 trillion

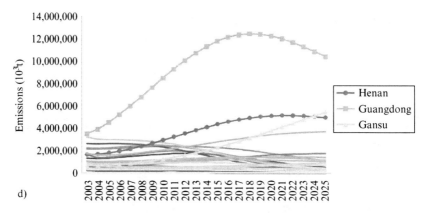

Figure 13.1d   Sulfur dioxide: forecasting results (scenario 6)

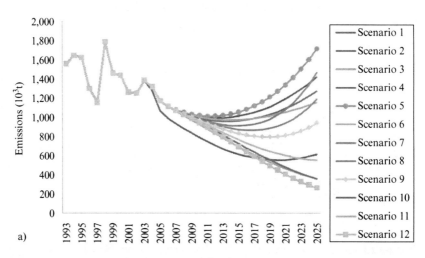

Figure 13.2a   Dust: forecasting results

foreign trade. The effects of stricter environmental regulations should be apparent in Guangdong in the coming decades.

The results for dust emissions are provided in Figure 13.2a. In more than half of the scenarios, the emissions decrease and then increase, though four scenarios show a decreasing trend. Here province level estimates are shown for scenarios 5, 9 and 12 (see Figures 13.2b–d). Shanxi and Sichuan show significantly high estimates. Next to these, Henan province shows the largest share. In scenario 12, Shanxi and Sichuan start decreasing around 2009 and 2013, respectively. Sichuan has been historically known as the

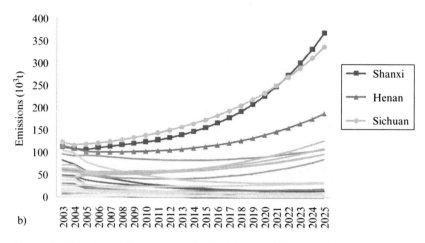

Figure 13.2b   Dust: forecasting results (scenario 5)

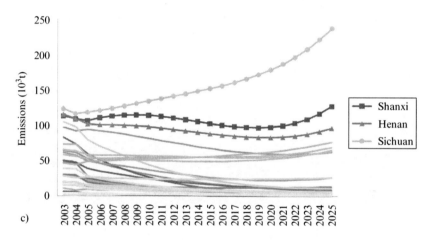

Figure 13.2c   Dust: forecasting results (scenario 9)

'Province of Abundance'. Sichuan is one of the major industrial bases of China. In addition to heavy industries such as coal, energy, iron and steel, it has established a light manufacturing sector comprising building materials, wood processing, food and silk processing. Figure 13.3a shows the results of soot emissions. As in the dust case, more than half of the scenarios present an increasing trend though some are decreasing. Scenarios 5, 11 and 12 are shown in detail in Figures 13.3b–d, respectively.

COD emissions are shown to decrease over time (Figure 13.4). A significant amount of investment has been used to construct waste treatment

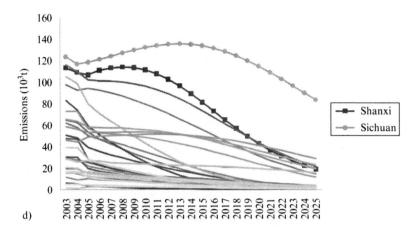

d)

Figure 13.2d   Dust: forecasting results (scenario 12)

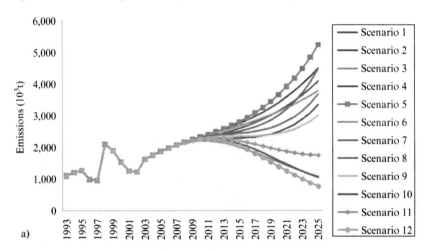

a)

Figure 13.3a   Soot: forecasting results

plants, and therefore emissions would be expected to decrease over time. Coal use is expected to increase for all cases in Figures 13.5a–c. In particular, from the results in scenario 9 of the most increasing trend and in scenario 3 of the least increasing trend, we can see the varying results. Guangdong shows the largest use of coal while Henan is second in scenario 9. However, in scenario 3, the level of Guangdong becomes constant after about 2022, and Henan becomes the largest in 2024.

On the other hand, fresh water uses are forecast to increase over time for more than half of the cases (see Figure 13.6a–d). Guangdong and

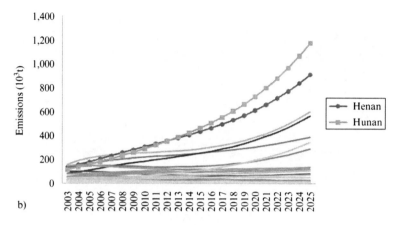

Figure 13.3b   Soot: forecasting results (scenario 5)

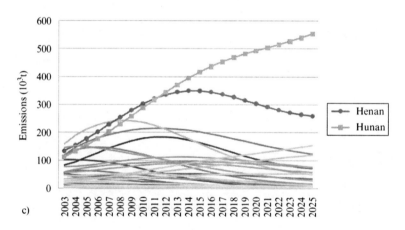

Figure 13.3c   Soot: forecasting results (scenario 11)

Zhejiang, in all cases, show a decreasing, increasing and finally decreasing trend. Northern agricultural provinces are expected to use more fresh water in the scenarios.

2   FINDINGS

From our forecasting modeling, it is clear that several emissions and resource uses continue to increase but others might decrease. Technological change is the key to solving the problem of increasing emissions as this

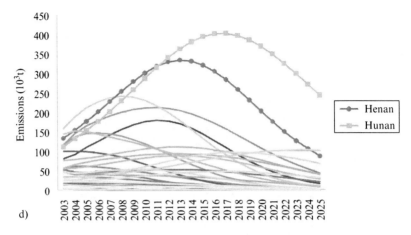

d)

Figure 13.3d   Soot: forecasting results (scenario 12)

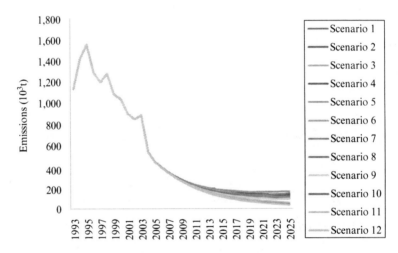

Figure 13.4   Chemical oxygen demand: forecasting results

book has shown. Technological change is central to maintaining standards of living in modern economies with finite resources and increasingly stringent environmental goals. Successful environmental policies can contribute to efficiency by encouraging, rather than inhibiting, technological innovation. Over time, economists have greatly improved our understanding of the role of technological change in economic growth and of the constituents of technological change. We have progressed from 'confessions of ignorance' based on mere observations that productivity increases over

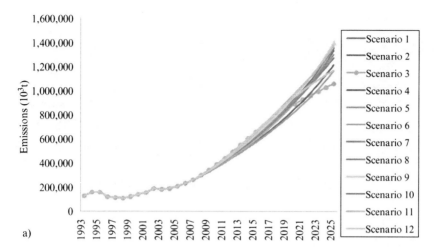

a)

Figure 13.5a   Coal: forecasting results

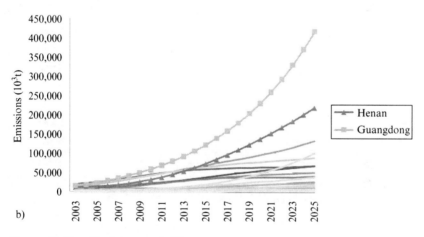

b)

Figure 13.5b   Coal (scenario 9)

time, to an increasingly sophisticated understanding of the mechanisms that drive technological change and empirical measures of various components of such change.

However, little research to date has focused on the design and implementation of environmental regulations that encourage technological progress, or in ensuring productivity improvements in the face of depletion of natural resources and increasing stringency of environmental regulations.

This book contributes to the literature in several ways. First, the research

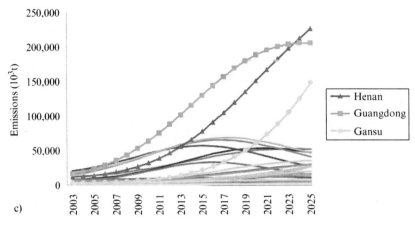

c)

Figure 13.5c   Coal (scenario 3)

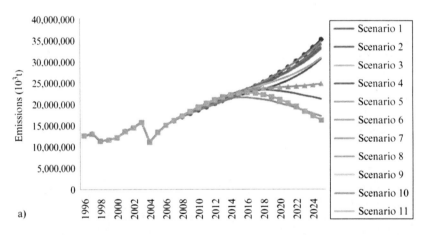

a)

Figure 13.6a   Fresh water: forecasting results

provides a comprehensive analysis of these issues within the Chinese context. It identifies and measures the impact of technological change both in market and environmental output sectors in the manufacturing industries, and takes steps to identify key causal relationships. A thorough understanding of the nature and role of technological change is essential for developing well-conceived policies that contribute to the long-term well-being of society. This book illustrates the importance of understanding the process of technological change, as well as the challenges that are faced in measuring, and particularly in forecasting technological change.

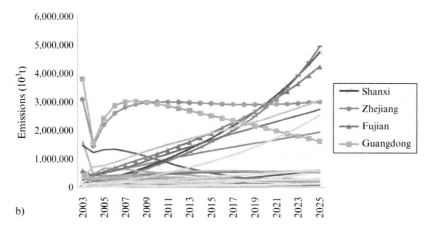

Figure 13.6b   Fresh water: forecasting results (scenario 4)

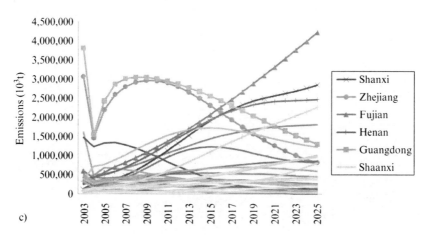

Figure 13.6c   Fresh water: forecasting results (scenario 11)

In forecasting, we are dealing explicitly with the realm of uncertainty, and no one can expect to formulate long-term predictions with a high degree of accuracy. Yet despite these challenges, the development of a sound policy requires an improved understanding of the nature and the role of technological change in shaping future living standards.

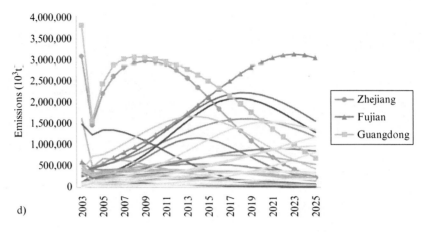

d)

Figure 13.6d   Fresh water: forecasting results (scenario 12)

Index

Abramovitz, M. 99
acid rain 53, 66, 85
acid rain control policies 66, 67,
    129–30
administrative status
    environmental protection agency 20,
        21, 31, 33, 91, 120
    environmental protection bureaus
        and offices 10, 13, 72–3
    local environmental agencies 12, 20,
        31, 120
    State Environmental Protection
        Administration (SEPA) 11, 12,
        13, 21, 66, 91, 120
'Agenda 21' 265
agricultural labor 7, 150, 151, 152, 153,
    154, 161
agricultural land 148, 149, 270, 275,
    282, 288, 290, 291
    see also cultivated land; grain
        harvested land; irrigated land
        area
agricultural machinery 148, 150, 151,
    153, 154, 161
agricultural sector
    and experts' judgment on the future
        perspective study 267, 274, 275,
        280–81, 282–3
    and forecasting pollution study 305
    and stagnancy of energy-related CO_2
        emissions study 199, 200, 201,
        202, 203, 204, 211, 212, 215
    see also water efficiency and
        agricultural production study
agricultural share of GDP 267, 274,
    280, 288, 289, 291
Aigner, D.J. 174–5
AIM Project Team 264, 266
air pollution
    and efficiency in environmental
        management study 53, 66

and efficiency in environmental
    management study II 83, 85, 91
and environmental Kuznets curve
    (EKC) study 33–4, 38–9
extent of 1, 19
and increasing returns to pollution
    abatement study 129–30
SEPA estimates 51, 83, 122
see also CO_2 (carbon dioxide)
    emissions; dust; SO_2 (sulfur
    dioxide) emissions; soot
air pollution control laws 12, 66, 67–8,
    91, 129
air pollution control policies 1, 2, 19,
    66, 129–30
air pollution control regulations 12,
    129–30
air quality standards 12, 129
Aitken, B. 99
Allen, F. 5–6
Anastasi, C. 265, 268
Andreoni, J. 121–2
Ang, B.W. 192, 198, 212, 223, 229,
    257–8
animal foodstuff consumption 270,
    275, 282
Aoyagi, S. 42, 47–8, 49–50
Arellano, M. 128
Asian financial crisis 62–3
Auffhammer, M. 197

Balk, B.M. 47, 55
bargaining power of enterprises 14, 39,
    72, 78
BAU perspective, in experts' judgment
    on the future perspective study
    293, 294, 295
Bayesian MCMC (Markov chain
    Monte Carlo) methods 139–43
Becker, G.S. 101, 106
Berman, E. 98

and water efficiency and agricultural production study 153
National Committee for Environmental Protection 12
National Congress of Environmental Protection 11, 13, 20, 120
National Environmental Protection Agency (NEPA) 2, 19
National People's Congress 10, 11, 12, 20, 21, 33, 63, 66, 91, 119–20, 129
natural gas consumption 199, 200, 201, 202, 210, 214, 226, 288
natural gas investment 244
natural gas supply 271, 276, 289
natural resource consumption 37, 265, 266
natural resource protection policies 2, 12, 33
natural water supply 147
new energy sources 138, 277, 288, 289, 292, 295
Ninth National People's Congress 11, 12, 21, 33, 66, 91
non-energy end use 232, 234, 237, 238, 239, 240
nonmarket resources 77, 79, 147
nonparametric models 26–8, 29–30, 31
see also DEA (data envelopment analysis); efficiency in environmental management study; increasing returns to pollution abatement study; iron and steel industry productivity study
Northeast China 150, 151, 152, 160, 161, 162, 167
Northern China 69, 171, 283
Northwest China 150, 151, 152, 160, 161, 167

OECD 191, 197, 228, 232
oil consumption
and efficiency in environmental management study 53, 54, 55, 56, 57, 63
and efficiency in environmental management study II 80, 83, 85, 86, 87–9, 90

and environmental Kuznets curve (EKC) study 33, 37–8
statistics 138
OLS (ordinary least squares) 26, 154, 158, 159, 160
Ortolano, L. 1, 2, 10, 12, 13, 19, 20, 31, 33, 72–3, 77, 99, 100, 109, 119, 120
ownership of enterprises 212–13, 215–16, 217, 219, 224, 250
see also privately-owned enterprises; state-owned enterprises

Palmer, K. 98
Panel Code of the People's Republic of China 12, 32–3
parametric models 26, 27, 28, 31, 32
see also efficiency in environmental management study II; foreign direct investment (FDI) and environmental policies study; SFA (stochastic frontier analysis)
Parker, E. 148, 149
Party Congress 2, 59, 62
passenger car ownership 264–5, 267, 270, 277, 284–5, 286–7, 288, 289
patents 98, 100, 104, 106, 109, 114
petroleum products 199, 200, 201, 202, 210, 214, 225
petroleum refining 242–3, 244, 245
Pittman, R.W. 79
pollutants 70, 71, 72, 77, 79, 80, 81, 91–2
see also chemical oxygen demand (COD); chromium six; CO_2 (carbon dioxide) emissions; dust; lead; pollution; SO_2 (sulfur dioxide) emissions; soot; TSP (total suspended particulate matter) pollution
pollution
and environmental Kuznets curve (EKC) 22–3, 120–21
and experts' judgment on the future perspective study 265, 271, 278, 279, 285, 288, 289, 290, 291, 292, 293, 294, 295
see also forecasting pollution study; pollutants
pollution abatement *see* increasing returns to pollution abatement

variable, in water efficiency and
agricultural production study
155–6, 157, 159–63, 167
and water management policies 168
see also water efficiency and
agricultural production study
water efficiency and agricultural
production study
conclusions 163
data 153
introduction 146–9
methodology 154–9
regional agricultural production
149–52
results 159–63, 167
water inefficiency 161–2, 181, 184, 185,
186, 187
water management policies 69–70, 89,
146, 168
water pollution
and efficiency in environmental
management study 69–70
and efficiency in environmental
management study II 83
and environmental Kuznets curve
(EKC) study 34–6, 38, 39
and iron and steel industry
productivity study 169, 173
SEPA estimates 51, 83, 122
see also chemical oxygen demand
(COD); chromium six; lead
water pollution control policies 1, 2, 19
water prices 185, 187
water productivity 180, 181, 182–4,
185, 186, 187–8
water recycling 22, 170, 173

water scarcity 69–70, 89, 146, 168, 171,
282, 283, 285
water supply 146, 147
water use efficiency (WUE) 146–7
Watson, R.T. 265
wheat production 146, 147, 150, 152,
154, 159, 160
Wheeler, D. 14, 78, 100
Williamson, R. 5
WLS (weighted least squares), in
environmental Kuznets curve
(EKC) study 26
Woo, W.T. 7, 168
World Bank 1, 6, 10, 11, 19, 70, 168
World Business Council for Sustainable
Development 124
Wu, L.B. 168, 223, 224, 240
Wu, Y. 8, 9, 148, 149, 171, 175

Yang, D. 146
Yao, Y. 26, 55, 86, 122
Ye, G. 174, 184, 185
*Yearbook of the Iron and Steel
Industry in China* (Ministry of
Metallurgical Industry) 174, 179
Yellow River 69, 70, 146, 149–50, 151,
152, 160, 161, 162, 167
Young, A. 7, 59, 87

Zhang, B. 148, 149
Zhang, F.Q. 198, 223, 229, 258
Zhang, X. 148, 149
Zhang, Y. 147
Zhang, Z.X. 191–2, 211, 212, 223
Zhejiang 305, 309, 310
Zhou, J.P. 219